Social and Sustainable Finance for Social Innovation and Sustainable Development Goals (SDGs)

Rosella Carè
University of Waterloo, Canada & University Magna Graecia of Catanzaro, Italy

IGI Global
Scientific Publishing
Publishing Tomorrow's Research Today

Vice President of Editorial Melissa Wagner
Director of Acquisitions Mikaela Felty
Director of Book Development Jocelynn Hessler
Production Manager Mike Brehm
Cover Design Jose Rosado

Published in the United States of America by
IGI Global Scientific Publishing
701 East Chocolate Avenue
Hershey, PA, 17033, USA
Tel: 717-533-8845
Fax: 717-533-7115
Website: https://www.igi-global.com E-mail: cust@igi-global.com

Library of Congress Cataloging-in-Publication Data

Names: Carè, Rosella editor http://id.loc.gov/rwo/agents/no2018124007
Title: Social and sustainable finance for social innovation and sustainable development goals (SDGs) / [edited by] Rosella Carè.
Description: Hershey, PA : IGI Global Scientific Publishing, [2026] | Includes bibliographical references and index. | Summary: "This book aims to explore the intersection of social and sustainable finance, social innovation, and the Sustainable Development Goals (SDGs). In an era where global challenges require innovative and coordinated responses, this book aims to provide an in-depth analysis of financial strategies that can drive positive social change"-- Provided by publisher.
Identifiers: LCCN 2025002870 (print) | LCCN 2025002871 (ebook) | ISBN 9798369395516 hardcover | ISBN 9798369395523 paperback | ISBN 9798369395530 ebook
Subjects: LCSH: Finance--Environmental aspects | Finance--Social aspects | Sustainable development http://id.loc.gov/authorities/subjects/sh92005743 | Social change--Economic aspects
Classification: LCC HG101 .S635 2025 (print) | LCC HG101 (ebook) | DDC 332--dc23/eng/20250313
LC record available at https://lccn.loc.gov/2025002870
LC ebook record available at https://lccn.loc.gov/2025002871

British Cataloguing in Publication Data
A Cataloguing in Publication record for this book is available from the British Library.

Editorial Advisory Board

Table of Contents

Detailed Table of Contents

The purpose of this study is to find out the current status of social and sustainable finance in a global context. A detailed bibliometric analysis was done on Vos Viewer software for the documents fetched with keywords social and sustainable finance retrieved from the Scopus database. Content analysis was done on 50 Indian companies based on Nifty Fifty (Indices of National Stock Exchange of India) based on the themes retrieved from 978 documents in bibliometric analysis. The study found the dynamic and geographically diverse research landscape for Social and Sustainable Finance. Initially dominated by the USA, now moving towards countries like China and India. A strong association between "Sustainable Finance" and keywords like "ESG" and "sustainable development" was found. The study also finds that Sustainable Development Goals (SDGs), corporate governance, and corporate social responsibility (CSR) are the most frequently disclosed themes in the annual reports of Indian companies.

The 2008–2009 financial crisis exposed vulnerabilities in the traditional banking system, leading to stricter regulations that restricted access to capital. This created space for the rise of alternative finance, which operates outside conventional banking and capital markets, offering innovative solutions. Simultaneously, sustainable finance has gained momentum by integrating ESG principles into investment strategies, channeling resources toward responsible economic activities. The intersection of these fields is significant, as alternative finance can fund sustainable projects often neglected by traditional financiers. Despite growing research, studies remain fragmented, with gaps in understanding their synergies. This study conducts a

future paths for embedding them into wider social finance frameworks, including blended finance and ESG-aligned models.

In response to growing social challenges compounded by stretched public and philanthropic resources, the international development sector has become increasingly interested in results-based funding mechanisms such as Development Impact Bonds (DIBs). This study contributes to the growing field of research on DIBs in low- and middle-income counties (LMICs) by exploring stakeholder perceptions on the model's benefits and costs thus far. Drawing on stakeholder interviews from 7 recent DIBs, the study finds that stakeholders wanted to test the effectiveness of DIBs, and that the DIB's provision of outcomes-focused risk capital helped enable a collaborative and adaptive approach to service delivery. This approach then generated evidence of blended returns and increased organizational capacity, as well as spurred cultural shifts towards more sustainable outcomes-based working. Stakeholders also experienced costs and challenges in implementation – especially around garnering institutional buy-in, negotiating contract terms, and managing changing relationships.

Achieving a resilient, net-zero future requires a fundamental shift in how economies and societies operate. Since the early 2000s, corporations have increasingly recognized the importance of non-financial factors—particularly environmental and social ones—in shaping performance and reputation. Integrating climate knowledge, data, and insights into decision-making and market strategies is essential for driving this transformation. This study explores the growing climate services (CS) market, which has emerged in response to urgent climate-related challenges. Through a comprehensive literature review, we propose the foundations for a tailored business model that supports the integration of climate services into organizational strategies. The study advances a taxonomy for climate services and examines its relevance to

Preface

In an era marked by unprecedented global challenges—climate change, rising inequality, geopolitical instability, and systemic health crises—the role of finance is undergoing a profound transformation. No longer confined to the pursuit of profit maximization, financial systems are increasingly called upon to serve broader societal and environmental objectives. This edited volume, *Social and Sustainable Finance for Social Innovation and SDGs*, responds to this imperative by exploring how innovative financial instruments and strategies can catalyze social innovation and contribute meaningfully to the achievement of the United Nations Sustainable Development Goals (SDGs).

FINANCE AS A LEVER FOR TRANSFORMATION

The traditional architecture of finance—centered on risk-adjusted returns and shareholder value—has proven insufficient to address the complexity of today's development challenges. The 2008–2009 financial crisis exposed deep structural vulnerabilities, prompting a wave of regulatory reforms and a rethinking of the social contract between finance and society. In this context, social finance and sustainable finance have emerged as complementary paradigms that seek to realign capital flows with long-term public value creation.

Social finance encompasses instruments such as impact investing, social impact bonds, and community-based lending, which aim to generate measurable social outcomes alongside financial returns. Sustainable finance, meanwhile, integrates environmental, social, and governance (ESG) criteria into investment decisions, directing capital toward activities that mitigate climate risks, foster inclusion, and promote resilience. Together, these approaches represent a shift from extractive to regenerative finance—one that prioritizes intergenerational equity, stakeholder engagement, and systemic impact.

THE NEXUS OF FINANCE, INNOVATION, AND THE SDGs

At the heart of this volume lies the recognition that financial innovation is essential to unlocking solutions for the SDGs. The 2030 Agenda calls for mobilizing trillions of dollars annually to meet targets across poverty eradication (SDG 1), decent work (SDG 8), climate action (SDG 13), and reduced inequalities (SDG 10), among others. Yet, traditional finance often fails to reach the communities, sectors, and initiatives most in need of support.

This book explores how alternative finance mechanisms—including crowdfunding, peer-to-peer lending, and blockchain-based solutions—can democratize access to capital and empower social enterprises, grassroots innovators, and underserved populations. These instruments not only fill funding gaps but also foster participatory governance, transparency, and trust, which are critical to the legitimacy and effectiveness of development interventions.

Moreover, the integration of digital technologies into financial services has accelerated the reach and efficiency of social and sustainable finance. From AI-driven credit scoring to decentralized finance (DeFi) platforms, digital innovation is reshaping the financial inclusion landscape. However, these advances also raise important questions about data ethics, regulatory oversight, and algorithmic bias, which the chapters in this volume critically examine.

BRIDGING THEORY AND PRACTICE

A distinctive feature of this volume is its commitment to bridging the gap between academic research and practical implementation. While scholarly interest in social and sustainable finance has grown exponentially, there remains a need to translate conceptual insights into actionable strategies. This book brings together contributions from researchers, practitioners, and policymakers to offer a pluralistic and grounded understanding of the field.

The chapters span diverse geographies, methodologies, and thematic areas—from bibliometric analyses of emerging trends to in-depth explorations of regulatory frameworks and financial innovations. They collectively underscore the importance of interdisciplinary collaboration, contextual sensitivity, and institutional learning in advancing the transformative potential of finance.

For example, the bibliometric chapter included in this volume reveals a thematic evolution from microfinance and banking (1999–2009) to crowdfunding and green finance (2010–2020), and more recently to cryptocurrencies and blockchain (2021–2024). This trajectory reflects not only the diversification of financial instruments but also the growing alignment between financial innovation and sustainability imperatives.

A RESOURCE FOR A DIVERSE AUDIENCE

This volume is designed to serve multiple audiences:

- Academic researchers and students will find rigorous analyses and conceptual frameworks to deepen their understanding of the evolving finance–sustainability nexus.
- Industry professionals and financial innovators will gain insights into emerging instruments, market dynamics, and impact measurement tools.
- Policy makers and regulators will benefit from comparative perspectives on enabling environments and governance models.
- Civil society organizations and social entrepreneurs will discover practical pathways to mobilize resources and scale their initiatives.

By addressing both theoretical foundations and real-world applications, the book aims to contribute to a more inclusive, resilient, and sustainable financial ecosystem.

STRUCTURE AND DEVELOPMENT OF THE VOLUME

This volume unfolds through a carefully curated sequence of nine chapters, each contributing to a multidimensional understanding of how social and sustainable finance can support social innovation and the achievement of the Sustainable Development Goals (SDGs). The structure reflects both thematic coherence and methodological diversity, offering readers a progressive journey through foundational concepts, empirical analyses, and emerging innovations.

The journey begins with **Chapter 1**, *Global Perspectives on Social and Sustainable Finance*, which lays the conceptual groundwork by exploring the diverse interpretations and applications of social and sustainable finance across global contexts. This opening chapter highlights the importance of aligning financial systems with inclusive development and sets the tone for the volume's interdisciplinary approach.

Building on this foundation, **Chapter 2**, *Bridging Finance and Sustainability: A Bibliometric Analysis of Alternative and Sustainable Finance for Advancing the Sustainable Development Goals*, provides a rigorous quantitative mapping of the field. Through bibliometric methods, the chapter identifies key research streams, influential authors, and thematic clusters, offering a panoramic view of how alternative finance mechanisms—such as microfinance, crowdfunding, and green bonds—have evolved in relation to the SDGs.

The analytical lens is further refined in **Chapter 3**, *Mapping the Intersection of Fintech and Social and Sustainable Finance: A Bibliometric Review*. Here, the focus shifts to the convergence between financial technology (Fintech) and sustainability-oriented finance. The chapter reveals how digital innovation is reshaping access to capital, impact measurement, and financial inclusion, particularly in underserved regions, and underscores the transformative potential of tech-enabled financial ecosystems.

The theme of innovation continues in **Chapter 4**, *Redefining Sustainable Energy Financing – The Disruptive Influence of Decentralised Finance (DeFi)*. This contribution explores how decentralized finance, powered by blockchain technologies, can disrupt traditional models of energy financing. It discusses the potential of DeFi to democratize investment in renewable energy and enhance transparency, while also addressing the regulatory and environmental challenges associated with these emerging tools.

Chapter 5, *The Evolution of Social Finance: From Social Impact Bonds to Technological Innovation for Social Good*, offers a historical and conceptual overview of social finance instruments. It traces the development of models such as social impact bonds (SIBs), highlighting how technological innovation is expanding their scope and effectiveness in addressing complex social challenges.

This discussion is deepened in **Chapter 6**, *Social Impact Bonds: Evolution, Challenges, and Future Directions in Outcome-Based Financing*. The chapter provides a detailed analysis of the SIB model, examining its contractual architecture, stakeholder dynamics, and implementation barriers. It also reflects on the enabling conditions for scaling outcome-based financing within broader social finance ecosystems.

Complementing this perspective, **Chapter 7**, *Results-Based Funding via Development Impact Bonds: Stakeholder Perceptions on Benefits and Costs*, presents empirical evidence on Development Impact Bonds (DIBs). Drawing on stakeholder interviews and case studies, the chapter explores perceived benefits, risks, and operational complexities, contributing to a nuanced understanding of how results-based funding can be tailored to development contexts.

The volume then turns to climate resilience in **Chapter 8**, *Foundations of a Tailored Business Model in Climate Services for a Resilient Future*. This chapter proposes a business model framework for climate services, emphasizing the role of financial innovation in supporting adaptation strategies and building institutional capacity for climate risk management. It bridges the gap between financial design and environmental governance, offering practical insights for policy and practice.

Finally, **Chapter 9**, *Integrating Double Materiality into the Criteria of European Sustainable Finance Labels: A Systematic Review of the Literature*, closes the volume with a critical examination of how the concept of double materiality is being integrated into European sustainable finance labels. Through a systematic review, the chapter discusses implications for ESG reporting, regulatory frameworks, and investor behavior, highlighting the need for more holistic and socially responsive financial standards.

By combining theoretical reflection, empirical analysis, and forward-looking perspectives, the volume provides a comprehensive resource for scholars, practitioners, and policymakers committed to advancing social and sustainable finance as a lever for transformative change.

TOWARD A NEW FINANCIAL ETHOS

This volume invites readers to reimagine finance not as a neutral or technical domain, but as a normative and political space—one that shapes the distribution of risks, resources, and opportunities across society. It challenges the notion that markets alone can deliver public goods and instead advocates for hybrid models that blend public, private, and civic logics.

Whether through outcome-based contracts like social impact bonds, ESG-linked lending, or digital platforms for microcredit, the chapters in this book demonstrate that finance can be a powerful enabler of social innovation—but only if designed with intentionality, accountability, and equity at its core.

As we move toward 2030 and beyond, the imperative is clear: finance must evolve from a system that extracts value to one that creates and sustains it. This volume offers both the analytical tools and the practical insights to support that transition.

POSITIONING THE VOLUME WITHIN THE LITERATURE

This volume emerges at a critical juncture in the evolution of financial thought and practice. In recent years, the academic and policy discourse has increasingly recognized the limitations of traditional finance in addressing complex social and environmental challenges. The rise of social and sustainable finance reflects a paradigmatic shift—one that repositions finance as a tool for systemic transformation rather than a mechanism for capital accumulation.

By integrating perspectives from sustainability science, financial management, social innovation, and digital transformation, I aim to contribute to a growing body of interdisciplinary literature that seeks to redefine the purpose and practice of finance. This book offers a timely and necessary response to the call for financial systems that are inclusive, accountable, and aligned with the Sustainable Development Goals (SDGs).

METHODOLOGICAL DIVERSITY AND INTERDISCIPLINARITY

A key strength of this volume lies in its methodological and disciplinary diversity. The chapters employ a wide range of approaches—including bibliometric analysis, systematic literature reviews, empirical case studies, stakeholder interviews, and conceptual modeling. This plurality of methods reflects the complexity of the field and enhances the volume's capacity to engage with multiple audiences.

The contributors come from diverse academic backgrounds—economics, finance, sociology, environmental studies, and information systems—bringing with them a rich tapestry of insights and analytical tools. This interdisciplinarity is not only a methodological asset but also a reflection of the real-world interconnectedness of financial, social, and environmental systems.

RELEVANCE TO POLICY AND PRACTICE

Beyond its academic contributions, the volume offers actionable insights for policymakers, financial institutions, and social innovators. It addresses pressing questions around regulatory frameworks, impact measurement, financial inclusion, and the role of technology in democratizing access to capital.

Several chapters provide direct implications for policy design—such as the integration of double materiality into sustainable finance labels, the governance of decentralized finance (DeFi), and the structuring of social impact bonds and development impact bonds. Others offer practical models for climate services, fintech applications, and results-based funding mechanisms. Together, these contributions form a knowledge base that is both theoretically robust and practically relevant.

EDITORIAL VISION AND ACKNOWLEDGMENT OF CONTRIBUTORS

The development of this volume has been guided by a clear editorial vision: to bridge the gap between theory and practice, and to foster dialogue across disciplines and sectors. Curating this book has been a deeply collaborative process, and I wish to express my sincere gratitude to all the authors who contributed their expertise and time. Their commitment to advancing the field of social and sustainable finance has been instrumental in shaping the richness and depth of this work.

I also thank the reviewers for their constructive feedback, and the editorial staff for their support throughout the process.

FINAL REFLECTIONS

As we approach the midpoint of the 2030 Agenda, the urgency of aligning financial systems with sustainability goals has never been greater. This volume does not claim to offer definitive answers, but rather aims to stimulate critical reflection, inspire innovation, and support the co-creation of financial models that serve people and planet.

I hope that readers—whether researchers, students, policymakers, or practitioners—will find in these pages not only knowledge, but also inspiration to rethink finance as a lever for inclusive and sustainable transformation.

Acknowledgments

I would like to sincerely thank the two young researchers who work alongside me every day—Rabia Fatima and Simone Taddeo—for their constant dedication and support throughout this journey.

My deepest gratitude also goes to Nathalie Lévy, who has stood by my side both as a colleague and a friend, and whose encouragement and contribution have been instrumental in the development of this volume.

I also wish to thank all those who have remained close to me—in sunshine and in storms. To those who never turned away when it would have been easier to do so, I have only one word: thank you.

Finally, I wish to thank my family—without you, none of this would be possible.

Chapter 1
Global Perspectives on Social and Sustainable Finance

Mayank Kumar
https://orcid.org/0000-0002-9643-5871
Christ University, Bengaluru, India

Nirakarnath Pandey
https://orcid.org/0000-0003-0287-0969
Christ University, Bengaluru, India

ABSTRACT

The purpose of this study is to find out the current status of social and sustainable finance in a global context. A detailed bibliometric analysis was done on Vos Viewer software for the documents fetched with keywords social and sustainable finance retrieved from the Scopus database. Content analysis was done on 50 Indian companies based on Nifty Fifty (Indices of National Stock Exchange of India) based on the themes retrieved from 978 documents in bibliometric analysis. The study found the dynamic and geographically diverse research landscape for Social and Sustainable Finance. Initially dominated by the USA, now moving towards countries like China and India. A strong association between "Sustainable Finance" and keywords like "ESG" and "sustainable development" was found. The study also finds that Sustainable Development Goals (SDGs), corporate governance, and corporate social responsibility (CSR) are the most frequently disclosed themes in the annual reports of Indian companies.

DOI: 10.4018/979-8-3693-9551-6.ch001

1. INTRODUCTION

The modern financial landscape is transforming significantly, driven by a growing global focus on sustainability, ethics, and social responsibility. With serious consequences arising due to climate change, inequality, and corporate accountability, the goal of finance has expanded beyond merely maximising shareholder value. This move has led to the emergence of social finance and sustainable finance, which emphasises on inclusion of environmental, social, and governance (ESG) principles into financial decision-making. Key components of this approach include green, blue, and inclusive finance. Recently, these concepts have been recognised worldwide, redefining how businesses, investors, and policymakers should allocate capital.

Social finance and sustainable finance encircle two interrelated yet distinct approaches to aligning financial objectives with broader societal aspirations. Social finance focuses on channelling capital to generate social impact and help remove serious problems like poverty, education, healthcare, and community development. A notable example is Bangladesh's Grameen Bank, which revolutionised the concept of microfinance by creating an appropriate platform of small loans for rural entrepreneurs, mainly women, empowering millions.

Sustainable finance takes a broader perspective and includes environmental, social, and governance (ESG) factors in investment and financing decisions (Rhee & Ha, 2022). Within this realm, green finance emphasises funding environmentally sustainable projects, such as solar and renewable energy. For instance, Tesla's green bonds have significantly adopted environment-friendly energy knowhows like solar plates and electric vehicles. Blue finance extends this idea to ocean-based industries, promoting the sustainable use of marine resources and the protection of aquatic ecosystems. The Seychelles Blue Bond, the world's first sovereign blue bond, exemplifies this approach, raising $15 million to support sustainable fisheries and marine conservation. ("Seychelles launches world's first sovereign blue bond," 2018). Additionally, inclusive finance strives to provide affordable financial services to underserved populations, particularly in low-income and marginalised communities. Kenya's M-Pesa mobile money transfer platform is a standout example, transforming financial inclusion by enabling millions to access banking services. These frameworks are increasingly recognised as vital tools for tackling global challenges and advancing the United Nations Sustainable Development Goals (SDGs). "Without environmental sustainability, economic stability and social cohesion cannot be achieved." (Harding, 2007)

The rise of social and sustainable finance reflects growing stakeholder expectations, with corporate investors driving ESG-focused practices. BlackRock, for example, has allocated over $560 billion to ESG investments, signalling rising demand. (*Investment Management & Financial Services | BlackRock*, 2024). Governments are also implementing policies to support this shift. Hong et al. (2023) highlight the welfare impact of sustainable finance through models favouring net-zero firms. As Prince Charles said, "The sustainability revolution will, hopefully, be the third major social and economic turning point in human history."

Social finance and sustainable finance originated in historical movements aimed at aligning financial practices with ethical and moral values (Setyowati, 2020). From religious teachings emphasising responsible resource management to the emergence of socially responsible investing (SRI) in the 20th century, these developments laid the groundwork for modern sustainable finance. However, the 21st century has seen a rapid expansion of these practices, propelled by factors such as globalisation, technological innovation, and the growing urgency to address environmental challenges.

The 2015 Paris Agreement and UN SDGs marked a turning point in integrating sustainability into finance, driving the growth of green and blue finance. ("Paris Agreement | UNFCCC," 2015) These initiatives have spurred governments and institutions to align financial strategies with sustainability goals. Inclusive finance efforts, like India's Jan Dhan Yojana, which opened over 540 million bank accounts, highlight the push for equitable financial access. ("Over 540 million bank accounts opened under Pradhan Mantri Jan Dhan Yojana," 2024)

Regional acceptance, adaptation and application of financial frameworks vary by cultural, economic, and regulatory contexts. European countries lead with stringent policies like the EU Taxonomy and SFDR ("Sustainability-related disclosure in the financial services sector," 2024); on the other side, the U.S. follows a market-driven approach by institutional investors. Meanwhile, emerging economies in Asia, Africa, and Latin America increasingly recognise the potential of inclusive and sustainable finance to drive growth and create a robust resilience system to safeguard economic and environmental vulnerabilities.

Danilov (2021), in their paper, have given an overview of concepts that validate the feasibility of moving from the conventional paradigm of finance to a new paradigm of sustainable finance. Social finance and sustainable finance are grounded in various theoretical frameworks that highlight the relationship between financial performance, social impact, and environmental responsibility. For example, stakeholder theory shifts the focus from a shareholder-centric approach to one that considers the interests of a broader range of stakeholders, such as employees, customers, communities, and the climate. Likewise, the concept of the triple bottom line approach emphasises the importance of balancing economic, social, and environmental goals, underscoring the interdependence of these factors in achieving sustainable outcomes over the long term.

Green finance supports projects that curb environmental degradation, promote renewable energy, and encourage sustainable land use. Germany's Energiewende policy, for example, leveraged green finance to cut carbon emissions by 40%

(1990–2020). ("Germany's Energiewende," 2021) Blue finance extends these principles to marine ecosystems, funding initiatives like Indonesia's mangrove restoration to combat erosion and enhance biodiversity. As a growing sector within climate finance, blue finance attracts global investment, fostering economic growth, job creation, and marine conservation. With the ocean economy projected to reach $3 trillion by 2030, innovative financial solutions are key to sustaining ocean health and expanding clean water access.

Inclusive finance builds on the premise of financial inclusion, aiming to empower underserved populations through access to affordable credit, savings, insurance, and payment systems. Rural Development Bank and community-based lending models have been instrumental in advancing inclusive finance, particularly in developing economies. According to the World Bank Group, financial inclusion is crucial in lowering extreme poverty and promoting prosperity for everybody. Since a transaction account enables people to send and receive payments and keep money, having access to one is a first step toward greater financial inclusion. Because a transaction account acts as a doorway to other financial services, the World Bank Group (WBG) is still focused on ensuring everyone has access to transaction accounts. (*Independent Evaluation Group*, 2021)

ESG integration serves as the foundation of sustainable finance, offering a systematic method for assessing the non-financial performance of companies and investments (Sisodia & Maheshwari, 2023). Environmental considerations include improving climatic conditions, making efficient use of renewable resources, and preserving biodiversity. Social aspects focus on labour rights, community engagement, and promoting diversity and inclusion. Governance emphasises transparency, accountability, and ethical decision-making. Collectively, these dimensions provide an all-inclusive framework for evaluating the sustainability and resilience of financial activities. Alshater et al. (2021) have shown through their Network analysis that the popularity of 'Sustainable finance' and 'ESG' topics has increased in the Journal of Sustainable Finance and Investment (JFSI) while that of 'Corporate governance' and 'Socially responsible investment' has declined. They have also shown through Bibliographic coupling analysis that the major themes published in JSFI involve four main clusters: 'Corporate social responsibility and sustainable development'; 'Sustainable finance and green bonds'; 'Corporate governance and ESG'; and 'Responsible investment and pension funds.

Impact investing, a vital aspect of social finance, involves intentionally deploying capital to achieve measurable social and environmental benefits alongside financial returns. By prioritising areas like renewable energy, affordable housing, and healthcare, impact investors aim to tackle critical societal issues while maintaining financial sustainability. Additionally, the growing domains of green and blue finance highlight the power of targeted investments in promoting environmental sustainability and conserving natural resources. Impact investing is when investors pursue strategies that create positive environmental or social benefits and strong investment returns. "Impact investing provides a way for investors to be more proactive with their investment dollars and partner together to make purposeful investments that can contribute to affecting real change across the globe," ("What is impact investing? Meaning, types and examples," 2024)

The growth of these financial paradigms is driven by a mix of demand- and supply-side factors. On the demand side, investors gradually seek opportunities that reflect their values and promote positive societal impacts. Millennial and Gen Z investors have shown a strong inclination toward ESG-compliant investments, reshaping capital flows toward sustainable, green, and blue assets. Additionally, the mounting evidence connecting strong ESG performance with improved financial outcomes has strengthened the business case for sustainability, motivating investors to include ESG factors in their investment strategies.

On the supply side, corporations and financial institutions increasingly acknowledge the strategic benefits of adopting sustainable practices. Improving ESG performance allows companies to mitigate risk, lower costs, and strengthen their competitive advantage. Access to sustainable financial tools like green bonds, blue bonds, and sustainability-linked loans provides organisations with capital on favourable terms, further encouraging ESG adoption. Additionally, inclusive finance initiatives, such as mobile banking and digital payment platforms, have widened financial access, especially in regions with limited traditional banking infrastructure.

Technological advancements have played a crucial role in driving these financial frameworks. The proliferation of big data, artificial intelligence, and blockchain technology has facilitated more accurate and transparent measurement of ESG performance, enabling investors to make informed decisions. Moreover, digital platforms and fintech innovations have democratised access to inclusive finance, empowering individual investors and small businesses to participate in the transition toward a sustainable economy.

Despite its increasing importance, social finance and sustainable finance encounter significant challenges that must be overcome to achieve their full impact. A major obstacle is the lack of global standardisation and consistency in ESG metrics and reporting. The absence of universally recognised frameworks for assessing and disclosing ESG performance has resulted in disintegration and instances of misleading claims, eroding investor trust and limiting the scalability of sustainable finance initiatives.

Balancing short-term financial pressures with long-term sustainability goals remains a challenge as organisations face competing stakeholder demands. Resource disparities and regulatory gaps further hinder the equitable adoption of sustainable finance, particularly in emerging markets. Bridging these gaps requires coordinated efforts from governments and financial institutions to strengthen frameworks and provide support. An estimated $600–800 billion is needed annually for land, forest, and water conservation, plus $550 billion for renewable energy projects, yet less than 15% of conservation funding is met. Mobilising additional resources is crucial to sustaining ecosystems on land and in oceans.

The increasing awareness of the interconnectedness between financial, social, and environmental systems opens up substantial opportunities for expanding these financial paradigms. The shift toward a low-carbon economy, for example, creates vast prospects for innovation and investment in areas such as renewable energy, energy efficiency, and sustainable infrastructure through green finance. Likewise, the growth of blue finance highlights the critical need for investments in ocean health and marine conservation, essential for maintaining the planet's ecological balance and supporting life.

Inclusive finance presents unique opportunities to address economic inequality by empowering underserved communities. The integration of digital technologies and innovative business models, such as peer-to-peer lending and mobile banking, can enhance financial inclusion and promote equitable access to resources. Furthermore, the expansion of new financial instruments and mechanisms, such as blue bonds, transition bonds, and sustainability-linked derivatives, expands the toolkit for achieving sustainability objectives.

Collaboration and partnerships will play a critical role in scaling these financial frameworks. By fostering cross-sectoral cooperation among governments, financial institutions, businesses, and civil society, stakeholders can leverage their collective expertise and resources to drive systemic change. Initiatives such as blended finance, which combines public and private capital to de-risk investments in sustainable projects, exemplify the potential of collaborative approaches to unlock new opportunities.

Financial objectives are frequently the foundation of a company's business strategy and operations. Nonetheless, corporate social responsibility (CSR) initiatives push company executives to think about corporate citizenship or the company's overall societal impact while making choices. Corporate social responsibility assists businesses in making sure that their activities are moral, secure, and, whenever feasible, have a good influence. Companies strive to reduce their environmental effect, help address societal issues like poverty and inequality, and make sure their brand identity aligns with their beliefs through corporate social responsibility (CSR) activities. As more workers look for companies that share their values, CSR may also assist draw in top talent and increase employee engagement and retention. Furthermore, taking a proactive stance on moral and societal concerns may help avoid penalties and other legal troubles (McGrath, 2023).

In a nutshell, social finance and sustainable finance represent a transformative shift in the global financial paradigm, aligning capital flows with the pressing needs of society and the environment. As the world contends with unparalleled challenges such as climate change, inequality, and economic instability, the integration of ESG principles into financial systems offers a pathway to resilience, inclusivity, and long-term prosperity. By addressing the challenges and harnessing the opportunities outlined in this chapter, stakeholders can collectively contribute to the realisation of a more sustainable and equitable global economy.

A new understanding of the value of companies and securities that considers social and environmental externalities, long-term value creation as the primary business objective, and the adaptive markets hypothesis are some of the fundamental components of the sustainable finance idea. All of these components are predicated on the original argument—which more and more investors are adopting—that firms must integrate non-financial (social and environmental) and financial objectives in their growth.

This book chapter aims to comprehensively examine the evolving landscape of social finance and sustainable finance across the globe. It seeks to analyse the current status and the various stages of growth that these financial approaches are experiencing in different geographical regions. By exploring regional trends and patterns, the chapter intends to provide a nuanced understanding of how social finance and sustainable finance practices are being adopted and integrated into financial systems worldwide. Furthermore, the chapter will engage in a detailed review of existing literature from across the globe to uncover the predominant areas of scholarly focus within the realm of social and sustainable finance. This includes identifying key themes that have attracted researchers' attention and mapping the interconnected disciplines that align with the study's central concepts. Such an approach helps in establishing a conceptual framework and contextual grounding for further analysis.

A distinctive component of this study involves examining how Indian corporations are implementing social and sustainable finance principles. This will be achieved through a methodical content analysis of annual reports published by these organisations. As defined by Weber (1988), content analysis involves classifying textual material into distinct categories based on specific, predetermined criteria. This technique enables researchers to identify the presence of particular words, phrases, or concepts within a body of text—be it books, academic essays, articles, or corporate documents. In the field of accounting and intellectual capital reporting, content analysis is widely recognised as a robust research method, as demonstrated by the works of Abeysekera & Guthrie (2005) and Adams et al. (1995). In this chapter, the texts—primarily annual reports—will be coded into thematic segments that reflect various social and sustainable finance dimensions. The themes selected for the study include but are not limited to, corporate governance, corporate social responsibility, climate finance, green finance, carbon finance, renewable energy finance, social finance, sustainable finance, sustainable development goals, impact investment, socially responsible investing, and blue finance. These themes serve as the analytical lens through which the implementation of these concepts by Indian companies will be evaluated. The methodology is consistent with the approach used by Vuontisjärvi (2006), and is designed to determine the extent to which these themes are embedded in corporate disclosures. Through this analysis, the chapter aspires to shed light on the strategic priorities of Indian firms in the context of sustainability and social responsibility.

Following is the Scheme of the Book Chapter: Chapter 1: Introduction, Chapter 2: Literature Review, Chapter 3: Research Methodology and Chapter 4: Analysis, Interpretation & Conclusions

2. LITERATURE REVIEW

The intersection of finance with social and environmental concerns has led to the emergence of two major financial paradigms: social finance and sustainable finance. While both are concerned about aligning financial flows with broader societal goals, their primary objectives, instruments, and philosophical underpinnings diverge. This literature review synthesises scholarly contributions to the fields of social and sustainable finance, critically evaluating their conceptual evolution, theoretical frameworks, operational mechanisms, and contemporary relevance

2.1 Social Finance

Social finance has emerged as a response to the limitations of traditional finance, which has historically prioritised profit maximisation without accounting for negative social or environmental externalities. The traditional financial model evaluates lending decisions based on profitability, liquidity, and risk metrics, often sidelining ethical or societal concerns. However, this paradigm has evolved with the recognition that finance can serve a dual purpose: generating financial returns while addressing social challenges. The emergence of social finance signifies a departure from purely profit-oriented financial systems towards more inclusive, ethical, and sustainable models of capital allocation (Nicholls & Emerson, 2015; Emerson, 2003).

At its core, social finance challenges the dominant investor logic by integrating social utility and environmental responsibility into investment decisions. The concept rests on the blended value proposition—that financial, social, and environmental returns are not mutually exclusive but can co-exist in a single investment vehicle (Emerson, 2003). This reimagined logic promotes long-term societal well-being over short-term profit extraction, making social finance a distinct and critical innovation within the broader financial ecosystem (Weber, 2012; Weber & Duan, 2012).

Chiapello and Knoll (2020) position social finance within broader socio-political transformations, linking it to welfare state reform, financialisation, and the restructuring of public governance. They argue that social finance is more than a financial innovation—it represents a new way of organising state-society-market relationships, influencing how public goods are funded and delivered. This interpretation aligns with Langley's (2018) view that social finance constructs a liberal, moral, and entrepreneurial social domain, transforming "the social" into a space governed by market dynamics.

Innovations such as microfinance, venture philanthropy, crowdfunding, and social impact bonds have facilitated the operationalisation of social finance. Andrikopoulos (2019) highlights that while these instruments redefine the landscape of public goods provision and entrepreneurial activity, they also face significant challenges. Chief among these are the lack of standardised impact metrics, difficulties attributing social outcomes to specific investments, and social ventures' small-scale, long-horizon nature.

Haigh (2014) identifies the strategic intent behind social finance as the effective allocation of capital toward projects with measurable environmental and social returns. This has necessitated the development of new organisational models and financial instruments that can mobilise resources while maintaining accountability for non-financial outcomes. In this context, Akcay and Hirshleifer (2020) introduce a paradigm based on social transmission biases, information asymmetries, and institutional influences, which shape investor preferences and market behaviours in the social finance space.

Social networks also play a pivotal role in shaping financial behaviour. Kuchler and Stroebel (2021) demonstrate how social relationships influence household investment decisions, reinforcing the embeddedness of finance within social contexts. These findings validate the broader claim that social finance is a response to market failures and a product of evolving social norms and networks.

Ozili (2021) expands the scope of social finance by linking it with green and digital finance. He proposes that digital technologies can streamline and democratise social investment, enabling more inclusive participation and efficient resource allocation. Carè and Weber (2023) further delineate the intellectual structure of the field by identifying four primary research hotspots—impact investing, social entrepreneurship, social impact bonds, and social innovation. They emphasise the growing institutionalisation of the field, mapping its evolution across academic institutions and practitioner communities.

Arifin et al. (2023) add a grassroots perspective by reviewing models of community financing. Their work underscores the importance of local capital mobilisation in fostering community empowerment and development, reaffirming the bottom-up potential of social finance.

2.1.1 Islamic Social Finance

Within the broader umbrella of social finance, Islamic Social Finance (ISF) offers a faith-based alternative that aligns financial practices with Shariah principles. It includes instruments such as zakat (obligatory almsgiving), waqf (endowments), infaq, and sadaqah (voluntary charity), which are explicitly designed to promote social welfare and economic justice.

Ascarya et al. (2022) propose an integrated model of Islamic commercial and social finance (IICSF), wherein Islamic banks establish separate Baitul Maal institutions to manage social finance instruments. These banks act as facilitators, ensuring the compliance and effective deployment of social funds.

ISF has demonstrated strong alignment with the Sustainable Development Goals (SDGs). Dirie et al. (2023) show that ISF mechanisms can contribute to 11 of the 17 SDGs, particularly in areas such as poverty alleviation, education, health, and clean water. Shahid et al. (2023) support this view, arguing that global ISF resources are sufficient to help Muslim-majority countries meet key SDG targets.

Despite its potential, Islamic Social Finance (ISF) faces challenges related to awareness, governance, and operational capacity. Umar et al. (2021) find that while ISF mechanisms like zakat positively impact poverty reduction, their effectiveness is limited by low public awareness and lack of integration into broader development strategies. Lanzara (2021) provides bibliometric evidence of a surge in scholarly interest in ISF, especially in the last five years, reflecting its growing relevance.

Kuanova et al. (2021) review ISF instruments' theoretical foundations and practical applications, highlighting their suitability for addressing contemporary challenges. Akhter et al. (2023) outline future research directions in ISF, such as Islamic fintech, economic recovery, sustainable development, and refugee support. Kasmon et al. (2024) explore how fintech innovations—crowdfunding, peer-to-peer lending, and blockchain—are being leveraged to modernise ISF practices across Asia.

2.1.2 The Current Landscape and Future Directions

The geographical diffusion of social finance remains uneven, with notable differences in institutional structures and policy environments across regions. Benedikter (2011) compares social banking systems in the U.S. and Europe, attributing their growth to long-standing traditions of ethical finance. He posits that social finance can complement traditional finance by acting as a model for ethical and sustainable practices.

Gonzalez-Ruiz et al. (2024) call for a deeper exploration of social banking models, especially their role in financial inclusion and community development. Silva et al. (2024) advocate for more rigorous studies on how social finance fosters systemic social innovation. Ozili (2024) stresses the need to examine the role of emerging technologies like blockchain and artificial intelligence (AI) in enhancing transparency, accountability, and efficiency in social finance markets.

2.2 Sustainable Finance

Sustainable finance builds upon the premise that financial systems must be economically viable, environmentally sustainable, and socially inclusive. It focuses on incorporating Environmental, Social, and Governance (ESG) considerations into investment decisions to drive long-term value creation. The rise of sustainable finance corresponds with increasing awareness of climate change, biodiversity loss, and growing socio-economic inequality, prompting financial institutions to reassess their role in global development.

The academic field of sustainable finance has gained momentum since the mid-2010s, particularly after landmark initiatives such as the Paris Agreement and the adoption of the SDGs (Singhania et al., 2023). Their bibliometric review highlights increased scholarly output and global collaboration while also noting the need for further theoretical development and empirical research.

Cunha et al. (2021) emphasise that sustainable finance is central to promoting global development. However, they identify major obstacles such as short-termism, under-theorization, and limited empirical evidence on impact. Edmans and Kacperczyk (2022) categorise the drivers of sustainable finance into three areas: financial relevance, non-financial contributions, and evolving investor preferences. These drivers reflect a shift in corporate and investor behaviour, where sustainability is now integral to strategic decision-making rather than a peripheral concern.

The global market for sustainable financial instruments, such as green, social, and sustainability-linked bonds (GSS+), has surged since 2007, reaching a cumulative market value of USD 3.9 trillion. This growth underscores stakeholder interest in aligning capital flows with environmental and social outcomes. Singhania et al. (2023) identify key research areas, including carbon trading, climate finance, greenwashing, and the role of blockchain and AI in sustainability reporting.

Setyowati (2020) cautions that while financial institutions have adopted sustainability frameworks and reporting standards, interpretations of what constitutes a “green” initiative vary widely. This ambiguity risks enabling token compliance and undermining the credibility of sustainable finance. The article calls for stronger regulatory frameworks and central bank interventions to foster genuine climate finance.

2.2.1 Theoretical Contributions and Sub-Themes

Ozili (2021) introduces six theoretical lenses for understanding sustainable finance: system disruption theory, peer emulation theory, priority theory, resource theory, life span theory, and positive signalling theory. These frameworks offer insights into how different actors prioritise sustainability, emulate peer behaviours, and allocate resources based on lifecycle assessments.

Olumekor and Oke (2024) find that support for sustainable finance is shaped more by demographic characteristics—such as age, gender, and urban versus rural residency—than by knowledge alone. Jayaram and Singh (2020) identify major sub-fields within sustainable finance, including climate finance, impact investing, sustainable banking, and microfinance, with climate finance and sustainable banking being the most promising areas for future inquiry.

Talan and Sharma (2019) emphasise the accountability potential of sustainable investing. They argue that financial markets must be held responsible for their social and environmental impacts, necessitating a shift from conventional investment practices to sustainability-focused models. Streimikiene et al. (2023) empirically validate the link between sustainable finance and SDG performance across Baltic Sea states, showing that countries with more robust sustainable finance frameworks make greater progress toward SDGs.

Naeem et al. (2022) confirm the alignment of sustainable finance with ongoing business trends in socially responsible investing and climate action. Luo et al. (2022) identify evolving research hotspots such as green finance, carbon credits, renewable energy, and low-carbon transitions, which dominate the academic discourse from 2000 to 2021.

2.2.2 Geographical Trends and Emerging Technologies

Kashi and Shah (2023) identify the U.S., Switzerland, Japan, China, and the UK as global hubs of sustainable finance research. Purnomo et al. (2021) find that while the UK leads in scholarly output, China is the largest source of research funding. Ziolo et al. (2020) link the achievement of SDGs to the presence of sustainable financial systems in OECD countries, showing that economic, environmental, and social sustainability are strongly associated with sustainable financial models.

Xu (2024) highlights the potential of AI in improving ESG data analytics and decision-making processes, while Ballandies et al. (2021) explore how blockchain can align financial incentives with ecological outcomes. Hilario-Caballero et al. (2020) call for a deeper understanding of how financial innovations can support the transition to integrated sustainability frameworks.

Svartzman et al. (2020) underscore the importance of green monetary policies and the role of central banks in promoting sustainability through tools like green quantitative easing and carbon stress testing. Malamas et al. (2023) identify fintech-driven solutions such as decentralised finance (DeFi), green digital banking, and tokenised green bonds as emerging frontiers for research and practice.

3. RESEARCH METHODOLOGY

The following section gives a comprehensive knowledge of the methodology used, data collection and framework used in this research study

3.1 Study Approach

In order to identify significant contributions from writers, organizations, journals, and nations, as well as to identify research hotspots and developing trends in the central banking approach to climate threats, this study uses the bibliometric research method. Price (1965) first used this methodology to assess and map academic publications (Bahoo et al., 2020; Zupic & Cater, 2013). It has been well-liked because of its cross-disciplinary approach and capacity to manage big datasets.

To explain the contributions of the study participants (e.g., authors, institutions, journals, and nations) to central banking operations and climate risks, performance analysis was done (Cobo et al., 2011; Donthu et al., 2021). Furthermore, science mapping methods were used to determine the connections between the research components, including co-citation analysis, co-authorship analysis, and co-word analysis.

VOS Viewer, which is one of the most potent software to study bibliometric networks, was used for science mapping and network analysis. At the same time, Microsoft Excel was utilised for the dataset selection and standardisation process.

Finding certain words or concepts in texts or collections of texts is essentially the goal of the research method known as content analysis. Books, book chapters, essays, yearly reports, articles, historical documents, etc. are considered as texts. An established technique for examining annual reports is content analysis, which has been applied extensively in the field of accounting research on intellectual capital reporting. Any text is coded or divided into manageable words, phrases, sentences, or subject groups for conducting content analysis. Themes have been adopted as a fundamental criterion for this investigation (Pandey, 2012). The objective is to verify the presence or absence of certain social and sustainable finance themes in each annual report of various Indian organisations under study.

3.2 Data Collection and Treatment

For analysing large volumes of scientific data, bibliometric analysis is a widely used accurate method. Bibliometric analysis comprehends interconnectedness among journal citations, co-authorship and keywords (Donthu et al., 2021).

Scopus database was used to fetch the data useful for the bibliometric analysis. The search was done on March 7, 2025. Documents were searched with the following keywords, namely a) Social Finance and b) Sustainable Finance. Articles from 1960 to till date were considered. A total of 991 articles were found, and finally, 978 documents were obtained based on the inclusion criteria of articles published in the English language. These documents were exported in CSV files.

Bibliometrics is a quantitative analysis method. VOS viewer is a bibliometric software, that introduces sample pieces of literature data into it and draws a knowledge map. It can present the overall external characteristics of subject areas, and the software has a unique advantage, especially in clustering analysis.

3.3 Output of Publication

The number of publications related to keywords retrieved from the Scopus database was counted. As discussed in Table 1, a total of 10 types of documents were recorded.

Table 1. Publication by document type

Rank	Type of Document	No of Documents	Percentage
1	Article	567	58
2	Conference Paper	271	27.5
3	Review	58	6.4
4	Book Chapter	31	2.9
5	Retracted	12	1.4
6	Book	12	1.2
7	Short Survey	11	1.1
8	Note	10	1
9	Conference Review	1	0.1
10	Data Paper	1	0.1
		978	100

Compiled by Researcher

4. ANALYSIS, INTERPRETATION & CONCLUSION

4.1 Analysis

4.1.1 Performance Analysis

4.1.1.1 Total Publications (TP) and Total Citations (TC)

The year-wise research growth in this research field is displayed in Fig. 1. The figure shows that research in the field experienced significant growth in the number of papers published. An effective structural variation in the growth pattern has been observed since 2024. The years 2020, 2021, and 2022, 2023 & 2024 collectively represent 69% of the entire sample when considering the number of articles published. This trend suggests that this topic has been attracting rising interest globally since 2020.

Figure 1. Article published from 2011 to 2025

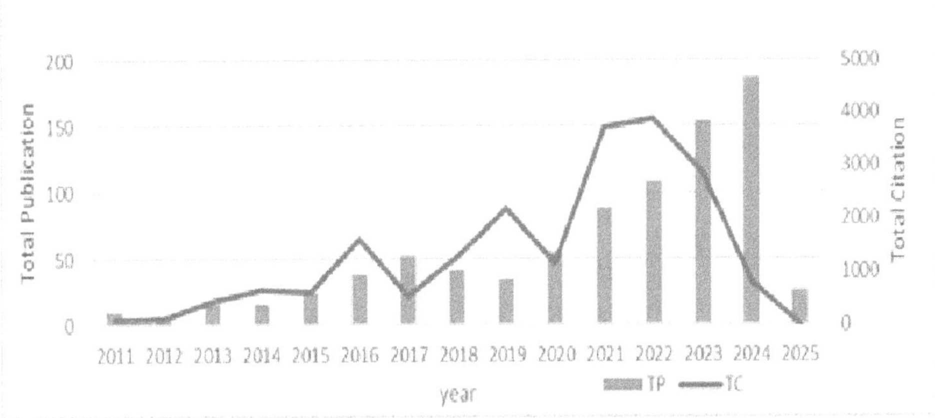

4.1.1.2 Most Contributing Authors (CA)

The author's data were collected from the Scopus database. There are 978 different scholars in the sample of articles analyzed. Surprisingly, 88.3% of the scholars contributed a single article on the topic, and only 11.7% of the scholars contributed to the field with more than one article. Table 2 ranks the most prolific scholars according to the number of articles published ($n \geq 2$).

Table 2. Top 15 Contributing Authors

Authors	Country	No of Publication
Ziolo M.; Bak I.; Cheba K.; Spoz A.	Poland	6
Li J.; Dong K.; Taghizadeh-Hesary F.; Wang K.	China	5
Zhang Y.	China	5
Adebayo T.S.; Kirikkaleli D.; Adeshola I.; Oluwajana D.; Akinsola G.D.; Osemeahon O.S.	Cyprus	4
Li X.; Li Y.; Cai J.; Cao Y.; Li L.	China	4
Majercáková D.; Mittelman A.	Slovakia	4
Wang L.	China	4
Chen X.; Wang J.	China	3
Jeyaretnam T.	USA	3
Li Q.	China	3
Liu Y.	China	3
Sun H.; Chen F.	China	3
Wang X.	China	3
Zhang D.	China	3
Bataev A.V.	Russian Federation	2

Compiled by Researcher

4.1.1.3 Most Cited Publications (CP)

Citation count and analysis can be considered as a useful tool to assist in identifying the most influential articles and authors (Liu, 1993). In general terms, the overall citations received by an article reflect its quality and influence (Shashi et al., 2020). Table 3 summarizes the top 20 articles that are most frequently cited. The table contains the title of the article, the author's name, the publishing journal, and the year of publication. The article The Long-term Benefits of Organizational Resilience through Sustainable Business Practices," published by Ortiz and Bansal (2016), emerged as the top-cited article, with 683 citations. Furthermore, the article entitled "Do Environmental, social, and Governance Activities Improve Corporate Financial Performance?" published by Xie et al. (2019), appeared as the second most cited paper, with 597 citations.

Table 3. Top 20 cited publications

Authors	Title	Source title	Cited by
Ortiz-de-Mandojana N.; Bansal P.	The long-term benefits of organizational resilience through sustainable business practices	Strategic Management Journal	683
Xie J.; Nozawa W.; Yagi M.; Fujii H.; Managi S.	Do environmental, social, and governance activities improve corporate financial performance?	Business Strategy and the Environment	597
Azapagic A.; Perdan S.	Indicators of sustainable development for industry: A general framework	Process Safety and Environmental Protection	457
Acheampong A.O.	Modelling for insight: Does financial development improve environmental quality?	Energy Economics	438
Zakari A.; Khan I.; Tan D.; Alvarado R.; Dagar V.	Energy efficiency and sustainable development goals (SDGs)	Energy	391
Ahmad M.; Jiang P.; Murshed M.; Shehzad K.; Akram R.; Cui L.; Khan Z.	Modelling the dynamic linkages between eco-innovation, urbanization, economic growth and ecological footprints for G7 countries: Does financial globalization matter?	Sustainable Cities and Society	346
Zhou G.; Liu L.; Luo S.	Sustainable development, ESG performance and company market value: Mediating effect of financial performance	Business Strategy and the Environment	329
Frias-Aceituno J.V.; Rodríguez-Ariza L.; Garcia-Sánchez I.M.	Explanatory Factors of Integrated Sustainability and Financial Reporting	Business Strategy and the Environment	326
Wang X.; Wang Q.	Research on the impact of green finance on the upgrading of China's regional industrial structure from the perspective of sustainable development	Resources Policy	298
Shahbaz M.; Mallick H.; Mahalik M.K.; Sadorsky P.	The role of globalization on the recent evolution of energy demand in India: Implications for sustainable development	Energy Economics	281
Zhang M.; Liu Y.	Influence of digital finance and green technology innovation on China's carbon emission efficiency: Empirical analysis based on spatial metrology	Science of the Total Environment	270
Cantele S.; Zardini A.	Is sustainability a competitive advantage for small businesses? An empirical analysis of possible mediators in the sustainability–financial performance relationship	Journal of Cleaner Production	265
Lin C.-H.; Yang H.-L.; Liou D.-Y.	The impact of corporate social responsibility on financial performance: Evidence from business in Taiwan	Technology in Society	251
Okafor A.; Adusei M.; Adeleye B.N.	Corporate social responsibility and financial performance: Evidence from U.S tech firms	Journal of Cleaner Production	231

continued on following page

Table 3. Continued

Authors	Title	Source title	Cited by
Sinha A.; Mishra S.; Sharif A.; Yarovaya L.	Does green financing help to improve environmental & social responsibility? Designing SDG framework through advanced quantile modelling	Journal of Environmental Management	229
Brewer E.; Demmer M.; Du B.; Ho M.; Kam M.; Nedevschi S.; Pal J.; Patra R.; Surana S.; Fall K.	The case for technology in developing regions	Computer	228
Nundy S.; Ghosh A.; Mesloub A.; Albaqawy G.A.; Alnaim M.M.	Impact of COVID-19 pandemic on socio-economic, energy-environment and transport sector globally and sustainable development goal (SDG)	Journal of Cleaner Production	219
Scholtens B.; Dam L.	Banking on the Equator. Are Banks that Adopted the Equator Principles Different from Non-Adopters?	World Development	215
Umar M.; Ji X.; Mirza N.; Naqvi B.	Carbon neutrality, bank lending, and credit risk: Evidence from the Eurozone	Journal of Environmental Management	214
Abbasi K.R.; Hussain K.; Haddad A.M.; Salman A.; Ozturk I.	The role of Financial Development and Technological Innovation towards Sustainable Development in Pakistan: Fresh insights from consumption and territory-based emissions	Technological Forecasting and Social Change	212

Compiled by Researcher

4.1.1.4 Most Contributing Journals (CJ)

All of the sample articles were published in 383 different journals. Table 4 shows a list of the top 15 journals in terms of publication counts and considers only those with at least 2 published articles. Regarding the journals' subject areas, Table 4 also highlights that the list is headed by the journal Sustainability, with more than 5% contributions in terms of publications.

Table 4. Top 15 contributing journals (n > 2)

Publication Titles	No of total Publication	Proportion of Total publication	Author Keywords
Sustainability (Switzerland)	55	5.65	ESG factors; Fuzzy cognitive mapping; MCDA; PROMETHEE; Risk; Sustainable finance; Sustainable financial systems
Resources Policy	49	5.03	Green finance; Industrial structure; Sustainable development
Journal of Cleaner Production	41	4.21	Competitive advantage; Corporate social responsibility; Firm performance; Small and medium enterprises; Sustainability
Journal of Environmental Management	22	2.26	Agenda 2030; Environmental and social responsibility; Green bonds; Green financing; Quantile; Wavelet
Environmental Science and Pollution Research	19	1.95	Clean energy; Green finance; Green financial volatility; OLS; R&D; South Asia
Energies	17	1.75	DEA; Energy efficiency; Regression; Sustainable economic development; Sustainable financial development
Energy Economics	12	1.23	CO₂ emissions; Economic growth; Energy intensity; Financial development
Renewable and Sustainable Energy Reviews	10	1.03	Economic growth; Energy trilemma; Energy use; Financial development; Top ten countries of the WETI 2020
Renewable Energy	10	1.03	CS-ARDL Approach; Economic globalization; Economic policy uncertainty; Financial development; Renewable energy consumption
Business Strategy and the Environment	9	0.92	corporate efficiency; corporate social responsibility; data envelopment analysis; ESG activities; ESG disclosure; stakeholder engagement; sustainable development
Energy and Environment	9	0.92	ecological footprint; economic efficiency; Environmental Kuznets curve; financial development; industrialization; renewable energy; super-efficiency SBM model
Technological Forecasting and Social Change	9	0.92	Economic globalization; Energy use; Financial development; Technological innovation
Environmental Impact Assessment Review	7	0.72	Adaptive management; Community development; Community relations; Corporate social responsibility; Greentape reduction; Sustainable development

continued on following page

Table 4. Continued

Publication Titles	No of total Publication	Proportion of Total publication	Author Keywords
International Journal of Environmental Research and Public Health	6	0.62	Agricultural technology innovation; Public health; Rural financial development; Sustainable development in agriculture
Procedia Computer Science	6	0.62	Business model; Corporate sustainability; Enterprises; Finance; Sustainability

Compiled by Researcher

4.1.1.5 Most Contributing Countries (CC)

An overview of the research centres and subgroups within this particular field of study may be obtained by concentrating on the research performance of nations, funding agencies, and organisations. The amount of research conducted at the national level may significantly rise among nations or areas that have largely created particular policies or as a result of funding initiatives in a particular field of study. The top 10 nations in terms of contributions ($n \geq 5$) are displayed in Table 5. Even if three or more writers from the same nation coauthored the publication, each nation is only included once when analysing nations' performance based on the authors' affiliation. The top 10 countries contribute 75% of the total articles. China emerged as the dominant region with 243 articles, followed by the United States with 100 articles, top 2 countries contribute around 35% of the total articles. Other eight countries contribute around 39% of the total articles.

Table 5. Top 10 contributing countries

Country	Documents	Citations	Total Link Strength
China	243	161	70
United States	100	39	33
United Kingdom	60	7403	36
Italy	54	154	10
India	52	556	32
Pakistan	52	7	52
Russian Federation	49	1502	8
Malaysia	48	303	43
Canada	38	1072	26
Germany	33	78	12

Compiled by Researcher

4.1.1.6 Keywords Analysis

In this section, the analysis of keywords was carried out to identify the linkages among different subtopics (Feng et al., 2017). Table 6 lists the most recurring keywords (n $\geq$ 10). The higher the frequency of occurrence of keywords, the higher the attention paid to the topic. Observing the table, the most frequently used keywords are "sustainable finance" (126), "sustainable development" (113), and "sustainability" (108).

Table 6. Frequent Keywords

Keyword	Occurrences	Total Link Strength
sustainable finance	126	175
sustainable development	113	122
sustainability	108	138
corporate social responsibility	74	106
green finance	66	87
esg	59	96
financial development	47	66
financial performance	41	60
sustainable development goals	35	44
economic growth	34	52
finance	33	34
renewable energy	31	47
natural resources	22	38
financial inclusion	20	22
social finance	20	27
environment	19	24
environmental	19	36
corporate governance	17	28
social responsibility	17	29
china	16	31
climate change	16	28
social	16	36
environmental sustainability	15	29
csr	14	25
impact investing	13	21
sdgs	13	21

continued on following page

Table 6. Continued

Keyword	Occurrences	Total Link Strength
carbon emissions	12	16
circular economy	12	18
co 2 emissions	12	21
digital finance	12	7
energy consumption	12	21
islamic social finance	12	12
economic development	11	12
fintech	11	15
globalization	11	19
social sustainability	11	18
corporate financial performance	10	12
sustainability reporting	10	15

Compiled by Researcher

4.1.2 Science Mapping

Explaining the dynamics and structure of scientific domains is the primary goal of science mapping (Shashi et al., 2020; Zupic & Cater, 2013). Scholars can identify the most influential research work by using this strategy, which has been shown to be a very effective instrument for obtaining a transparent, systematic, and reproducible review process (Zupic & Cater, 2013) (Huertas-Valdivia et al., 2020). To obtain a deeper understanding, we used co-citation, co-authorship, and keyword co-occurrence analysis under science mapping. Table 7 presents an overview of this study's primary science mapping techniques.

Table 7. Applied technique for science mapping

Technique	Purpose	Unit of Analysis	Data Requirement
Co-citation analysis	To investigate the relationships between cited publications in order to identify the foundational themes.	Documents	References
Co-author analysis	To identify scholars who are actively participating in the advancement of the research field.	Authors	Authors Affiliation (country and organizations)
Co-word Analysis	To explore the current or potential relationships between topics in the research field by analyzing the keywords.	Keywords	Article Title Abstract Index keywords Author keywords Full text

Compiled by Researcher

4.1.2.1 Co-Citation Analysis

Co-citation analysis constructs structural images of scientific fields by using bibliographic data from selected databases (Zupic & Cater, 2013). In particular, co-citation analysis is used to analyze the frequency with which two items (publications) are cited together (Small, 1973), which mainly elucidates that their content is related (Zupic & Cater, 2013). This study applied author co-citation analysis to identify the most important authors in this research field and link them through citation records (White & McCain, 1998). Within the 978 selected sample articles, 47861 cited references were identified. Authors with at least 5 citations were considered. As a consequence, 65 authors out of 47861 citations met this threshold criterion. Out of these 65 authors, only 61 are interconnected. In Fig. 2, the thickness of nodes in the network shows the authors' co-citation ties, while closer links show the proximity among the nodes. The co-citation network revealed 8 clusters of the cited 61 research studies/reports with 223 links and a total link strength of 397.

As represented in Fig. 2,

1. The red cluster contains 14 studies and outlines corporate social responsibility
2. Orange cluster contains 11 studies and outlines sustainable finance.
3. The blue cluster contains 9 studies and outlines renewable energy.
4. Golden cluster contains 7 studies and outlines natural resources and environment.
5. The purple cluster contains 7 studies and outlines energy.
6. Sky Blue cluster contains 5 studies and outlines ESG and green finance
7. Dark Orange contains 5 studies and outlines resources
8. Brown cluster contains 3 studies and outlines the competitive advantage

Figure 2. Co-citation

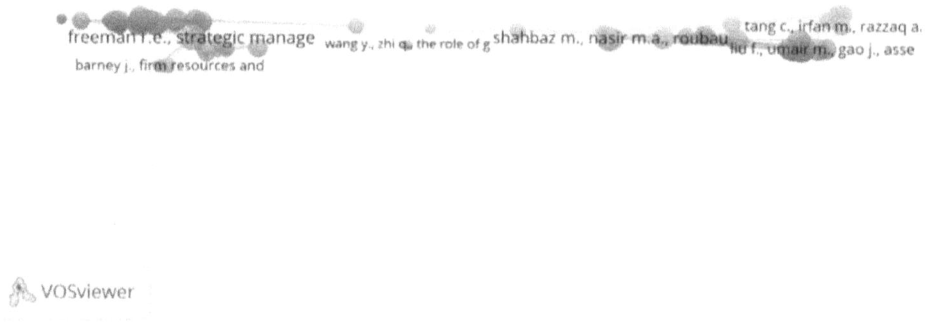

Compiled by Researcher

4.1.2.2 Co-author analysis

Co-author analysis identifies the social network among researchers (Paltrinieri et al., 2019; Zupic & Cater, 2013). The main reason behind conducting this analysis was to recognise those scholars who are actively contributing together in this research field (Migliavacca et al., 2022). For the purpose of the analysis, the minimum document scale was confined to 3 with a minimum citation of 50. Fig. 3 reveals six main groups comprising 10 researchers working jointly on multiple aspects of central bank activities and climate-related risk. Table 8 provides details of these authors.

Table 8. Social network of authorship

Author	Documents	Citations	Total link strength
adebayo, tomiwa sunday	7	447	1
agyabeng-mensah, yaw	3	332	0
bak, iwona	4	158	11
cheba, katarzyna	4	158	11
filipiak, beata zofia	3	152	9
irfan, muhammad	6	322	1
lee, chien-chiang	3	149	0
ullah, farid	3	73	0
zhang, dongyang	3	235	0
ziolo, magdalena	6	233	11

Compiled by Researcher

Figure 3. Co-authorship analysis

Compiled by Researcher

4.1.2.3 Co-word analysis

A content analysis method called co-word analysis makes use of keywords in texts to create connections and develop a theoretical framework for the field of study (Zupic & Cater, 2013).

To identify frequently occurring terms together in a given text corpus, a quantitative technique known as co-occurrence analysis was employed. This method is particularly helpful for understanding the relationships and connections among concepts within a certain topic. Based on the authors' chosen keywords related to the chapter, the bibliometric data of 974 articles were obtained from the Scopus database and cooccurrence analysis was performed using network visualization.

The least number of occurrences of keywords was set to 25. Out of 6638 keywords, 77 keywords met the threshold. Out of these 77 keywords, all keywords were identified by the author, matching the theme and subtheme of the paper. Based on these 77 keywords network visualization was applied in VOS Viewer. Based on the three components of the chapter title network visualization image was created as

Figure 4. Overlay visualization map

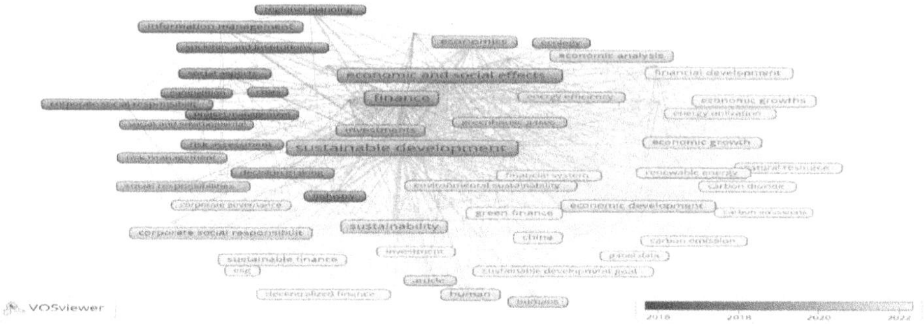

Compiled by Researcher

4.1.2.4 Country-wise Citation Analysis

Figure 5. Overlay visualization map

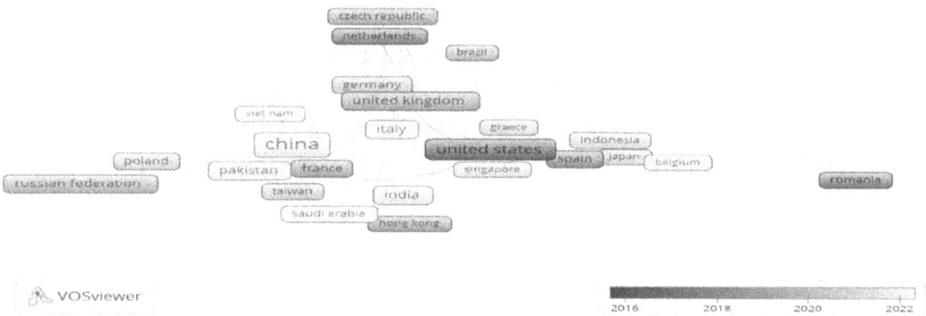

Compiled by Researcher

4.1.3 Cluster Analysis

The cluster analysis built upon the keyword network is a noteworthy output of the bibliometric technique. As a result, the following sections examine the five clusters, highlighting the connections between various keywords within each group.

The cluster technique has been used to highlight the four clusters containing keywords associated with the central theme of this article i.e Social and Sustainable Finance. Figure 4 depicts the Co-occurrence analysis for the network visualisation that emerged in the scientific papers. The cloud map shows the number of occurrences of the word in the article and the relationship of the keywords. Out of 5 colours in Figure 4, each colour represents a group of terms merged into clusters, and the length of curved lines specifies the approximate connection of the repetition of the term. In contrast, the thickness of one shows the strength of pairs of topic areas or keywords. A total of five clusters have been identified: Cluster One contains thirty-two keywords, Cluster Two contains twenty-nine keywords, Cluster Three contains nine keywords, Cluster Four contains five keywords, and Cluster Five contains two keywords. Cluster 1 contains the article keywords social and sustainable finance. Important keywords associated with article keywords are sustainable development, sustainability, ESG, social responsibility, and corporate social responsibility.

Figure 4 shows the trends related to the keyword during the researched period. It is evident from Figure 4 that around the year 2020, keywords like sustainability, CSR, climate change and energy efficiency were the topics researched. This followed keywords like environmental economics, economic development, carbon, and economic growth were the researched keywords. Post 2021 keywords like sustainable finance, ESG, Sustainable development goals (SDG), green finance carbon emission, renewable energy, etc, are main themes for researchers.

The article keyword sustainable finance is associated mostly with cluster 1 marked in yellow. In addition to cluster 1, this keyword is also associated with two other clusters attached with keywords like economic and social effect from one cluster and climate change from another cluster. Figure 4 shows the association of the article keyword sustainable finance with keywords like sustainable development goals (SDG), ESG, sustainability, investments, corporate governance, CSR, environmental impact, finance, investments and sustainable developments. It's evident that the article keyword sustainable finance is researched along with sustainable developments by the highest number of researchers.

Figure 4 shows that in literature, social finance is only associated with sustainable finance, and it has always been considered sustainable finance.

4.1.4 Content Analysis

4.1.4.1 Definition of Themes

The themes are social finance, sustainable finance, sustainable development goals, socially responsible investing, impact investing, climate financing, green financing, carbon financing, renewable energy financing, blue financing, corporate governance and corporate social responsibilities. The themes were selected based on the frequency of the themes that appeared in 978 research articles from the Scopus database based on bibliometric analysis of keywords.

4.1.4.2 Disclosure of Themes Related to Social Finance and Sustainable Finance in Corporate Annual Reports

An annual report is a comprehensive document published by companies at the end of each financial year, designed to communicate vital information to a wide array of stakeholders, including shareholders, potential investors, regulators, and the general public. Its primary objective is to present a holistic picture of the company's financial health, operational performance, strategic direction, and broader business activities over the reporting period. A key component of the annual report is the Chairman's or CEO's message, which gives the overview of the company's major achievements and challenges during the year. This message also outlines the leadership's vision and strategic roadmap for the future and sets the tone for the rest of the document.

Apart from this message, the annual report offers a business overview detailing the company's core operations, competitive position within the market, and relevant industry trends. This section helps readers understand the business model and the external factors influencing its performance. The financial statements section of the report includes essential documents such as the Balance Sheet, Income Statement, and Cash Flow Statement, along with accompanying notes. These statements are mandatorily audited by independent external auditors, ensuring their accuracy and reliability, and they provide stakeholders with quantitative insights into the company's financial standing. Another important section is the Management Discussion and Analysis (MD&A), which presents a detailed commentary on the financial results, identifies key business risks, and discusses the company's future outlook. This discussion allows stakeholders to interpret the numbers presented in the financial statements within a broader strategic and operational context.

Another section of the report includes a Corporate Governance Report, which outlines the structure and practices of the company's board of directors, executive compensation policies, and adherence to governance standards. This section critically evaluates the company's leadership transparency and accountability mechanisms. In recent years, there has been growing emphasis on including Corporate Social Responsibility (CSR) and Environmental, Social, and Governance (ESG) reporting within annual reports. These segments highlight the company's initiatives and performance related to social impact, environmental stewardship, and ethical governance, reflecting a broader commitment to sustainability and responsible business practices. Together, these elements of the annual report provide stakeholders with a well-rounded understanding of a company's past performance, present condition, and future direction, making it a crucial tool for informed decision-making.

Annual reports are compulsory for publicly traded companies and are often filed with regulatory bodies like the SEBI (India), SEC (U.S.), or Companies House (U.K.). Disclosing all necessary information in an annual report is a regulatory necessity and a strategic advantage. It builds trust, ensures compliance, enhances financial credibility, and attracts investment, all contributing to long-term sustainability. Proper disclosures not only ensure accountability and ethical corporate governance but also align with global best practices, enhancing cross-border investment opportunities. We have selected fifty NIFTY-based companies listed on the National Stock Exchange of India. NIFTY (also known as NIFTY 50) is the benchmark stock market index of the National Stock Exchange of India (NSE). It represents the 50 largest and most liquid companies listed on the NSE across various sectors of the Indian economy.

4.1.4.3 Key Features of NIFTY 50:

The NIFTY 50 is a benchmark equity index representing a diversified portfolio of 50 of India's most frequently traded and financially robust companies listed on the National Stock Exchange (NSE). These companies represent various sectors, contributing to the index's broad-based and inclusive nature, which helps capture the overall market performance across different industries (India, 2025). Launched in 1996, the NIFTY 50 uses the year 1995 as its base year, with a base index value set at 1,000 points. This historical foundation provides a consistent reference point for tracking the long-term movement and growth of the Indian equity market. The Nifty 50 index is constructed using the free-float market capitalisation method. This approach assigns weight to each company based on its market capitalisation that is readily available for trading in the market, rather than its total market capitalisation. As a result, companies with larger free-float market capitalisation exert a greater influence on the index's movements, reflecting the actual market sentiment more accurately. It includes constituents from diverse sectors such as banking, information technology, energy, pharmaceuticals, fast-moving consumer goods (FMCG), etc., offering investors a snapshot of the broader Indian economy. To maintain its relevance and accuracy in reflecting current market dynamics, the composition of the NIFTY 50 is reviewed and updated semi-annually by the National Stock Exchange (NSE). This periodic revision ensures that the index continues to represent the most significant and liquid stocks in the Indian capital market.

Table 9. LIST OF NIFTY-BASED COMPANIES WITH MARKET CAPITALISATION

Serial No.	Name of Companies	Market Capitalization as on 28/01/2025 (in crores)
1	BAJFINANCE	4,71,056.31
2	AXISBANK	3,04,386.70
3	SHRIRAMFIN	99,627.37
4	BAJAJFINSV	2,82,625.16

continued on following page

Table 9. Continued

Serial No.	Name of Companies	Market Capitalization as on 28/01/2025 (in crores)
5	HDFCBANK	12,79,792.64
6	TATAMOTORS	2,69,421.53
7	CIPLA	1,15,246.52
8	TATASTEEL	1,60,975.08
9	ICICIBANK	8,80,834.49
10	M&M	3,57,551.84
11	ADANIENT	2,66,390.68
12	BHARTIARTL	9,24,850.38
13	INDUSINDBK	73,016.62
14	WIPRO	3,23,525.38
15	MARUTI	3,83,473.68
16	TRENT	1,96,549.02
17	INFY	7,67,880.17
18	RELIANCE	16,77,134.64
19	HEROMOTOCO	81,788.81
20	SBIN	6,75,995.34
21	APOLLOHOSP	96,982.03
22	BAJAJ-AUTO	2,40,672.58
23	TITAN	2,97,936.60
24	KOTAKBANK	3,80,695.49
25	HDFCLIFE	1,33,581.41
26	ADANIPORTS	2,34,990.72
27	TECHM	1,63,754.30
28	ULTRACEMCO	3,32,622.89
29	HINDUNILVR	5,61,564.06
30	SBILIFE	1,46,109.59
31	TATACONSUM	94,898.98
32	ASIANPAINT	2,12,630.17
33	ONGC	3,16,104.68
34	TCS	14,81,588.75
35	JSWSTEEL	2,28,759.99
36	NESTLEIND	2,09,868.09
37	POWERGRID	2,67,113.34
38	NTPC	3,11,650.85

continued on following page

Table 9. Continued

Serial No.	Name of Companies	Market Capitalization as on 28/01/2025 (in crores)
39	EICHERMOT	1,41,847.10
40	BPCL	1,10,284.81
41	LT	4,74,028.16
42	HCLTECH	4,63,385.45
43	COALINDIA	2,32,581.37
44	DRREDDY	99,012.75
45	ITC	5,42,257.53
46	BEL	1,95,134.55
47	GRASIM	1,61,756.31
48	HINDALCO	1,30,631.28
49	BRITANNIA	1,21,571.05
50	SUNPHARMA	4,12,541.65

Compiled by Researcher

4.1.4.4 Theme and Frequency Table

As mentioned in the introduction, the objective of this study is to verify the presence or absence of certain themes on social finance and sustainable finance in each annual report of various Indian organizations under study. Hence, a detailed content analysis of annual reports for the Financial Year 2023-2024 for all the 50 companies based on Nifty (refer to Table-9) has been carried out, and results are mentioned in Table 10 under the heading "The list of themes and their frequencies of disclosure".

Table 10. List of Themes and Frequency of Disclosure

Serial No.	Themes	Nos. of Companies (Out of 50)	Frequency Percentage (%)
1	Social finance	9	18
2	Sustainable finance	12	24
3	Sustainable development goals	50	100
4	Socially responsible investing	4	8
5	Impact investing	6	12
6	Climate financing	18	36
7	Green financing	12	24

continued on following page

Table 10. Continued

Serial No.	Themes	Nos. of Companies (Out of 50)	Frequency Percentage (%)
8	Carbon financing	22	44
9	Renewable energy financing	34	68
10	Blue financing	6	12
11	Corporate governance	50	100
12	Corporate social responsibilities	50	100

Compiled by Researcher

4.2 Interpretation

4.2.1 Bibliometric Analysis

The bibliometric mapping reveals a dynamic intellectual landscape within the domain of sustainable finance and development, showcasing both historical depth and contemporary evolution. Figure 2 offers a nuanced view of the intellectual structure of the field. On the left side of the map, clusters shaded in red, brown, and orange include seminal scholars such as Freeman R.E., known for stakeholder theory, and Barney J., associated with the resource-based view. These foundational theorists anchor the theoretical underpinnings of sustainable finance and provide the conceptual scaffolding for subsequent research. Their positioning on the map suggests enduring influence, serving as key nodes from which modern applications and frameworks have developed. Transitioning toward the centre of the map, green and light-blue clusters highlight scholars such as Shahbaz M. and Nasir M.A., who frequently contribute to research in environmental economics and sustainability. These authors represent a bridging generation, connecting classical theories to current ecological and economic balance concerns. On the far right, blue, purple, and yellow clusters contain newer and emerging scholars, including Umair M., Liu R., Tang C., and Irfan M. Their research tends to emphasise practical and applied dimensions such as sustainable supply chains, carbon neutrality, and green finance mechanisms. The spatial arrangement on the map thus visually demonstrates the chronological and thematic development of the field, where classical theories are continuously adapted and extended to address emerging environmental and financial imperatives.

Figure 3 adds another dimension to this analysis by visualising author collaboration networks. Here, distinct clusters—such as the one involving Ziolo, Magdalena, and Filipiak, Beata Zofia—indicate cohesive research teams with consistent scholarly output. Their strong interconnections suggest shared research agendas and methodological alignment. In contrast, more isolated authors like Zhang, Dongyang, and Lee, Chien-Chiang occupy peripheral positions, which may reflect individual scholarly pursuits or limited co-authorship in the bibliometric dataset. This network structure offers insight into how ideas, theories, and collaborative interactions shape academic knowledge in sustainable finance. Such patterns of scholarly engagement can be meaningfully connected to the theoretical framework of the chapter by showing how different research communities either converge around or diverge from dominant paradigms.

The keyword co-occurrence map presented in Figure 4 provides a thematic overview of the literature, uncovering the conceptual architecture underpinning sustainable finance and development. Central keywords like "sustainable development," "finance," and "economic development" act as foundational anchors around which various research clusters form. These terms represent the core pillars of the field, reinforcing its interdisciplinary character. Surrounding these central themes are clusters highlighting corporate social responsibility, green finance, environmental sustainability, and carbon emissions—suggesting well-established yet evolving domains of inquiry. The colour gradient from purple to yellow indicates a chronological trajectory of scholarly attention. Emerging keywords such as "decentralised finance," "carbon neutrality," and "energy utilisation" appear in yellow, pointing to growing research interest in recent years. This temporal layering not only reflects shifts in academic priorities but also illustrates how newer themes are expanding the traditional theoretical boundaries of the field.

Figure 5 complements the previous visualisations by mapping country-level contributions and collaboration patterns. This geographical perspective provides context for how sustainable finance research is distributed across different national and regional settings. Countries like China, the United States, and the United Kingdom are represented with larger nodes, denoting high publication output and centrality. The colour gradient captures temporal dynamics, with countries like China, Pakistan, and Saudi Arabia becoming more prominent contributors in recent years (as indicated by yellow nodes). Conversely, countries such as Russia, the Czech Republic, and Romania were more active during earlier phases (represented in blue). This longitudinal and chronological analysis reveals important shifts in the global research agenda, where emerging economies increasingly participate in and influence the discourse on sustainability and finance. This growing diversification aligns with theoretical discussions on global environmental governance and inclusive financial systems, thereby reinforcing the need for context-specific adaptations of existing frameworks.

In totality, these facts and figures present a comprehensive bibliometric landscape that maps out the intellectual and collaborative structure of the field and highlights the evolving nature of its themes and global engagement.

4.2.2 Content Analysis

The content analysis of sustainability disclosures across 50 companies reveals the prominence and distribution of key themes aligned with sustainable finance and corporate responsibility. As illustrated in the table, certain themes such as Sustainable Development Goals (SDGs), Corporate Governance, and Corporate Social Responsibility (CSR) appear in all 50 companies, reflecting a strong institutional commitment to global sustainability agendas and responsible corporate behaviour. This universal presence indicates the entrenchment of these concepts as foundational pillars in the discourse of corporate sustainability and aligns with theoretical frameworks such as stakeholder theory and legitimacy theory, which posit that firms seek societal approval through transparent and accountable governance practices.

Notably, Renewable Energy Financing also emerges as a dominant theme in 68% of the companies. This suggests a widespread shift towards clean energy initiatives, likely driven by international policy mandates and investor expectations. Similarly, Carbon Financing (44%) and Climate Financing (36%) are also prominently featured, emphasising the growing integration of climate-related risk management into financial strategy—a trend consistent with evolving regulatory frameworks like the Task Force on Climate-related Financial Disclosures (TCFD). These findings support the relevance of environmental finance literature that frames climate adaptation and mitigation as critical financial and operational imperatives.

Themes such as Sustainable Finance (24%) and Green Financing (24%) are moderately represented, indicating that while companies increasingly adopt sustainability language, the direct financial mechanisms supporting sustainability may still be developing or unevenly reported. Social Finance (18%), Impact Investing (12%), and Blue Financing (12%) appear less frequently, suggesting that these niche or emerging instruments are still in the early stages of corporate integration or may be relevant to specific sectors. Socially Responsible Investing (SRI) is mentioned by only 8% of companies, which may reflect either limited direct investor communication or the embedding of SRI within broader ESG strategies without explicit labelling.

The distribution of themes reflects maturity and emerging trends within sustainable finance practices. High-frequency themes such as SDGs and CSR represent institutionalised norms, while moderate and low-frequency themes point to emerging strategic priorities or areas requiring further standardisation and integration. This analytical pattern supports a layered understanding of how corporations operationalise sustainability concepts, reinforcing the theoretical propositions that firms vary in their commitment and capacity to implement sustainability strategies based on sectoral, geographic, or regulatory context. By linking this empirical output with bibliometric patterns—such as the rising prominence of terms like "green finance," "carbon emissions," and "renewable energy" in keyword analyses—the content analysis provides a grounded understanding of how theoretical commitments to sustainability are translated into corporate discourse and action.

CONCLUSION

Integrating bibliometric and content analyses provides a multi-layered understanding of how sustainable finance and development have evolved as both academic fields and corporate imperatives. The bibliometric analysis reveals the progress path, beginning with foundational theories such as stakeholder theory and the resource-based view and progressing toward emergent areas like green finance, decentralised finance, and carbon neutrality. Co-citation and co-authorship figures demonstrate how early theoretical frameworks continue to shape the field, while collaboration networks and keyword co-occurrences highlight the growing complexity and interdisciplinarity of research in response to evolving environmental and financial challenges. Notably, the geographic analysis uncovers an important shift: emerging economies such as China, Pakistan, and Saudi Arabia are becoming increasingly central to the discourse, reflecting a broader, more globally inclusive research ecosystem.

The content analysis further enriches this picture by empirically tracing how sustainability themes are embedded within corporate narratives. The universal adoption of frameworks such as the Sustainable Development Goals, Corporate Governance, and CSR underscores their status as institutionalised norms. Meanwhile, the substantial focus on renewable energy and climate finance in company disclosures echoes the thematic priorities identified in the academic literature, reinforcing the alignment between scholarly discourse and business practice. Conversely, the limited representation of emerging concepts like blue finance and socially responsible investing suggests a developmental gap that merits further exploration.

The above findings confirm that sustainable finance is a dynamic field but one characterised by dynamic interaction between theory and practice. Foundational theories provide the conceptual base, while corporate disclosures reflect the practical translation of these ideas under varied regulatory, regional, and market conditions. This dual analytical approach strengthens the theoretical coherence of the study by demonstrating how intellectual traditions are preserved and continuously reinterpreted in light of contemporary sustainability imperatives.

IMPLICATIONS FOR RESEARCHERS

Future research in social finance and sustainable finance presents several promising avenues that can contribute to the evolution of financial models aligned with environmental, social, and governance (ESG) objectives. Researchers can explore integrating emerging technologies such as artificial intelligence (AI), blockchain, and decentralised finance (DeFi) to enhance transparency, efficiency, and impact measurement within social finance markets. Additionally, studying the role of regulatory frameworks and financial policies in promoting sustainable finance can provide insights into fostering a more resilient and inclusive financial ecosystem. There is also a need to examine the intersection of social finance with digital finance to assess how technological advancements facilitate Impact investments and financial inclusion. Comparative studies across geographies can help understand the diverse implementation models of sustainable finance, particularly in developing economies.

REFERENCES

Independent Evaluation Group. (2021). https://ieg.worldbankgroup.org/sites/default/files/Data/reports/ap_driveforfinancialinclusion.pdf

Investment Management & Financial Services. (2024). BlackRock. https://www.blackrock.com/us/individual/literature/annual-financial-statements/afs-retail-blackrock-funds.pdf

Abeysekera, I., & Guthrie, J. (2005). An empirical investigation of annual reporting trends of intellectual capital in Sri Lanka. *Critical Perspectives on Accounting*, *16*(3), 151–163. DOI: 10.1016/s1045-2354(03)00059-5

Adams, C. A., Coutts, A., & Harte, G. (1995). Corporate equal opportunities (non-) disclosure. *The British Accounting Review*, *27*(2), 87–108. DOI: 10.1006/bare.1994.0005

Akcay, E., & Hirshleifer, D. (2020). Social finance: Cultural evolution, transmission bias and market dynamics. https://doi.org/DOI: 10.3386/w27745

Akhter, A., Javed, M. Y., & Akhter, J. (2023). Research trends in the field of Islamic social finance: A bibliometric analysis from 1914 to 2022. *International Journal of Ethics and Systems*. https://doi.org/DOI: 10.1108/ijoes-03-2023-0044

Alshater, M. M., Atayah, O. F., & Hamdan, A. (2021). Journal of sustainable finance and investment: A bibliometric analysis. *Journal of Sustainable Finance & Investment*, *13*(3), 1131–1152. DOI: 10.1080/20430795.2021.1947116

Andrikopoulos, A. (2019). Delineating social finance. SSRN *Electronic Journal*. https://doi.org/DOI: 10.2139/ssrn.3510056

Arifin, M. R., Raharja, B. S., Aligarh, F., & Nugroho, A. (2023). A systematic literature review on community financing: Avenues for further research. *Cogent Business & Management*, *10*(2). Advance online publication. DOI: 10.1080/23311975.2023.2211208

Ascarya, A., Suharto, U., & Husman, J. A. (2022). Proposed model of integrated Islamic commercial and social finance for Islamic bank in Indonesia. *Eurasian Economic Review*, *12*(1), 115–138. DOI: 10.1007/s40822-022-00201-z

Bahoo, S., Alon, I., & Paltrinieri, A. (2020). Sovereign wealth funds: Past, present and future. *International Review of Financial Analysis*, *67*, 101418. DOI: 10.1016/j.irfa.2019.101418

Ballandies, M. C., Dapp, M. M., Degenhart, B. A., Helbing, D., Klauser, S., & Pardi, A. (2021). Finance 4.0—A socio-ecological finance system. *SpringerBriefs in Applied Sciences and Technology*, 53-89. https://doi.org/DOI: 10.1007/978-3-030-71400-0_4

Benedikter, R. (2011). *Social banking and social finance.* SpringerBriefs in Business., DOI: 10.1007/978-1-4419-7774-8

Carè, R., Fatima, R., & Boitan, I. (2024). Central banks and climate risks: Where we are and where we are going? *International Review of Economics & Finance, 92*, 1200–1229. DOI: 10.1016/j.iref.2024.01.057

Carè, R., & Weber, O. (2023). What's in a name? Exploring the intellectual structure of social finance. *International Journal of Emerging Markets.* Advance online publication. DOI: 10.1108/ijoem-07-2022-1142

Chiapello, E., & Knoll, L. (2020). Social Finance and Impact Investing. Governing Welfare in the Era of Financialization. *Historical Social Research / Historische Sozialforschung, Special Issue: Social Finance, Impact Investing, and the Financialization of the Public Interest, 45*(3), 7-30. https://www.jstor.org/stable/26918402

Cobo, M., López-Herrera, A., Herrera-Viedma, E., & Herrera, F. (2011). An approach for detecting, quantifying, and visualizing the evolution of a research field: A practical application to the fuzzy sets theory field. *Journal of Informetrics, 5*(1), 146–166. DOI: 10.1016/j.joi.2010.10.002

Cunha, F. A., Meira, E., & Orsato, R. J. (2021). Sustainable finance and investment: Review and research agenda. *Business Strategy and the Environment, 30*(8), 3821–3838. DOI: 10.1002/bse.2842

Danilov, Y. (2021). Sustainable finance: A new theoretical paradigm. *World Economy and International Relations, 65*(9), 5–13. DOI: 10.20542/0131-2227-2021-65-9-5-13

Dirie, K. A., Alam, M. M., & Maamor, S. (2023). Islamic social finance for achieving sustainable development goals: A systematic literature review and future research agenda. *International Journal of Ethics and Systems, 40*(4), 676–698. DOI: 10.1108/ijoes-12-2022-0317

Donthu, N., Kumar, S., Mukherjee, D., Pandey, N., & Lim, W. M. (2021). How to conduct a bibliometric analysis: An overview and guidelines. *Journal of Business Research, 133*, 285–296. DOI: 10.1016/j.jbusres.2021.04.070

Edmans, A., & Kacperczyk, M. (2022). Sustainable finance. *Review of Finance, 26*(6), 1309–1313. DOI: 10.1093/rof/rfac069

Emerson, J. (2003). The blended value proposition: Integrating social and financial returns. *California Management Review, 45*(4), 35–51. DOI: 10.2307/41166187

Feng, Y., Zhu, Q., & Lai, K. (2017). Corporate social responsibility for supply chain management: A literature review and bibliometric analysis. *Journal of Cleaner Production, 158*, 296–307. DOI: 10.1016/j.jclepro.2017.05.018

Germany's Energiewende. (2021, May 27). World Nuclear Association. https://world-nuclear.org/information-library/energy-and-the-environment/energiewende

Gonzalez-Ruiz, J. D., Marín-Rodríguez, N. J., & Weber, O. (2024). New insights on social finance research in the sustainable development context. *Business Strategy & Development, 7*(1). Advance online publication. DOI: 10.1002/bsd2.342

Haigh, M. (2014). Call for papers for the social finance and sustainable finance stream: The 14th finance, risk and accounting perspectives conference oriel college, University of Oxford 22nd–24th September 2014 conference pages HTTP://www.acrn.eu/finance. *Journal of Sustainable Finance & Investment, 4*(2), 210-210. https://doi.org/DOI: 10.1080/20430795.2014.891968

Harding, P. (2007). Quotes on sustainability, climate change, population - Quotes corner. *philharding.net - Environmental sustainability, Green Belt advocate and photographer*. https://www.philharding.net/quotes-corner/quotes-corner-1sd.htm

Hilario-Caballero, A., Garcia-Bernabeu, A., Salcedo, J. V., & Vercher, M. (2020). Tri-criterion model for constructing low-carbon mutual fund portfolios: A preference-based multi-objective genetic algorithm approach. *International Journal of Environmental Research and Public Health, 17*(17), 6324. DOI: 10.3390/ijerph17176324 PMID: 32878037

Hong, H., Wang, N., & Yang, J. (2023). Welfare consequences of sustainable finance. *Review of Financial Studies, 36*(12), 4864–4918. DOI: 10.1093/rfs/hhad048

Huertas-Valdivia, I., Ferrari, A. M., Settembre-Blundo, D., & García-Muiña, F. E. (2020). Social life-cycle assessment: A review by bibliometric analysis. *Sustainability, 12*(15), 6211. DOI: 10.3390/su12156211

India, N. (2025, January 28). *Corporate filings annual reports - Equity, SME - NSE India*. NSE India. https://www.nseindia.com/companies-listing/corporate-filings-annual-reports

Jayaram, R., & Singh, S. (2020). Sustainable finance: A systematic review. *International Journal of Indian Culture and Business Management, 21*(3), 317. DOI: 10.1504/ijicbm.2020.110452

Kashi, A., & Shah, M. E. (2023). Bibliometric review on sustainable finance. *Sustainability, 15*(9), 7119. DOI: 10.3390/su15097119

Kasmon, B., Ibrahim, S. S., Daud, D., Raja Hisham, R. R., & Dian Wisika Prajanti, S. (2024). FinTech application in Islamic social finance in Asia region: A systematic literature review. *International Journal of Ethics and Systems*. https://doi.org/DOI: 10.1108/ijoes-07-2023-0155

Kuanova, L. A., Sagiyeva, R., & Shirazi, N. S. (2021). Islamic social finance: A literature review and future research directions. *Journal of Islamic Accounting and Business Research, 12*(5), 707–728. DOI: 10.1108/jiabr-11-2020-0356

Kuchler, T., & Stroebel, J. (2021). Social finance. *Annual Review of Financial Economics, 13*(1), 37–55. DOI: 10.1146/annurev-financial-101320-062446

Langley, P. (2018). The folds of social finance: Making markets, remaking the social. *Environment and Planning A. Economy and Space, 52*(1), 130–147. DOI: 10.1177/0308518x17752682

Lanzara, F. (2021). Islamic finance as social finance: A bibliometric analysis from 2000 to 2021. *International Journal of Business and Management, 16*(9), 107. DOI: 10.5539/ijbm.v16n9p107

LIU, M. (1993). Progress in documentation the complexities of citation practice: A review of citation studies. *The Journal of Documentation, 49*(4), 370–408. DOI: 10.1108/eb026920

Luo, W., Tian, Z., Zhong, S., Lyu, Q., & Deng, M. (2022). Global evolution of research on sustainable finance from 2000 to 2021: A bibliometric analysis on wos database. *Sustainability, 14*(15), 9435. DOI: 10.3390/su14159435

Malamas, V., Dasaklis, T. K., Arakelian, V., & Chondrokoukis, G. (2023). A blockchain framework for digitizing securities issuance: The case of green bonds. *Journal of Sustainable Finance & Investment, 14*(3), 569–595. DOI: 10.1080/20430795.2023.2275212

McGrath, A. (2023, December 22). *What is corporate social responsibility (CSR)?* IBM - United States. https://www.ibm.com/think/topics/corporate-social -responsibility

Migliavacca, M., Patel, R., Paltrinieri, A., & Goodell, J. W. (2022). Mapping impact investing: A bibliometric analysis. *Journal of International Financial Markets, Institutions and Money, 81*, 101679. DOI: 10.1016/j.intfin.2022.101679

Naeem, M. A., Karim, S., Rabbani, M. R., Bashar, A., & Kumar, S. (2022). Current state and future directions of green and sustainable finance: A bibliometric analysis. *Qualitative Research in Financial Markets*, *15*(4), 608–629. DOI: 10.1108/qrfm-10-2021-0174

Nicholls, A., & Emerson, J. (2015). Social finance. *Social Finance*, 1-42. https://doi.org/DOI: 10.1093/acprof:oso/9780198703761.003.0001

Olumekor, M., & Oke, A. (2024). Support for sustainable finance and investment in Europe. *Journal of Cleaner Production*, *449*, 141769. DOI: 10.1016/j.jclepro.2024.141769

Over 540 million bank accounts opened under Pradhan Mantri Jan Dhan Yojana. (2024, December 12). *Mint*. https://www.livemint.com/industry/banking/pradhan-mantri-jan-dhan-yojana-jan-dhan-accounts-financial-inclusion-financial-literacy-msmes-credit-gap-rupay-11733996410678.html

Ozili, P. K. (2021). Digital finance, green finance and social finance: Is there a link? SSRN *Electronic Journal*. https://doi.org/DOI: 10.2139/ssrn.3786881

Ozili, P. K. (2024). *Social finance: What is social about it*. Reference Module in Social Sciences., DOI: 10.1016/b978-0-44-313776-1.00286-5

Paltrinieri, A., Hassan, M. K., Bahoo, S., & Khan, A. (2019). A bibliometric review of sukuk literature. *International Review of Economics & Finance*, *86*, 897–918. DOI: 10.1016/j.iref.2019.04.004

Pandey, N. (2012). Human resources. *Management and Labour Studies*, *37*(4), 323–335. DOI: 10.1177/0258042x13484869

Price, D. J. (1965). Networks of scientific papers. *Science*, *149*(3683), 510–515. DOI: 10.1126/science.149.3683.510 PMID: 14325149

Purnomo, A., Sari, A. K., Susanti, T., Mannan, S. S., & Lumentut, T. M. (2021). Sustainable finance study of bibliometric overview. *IOP Conference Series. Earth and Environmental Science*, *729*(1), 012124. DOI: 10.1088/1755-1315/729/1/012124

Rhee, W. W., & Ha, H. (2022). Does public-loan management matter for sustainable finance and operation risk? *Sustainability*, *14*(3), 1453. DOI: 10.3390/su14031453

Setyowati, A. B. (2020). Governing sustainable finance: Insights from Indonesia. *Climate Policy*, *23*(1), 108–121. DOI: 10.1080/14693062.2020.1858741

Seychelles launches world's first sovereign blue bond. (2018, October 29). World Bank. https://www.worldbank.org/en/news/press-release/2018/10/29/seychelles-launches-worlds-first-sovereign-blue-bond

Shahid, M., Sulub, Y. A., Mohtesham, M. M., & Abdullah, M. (2023). Analyzing the commonalities between Islamic social finance and sustainable development goals. *International Journal of Ethics and Systems*, *40*(2), 381–394. DOI: 10.1108/ijoes-04-2022-0082

Shashi, Centobelli, P., Cerchione, R., & Mittal, A. (2020). Managing sustainability in luxury industry to pursue circular economy strategies. *Business Strategy and the Environment*, *30*(1), 432–462. DOI: 10.1002/bse.2630

Silva, H. P., Lehoux, P., & Sabio, R. P. (2024). The multifaceted role of social finance in supporting social entrepreneurship: A qualitative inquiry into business tools and value-adding and subtracting activities. *Journal of Social Entrepreneurship*, •••, 1–26. DOI: 10.1080/19420676.2024.2418867

Singhania, M., Chadha, G., & Prasad, R. (2023). Sustainable finance research: Review and agenda. *International Journal of Finance & Economics*, *29*(4), 4010–4045. DOI: 10.1002/ijfe.2854

Sisodia, A., & Maheshwari, G. C. (2023). Exploring sustainable finance: A review and future research agenda. *Vision: The Journal of Business Perspective*. https://doi.org/DOI: 10.1177/09722629231209177

Small, H. (1973). Co-citation in the scientific literature: A new measure of the relationship between two documents. *Journal of the American Society for Information Science*, *24*(4), 265–269. DOI: 10.1002/asi.4630240406

Streimikiene, D., Mikalauskiene, A., & Burbaite, G. (2023). The role of sustainable finance in achieving sustainable development goals. *Economia e Sociologia*, *16*(1), 271–298. DOI: 10.14254/2071-789x.2023/16-1/17

Sustainability-related disclosure in the financial services sector. (2024, May 3). Finance. https://finance.ec.europa.eu/sustainable-finance/disclosures/sustainability-related-disclosure-financial-services-sector_en

Svartzman, R., Bolton, P., Despres, M., Pereira Da Silva, L. A., & Samama, F. (2020). Central banks, financial stability and policy coordination in the age of climate uncertainty: A three-layered analytical and operational framework. *Climate Policy*, *21*(4), 563–580. DOI: 10.1080/14693062.2020.1862743

Talan, G., & Sharma, G. D. (2019). Doing well by doing good: A systematic review and research agenda for sustainable investment. *Sustainability*, *11*(2), 353. DOI: 10.3390/su11020353

Umar, U. H., Baita, A. J., Haron, M. H., & Kabiru, S. H. (2021). The potential of Islamic social finance to alleviate poverty in the era of COVID-19: The moderating effect of ethical orientation. *International Journal of Islamic and Middle Eastern Finance and Management, 15*(2), 255–270. DOI: 10.1108/imefm-07-2020-0371

Vuontisjärvi, T. (2006). Corporate social reporting in the European context and human resource disclosures: An analysis of Finnish companies. *Journal of Business Ethics*, *69*(4), 331–354. DOI: 10.1007/s10551-006-9094-5

Weber, O. (2012). Sustainable banking – History and current developments. SSRN *Electronic Journal*. https://doi.org/DOI: 10.2139/ssrn.2159947

Weber, O., & Duan, Y. (2012). Social finance and banking. *Socially Responsible Finance and Investing*, 161-180. https://doi.org/DOI: 10.1002/9781118524015.ch9

Weber, R. P. (1988). Basic content analysis. *Sage University Paper Series on Quantitative Applications in the Social Sciences*, *07*(49). Advance online publication. DOI: 10.4135/9781412983488

What is impact investing? Meaning, types and examples. (2024, April 5). Fintrakk: Personal Finance Blog. https://fintrakk.com/what-is-impact-investing-meaning-types-examples/

White, H. D., & McCain, K. W. (1998). Visualizing a discipline: An author Co-citation analysis of information science, 1972–1995. *Journal of the American Society for Information Science*, *49*(4), 327–355. DOI: 10.1002/(sici)1097-4571(19980401)49:43.0.co;2-4

Xu, J. (2024). AI in ESG for financial institutions: An industrial survey. https://doi.org/DOI: 10.2139/ssrn.4949354

Ziolo, M., Bak, I., & Cheba, K. (2020). The role of sustainable finance in achieving sustainable development goals: Does it work? *Technological and Economic Development of Economy*, *27*(1), 45–70. DOI: 10.3846/tede.2020.13863

Zupic, I., & Cater, T. (2013). Bibliometric methods in management and organization: A review. SSRN *Electronic Journal*. https://doi.org/DOI: 10.2139/ssrn.2267251

Chapter 2
Bridging Finance and Sustainability:
A Bibliometric Analysis of Alternative and Sustainable Finance for Advancing the Sustainable Development Goals

Rabia Fatima
https://orcid.org/0000-0002-3471-9756
HAN University of Applied Sciences, The Netherlands

Nathalie Lévy
https://orcid.org/0000-0001-5243-9953
University of Tours, France

ABSTRACT

The 2008–2009 financial crisis exposed vulnerabilities in the traditional banking system, leading to stricter regulations that restricted access to capital. This created space for the rise of alternative finance, which operates outside conventional banking and capital markets, offering innovative solutions. Simultaneously, sustainable finance has gained momentum by integrating ESG principles into investment strategies, channeling resources toward responsible economic activities. The intersection of these fields is significant, as alternative finance can fund sustainable projects often neglected by traditional financiers. Despite growing research, studies remain fragmented, with gaps in understanding their synergies. This study conducts a bibliometric analysis to examine trends, key contributors, and research gaps in alternative and sustainable finance. The findings offer insights into how alternative

DOI: 10.4018/979-8-3693-9551-6.ch002

finance mechanisms contribute to sustainable development, supporting researchers, policymakers, and practitioners navigating the evolving landscape of finance and sustainability.

1. INTRODUCTION

The 2008-2009 financial crisis exposed systemic vulnerabilities in the traditional banking system and financial markets, leading to global regulatory reforms that significantly restricted access to capital (Motylska-Kuźma, 2018). This regulatory shift created fertile ground for the emergence of alternative finance, which operates outside conventional banking structures and capital markets (Baeck et al., 2014). Often associated with shadow banking, alternative finance includes innovative mechanisms such as crowdfunding, peer-to-peer lending and microfinance. These instruments prioritize flexibility and accessibility, offering new financial opportunities to individuals and businesses (Financial Stability Board (FSB), 2012).

Simultaneously, sustainable finance has become increasingly prominent by integrating environmental, social, and governance (ESG) criteria into investment strategies. By redirecting institutional capital towards responsible economic activities, sustainable finance addresses long-term environmental and social challenges while complementing alternative finance's emphasis on inclusivity and innovation (Schoenmaker & Schramade, 2019). The financial stakes involved in achieving the United Nations' Agenda 2030 and the Sustainable Development Goals (SDGs) have underscored the urgency of financing climate and societal transitions (United Nations, 2024). Sustainable finance has emerged as a critical lever for channeling financial flows towards activities that mitigate climate risks while promoting social equity.

However, neither traditional nor sustainable finance fully addresses the challenges of sustainable development. Investments required for long-term projects with limited returns or perceived risks remain largely neglected. In this context, the intersection between alternative and sustainable finance holds particular promise. While traditional finance struggles to adequately support the transition to a low-carbon economy or address global sustainability imperatives, alternative finance mechanisms can direct capital towards projects often overlooked by traditional financiers. The synergy between alternative and sustainable finance thus represents a unique opportunity to bridge existing gaps and drive transformative change.

Numerous studies have explored alternative finance (Carè et al., 2018; Motylska-Kuźma, 2018) and sustainable finance (e.g., Schoenmaker & Schramade, 2019; Lagoarde-Segot, 2019; Fatima et al., 2022; CE, 2024). However, existing research remains fragmented with notable gaps in understanding their synergies (Carè et al., 2018; Fatima et al., 2022). This chapter adopts an integrative perspective to explore the intersection between these fields using bibliometric methods. It aims to uncover how the inclusivity of alternative finance complements the institutional focus of sustainable finance to address global sustainability challenges more effectively. Bibliometric analysis provides a systematic approach to mapping intellectual structures, identifying key contributors, and revealing emerging trends across disciplines while minimizing subjective bias (Zupic & Čater, 2015; Donthu et al., 2021).

Specifically, this chapter seeks to (i) analyze the evolution of research on alternative and sustainable finance in the context of sustainable development; (ii) identify the key articles, journals and authors in the field; (iii) highlight the main research streams in the literature; (iv) identify controversies, gaps and opportunities for future research. The chapter is organized into six sections. Section 2 describes the bibliometric methodology used for analyzing the scientific corpus. Section 3 focuses on performance analysis by assessing the main contributions of influential authors, articles, and journals in the field. Section 4 maps the main thematic clusters identified - microfinance, crowdfunding, green finance, and cryptocurrencies - and explores their respective contributions to the SDGs. Section 5 critically discusses findings by addressing controversies, under-researched dimensions, and proposing future research directions. Finally, Section 6 synthesizes key conclusions while acknowledging methodological limitations.

2. RESEARCH METHODOLOGY

This study aims to examine the conceptual structure and the role of alternative and sustainable finance in achieving sustainable development through bibliometric analysis of published research articles until September (Q3)[1] 2024. Bibliometric analysis identifies the most contributing researchers, scientific studies, and journals while mapping prominent research themes and evolving trends in alternative and sustainable finance. The bibliometric method has gained popularity due to its cross-disciplinary applicability, capability to manage large datasets (Donthu et al., 2021; Khan et al., 2022), and its ability to map research fields without subjective bias (Zupic & Čater, 2015). The study employs both performance analysis and science mapping approaches (see Figure 1) (Cobo et al., 2011; Zupic & Čater, 2015; Donthu et al., 2021).

Performance analysis was used to explain the contributions of the main research constituents, such as authors, publications, and journals in the areas of alternative and sustainable finance (Ramos-Rodríguez & Ruíz-Navarro, 2004; Cobo et al., 2011; Donthu et al., 2021). Science mapping techniques, including co-word analysis and thematic analysis were employed to illustrate the relationships among these research constituents (Cobo et al., 2011; Zupic & Čater, 2015; Aria & Cuccurullo, 2017; Tennekes, 2018; Donthu et al., 2021).

For data analysis, Microsoft Excel was used initially for data collection, selection and keyword standardization, followed by the use of VOSviewer for network analysis, as it is recognized as the most powerful network visualization software for distance-based mapping techniques (van Eck & Waltman, 2010; van Eck & Waltman, 2014; Paltrinieri et al., 2023).

2.1 Data Selection, and Cleaning Procedure

SCOPUS and Web of Science are the most used data collection platforms for bibliometric analysis in the social sciences (Zupic & Čater, 2015; Singh et al., 2021). We selected the Scopus database for data collection because of its broader coverage of peer-reviewed research papers (Norris & Oppenheim, 2007; Singh et al., 2021; Carè et al., 2025) and because many previous studies widely recognize and frequently use Scopus for quantitative analyses, especially bibliometric analysis (Sas et al., 2019; Baker et al., 2020).

For data collection, a three-step procedure was conducted to develop the list of search keywords for Scopus. First, a preliminary literature review was carried out to identify relevant key terms. Second, key terms that were too specific, too general, irrelevant, redundant, or duplicated were eliminated. Lastly, the selected key terms were converted into search queries (see Figure 1) (Carè et al., 2024).

After finalizing the key terms and search queries, the search was conducted on Scopus using the "TITLE-ABS-KEY" fields, which include the article title, abstract, and keywords. The search focused exclusively on research articles ("ar") published in English from 1999 to 2024 (Q3) (Tian et al., 2018; Shashi et al., 2021). This focus on journal articles was intentional, as this document type is regarded as "certified knowledge" (Ramos-Rodríguez & Ruíz-Navarro, 2004; Fernandez-Alles & Ramos-Rodríguez, 2009; Carè et al., 2024) and is likely to have a significant impact in the scientific field (Podsakoff et al., 2005; Crossan & Apaydin, 2010). The dataset was limited to three specific subject areas: economics, econometrics, and finance ("ECON"), business, management, and accounting ("BUSI"), and social sciences ("SOCI"). It was decided not to restrict the search query exclusively to the area of finance in order to obtain a more comprehensive view of research in alternative and sustainable finance (Carè & Weber, 2023). After conducting the search for all selected key terms and merging the results, a total of 448 articles were retrieved, all considered relevant for analysis by both researchers. The datasets were then downloaded in Excel (.csv) format for the standardization process. Figure 1 displays the methodological framework applied in this research study.

Figure 1. Methodological Framework

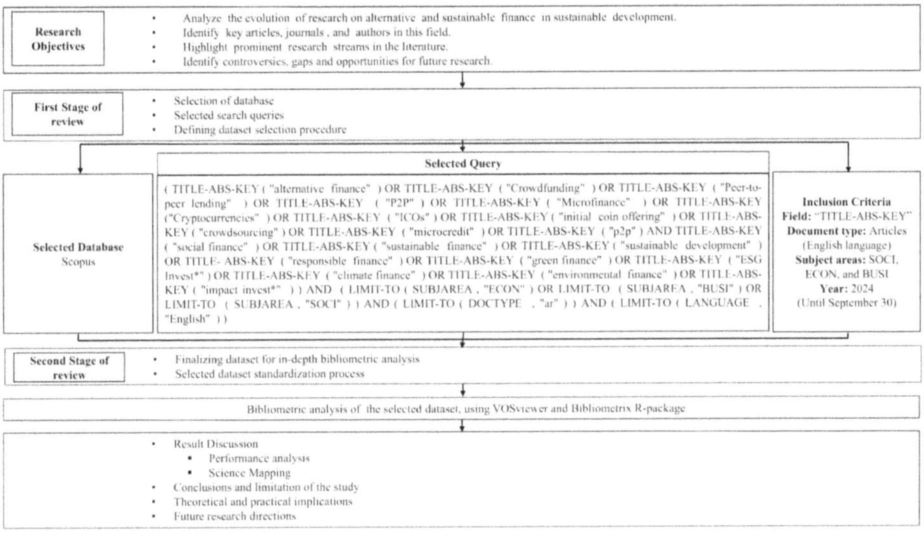

Source: Partially adapted from the study of Agrawal et al. (2022)

2.2 Data Standardization

The steps of the standardization process have been applied, following the research by Carè et al. (2023, 2024). The steps were applied in a separate thesaurus (.csv) Excel file. A VOSviewer thesaurus file is used to standardize different variants of, for instance, an author name, a source title, a cited reference, an organization name, or a keyword (Van Eck & Waltman, 2023). In total, the sample of 448 articles yielded 595 different authors' keywords.

3. PERFORMANCE ANALYSIS

Performance analysis evaluates the contributions of various research elements within a specific field, such as authors, journals, countries, and institutions (Ramos-Rodrígue & Ruíz-Navarro, 2004; Cobo et al., 2011; Donthu et al., 2021). This analysis focuses on the productivity of these research constituents, which can be measured using publication metrics like total publications (TP), most contributing authors (CA), publications (CP), and journals (CJ). Productivity per active publication year is calculated by dividing the total number of citations by the number of active years of publication (PAY = TC ÷ NAY) (see Table 1 for details) (Donthu et al., 2021). In the analysis, indicators such as publication count are often employed to assess productivity, while citation count serves as a measure of impact and influence (Carè et al., 2024). Furthermore, the h-index is frequently used to evaluate the combined output and influence of authors or journals, as it accounts for both the number of publications and their citations (Carè et al., 2024). Table 1 provides a summary of the metrics utilized in this study for conducting the performance analysis.

Table 1. Performance Analysis Key Metrics

Metric	Description
Publication-related metrics	
Total publications (TP)	Total number of articles ('ar') published from 1999 to 2024 (Q3)
Total citations (TC)	Total number of citations received by selected articles from 1999 to 2024 (Q3)
Author-related metrics	
Contributing authors (CA)	Authors with a total of 3 or more than 3 publications
Number of publications per authors (NPA)	Total number of publications authored by each author.
Contributing author total citations (CAC)	Total citations received by selected authors' publications in the dataset.
h-index (h)	Explain the influence and impact of each research author
Proportion of total publications of author articles (PJP)	(NPA ÷ TP)*100
Publication-and-Citation related metrics	
Most cited papers (CP)	Top 9 most influential research articles, selected as per highest citations (n≥180).
Published articles total citations (PTC)	total number of received citations received by each article.
Average citations per year (ACY)	PTC ÷ total number of active publication years (NAY) (e.g., from publication year to 2024).
Journal-related metrics	
Most contributing journals (CJ)	Top 7 most influential journals, selected as per highest number of publications (n≥3).
Total number of publications per journal (NPJ)	Total articles published.
Proportion of total journal publications (PJP)	(NPJ ÷ TP)*100
h-index (h)	Describe the influence and impact of each journal

Source: Partially adapted from Donthu et al. (2021)

3.1 Total Publications (TP) And Citations (TC)

Figure 2 illustrates the annual growth in the research domains of alternative finance, sustainable finance, and sustainable development. While the first paper in this field was published in 1999, the data reveals that these research areas garnered significant scholarly attention after 2015.

Figure 2. Published articles and received citations from 1999 to 2024 (Q3)

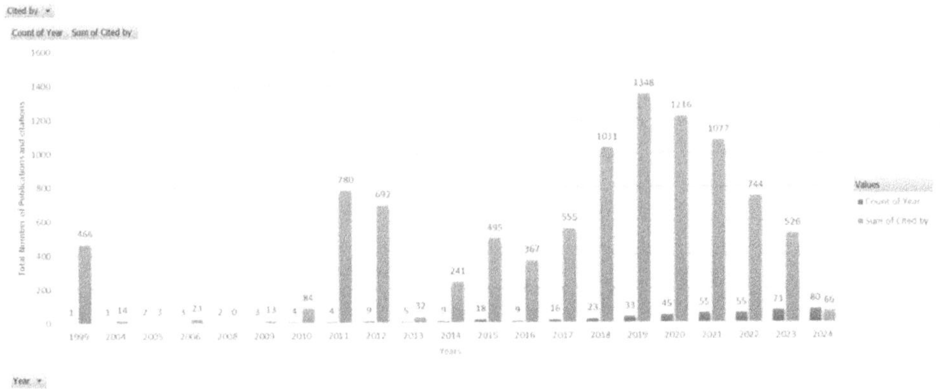

3.2 Contributing Authors (CA)

The data were collected from the Scopus database, identifying 1,248 distinct scholars contributing to various aspects of alternative finance, sustainable finance, and sustainable development research. Most of the scholars in this field are primarily from Asian countries, such as Bangladesh, China, Singapore, and Thailand, or from just two European countries, Italy and Germany. Interestingly, since 1999, 95% of these scholars have published only a single article in these research areas, while only 5% have contributed more than one article. The most active contributors in this field are Md Aslam Mia (8 articles), Andrea Gatto (5 articles), and Jacob Hörisch (5 articles). Table 2 ranks the leading scholars who have published at least three articles ($n \geq 3$).

Table 2. Contributing authors (CA) (n≥3)

Authors	Publications (NPA)*	Citations[2] (CAC)*	Country	Affiliation	h-Index (h)*	% of 448 (PJP)*
Mia, M.A.	8	117	Bangladesh	International University of Business Agriculture and Technology	13	1.8%
Gatto, A.	5	89	China	Wenzhou-Kean University	23	1.1%
Hörisch, J.	5	383	Germany	Leuphana Universität Lüneburg	26	1.1%
Tenner, I.	4	164	Germany	Leuphana Universität Lüneburg	5	0.9%
Green, W.N.	3	27	Singapore	National University of Singapore	12	0.7%
Huruta, A.D.	3	58	Indonesia	Satya Wacana Christian University	9	0.7%
Kim, M.J.	3	56	Thailand	Prince of Songkla University	32	0.7%
Moro-Visconti, R.	3	92	Italy	Università Cattolica del Sacro Cuore	7	0.7%
Sukmana, R.	3	19	Indonesia	Universitas Airlangga	12	0.7%
Testa, S.	3	85	Italy	Università degli Studi di Genova	20	0.7%

For more details, refer to Table 1 in the sub-section 'Publication-Related Metrics'
Source: Authors' elaboration

3.3 Prominent Publications (CP)

The total citation count was utilized as a proxy to identify the most influential articles and authors (Carè et al., 2024). In general, the total number of citations an article receives reflects its quality and influence (Shashi et al., 2021). Table 3 ranks the most prominent publications that have accumulated at least 180 citations (n≥180) as of September 30, 2024. Qualitative measures such as PTC and ACY were employed to identify the most contributing research articles in these fields, while the field-weighted citation impact (FWCI), a metric that normalizes for article age and field, was used to assess scientific visibility and impact (Zanotto & Carvalho, 2021). According to SciVal® guidelines, an article with an FWCI ≥ 1 signifies that it has received more citations than the global average for that specific topic since its publication (Huggett et al., 2018; Zanotto & Carvalho, 2021, p. 2867; Carè & Weber, 2023). In the dataset analyzed, Pretty et al. (2011) emerged as the top-cited article with 776 citations (PTC) and an average citation score (ACY) of just over 55 per year.

Table 3. Most Cited Papers (n≥180)

Paper Title	Author(s)	Source Title	FWCI	Year of Publication	<2017	2018	2019	2020	2021	2022	2023	2024*	Total Citations (PTC)*	Average citations per Year (ACY)*
Sustainable intensification in African agriculture	Pretty J.; Toulmin C.; Williams S.	International Journal of Agricultural Sustainability	23.81	2011	309	85	64	90	69	68	51	40	776	55.43
Can farmers' adaptation to climate change be explained by socio-economic household-level variables?	Below T.B.; Mutabazi K.D.; Kirschke D.; Franke C.; Sieber S.; Siebert R.; Tscherning K.	Global Environmental Change	8.13	2012	125	43	61	58	84	63	51	37	522	40.15
Micro-credit initiatives for equitable and sustainable development: Who pays?	Rahman A.	World Development	14.42	1999	314	23	26	28	22	22	20	11	466	17.92
Mapping citizen science contributions to the UN sustainable development goals	Fraisl D.; Campbell J.; See L.; Wehn U.; Wardlaw J.; Gold M.; Moorthy I.; Arias R.; Piera J.; Oliver J.L.; Masó J.; Penker M.; Fritz S.	Sustainability Science	17.38	2020				9	44	59	71	42	225	45.00
Enhancing sustainable urban development through smart city applications	Angelidou M.; Psaltoglou A.; Komninos N.; Kakderi C.; Tsarchopoulos P.; Panori A.	Journal of Science and Technology Policy Management	11.10	2018		1	18	38	42	36	38	37	210	30.00
Sharing versus collaborative economy: how to align ICT developments and the SDGs in tourism?	Gössling S.; Michael Hall C.	Journal of Sustainable Tourism	10.50	2019			7	33	33	44	34	38	189	31.50
Sustainability in equity crowdfunding	Vismara S.	Technological Forecasting and Social Change	12.78	2019			9	18	38	39	35	50	189	31.50
Sustainability of the sharing economy in question: When second-hand peer-to-peer platforms stimulate indulgent consumption	Parguel B.; Lunardo R.; Benoit-Moreau F.	Technological Forecasting and Social Change	7.60	2017	2	10	20	27	31	26	32	32	180	22.50
Crowdfunding for environmental ventures: An empirical analysis of the influence of environmental orientation on the success of crowdfunding initiatives	Hörisch J.	Journal of Cleaner Production	3.02	2015	7	19	24	21	33	23	25	28	180	18.00

* For more details, refer to Table 1 in the sub-section 'Citation-and-publication related metrics'

** Record until September 30, 2024

Source: Authors' elaboration

3.4 Most Contributing Journals (CJ)

The selected sample articles were distributed across 251 different journals. Interestingly, only 25% of these journals have published more than one paper since 1999, whereas the majority, accounting for 75%, have published just a single article. This distribution suggests that research papers integrating themes such as sustainable finance, alternative finance, and sustainable development are relatively dispersed across diverse journals. Table 4 highlights the most significant journals contributing at least 5 or more publications.

Additionally, the table provides details on the impact factor, h-Index, and primary subject areas of these journals. Notably, only two journals belong to the field of Economics, Econometrics, and Finance. Most of the journals publishing in this domain are multidisciplinary in scope.

Table 4. Most contributing journals (n≥3)

Publication Titles	Total Number (NPJ)*	% of 448 (PJP)*	IF**	H-INDEX*** (h)*	Subject Area***
Sustainability Switzerland	51	11.38%	3.3	169	A; B; C; D
Journal Of Cleaner Production	27	6.03%	9.8	309	B; E; F; C
Technological Forecasting And Social Change	14	3.13%	12.9	179	E; G
Resources Policy	10	2.23%	13.4	114	C; D; H
Enterprise Development And Microfinance	8	1.79%	n.a.	20	D
Technology In Society	5	1.12%	10.1	88	D; E
Venture Capital	5	1.12%	3.9	63	E; H

n.a.: Data not available

* For more details, refer to Table 1 in the sub-section 'Journal-related metrics'

** Data regarding Impact factor (IF) were obtained from the Journal's official website.

***Assigned by SCImago (https://www.scimagojr.com/): Legend: "Computer Science" = A; "Energy" = B; "Environmental Science" = C; "Social Sciences" = D; "Business, Management and Accounting" = E; "Engineering" = F; "Psychology" = G; "Economics, Econometrics and Finance" = H

Source: Authors' elaboration

3.5 Keywords Analysis

The analysis of keywords was conducted to identify the connections between different research themes. Table 5 presents the keywords most frequently observed, with a threshold level of 5 (n≥5). A higher occurrence of a keyword signifies greater focus on the respective topic. Within the selected dataset, the most frequently occurring keywords are "sustainable development" (127), "microfinance" (76), and "crowdfunding" (59).

Table 5. Frequent keywords

Cluster/color	Keywords and Frequencies
#1: Red Cluster	Cash waqf (9), Covid 19 (17), financial inclusion (26), financial sustainability (7), Islamic microfinance (11), Islamic social finance (8), microcredit (26), microfinance (76), microfinance institutions (20), poverty alleviation (21), SDGs (40), self-help groups (7), social performance (5), women empowerment (7).
#2: Green Cluster	Banks (6), climate change (9), crowdfunding (59), crowdsourcing (29), entrepreneurial finance (6), entrepreneurship (13), equity crowdfunding (9), green finance (11), open innovation (6), renewable energy investment (7), small & medium enterprises (9), sustainable development (127), sustainable entrepreneurship (6).
#3: Blue Cluster	Alternative finance (6), financial innovation (5), impact investing (16), peer-to-peer lending (12), sharing economy (12), social enterprise (6), social entrepreneurship (5), social finance (16), sustainable finance (13).
#4: Yellow Cluster	Bitcoin (8), Blockchain (20), cryptocurrencies (22), environmental sustainability (7), financial technology (16), green bonds (6), natural resources (5), Shariah compliance (5).

Source: Authors' elaboration

4. SCIENCE MAPPING

The science mapping method is a valuable tool for understanding the structure and progression of research fields (Zupic & Čater, 2015; Shashi et al., 2021). This method provides a systematic, transparent, and reproducible way to review literature, helping researchers pinpoint key contributions in the field (Zupic & Čater, 2015; Huertas-Valdivia et al., 2020).

4.1 Keyword Analysis

In this study, we employed keyword (or co-word) analysis, a content analysis approach that identifies relationships between keywords in academic documents to build a conceptual representation of the research domain (Zupic & Čater, 2015). Before performing the analysis, we standardized the authors' keywords to ensure consistency. Following Kwong et al. (2023) and Guan et al. (2024), we included only keywords with a minimum frequency of 5 occurrences. Figure 3 illustrates the most significant keywords, selected based on a frequency threshold of 5 occurrences and a cluster size of at least 5. In the network visualization, the size of each node represents the keyword's frequency, indicating its importance, while the thickness of the links reflects the strength of the connections between keywords (Montalván-

Burbano et al., 2021; van Eck & Waltman, 2023). The map identifies four distinct clusters containing 45 keywords (nodes) and 263 links, with a combined link strength of 584 (see Table 5 for details).

Figure 3. Network Visualization Map

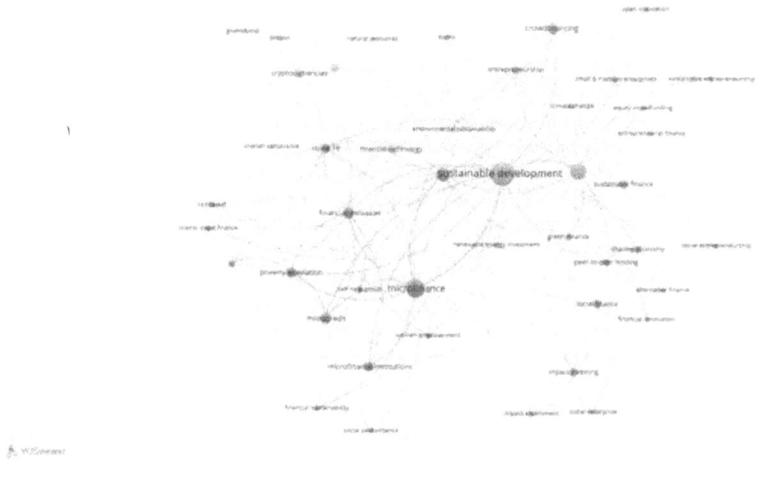

In the overlay visualization map, the color of each node (representing a keyword) reflects a specific property associated with that node (van Eck & Waltman, 2014). This map highlights emerging research directions, offering valuable insights for decision-makers and analysts (Rotolo et al., 2017). More specifically, the color of the nodes represents the year, which is derived from the publication dates of the articles from which the authors' keywords were sourced (see Figure 4). For example, yellow-colored nodes indicate recently emerging research areas or key topics, such as cryptocurrencies, bitcoin, green bonds, shariah compliance, and small and medium enterprises (SMEs).

Figure 4. Overlay Visualization Map

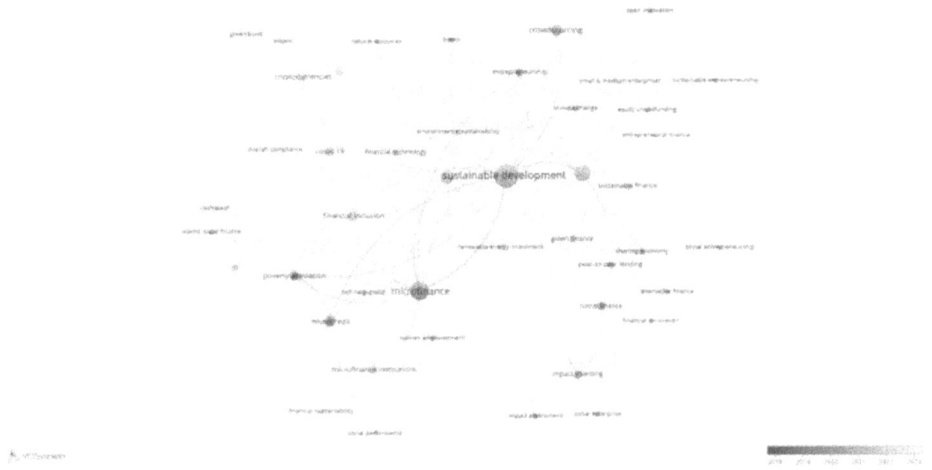

4.2 Cluster Analysis

To identify the main clusters, a co-occurrence analysis was applied, and selected authors' keywords were used as the unit of analysis. This method resulted in the segmentation of 45 keywords across four main clusters, as illustrated in Figure 3. The detailed characteristics of each cluster are comprehensively explained below.

4.2.1 Cluster 1: Microfinance and microcredit: Pathways to financial inclusion and SDGs

This cluster focuses on alternative and sustainable financial systems that contribute to achieving the SDGs (40). Central concepts include microfinance (76), microcredit (26), and financial inclusion (26), which are closely linked to poverty alleviation (21), women's empowerment (7), and social performance (5). World Bank Group President David Malpass, in his speech, mentioned that the COVID-19 "pandemic and global recession have pushed over 1.4% of the world's population into extreme poverty" (World Bank, 2020). The cluster highlights the importance of tools like microfinance institutions, self-help groups, and microcredit in promoting financial access and economic resilience. The concept of microfinance emphasizes that financial institutions should contribute to sustainable economic and financial system development by providing credit access to individuals who are usually excluded from the traditional banking system (Lopatta et al., 2017). The mission of microfinance and microfinance institutions (MFIs) is to contribute to SDGs, social welfare, and progress (Schreiner, 2002; Hudon, 2009; Hassan et al., 2011; Begum et al., 2018; Mia et al., 2019) by speeding up financial development and economic growth (Delia, 2011; Swamy & Tulasimala, 2011; Vanroose & D'Espallier, 2013; Lopatta & Tchikov, 2016) and accounting for poverty alleviation (Morduch, 1999; Barr, 2004; Prior & Argandoña, 2009; Imai et al., 2012; Kleynjans & Hudon, 2016; Casselman et al., 2015; Mazumder, 2015). However, self-help groups (SHGs), typically consisting of 10–20 members, primarily women, are formed to facilitate savings and access to microfinance, which is an important initiative to provide access to capital and promote livelihoods among indigenous rural communities (Saha et al., 2015). According to Robert et al. (2021), the success of microfinancing is a cooperative effort between SHGs, non-profit organizations (NGOs), and banks. More specifically, the SHG interventions have a significant positive association with the socio-cultural and economic empowerment of rural women (Ghosh et al., 2024), ultimately contributing to achieving five specific SDGs, i.e., (SDG 1) no poverty, (SDG 2) zero hunger, (SDG 3) good health and well-being, (SDG 4) quality education, and (SDG 5) gender equality (Basak & Roy Chowdhury, 2024).

Microcredit is a microfinancing instrument that involves providing small, unsecured loans to individuals or groups to help them start or grow business ventures (Khavul, 2010; Etzion et al., 2017). From a broader perspective, microcredit has led to several significant positive impacts. Its widespread adoption and growth gave rise to the broader field of microfinance, which now includes a variety of services such as credit, savings, mortgages, insurance, and retirement plans. All these services are offered in small amounts, making them accessible to individuals who were previously excluded from traditional financial systems (Khavul, 2010; Conning & Morduch, 2011; Etzion et al., 2017). According to Vizcaíno et al. (2024), facilitating access to microcredit is one of the key solutions to achieve the targets proposed in the SDGs. Since 2010, more than 55 countries have also made commitments to financial inclusion, as it has been identified as an enabler for seven SDGs, specifically those addressing poverty (SDG 1), hunger (SDG 2), health (SDG 3), gender equality (SDG 5), decent work (SDG 8), industry, innovation, and infrastructure (SDG 9), and reducing inequalities (SDG 10). The concept of "financial inclusion means that individuals and businesses have access to useful and affordable financial products and services that meet their needs – transactions, payments, savings, credit, and insurance – delivered in a responsible and sustainable way" (World Bank, 2022, para. 1). However, it is important to mention that financial inclusion, through microfinance, is an important phenomenon to achieve individual-level socio-economic development by mitigating poverty (Noreen et al., 2011; Bruton et al., 2015; Lopatta & Tchikov, 2017; Das, 2019) and improving the livelihoods of individuals (Solesbury, 2003; Montgomery & Weiss, 2011; Niaz, 2022).

Numerous research studies emphasize the significance of implementing Islamic finance models, such as Islamic microfinance (11), cash waqf (9), and Islamic social finance (8), as effective tools for advancing social performance and promoting financial inclusion. Islamic microfinance is a specific branch of Islamic finance that adheres to Shari'ah principles, particularly the prohibition of riba (interest)-based transactions (Begum et al., 2018). However, it stands apart from other forms of Islamic finance in several key ways. First, Islamic microfinance places a strong emphasis on the well-being of the community, prioritizing financial inclusion for its most impoverished members. Second, it promotes the provision of collateral-free loans (Qard-al-Hasan) to micro-entrepreneurs who often lack access to funding from traditional Islamic banks. Finally, Islamic microfinance seeks to mitigate the high transaction costs typically associated with the Islamic financial system (Widiarto & Emrouznejad, 2015; Hassan et al., 2021). Moreover, the cash waqf funds aim to support underprivileged individuals through Islamic microfinance, serving to promote socio-economic justice within Muslim communities (Zauro et al., 2020; Ascarya et al., 2022).

4.2.2 Cluster 2: Innovative financial mechanisms for sustainable development

The green cluster centers around themes of sustainable development, highlighting innovative financial mechanisms like crowdfunding, crowdsourcing, green finance, renewable energy investment, and entrepreneurial finance to support entrepreneurial and environmental sustainability. Key areas of focus include fostering small and medium enterprises (SMEs), promoting sustainable entrepreneurship, and addressing global challenges such as climate change. Several scholars emphasize that sustainable entrepreneurship represents the most effective approach to corporate sustainability management (e.g., Schaltegger, 2002; Schaper, 2010; Schaltegger & Wagner, 2011). Unlike conventional forms of sustainability management, such as environmental administration or management, sustainable entrepreneurship extends beyond merely mitigating the negative environmental and social impacts of business activities. Instead, it focuses on addressing specific sustainability challenges by integrating sustainability goals into the core of its operations (Schaltegger, 2002; Schaper, 2010; Schaltegger & Wagner, 2011). As Lehner explains, sustainable entrepreneurship can be broadly defined as “all kinds of ventures that have a social or environmental mission as their primal goal, which aim to be financially and legally independent and strive to become self-sustainable by means of the market” (2013, p. 299).

Ortas et al. (2013) emphasize that insufficient funding serves as a key barrier to achieving sustainable development. More precisely, sustainability entrepreneurship commonly experiences difficulties in raising sufficient funding (Fedele & Miniaci,

2010). Crowdsourcing and crowdfunding have created a new opportunity to bridge this funding gap (Bento et al., 2019). According to Howe (2006), crowdsourcing refers to the process by which an institution or company outsources a task, previously handled by workers, to a large and undefined network of individuals through an open call. This can involve collaborative peer production or be performed by individuals working alone. The key element is the open call format and the extensive network of potential contributors (Howe, 2006; Hosseini et al., 2015). Crowdsourcing can serve as a valuable tool for entrepreneurs, enabling them to drive innovation and grow their businesses (Raineri & Reno, 2022). Studies in this cluster primarily explore the role of crowdsourcing in entrepreneurship and its key features (Richter, 2015; Dellermann et al., 2020; Watson et al., 2023). Additionally, Morschheuser et al. (2019) examine factors that influence participation in crowdsourcing, as well as its sustainable aspects (Konhäusner, 2021). Crowdsourcing has also been proposed as an effective strategy in response to the COVID-19 pandemic (e.g., Tangcharoensathien et al., 2020; Liu et al., 2021; Vermicelli et al., 2021, 2022).

However, crowdfunding is a broad term encompassing various alternative methods of raising funds, usually through the internet, where individuals collectively contribute money to achieve a specific objective (Ahlers et al., 2015). The four primary types of crowdfunding are reward-based, donation-based, lending-based, and equity-based (Vismara, 2019). In the donation-based model, contributors provide financial support to projects without expecting any return. In the reward-based model, contributors receive a non-financial reward proportional to their level of funding, often in the form of the product or service the project aims to commercialize. The lending-based model involves contributors lending money to the project creator, typically with an agreed-upon interest rate. In the equity-based model, contributors fund the project in exchange for equity shares (Messeni Petruzzelli et al., 2019). Crowdfunding provides a novel financing option that is often believed to support environmentally focused projects (Hörisch, 2015). More precisely, crowdfunding is increasingly highlighted in the media as an alternative means of finance, particularly for sustainability-focused enterprises and clean production technologies (Testa et al., 2020). Thus, the review of extant literature shows that crowdfunding offers several advantages for entrepreneurs: i) financing, by providing funding for new ideas or existing ventures (Lehner, 2013); ii) marketing, as it increases visibility among potential customers, the general public, and the media (Burtch et al., 2014; Mollick, 2014; Hörisch, 2018); iii) market testing, by signaling potential user interest in the offerings of a crowdfunding campaign (Belleflamme et al., 2014; Lam & Law, 2016); and iv) legitimization, by using crowd support to demonstrate public approval and endorsement of the project or cause (Lehner & Nicholls, 2014; Vasileiadou et al., 2016). Furthermore, the connection between crowdfunding and crowdsourcing is often discussed, as crowdfunding is built upon the broader crowdsourcing concept, where a company or individual can gather ideas, support, or feedback from the public, typically via the Internet (Belleflamme et al., 2014; Brem et al., 2019).

Furthermore, many research studies grouped in this cluster also explain the concept of green finance and entrepreneurial finance. As green investments are crucial for decarbonizing the energy system (Allen et al., 2018, p. 21–22), green finance, which involves redirecting significant financial flows toward climate-friendly assets, is expected to gain momentum. This shift is being encouraged by international organizations (e.g., OECD, 2017; TCFD, 2023). A growing body of literature has started to focus on this issue, examining various investment vehicles and strategies, such as green bonds, impact investing, and carbon pricing (see, for instance, Clark et al., 2018; Hafner et al., 2020). Despite the growing connection between finance and sustainability, research in entrepreneurial finance remains in its early stages (Vismara, 2019). Martino et al. (2022) note that entrepreneurial finance encompasses a variety of capital sources, including angel investors, venture capital, equity, and debt financing, as well as innovative funding methods such as initial coin offerings and crowdfunding (see Bruton et al., 2015; Block et al., 2021).

4.2.3 Cluster 3: Innovative finance for sustainable futures: exploring alternative financial mechanisms

The blue cluster focuses on alternative means of finance, highlighting innovative financial mechanisms aimed at addressing societal challenges and promoting sustainable development. Central themes include social finance (16), impact investing (16), sustainable finance (13), alternative finance (6), and social entrepreneurship (5), with a particular emphasis on models like peer-to-peer lending (12) and the sharing economy (12). These concepts reflect a growing trend toward financial systems that prioritize social welfare and environmental sustainability alongside economic growth. The cluster also explores how financial innovation (5) and impact assessment (7) contribute to more inclusive financial ecosystems, supporting social enterprises (6) and advancing the SDGs by offering accessible financing options for underserved communities.

The financial crisis of 2007-2008 revealed the weaknesses within the traditional banking system and financial markets (Motylska-Kuzma, 2018). The concepts of social finance and sustainable finance gained significant attention from regulators, researchers, and practitioners, particularly following the financial crisis (see, Lehner & Nicholls, 2014; Nicholls et al., 2015; Lauesen, 2016; Weber, 2019; Lagoarde-Segot, 2019; Rizzello & Kabli, 2020; Fatima et al., 2022; European Commission, 2024). Social and sustainable finance pertain to the raising of funds for projects that achieve sustainable goals or drive social change. It is not merely a fiscal obligation for states; rather, it opens avenues for various fundraising channels, including private sector institutions and markets (Chiu & Greene, 2019). These new fields of finance also support the shifting boundaries in the official roles, capacities, and responsibilities of public, private, and civil society organizations, as well as the hybrid agendas or goals that these actors promote (Chiu & Greene, 2019). Moreover, in the context of developing countries, impact investing—defined as investments aimed at generating both positive social and financial returns—plays a crucial role in financing companies that can address social issues through business solutions (Jochnick, 2012). In simple words, impact investing (or impact investments) is 'intended to create positive significant impact beyond financial return (O'Donohoe et al., 2010; Lehner & Nicholls, 2014). Many scholars emphasize that impact investing is a form of 'alternative finance' that primarily operates in non-listed, private markets, providing privileged access to the ultra-wealthy (e.g., see Stolz & Lai, 2020; Benquet & Bourgeron, 2022; Golka, 2024). According to Park & Jun (2024), among various impact investments, microfinance has seen significantly in developing economies (also, see Dileo, 2011; Hummels & Leede, 2014; Meyer & Krauss, 2021).

Further, in response to escalating 2007-2008 financial crises challenges, governments and regulators in several countries have implemented additional restrictions that impede access to financial capital (Motylska-Kuzma, 2018). This situation has particularly impacted the small and medium-sized enterprises (SME) sector, as well as startups. Therefore, these entities have begun exploring alternative financing methods, such as crowdfunding (Motylska-Kuzma, 2018; Mc Laren & Baldegger, 2021), crowdsourcing (Deflorian, 2023), and peer-to-peer lending, which contributes in achieving sustainable development (Léautier, 2018). More precisely, the International Union for the Conservation of Nature (IUCN) recommends adopting alternative finance mechanisms that can help in achieving financial sustainability (Emerton et al., 2006). Another alternative finance mechanism is the social and/or environmental impact bond, which is a subset of impact investing and an example of a results-based contract or pay-for-success (O'Flynn et al., 2022). In recent years, individuals are increasingly engaging in peer-to-peer economic interactions, such as micro-credit, currency exchange, online marketplace lending, cryptocurrencies, and the sharing economy (Park & Jun, 2024). Many of these initiatives aim to 'resocialize' finance by leveraging various informal, peer-to-peer, and collaborative relationships (Clarke & Tooker, 2018). The rise of the sharing economy, where access replaces ownership (Belk, 2014; Botsman & Rogers, 2010), can be partly attributed to the public's increasing environmental concerns. Rather than purchasing and owning goods, consumers now seek temporary access to the items they need (Bardhi & Eckhardt, 2012). Carsharing has been considered as one of the most prominent practices in the sharing economy (See Habibi et al., 2017; Hartl et al., 2018). Lastly in this cluster, various academic studies have examined the effectiveness of environmental impact assessments and carbon pricing systems in decreasing fossil fuel consumption, promoting sustainable practices, as well as encouraging environmentally responsible behavior (e.g., see Mintz-Woo et al., 2021; Zhang, 2023; Chen et al., 2024), thus assisting the countries in achieving its goals of greater sustainability (Chen et al., 2024).

4.2.4 Cluster 4: Cryptocurrencies and green bonds: synergies for a sustainable future

The yellow cluster focuses on cryptocurrencies (22), blockchain technology (20), and financial technology (FinTech) (33), emphasizing their role in advancing environmental sustainability (13) and the management of natural resources (5). Key themes include the use of cryptocurrencies for green bonds (6), the environmental implications of cryptocurrency adoption (e.g., Bitcoin), and their integration with sustainable practices. The cluster also touches on ethical frameworks like Shariah compliance and explores how these technologies intersect with global challenges such as COVID-19.

Cryptocurrencies were initially promoted for their capacity to function in a fair and equitable manner, independent of financial institutions and government oversight. Cryptocurrencies, a new form of digital money, were initially introduced in the Bitcoin whitepaper as an alternative currency (Nakamoto, 2008; Vaz & Brown, 2020). They operate through a peer-to-peer payment mechanism on open-access blockchain technology, which eliminates the need for intermediaries and financial institutions. Blockchain-based cryptocurrencies, such as Bitcoin, claim to offer greater access to and a fairer financial system (See Vigna & Casey, 2015; Scott, 2016; Vaz & Brown, 2020). More in detail, Vaz & Brown (2020) evaluated the cryptocurrencies within the UN 2030 agenda for sustainable development, especially its contribution to SDG 7, SDG 8, SDG 10, SDG 16, and SDG 17. The findings of this paper clearly indicate that technologists believe they have created viable alternatives to traditional money; however, several issues related to the sustainability of this form of finance persist (Vaz & Brown, 2020). The major concerns include energy consumption, the reward system that favors those with greater computing power (leading to inequality), and challenges associated with loss sharing when exchanges or user nodes are hacked and/or digital wallets are lost (Vaz & Brown, 2020). Tomlinson et al. (2021) stated that blockchain for good projects are unlikely to contribute to a sustainable future due to technical limitations and a conceptual framing that favors the status quo rather than transformative change. Blockchain also has the capability to mediate and harmonize differing Shariah compliance regimes, thereby facilitating the establishment of a unified digital market for Islamic financial services and products (Dahdal et al., 2022). Moreover, green cryptocurrencies are emerging as significant assets in the development of sustainable finance, which involves considering the environmental, social, and governance (ESG) impacts of investment decisions (Lobão, 2022). Also, the study by Dogan et al. (2022) suggests that the energy consumption associated with Bitcoin can be powered by clean energy, which helps mitigate its environmental impact. The study by Gunay et al. (2023) suggests that implementing and widely adopting blockchain technology through innovative business models could enhance global environmental sustainability due to the transparency, cost-effectiveness, and security it offers. According to Huynh (2022) investing in green bonds is one of many safest avenues. Green bonds, due to increased focus on environmental sustainability, outperformed most other financial instruments, especially after Covid 19 (Yi et al., 2021; Liu, 2022). A recent area of research has examined the relationship between green bonds and cryptocurrencies. Naeem and Karim (2021) reported that green bonds possess hedging properties against Bitcoin (BTC). In their empirical findings, Le et al. (2021) identified time and frequency domain connectedness and spillover effects among fintech, green bonds, and cryptocurrencies. Using a time-varying parameter vector autoregression (TVP-VAR) network connectedness model, Pham et al. (2021) demonstrated that spillovers between cryptocurrency, green, and fossil fuel assets fluctuate over time and become more pronounced during crisis periods. Additionally, the study revealed that the spillovers among these assets are asymmetric, with negative return spillovers being greater than positive return spillovers. Kamal and Hassan (2022) highlighted the role of cryptocurrencies as asset diversifiers in conjunction with the performance of green bonds. The study by Husain et al. (2023) revealed that less emphasis should be placed on the weightings of green cryptocurrencies in a portfolio, while greater emphasis should be placed on green bonds and gold during times of financial distress.

4.3 Thematic Analysis

We conducted a thematic analysis to examine the evolution of key themes in alternative and sustainable finance, as well as sustainable development research, from 1999 to 2024 (Q3) (Tennekes, 2018). Using the Bibliometrix R-package (Aria & Cuccurullo, 2017), we identified trends over time, categorizing articles into four groups based on publication patterns (see Figure 5). These fields gained notable attention after 2015, following the release of the European Commission's 2030 Agenda. Group 1 (1999–2009) included 12 articles focused on microfinance and banking, laying the groundwork for future studies. Group 2 (2010–2015) encompassed 49 articles that explored microcredit, microfinance, and the role of crowdfunding in achieving sustainable development, particularly the SDGs. Group 3 (2016–2020) reflected a surge in interest, with 126 articles discussing sustainable finance, green finance, alternative finance, and sustainable development. Group 4

(2021–2024) consisted of 261 articles focusing on emerging research areas such as crowdsourcing, the sharing economy, and social entrepreneurship, emphasizing their role in achieving the 2030 Agenda. The Sankey diagram in Figure 5 illustrates the thematic evolution, showing how early studies concentrated on “microfinance” and “banking,” while later periods introduced themes like “microcredit,” “crowdfunding,” and ultimately “sustainable development” and related financial concepts. Recent research highlights alternative mechanisms like crowdsourcing, waqf, and the sharing economy, which facilitate sustainable development, while the inclusion of “cryptocurrencies” in studies from 2021 to 2024 underscores the growing interest in energy-efficient financial models with positive environmental impacts.

Figure 5. Thematic Analysis

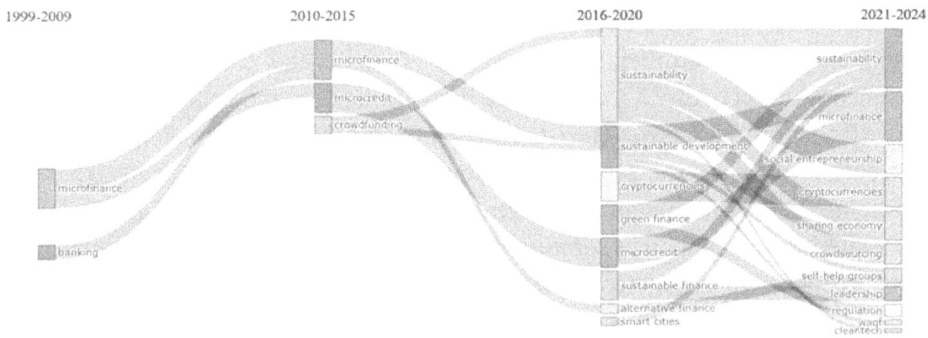

5. DISCUSSION OF RESULTS

Section 5 provides a critical review of the bibliometric evidence to address three key dimensions. Firstly, it explores the differentiated approaches of alternative and sustainable finance, emphasizing their complementary roles in advancing the Sustainable Development Goals (SDGs). Secondly, it discusses controversial and underexplored issues within the identified clusters, including structural limitations, regulatory gaps, and transparency challenges. Finally, the section identifies structural challenges and outlines future research directions to enhance the scalability and impact of these financial mechanisms.

5.1 Differentiated Approaches to Alternative and Sustainable Finance

The complementary nature of alternative and sustainable finance lies in their differentiated approaches, which respond to distinct but converging needs to achieve the SDGs. While transparency is an essential lever for ensuring the credibility of financial mechanisms aligned with the SDGs, it manifests itself differently in sustainable and alternative finance. Sustainable finance operates on a global scale, mobilizing institutional capital to finance projects aligned with ESG criteria. Green bonds exemplify this approach, providing institutional investors with detailed reports that enable them to assess the environmental impact of their investments (Hafner et al., 2020). However, this approach remains limited by the absence of robust social indicators to fully assess its impact beyond the environmental dimension. Alternative finance, on the other hand, places greater emphasis on local conditions through inclusive instruments such as microfinance and crowdfunding. These mechanisms promote direct transparency between lenders and beneficiaries thanks to their decentralized nature (Hörisch, 2015). Crowdfunding, for example, enables contributors to follow the progress of the projects they finance directly, thereby reinforcing their commitment and increasing the accountability of project owners. Financial education is another common objective, but it is expressed differently in the two approaches. Microfinance often includes financial education programs to help beneficiaries manage their financial resources more effectively and maximize the impact of the loans they receive (Morduch, 1999). Conversely, sustainable finance focuses on raising institutional investors' awareness of ESG issues in order to promote responsible capital allocation (Carè & Weber, 2023). While these approaches address distinct needs, they also face structural limitations and controversies that hinder their full potential in achieving the SDGs.

5.2 Key Controversies and Under-Explored Issues in the Clusters

The bibliometric analysis highlights key controversies within the clusters identified, reflecting the structural challenges and academic debates surrounding financing mechanisms to achieve the SDGs. These controversies highlight both the limitations of these instruments and the opportunities to improve their design and implementation for greater impact.

5.2.1 Microfinance: structural limitations and over-indebtedness

While widely recognized as a tool for financial inclusion, microfinance has been criticized for its structural limitations. One recurring problem is over-indebtedness, particularly in regions where borrowers take out multiple loans from different microfinance institutions (MFIs) (Banerjee et al., 2015). High interest rates charged by these institutions are highlighted as a factor exacerbating the economic vulnerability of poor households. These rates, justified by the high operational costs and risks associated with unbanked borrowers (Cull et al., 2009), limit borrowers' ability to invest in income-generating activities, thus reducing the expected positive impact. These criticisms underline the need for stricter regulation to protect borrowers while ensuring that institutional practices remain aligned with their social mission.

5.2.2 Crowdfunding: balancing innovation and investor protection

Crowdfunding has been celebrated for mobilizing resources for sustainable projects through participatory models. It promotes direct transparency between contributors and project leaders, thereby increasing stakeholder engagement (Hörisch, 2015). However, the lack of regulation has historically exposed investors to increased risks, particularly due to the possibility of fraud or mismanagement of funds raised. This absence of protection can limit investor confidence and hinder wider adoption of this tool (Vismara, 2019). Recent regulatory developments have sought to address its limitations. In the United States, updates to the JOBS Act have raised funding caps for equity crowdfunding campaigns, enabling startups to access greater capital without pursuing a full IPO (Passador, 2023). Similarly, Europe's adoption of the European Crowdfunding Service Providers Regulation (ECSPR) in 2021 has harmonized rules across member states, enhancing investor protection and facilitating cross-border funding flows (Alhammad et al., 2021). These measures aim to improve transparency, risk disclosures, and accountability while fostering innovation. However, stricter requirements around financial reporting and compliance can impose higher costs on smaller creators, potentially limiting their participation on regulated platforms (Lee, 2021). While crowdfunding effectively mobilizes resources for local initiatives such as renewable energy projects, its overall impact remains difficult to quantify due to the lack of standardized indicators, making it challenging to demonstrate alignment with the SDGs.

5.2.3 Green Finance: greenwashing and transparency

Green finance, notably through green bonds, has played a decisive role in financing the energy transition. However, it has been criticized for "greenwashing" when environmental benefits are not clearly demonstrated or independently verified (Flammer, 2020). This controversy highlights the importance of rigorous certification processes and increased transparency in building trust in these financial instruments.

5.2.4 Cryptocurrencies: regulatory fragmentation and environmental concerns

Cryptocurrencies face increasing scrutiny as regulators seek to address challenges such as financial volatility, high energy consumption, and risks of illicit activities. Recent regulatory developments reveal divergent approaches across jurisdictions. In the European Union, the Markets in Crypto-Assets Regulation (MiCAR) establishes a unified framework for crypto-assets, requiring licensing for service providers and mandatory risk disclosures (European Parliament, 2024; PwC, 2023). Conversely, the United States adopts a fragmented approach, with overlapping responsibilities between the SEC and CFTC, limiting coordination on investor protection and market integrity (Global Legal Insights, 2025; CCAF, 2024).

Environmental concerns further complicate the adoption of cryptocurrencies. An analysis by Krause and Tolaymat (2018) highlighted the significant energy consumption of proof-of-work mechanisms like Bitcoin and Ethereum prior to its transition to proof-of-stake (PoS). Following this transition in September 2022, Ethereum's energy consumption has reportedly decreased by approximately 99%, according to data from the Crypto Carbon Ratings Institute cited by Ethereum.org (2023). However, concerns remain regarding the centralization of validators and the uneven adoption of PoS across other cryptocurrencies (Dogan et al., 2022).

These dual challenges—regulatory fragmentation and environmental sustainability—highlight structural barriers that limit the scalability of cryptocurrencies as tools for sustainable development while raising questions about their alignment with global financial systems.

5.2.5 Decentralized Finance (DeFi) and Stablecoins

While these frameworks represent progress, significant challenges remain in regulating decentralized finance (DeFi) platforms due to their lack of intermediaries. Regulators are increasingly targeting DeFi platforms by introducing Know Your Customer (KYC) measures, Anti-Money Laundering (AML) compliance requirements, and mandatory registration with authorities (BIS, 2022; PwC, 2023). Additionally, stablecoins are facing stricter global regulations aimed at improving transparency and ensuring reserve backing standards to mitigate risks to financial stability (FSB, 2025). Despite these measures, global coordination remains crucial to address persistent issues such as pseudonymity, decentralized governance structures, and regulatory arbitrage within the crypto sector (CCAF, 2024; Atlantic Council, 2025).

These dual challenges underscore the complexity of integrating DeFi platforms and stablecoins into sustainable financial systems while ensuring compliance and reducing systemic risks. The lack of intermediaries in DeFi raises questions about accountability and governance structures, while the rapid growth of stablecoins highlights the need for robust frameworks to prevent destabilizing effects on global financial markets.

5.2.6 Environmental sustainability and financial volatility

Cryptocurrencies present both opportunities and challenges in advancing SDGs. Their potential for promoting financial inclusion—particularly in underserved regions—remains promising but underexplored. However, concerns about their environmental impact, financial volatility, and regulatory fragmentation raise questions about their long-term viability as tools for sustainable development. Ethical models such as green crypto-assets or Shariah-compliant cryptocurrencies could provide pathways to align these technologies more closely with sustainability principles and cultural or religious contexts. These innovations warrant further research to evaluate their effectiveness in addressing global development challenges while ensuring inclusivity and environmental responsibility (Husain et al., 2023; Atlantic Council, 2025).

5.2.7 Under-explored research themes

In addition to these controversies, which highlight academic challenges and debates, there are under-explored research themes within the clusters, which limit the overall understanding of alternative and sustainable finance mechanisms to the SDGs. These include: (i) the impact of microfinance on social well-being, community resilience or social capital; (ii) the role of crowdfunding in supporting technological innovation adapted to the specific challenges of developing countries (iii) ; the social impacts of green finance beyond environmental benefits, such as the ability to act against social inequalities or support marginalized communities; (iv) finally, ethical or religiously compliant crypto-currencies (e.g., Shariah-compliant models) as a route to financial inclusion in specific cultural or religious contexts.

5.3 Structural Challenges and Future Research Directions

Analysis of the bibliometric results of our research highlights several structural challenges and underexplored topics that deserve greater attention from researchers to maximize the contribution of alternative and sustainable financial mechanisms to the SDGs.

Firstly, the lack of robust regulatory frameworks remains a significant obstacle to the credibility and scalability of alternative finance mechanisms like crowdfunding and cryptocurrencies. Without clear regulations, these instruments expose investors to heightened risks, including fraud, mismanagement, and financial instability. Recent regulatory advancements, such as the Markets in Crypto-Assets Regulation (MiCAR) in the European Union, aim to address these issues by introducing mandatory disclosure of risks, licensing requirements for crypto-asset service providers (CASPs), and prudential safeguards like minimum capital requirements (European Parliament, 2024; PwC, 2023). However, the fragmented approach in the United States, with overlapping responsibilities between the SEC and CFTC, complicates cross-border compliance and limits coordinated efforts to combat illicit activities effectively (CCAF, 2024). Future research should explore how balanced regulatory frameworks can protect investors while promoting innovation and transparency, particularly in the context of DeFi platforms and stablecoins.

Secondly, the development of robust social indicators is essential to enhance the overall assessment of green finance instruments like green bonds. While these bonds have played a decisive role in financing the energy transition, they often lack transparency on social impacts, limiting their alignment with broader SDGs. Future studies should focus on creating standardized metrics that evaluate both environmental and social contributions, enabling a holistic understanding of the effectiveness of these instruments. For example, research could explore how green bonds contribute to community resilience, social equity, or support for marginalized communities (IFC, 2023).

Thirdly, criticisms like greenwashing and financial volatility highlight the need for rigorous certification processes and increased transparency to build investor confidence. Green finance instruments, particularly green bonds, have been criticized for lacking independent verification of their environmental benefits, leading to concerns about greenwashing (Flammer, 2020). Similarly, cryptocurrencies face scrutiny due to their high energy consumption and financial volatility, raising questions about their long-term viability as tools for sustainable development. Future research should explore how blockchain technology can enhance transparency by providing immutable records of transactions and impact metrics (Zhao, 2022).

Additionally, institutional players like multilateral development banks and governments can play a catalytic role by implementing public policies that promote financial transparency, and by directly supporting mechanisms such as green bonds or microcredit programs. Future research could explore how these institutions can catalyze the adoption of green crypto-currencies or facilitate crowdfunding for innovative projects in emerging markets.

Finally, an interdisciplinary approach integrating social economics, political ecology and technological innovation is essential to maximize the global impact of these financial mechanisms. By combining these perspectives, future research can design and evaluate more inclusive and sustainable solutions that meet local needs while contributing to global development goals. For instance, ethical models such as green crypto-assets or Shariah-compliant cryptocurrencies could provide pathways to align these technologies with sustainability principles and cultural or religious contexts (Husain et al., 2023; Atlantic Council, 2025). This approach could also address under-explored themes like microfinance's impact on social well-being or crowdfunding's role in technological innovation for developing countries.

6. CONCLUSIONS AND LIMITATIONS

This bibliometric analysis highlighted an exponential growth in publications on alternative and sustainable finance since 2015, linked to the adoption of the United Nations' Agenda 2030. Between 1999 and 2024, 448 articles extracted from the Scopus database were published, with a strong geographical concentration in Asia (Bangladesh, China) and Western Europe (Italy, Germany). Most authors contributed a single article, while prolific researchers such as Mia M.A. stand out for their sustained output. These results reflect a growing specialization in this field. In terms of academic impact, the most cited article is by Pretty et al. (2011), which highlights the links between sustainable finance and environmental development, underlining the key role of innovative financial instruments in the transition to sustainable economic models. Thematic evolution shows a clear progression in the topics addressed over time. Between 1999 and 2009, work focused on microfinance as a tool for financial inclusion (Morduch, 1999). Between 2010 and 2015, crowdfunding emerged as an important mechanism for financing projects aligned with the SDGs (Hörisch, 2015). From 2016 to 2020, green finance gained in popularity thanks to instruments such as green bonds (Hafner et al., 2020). Finally, between 2021 and 2024, cryptocurrencies and blockchain became central topics due to their potential to improve financial transparency while exploring responsible energy models (Pham et al., 2023). Geographically, publications are dominated by Asian researchers working on microfinance (notably around the Grameen Bank model) and European pioneers in the development of green bonds. This evolution reflects a gradual diversification of financial mechanisms to meet global challenges while adapting to local needs. However, addressing structural challenges such as regulatory fragmentation or greenwashing remains crucial to fully realize their potential for advancing the SDGs.

6.1 Policy Implications and Practical Applications

Our results indicate that alternative finance is an essential lever for achieving the SDGs, complementing sustainable finance with innovative solutions tailored to local needs. While sustainable finance acts at the institutional level by redirecting financial flows towards ESG-focused projects, alternative finance focuses on local, inclusive solutions such as microcredit or crowdfunding. Together, these approaches provide a global response to specific challenges while supporting global objectives. However, their effectiveness will depend on their ability to overcome structural difficulties. The lack of regulation in areas such as crowdfunding and crypto currencies undermines their credibility and hinders their widespread adoption. Balanced regulatory frameworks are necessary to protect investors while fostering innovation. For example, the adoption of the European Crowdfunding Service Providers Regulation (ECSPR) in 2021 aims to harmonize rules across member states, enhancing investor protection and facilitating cross-border funding flows (Alhammad et al., 2021). Similarly, the Markets in Crypto-Assets Regulation (MiCAR) in Europe introduces key requirements to improve transparency and financial stability (European Parliament, 2024). The absence of robust social indicators limits the ability to fully assess the impact of green finance beyond the environmental dimension. More comprehensive evaluation frameworks are needed to integrate both social and environmental outcomes. For instance, future studies could focus on creating standardized metrics to evaluate how green bonds contribute to community resilience or social equity (IFC, 2023). Criticism of greenwashing and financial volatility further underlines the need to improve transparency and governance. Governments and multilateral banks can play an essential role by directly supporting innovative financial mechanisms, while promoting balanced regulation that protects investors without stifling innovation. For example, public policies could encourage financial transparency and directly support mechanisms like green bonds or microcredit programs. Finally, this article highlights the importance of an interdisciplinary approach to maximize the impact of these innovative financial mechanisms. These orientations offer promising avenues for future research in this field.

6.2 Limitations of the Study

However, this research study also has certain limitations. Although Scopus offers extensive coverage of academic literature, relying solely on this database may have led to the omission of relevant studies indexed elsewhere, potentially affecting the scope of our analysis. Additionally, while citation metrics are commonly used to assess research influence, they may not fully capture the significance of studies on niche or emerging topics that have yet to gain broader recognition. Despite these limitations, our study offers a robust quantitative overview, and future research could incorporate multiple databases or qualitative assessments to provide a holistic perspective.

REFERENCES

Agrawal, R., Wankhede, V. A., Kumar, A., Luthra, S., & Huisingh, D. (2022). Progress and trends in integrating Industry 4.0 within Circular Economy: A comprehensive literature review and future research propositions. *Business Strategy and the Environment*, *31*(1), 559–579.

Ahlers, G. K. C., Cumming, D., Günther, C., & Schweizer, D. (2015). Signaling in Equity Crowdfunding. *Entrepreneurship Theory and Practice*, *39*(4), 955–980. DOI: 10.1111/etap.12157

Alhammad, M. M., AlOthman, R., & Tan, C. (2021). Review of Crowdfunding Regulations Across Countries: A Systematic Review Study. *Journal of Information Systems Engineering & Management*, *6*(4), em0145. Advance online publication. DOI: 10.21601/jisem/11395

Allen, M., Babiker, M., Chen, Y., Coninck, H. de, Connors, S., Diemen, R. van, Dube, O. P., Ebi, K. L., Engelbrecht, F., Ferrat, M., Ford, J., Forster, P., Fuss, S., Guillén Bolanos, T., Harold, J., Hoegh-Guldberg, O., Hourcade, J.-C., Huppmann, D., Jacob, D., … Zickfeld, K. (2018). *Global Warming of 1.5 °C. Summary for Policymakers*. 26.

Aria, M., & Cuccurullo, C. (2017). bibliometrix: An R-tool for comprehensive science mapping analysis. *Journal of Informetrics*, *11*(4), 959–975. DOI: 10.1016/j.joi.2017.08.007

Ascarya, A., Sukmana, R., Rahmawati, S., & Masrifah, A. R. (2022). Developing cash waqf models for Baitul Maal wat Tamwil as integrated Islamic social and commercial microfinance. *Journal of Islamic Accounting and Business Research*, *14*(5), 699–717. DOI: 10.1108/JIABR-09-2020-0267

Atlantic Council. (2025). *The 2025 Crypto Policy Landscape: Looming EU and US Divergences?* Retrieved from https://www.atlanticcouncil.org/blogs/econographics/the-2025-crypto-policy-landscape-looming-eu-and-us-divergences/

Baeck, P., Collins, L., & Zhang, B. (2014). Understanding alternative finance. *The UK alternative finance industry report*. Retrieved from https://media.nesta.org.uk/documents/understanding-alternative-finance-2014.pdf

Baker, H. K., Kumar, S., & Pattnaik, D. (2020). Twenty-five years of Review of Financial Economics: A bibliometric overview. *Review of Financial Economics*, *38*(1), 3–23. DOI: 10.1002/rfe.1095

Banerjee, A., Duflo, E., & Glennerster, R. (2015). The Miracle of Microfinance? Evidence from a Randomized Evaluation. *American Economic Journal. Applied Economics*.

Banerjee, A., Karlan, D., & Zinman, J. (2015). Six Randomized Evaluations of Microcredit: Introduction and Further Steps. *American Economic Journal. Applied Economics*, *7*(1), 1–21. DOI: 10.1257/app.20140287

Bardhi, F., & Eckhardt, G. M. (2012). Access-Based Consumption: The Case of Car Sharing. *The Journal of Consumer Research*, *39*(4), 881–898. DOI: 10.1086/666376

Barr, M. (2004). Microfinance and Financial Development. *Articles*, 271.

Basak, D., & Roy Chowdhury, I. (2024). Role of self-help groups on socioeconomic development and the achievement of Sustainable Development Goals (SDGs) among rural women in Cooch Behar District, India. *Regional Sustainability*, *5*(2), 100140. DOI: 10.1016/j.regsus.2024.100140

Begum, H., Alam, A. S. A. F., Mia, M. A., Bhuiyan, F., & Ghani, A. B. A. (2018). Development of Islamic microfinance: A sustainable poverty reduction approach. *Journal of Economic and Administrative Sciences*, *35*(3), 143–157. DOI: 10.1108/JEAS-01-2018-0007

Belk, R. (2014). You are what you can access: Sharing and collaborative consumption online. *Journal of Business Research*, *67*(8), 1595–1600. DOI: 10.1016/j.jbusres.2013.10.001

Belleflamme, P., Lambert, T., & Schwienbacher, A. (2014a). Crowdfunding: Tapping the right crowd. *Journal of Business Venturing*, *29*(5), 585–609. DOI: 10.1016/j.jbusvent.2013.07.003

Belleflamme, P., Lambert, T., & Schwienbacher, A. (2014b). Crowdfunding: Tapping the right crowd. *Journal of Business Venturing*, *29*(5), 585–609. DOI: 10.1016/j.jbusvent.2013.07.003

Benquet, M., & Bourgeron, T. (2022). *Alt-Finance: How the City of London Bought Democracy*. https://hal.science/hal-03879329

Bento, N., Gianfrate, G., & Thoni, M. H. (2019). Crowdfunding for sustainability ventures. *Journal of Cleaner Production*, *237*, 117751. DOI: 10.1016/j.jclepro.2019.117751

BIS Committee on Banking Supervision [BIS]. (2022). *Prudential Treatment of Cryptoasset Exposures*. Retrieved from https://www.bis.org/bcbs/publ/d545.pdf

Block, J. H., Groh, A., Hornuf, L., Vanacker, T., & Vismara, S. (2021). The entrepreneurial finance markets of the future: A comparison of crowdfunding and initial coin offerings. *Small Business Economics*, *57*(2), 865–882. DOI: 10.1007/s11187-020-00330-2

Botsman, R., & Rogers, R. (2010, October 1). Beyond Zipcar: Collaborative Consumption. *Harvard Business Review*. https://hbr.org/2010/10/beyond-zipcar-collaborative-consumption

Brem, A., Bilgram, V., & Marchuk, A. (2019). How crowdfunding platforms change the nature of user innovation – from problem solving to entrepreneurship. *Technological Forecasting and Social Change*, *144*, 348–360. DOI: 10.1016/j.techfore.2017.11.020

Bruton, G., Khavul, S., Siegel, D., & Wright, M. (2015). New Financial Alternatives in Seeding Entrepreneurship: Microfinance, Crowdfunding, and Peer–to–Peer Innovations. *Entrepreneurship Theory and Practice*, *39*(1), 9–26. DOI: 10.1111/etap.12143

Burtch, G., Ghose, A., & Wattal, S. (2014). Cultural Differences and Geography as Determinants of Online Prosocial Lending. *Management Information Systems Quarterly*, *38*(3), 773–794.

Cambridge Centre for Alternative Finance [CCAF]. (2024). *2nd Global Cryptoasset Regulatory Landscape Study*. University of Cambridge. Retrieved from https://www.jbs.cam.ac.uk/wp-content/uploads/2024/10/2024-2nd-global-cryptoasset-regulatory-landscape-study.pdf

Carè, R., Carè, S., Lévy, N., & Fatima, R. (2023). Missing finance in social impact bond research? A bibliometric overview between past and future research. *Corporate Social Responsibility and Environmental Management*, *30*(5), 2101–2120. DOI: 10.1002/csr.2496

Carè, R., Fatima, R., & Agnese, P. (2025). Crowdfunding and sustainable development: A systematic review. *Finance Research Letters*, *78*, 107220. DOI: 10.1016/j.frl.2025.107220

Carè, R., Fatima, R., & Boitan, I. A. (2024). Central banks and climate risks: Where we are and where we are going? *International Review of Economics & Finance*. Advance online publication. DOI: 10.1016/j.iref.2024.01.057

Carè, R., & Weber, O. (2023). How much finance is in climate finance? A bibliometric review, critiques, and future research directions. *Research in International Business and Finance*, *64*, 101886. DOI: 10.1016/j.ribaf.2023.101886

Casselman, R. M., Sama, L. M., & Stefanidis, A. (2015). Differential Social Performance of Religiously-Affiliated Microfinance Institutions (MFIs) in Base of Pyramid (BoP) Markets. *Journal of Business Ethics, 132*(3), 539–552. DOI: 10.1007/s10551-014-2360-z

Chen, F., She, W., Zeng, F., Gao, M., Wen, C., Liu, G., Wu, L., Wu, Y., & Zhang, C. (2024). Resource depletion and conservation: Balancing demands on resources for green recovery and sustainability. *Resources Policy, 89*, 104544. DOI: 10.1016/j.resourpol.2023.104544

Chiu, I. H. Y., & Greene, E. F. (2019). The Marriage of Technology, Markets and Sustainable (and) Social Finance: Insights from ICO Markets for a New Regulatory Framework. *European Business Organization Law Review, 20*(1), 139–169. DOI: 10.1007/s40804-019-00138-y

Clark, R., Reed, J., & Sunderland, T. (2018). Bridging funding gaps for climate and sustainable development: Pitfalls, progress and potential of private finance. *Land Use Policy, 71*, 335–346. DOI: 10.1016/j.landusepol.2017.12.013

Clarke, C., & Tooker, L. (2018). Social Finance Meets Financial Innovation: Contemporary Experiments in Payments, Money and Debt. *Theory, Culture & Society, 35*(3), 3–11. DOI: 10.1177/0263276417746467

Cobo, M. j., López-Herrera, A. g., Herrera-Viedma, E., & Herrera, F. (2011). Science mapping software tools: Review, analysis, and cooperative study among tools. *Journal of the American Society for Information Science and Technology, 62*(7), 1382–1402. DOI: 10.1002/asi.21525

Conning, J., & Morduch, J. (2011). Microfinance and Social Investment. *Annual Review of Financial Economics, 3*(Volume 3, 2011), 407–434. https://doi.org/DOI: 10.1146/annurev-financial-102710-144909

Crossan, M. M., & Apaydin, M. (2010). A Multi-Dimensional Framework of Organizational Innovation: A Systematic Review of the Literature. *Journal of Management Studies, 47*(6), 1154–1191. DOI: 10.1111/j.1467-6486.2009.00880.x

Cull, R., Demirguc-Kunt, A. A., & Morduch, J. (2009). Microfinance Meets the Market. *The Journal of Economic Perspectives, 23*(1), 167–192. DOI: 10.1257/jep.23.1.167

Dahdal, A., Truby, J., & Ismailov, O. (2022). The Role and Potential of Blockchain Technology in Islamic Finance. *European Business Law Review, 33*(2). https://kluwerlawonline.com/api/Product/CitationPDFURL?file=Journals\EULR\EULR2022005.pdf

Das, T. (2019). Does credit access lead to expansion of income and multidimensional poverty? A study of rural Assam. *International Journal of Social Economics*, *46*(2), 252–270. DOI: 10.1108/IJSE-12-2017-0592

Deflorian, M. (2023). Crowdsourcing infrastructures of green everyday life: How sustainable sharing, swapping and gardening initiatives in Vienna tackle the lack of transformative agency in eco-politics. *Environmental Politics*, *32*(7), 1231–1254. DOI: 10.1080/09644016.2022.2164212

Delia, E. P. (with APS Bank). (2011). *Microcredit as a tool of ethical financing for sustainable development*. APS Bank.

Dellermann, D., Lipusch, N., Ebel, P., & Leimeister, J. M. (2020). The potential of collective intelligence and crowdsourcing for opportunity creation. *International Journal of Entrepreneurial Venturing*, *12*(2), 183–207. DOI: 10.1504/IJEV.2020.105569

Dileo, P. (2011). Repositioning microfinance with impact investors: Codes of conduct and 'social first' MFIs. *Enterprise Development & Microfinance*, *22*(4), 276–290. DOI: 10.3362/1755-1986.2011.031

Dogan, E., Majeed, M. T., & Luni, T. (2022). Are clean energy and carbon emission allowances caused by bitcoin? A novel time-varying method. *Journal of Cleaner Production*, *347*, 131089. DOI: 10.1016/j.jclepro.2022.131089

Donthu, N., Kumar, S., Mukherjee, D., Pandey, N., & Lim, W. M. (2021). How to conduct a bibliometric analysis: An overview and guidelines. *Journal of Business Research*, *133*, 285–296. DOI: 10.1016/j.jbusres.2021.04.070

Emerton, L., Bishop, J., & Thomas, L. (2006). *Sustainable Financing of Protected Areas: A Global Review of Challenges and Options*. IUCN.

Ethereum.org. (2023). *Ethereum energy consumption: Sustainability benefits of proof-of-stake*. Retrieved from https://ethereum.org/en/energy-consumption/

Etzion, D., Gehman, J., Ferraro, F., & Avidan, M. (2017). Unleashing sustainability transformations through robust action. *Journal of Cleaner Production*, *140*, 167–178. DOI: 10.1016/j.jclepro.2015.06.064

European Commission. (2024). *Overview of sustainable finance*. https://finance.ec.europa.eu/sustainable-finance/overview-sustainable-finance_en

European Parliament. (2024). *Proposal for a Regulation on Markets in Crypto-assets*. Retrieved from https://www.europarl.europa.eu/legislative-train/theme-a-europe-fit-for-the-digital-age/file-crypto-assets-1

Fatima, R., Boitan, I. A., & Carè, R. (2022). How Many Shades Are There in Sustainable Finance?: A Bibliometric Review. In Gok, I. Y. (Ed.), *Handbook of Research on Global Aspects of Sustainable Finance in Times of Crises* (pp. 1–26). IGI Global., DOI: 10.4018/978-1-7998-8501-6.ch001

Fedele, A., & Miniaci, R. (2010). Do Social Enterprises Finance Their Investments Differently from For-profit Firms? The Case of Social Residential Services in Italy. *Journal of Social Entrepreneurship*, *1*(2), 174–189. DOI: 10.1080/19420676.2010.511812

Fernandez-Alles, M., & Ramos-Rodríguez, A. (2009). Intellectual structure of human resources management research: A bibliometric analysis of the journal Human Resource Management, 1985–2005. *Journal of the American Society for Information Science and Technology*, *60*(1), 161–175. DOI: 10.1002/asi.20947

Financial Stability Board [FSB]. (2012). *Global shadow banking monitoring report 2012*. Financial Stability Board. Retrieved from https://www.fsb.org/2012/11/r_121118c/

Financial Stability Board [FSB]. (2025). *Thematic Peer Review on FSB Global Regulatory Framework for Crypto Asset Activities*. Retrieved from https://www.fsb.org/2025/02/thematic-peer-review-on-fsb-global-regulatory-framework-for-crypto-asset-activities/

Flammer, C. (2020). Green bonds: Effectiveness and implications for public policy. *Environmental and Energy Policy and the Economy*, *1*(1), 95–128. DOI: 10.1086/706794

Ghosh, S., Mahapatra, M. S., Tandon, N., & Tandon, D. (2024). Achieving Sustainable Development Goal of Women Empowerment: A Study among Self-help Groups in India. *FIIB Business Review*, *13*(4), 477–491. DOI: 10.1177/23197145231169074

Global Legal Insights. (2025). *Blockchain & Cryptocurrency Laws & Regulations*. Retrieved from https://www.globallegalinsights.com/practice-areas/blockchain-cryptocurrency-laws-and-regulations/usa/

Golka, P. (2024). Epistemic gerrymandering: ESG, impact investing, and the financial governance of sustainability. *Review of International Political Economy*, *31*(6), 1894–1918. DOI: 10.1080/09692290.2024.2382241

Guan, L., Merigó, J. M., Löfstedt, R. E., & Wardman, J. K. (2024). Twenty-five years of the Journal of Risk Research: A bibliometric overview. *Journal of Risk Research*, •••, 1–44. DOI: 10.1080/13669877.2024.2377093

Gunay, S., Sraieb, M. M., Kaskaloglu, K., & Yıldız, M. E. (2023). Cryptocurrencies and global sustainability: Do blockchained sectors have distinctive effects? *Journal of Cleaner Production*, *425*, 138943. DOI: 10.1016/j.jclepro.2023.138943

Habibi, M. R., Davidson, A., & Laroche, M. (2017). What managers should know about the sharing economy. *Business Horizons*, *60*(1), 113–121. DOI: 10.1016/j.bushor.2016.09.007

Hafner, S., Jones, A., Anger-Kraavi, A., & Pohl, J. (2020). Closing the green finance gap – A systems perspective. *Environmental Innovation and Societal Transitions*, *34*, 26–60. DOI: 10.1016/j.eist.2019.11.007

Hartl, B., Sabitzer, T., Hofmann, E., & Penz, E. (2018). *"Sustainability is a nice bonus"* the role of sustainability in carsharing from a consumer perspective. *Journal of Cleaner Production*, *202*, 88–100. DOI: 10.1016/j.jclepro.2018.08.138

Hassan, M. K., Alshater, M. M., Hasan, R., & Bhuiyan, A. B. (2021). Islamic microfinance: A bibliometric review. *Global Finance Journal*, *49*, 100651. DOI: 10.1016/j.gfj.2021.100651

Hassan, M. K., Sanchez, B., & Yu, J.-S. (2011). Financial development and economic growth: New evidence from panel data. *The Quarterly Review of Economics and Finance*, *51*(1), 88–104. DOI: 10.1016/j.qref.2010.09.001

Hörisch, J. (2015). Crowdfunding for environmental ventures: An empirical analysis of the influence of environmental orientation on the success of crowdfunding initiatives. *Journal of Cleaner Production*, *107*, 636–645. DOI: 10.1016/j.jclepro.2015.05.046

Hörisch, J. (2018). "Think big" or "small is beautiful"? An empirical analysis of characteristics and determinants of success of sustainable crowdfunding projects. *International Journal of Entrepreneurial Venturing*, *10*(1), 111–129. DOI: 10.1504/IJEV.2018.090982

Hosseini, M., Shahri, A., Phalp, K., Taylor, J., & Ali, R. (2015). Crowdsourcing: A taxonomy and systematic mapping study. *Computer Science Review*, *17*, 43–69. DOI: 10.1016/j.cosrev.2015.05.001

Howe, J. (2006). The rise of crowdsourcing. *Wired Magazine*, *14*(6), 176–183.

Hudon, M. (2009). Should Access to Credit be a Right? *Journal of Business Ethics*, *84*(1), 17–28. DOI: 10.1007/s10551-008-9670-y

Huertas-Valdivia, I., Ferrari, A. M., Settembre-Blundo, D., & García-Muiña, F. E. (2020). Social Life-Cycle Assessment: A Review by Bibliometric Analysis. *Sustainability*, *12*(15), 15. Advance online publication. DOI: 10.3390/su12156211

Huggett, S., James, C., & Palmaro, E. (2018). Field-Weighting Readership: How Does It Compare to Field-Weighting Citations? In Erdt, M., Sesagiri Raamkumar, A., Rasmussen, E., & Theng, Y.-L. (Eds.), *Altmetrics for Research Outputs Measurement and Scholarly Information Management* (pp. 96–104). Springer., DOI: 10.1007/978-981-13-1053-9_8

Hummels, H., & de Leede, M. (2014). The emergence of impact investments: The case of microfinance. In *Socially Responsible Investment in the 21st Century: Does it Make a Difference for Society?* (world; Vol. 7, pp. 91–115). Emerald Group Publishing Limited. https://doi.org/DOI: 10.1108/S2043-905920140000007004

Husain, A., Yii, K.-J., & Lee, C.-C. (2023). Are green cryptocurrencies really green? New evidence from wavelet analysis. *Journal of Cleaner Production*, *417*, 137985. DOI: 10.1016/j.jclepro.2023.137985

Huynh, T. L. D. (2022). When 'green' challenges 'prime': Empirical evidence from government bond markets. *Journal of Sustainable Finance & Investment*, *12*(2), 375–388. DOI: 10.1080/20430795.2020.1769984

Imai, K. S., Gaiha, R., Thapa, G., & Annim, S. K. (2012). Microfinance and Poverty—A Macro Perspective. *World Development*, *40*(8), 1675–1689. DOI: 10.1016/j.worlddev.2012.04.013

International Finance Corporation [IFC]. (2023). *Green and Social Bond Impact Report*. Retrieved from https://www.ifc.org/en/insights-reports/2024/green-social-bond-impact-report-fy23

Jochnick, C. (2012). *Systems, power, and agency in market-based approaches to poverty. Oxfam America Research Backgrounder Series*. Oxfam America., https://beamexchange.org/uploads/filer_public/2f/64/2f64190f-1213-486b-bf25-ac90553195be/systems_poweragency.pdf

Kamal, J. B., & Hassan, M. K. (2022). Asymmetric connectedness between cryptocurrency environment attention index and green assets. *Journal of Economic Asymmetries*, *25*, e00240. DOI: 10.1016/j.jeca.2022.e00240

Khan, A., Goodell, J. W., Hassan, M. K., & Paltrinieri, A. (2022). A bibliometric review of finance bibliometric papers. *Finance Research Letters*, *47*, 102520. DOI: 10.1016/j.frl.2021.102520

Khavul, S. (2010). Microfinance: Creating Opportunities for the Poor? *The Academy of Management Perspectives*, *24*(3), 58–72.

Kleynjans, L., & Hudon, M. (2016). A Study of Codes of Ethics for Mexican Microfinance Institutions. *Journal of Business Ethics, 134*(3), 397–412. DOI: 10.1007/s10551-014-2434-y

Konhäusner, P. (2021). Crowdsourcing in Sustainable Retail—A Theoretical Framework of Success Criteria. *Journal of Risk and Financial Management, 14*(2), 2. Advance online publication. DOI: 10.3390/jrfm14020087

Krause, M., & Tolaymat, T. (2018). Quantification of energy and carbon costs for mining cryptocurrencies. *Nature Sustainability, 1*(11), 711–718. DOI: 10.1038/s41893-018-0152-7

Kwong, R., Kwok, M. L. J., & Wong, H. S. M. (2023). Green FinTech Innovation as a Future Research Direction: A Bibliometric Analysis on Green Finance and FinTech. *Sustainability, 15*(20), 20. Advance online publication. DOI: 10.3390/su152014683

Lagoarde-Segot, T. (2019). Sustainable finance. A critical realist perspective. *Research in International Business and Finance, 47*, 1–9.

Lam, P. T. I., & Law, A. O. K. (2016). Crowdfunding for renewable and sustainable energy projects: An exploratory case study approach. *Renewable & Sustainable Energy Reviews, 60*, 11–20. DOI: 10.1016/j.rser.2016.01.046

Lauesen, L. M. (2016). The landscape and scale of social and sustainable finance. In Lehner, O. M. (Ed.), *Routledge Handbook of Social and Sustainable Finance* (pp. 5–16). Routledge., DOI: 10.4324/9781315772578

Le, T.-L., Abakah, E. J. A., & Tiwari, A. K. (2021). Time and frequency domain connectedness and spill-over among fintech, green bonds and cryptocurrencies in the age of the fourth industrial revolution. *Technological Forecasting and Social Change, 162*, 120382. DOI: 10.1016/j.techfore.2020.120382 PMID: 33100414

Léautier, F. A. (2018). Can using geographical factors leverage private equity to deliver sustainable development results? In *Africa in the Post-2015 Development Agenda*. Routledge.

Lee, J. (2021). *Investor Protection on Crowdfunding Platforms*. In *The EU Crowdfunding Regulation*. Oxford University Press. Available at *SSRN*: https://ssrn.com/abstract=3968572

Lehner, O. M. (2013). Crowdfunding social ventures: A model and research agenda. *Venture Capital, 15*(4), 289–311. DOI: 10.1080/13691066.2013.782624

Lehner, O. M., & Nicholls, A. (2014). Social finance and crowdfunding for social enterprises: A public–private case study providing legitimacy and leverage. *Venture Capital, 16*(3), 271–286. DOI: 10.1080/13691066.2014.925305

Lehner, O. M., & Nicholls, A. (2016). Social finance and crowdfunding for social enterprises: A public–private case study providing legitimacy and leverage. In *Crowdfunding and Entrepreneurial Finance*. Routledge.

Liu, M. (2022). The driving forces of green bond market volatility and the response of the market to the COVID-19 pandemic. *Economic Analysis and Policy, 75*, 288–309. DOI: 10.1016/j.eap.2022.05.012

Liu, Z.-J., Panfilova, E., Mikhaylov, A., & Kurilova, A. (2021). Assessing Stability in the Relationship Between Parties in Crowdfunding and Crowdsourcing Projects During the COVID-19 Crisis. [JGIM]. *Journal of Global Information Management, 30*(4), 1–18. DOI: 10.4018/JGIM.297905

Lobão, J. (2022). Herding Behavior in the Market for Green Cryptocurrencies: Evidence from CSSD and CSAD Approaches. *Sustainability, 14*(19), 19. Advance online publication. DOI: 10.3390/su141912542

Lopatta, K., & Tchikov, M. (2016). Do microfinance institutions fulfil their promise? Evidence from cross-country data. *Applied Economics, 48*(18), 1655–1677. DOI: 10.1080/00036846.2015.1105924

Lopatta, K., & Tchikov, M. (2017). The Causal Relationship of Microfinance and Economic Development: Evidence from Transnational Data. *International Journal of Financial Research, 8*(3), 3. Advance online publication. DOI: 10.5430/ijfr.v8n3p162

Lopatta, K., Tchikov, M., Jaeschke, R., & Lodhia, S. (2017). Sustainable Development and Microfinance: The Effect of Outreach and Profitability on Microfinance Institutions' Development Mission. *Sustainable Development, 25*(5), 386–399. DOI: 10.1002/sd.1663

Martino, P., Bell, G., Rasheed, A. A., & Bellavitis, C. (2022). Entrepreneurial Finance and Governance. In *Oxford Research Encyclopedia of Business and Management*. https://doi.org/DOI: 10.1093/acrefore/9780190224851.013.384

Mazumder, M. S. U. (2015). Role of Microfinance in Sustainable Development in Rural Bangladesh. *Sustainable Development, 23*(6), 396–413. DOI: 10.1002/sd.1599

Mc Laren, E. M., & Baldegger, R. (2021). Crowd funders' motivations to support impact-oriented projects. *Journal of the International Council for Small Business, 2*(4), 334–339. DOI: 10.1080/26437015.2021.1938749

Messeni Petruzzelli, A., Natalicchio, A., Panniello, U., & Roma, P. (2019). Understanding the crowdfunding phenomenon and its implications for sustainability. *Technological Forecasting and Social Change, 141*, 138–148. DOI: 10.1016/j.techfore.2018.10.002

Meyer, J., & Krauss, A. (2021). The social performance of microfinance investment vehicles. *Journal of Sustainable Finance & Investment, 11*(2), 163–186. DOI: 10.1080/20430795.2020.1715094

Mia, M. A., Zhang, M., Zhang, C., & Kim, Y. (2019). Are microfinance institutions in South-East Asia pursuing objectives of greening the environment? In *Climate Change Mitigation and Sustainable Development*. Routledge.

Mintz-Woo, K., Dennig, F., Liu, H., & Schinko, T. (2021). Carbon pricing and COVID-19. *Climate Policy, 21*(10), 1272–1280. DOI: 10.1080/14693062.2020.1831432

Mollick, E. (2014). The dynamics of crowdfunding: An exploratory study. *Journal of Business Venturing, 29*(1), 1–16. DOI: 10.1016/j.jbusvent.2013.06.005

Montalván-Burbano, N., Velastegui-Montoya, A., Gurumendi-Noriega, M., Morante-Carballo, F., & Adami, M. (2021). Worldwide Research on Land Use and Land Cover in the Amazon Region. *Sustainability, 13*(11), 11. Advance online publication. DOI: 10.3390/su13116039

Montgomery, H., & Weiss, J. (2011). Can Commercially-oriented Microfinance Help Meet the Millennium Development Goals? Evidence from Pakistan. *World Development, 39*(1), 87–109. DOI: 10.1016/j.worlddev.2010.09.001

Morduch, J. (1999). The Microfinance Promise. *Journal of Economic Literature, 37*(4), 1569–1614. DOI: 10.1257/jel.37.4.1569

Morschheuser, B., Hamari, J., & Maedche, A. (2019). Cooperation or competition – When do people contribute more? A field experiment on gamification of crowdsourcing. *International Journal of Human-Computer Studies, 127*, 7–24. DOI: 10.1016/j.ijhcs.2018.10.001

Motylska-Kuzma, A. (2018). Crowdfunding and Sustainable Development. *Sustainability, 10*(12), 12. Advance online publication. DOI: 10.3390/su10124650

Naeem, M. A., & Karim, S. (2021). Tail dependence between bitcoin and green financial assets. *Economics Letters, 208*, 110068. DOI: 10.1016/j.econlet.2021.110068

Nakamoto, S. (2008). Bitcoin: A peer-to-peer electronic cash system. *Satoshi Nakamoto*. https://static.upbitcare.com/931b8bfc-f0e0-4588-be6e-b98a27991df1.pdf

NFGS. (2019). *A call for action: Climate change as a source of financial risk.* https://www.tcfdhub.org/resource/a-call-for-action-climate-change-as-a-source-of-financial-risk/

Niaz, M. U. (2022). Socio-Economic development and sustainable development goals: A roadmap from vulnerability to sustainability through financial inclusion. *Economic Research-Ekonomska Istraživanja, 35*(1), 3243–3275. DOI: 10.1080/1331677X.2021.1989319

Nicholls, A., Paton, R., & Emerson, J. (2015). *Social finance.* Oxford University Press.

Noreen, U., Imran, R., Zaheer, A., & Saif, M. I. (2011). Impact of microfinance on poverty: A case of Pakistan. *World Applied Sciences Journal, 12*(6), 877–883.

Norris, M., & Oppenheim, C. (2007). Comparing alternatives to the Web of Science for coverage of the social sciences' literature. *Journal of Informetrics, 1*(2), 161–169. DOI: 10.1016/j.joi.2006.12.001

O'Donohoe, N., Leijonhufvud, C., Saltuk, Y., Bugg-Levine, A., & Brandenburg, M. (2010). Impact investments. *An Emerging Asset Class, 96*, 1–96.

O'Flynn, L., Schweinsberg, S., & Wearing, S. (2022). Financing Protected Areas: The Social and Environmental Impact Bond's Role in Terrestrial Protected Area Sustainability. *Journal of Park and Recreation Administration, 40*(3), 123–139. DOI: 10.18666/JPRA-2021-10870

OECD. (2017). *Mobilising financing for the transition.* OECD., DOI: 10.1787/9789264273528-9-

Ortas, E., Burritt, R. L., & Moneva, J. M. (2013). Socially Responsible Investment and cleaner production in the Asia Pacific: Does it pay to be good? *Journal of Cleaner Production, 52*, 272–280. DOI: 10.1016/j.jclepro.2013.02.024

Paltrinieri, A., Hassan, M. K., Bahoo, S., & Khan, A. (2023). A bibliometric review of sukuk literature. *International Review of Economics & Finance, 86*, 897–918. DOI: 10.1016/j.iref.2019.04.004

Park, K., & Jun, H. (2024). Win-win or tradeoff? Investigating the hybridity of impact investing in Cambodia's microfinance industry. *Journal of International Development, n/a*(n/a). https://doi.org/DOI: 10.1002/jid.3954

Passador, M. L. (2023). *Crowdfunding Regulation.* In *The Palgrave Encyclopedia of Private Equity* (edited by D. Cumming & B. Hammer, forthcoming 2024). Palgrave Macmillan. Available at *SSRN*: https://ssrn.com/abstract=4603816

Pham, L., Huynh, T. L. D., & Hanif, W. (2023). Time-varying asymmetric spillovers among cryptocurrency, green and fossil-fuel investments. *Global Finance Journal, 58*, 100891. DOI: 10.1016/j.gfj.2023.100891

Podsakoff, P. M., MacKenzie, S. B., Bachrach, D. G., & Podsakoff, N. P. (2005). The influence of management journals in the 1980s and 1990s. *Strategic Management Journal, 26*(5), 473–488. DOI: 10.1002/smj.454

Pretty, J. N., Williams, S., & Toulmin, C. (2011). Sustainable intensification: Increasing productivity in African food and agricultural systems. *International Journal of Agricultural Sustainability, 9*(1), 3–289. DOI: 10.3763/ijas.2011.91ED

Prior, F., & Argandoña, A. (2009). Credit accessibility and corporate social responsibility in financial institutions: The case of microfinance. *Business Ethics (Oxford, England), 18*(4), 349–363. DOI: 10.1111/j.1467-8608.2009.01568.x

PwC. (2023). *Global Crypto Regulation Report*. Retrieved from https://www.pwc.com/gx/en/new-ventures/cryptocurrency-assets/pwc-global-crypto-regulation-report-2023.pdf

Raineri, E. M., & Reno, L. S. E. (2022). A Study of Crowdsourcing in Undergraduate Entrepreneurship Education. *Journal of Higher Education Theory and Practice, 22*(5), 5. https://articlearchives.co/index.php/JHETP/article/view/3398

Ramos-Rodríguez, A.-R., & Ruíz-Navarro, J. (2004). Changes in the intellectual structure of strategic management research: A bibliometric study of the Strategic Management Journal, 1980–2000. *Strategic Management Journal, 25*(10), 981–1004. DOI: 10.1002/smj.397

Richter, C. (2015). Crowdcreation as a dimension of crowdsourcing: Conditions for entrepreneurs. *International Journal of Entrepreneurial Venturing, 7*(4), 324–340. DOI: 10.1504/IJEV.2015.073645

Rizzello, A., & Kabli, A. (2020). Social Finance and Sustainable Development Goals: A Literature Synthesis, Current Approaches and Research Agenda. *ACRN Journal of Finance and Risk Perspectives, 9*.

Robert, F. C., Frey, L. M., & Sisodia, G. S. (2021). Village development framework through self-help-group entrepreneurship, microcredit, and anchor customers in solar microgrids for cooperative sustainable rural societies. *Journal of Rural Studies, 88*, 432–440. DOI: 10.1016/j.jrurstud.2021.07.013

Rotolo, D., Rafols, I., Hopkins, M. M., & Leydesdorff, L. (2017). Strategic intelligence on emerging technologies: Scientometric overlay mapping. *Journal of the Association for Information Science and Technology, 68*(1), 214–233. DOI: 10.1002/asi.23631

Saha, S., Kermode, M., & Annear, P. L. (2015). Effect of combining a health program with a microfinance-based self-help group on health behaviors and outcomes. *Public Health, 129*(11), 1510–1518. DOI: 10.1016/j.puhe.2015.07.010 PMID: 26304181

Sas, A., Lw, M., & Sm, M. (2019). Comparing Bibliometric Analysis Using PubMed, Scopus, and Web of Science Databases. *Journal of Visualized Experiments, 152*. Advance online publication. DOI: 10.3791/58494

Schaltegger, S. (2002). A Framework for Ecopreneurship: Leading Bioneers and Environmental Managers to Ecopreneurship. *Greener Management International, 38*, 45–58.

Schaltegger, S., & Wagner, M. (2011). Sustainable entrepreneurship and sustainability innovation: Categories and interactions. *Business Strategy and the Environment, 20*(4), 222–237. DOI: 10.1002/bse.682

Schaper, M. (2010). Understanding the Green Entrepreneur. In *Making Ecopreneurs* (2nd ed.). Routledge.

Schoenmaker, D., & Schramade, W. (2019). Investing for long-term value creation. *Journal of Sustainable Finance & Investment, 9*(4), 356–377. DOI: 10.1080/20430795.2019.1625012

Schreiner, M. (2002). Aspects of outreach: A framework for discussion of the social benefits of microfinance. *Journal of International Development, 14*(5), 591–603. DOI: 10.1002/jid.908

Scott, B. (2016). *How can cryptocurrency and blockchain technology play a role in building social and solidarity finance?* (Working Paper 2016–1). UNRISD Working Paper. https://www.econstor.eu/handle/10419/148750

Shashi, Centobelli, P., Cerchione, R., & Mittal, A. (2021). Managing sustainability in luxury industry to pursue circular economy strategies. *Business Strategy and the Environment, 30*(1), 432–462. DOI: 10.1002/bse.2630

Singh, V. K., Singh, P., Karmakar, M., Leta, J., & Mayr, P. (2021). The journal coverage of Web of Science, Scopus and Dimensions: A comparative analysis. *Scientometrics, 126*(6), 5113–5142. DOI: 10.1007/s11192-021-03948-5

Solesbury, W. (2003). *Sustainable livelihoods: A case study of the evolution of DFID policy*. Overseas Development Institute London. https://cdn.odi.org/media/documents/172.pdf

Stolz, D., & Lai, K. P. Y. (2020). Impact Investing, Social Enterprise and Global Development. In *The Routledge International Handbook of Financialization*. Routledge.

Swamy, V., & Tulasimala, B. K. (2011). Financial Intermediaries and Economic Development: Evidence on Transaction Costs of Borrowing by the Poor. *International Journal of Banking and Finance*, *8*(3), 3.

Tangcharoensathien, V., Calleja, N., Nguyen, T., Purnat, T., D'Agostino, M., Garcia-Saiso, S., Landry, M., Rashidian, A., & Hamilton, C., AbdAllah, A., Ghiga, I., Hill, A., Hougendobler, D., Andel, J. van, Nunn, M., Brooks, I., Sacco, P. L., Domenico, M. D., Mai, P., … Briand, S. (2020). Framework for Managing the COVID-19 Infodemic: Methods and Results of an Online, Crowdsourced WHO Technical Consultation. *Journal of Medical Internet Research*, *22*(6), e19659. DOI: 10.2196/19659 PMID: 32558655

TCFD. (2023). *2023 TCFD Status Report: Task Force on Climate-related Financial Disclosures*. https://www.fsb.org/uploads/P121023-2.pdf

Tennekes, M. (2018). tmap: Thematic Maps in R. *Journal of Statistical Software*, *84*, 1–39. DOI: 10.18637/jss.v084.i06

Testa, S., Roma, P., Vasi, M., & Cincotti, S. (2020). Crowdfunding as a tool to support sustainability-oriented initiatives: Preliminary insights into the role of product/service attributes. *Business Strategy and the Environment*, *29*(2), 530–546. DOI: 10.1002/bse.2385

Tian, X., Geng, Y., Sarkis, J., & Zhong, S. (2018). Trends and features of embodied flows associated with international trade based on bibliometric analysis. *Resources, Conservation and Recycling*, *131*, 148–157. DOI: 10.1016/j.resconrec.2018.01.002

Tomlinson, B., Boberg, J., Cranefield, J., Johnstone, D., Luczak-Roesch, M., Patterson, D. J., & Kapoor, S. (2021). Analyzing the sustainability of 28 'Blockchain for Good' projects via affordances and constraints. *Information Technology for Development*, *27*(3), 439–469. DOI: 10.1080/02681102.2020.1828792

United Nations. (2024). *The Sustainable Development Goals Report 2024*. United Nations. Retrieved from https://unstats.un.org/sdgs/report/2024/The-Sustainable-Development-Goals-Report-2024.pdf

van Eck, N., & Waltman, L. (2010). Software survey: VOSviewer, a computer program for bibliometric mapping. *Scientometrics*, *84*(2), 523–538. DOI: 10.1007/s11192-009-0146-3 PMID: 20585380

van Eck, N. J., & Waltman, L. (2014). Visualizing Bibliometric Networks. In Ding, Y., Rousseau, R., & Wolfram, D. (Eds.), *Measuring Scholarly Impact: Methods and Practice* (pp. 285–320). Springer International Publishing., DOI: 10.1007/978-3-319-10377-8_13

Van Eck, N. J., & Waltman, L. (2023). VOSviewer manual. *Leiden. Univeristeit Leiden, 1*(1), 1–54.

Vanroose, A., & D'Espallier, B. (2013). Do microfinance institutions accomplish their mission? Evidence from the relationship between traditional financial sector development and microfinance institutions' outreach and performance. *Applied Economics, 45*(15), 1965–1982. DOI: 10.1080/00036846.2011.641932

Vasileiadou, E., Huijben, J. C. C. M., & Raven, R. P. J. M. (2016). Three is a crowd? Exploring the potential of crowdfunding for renewable energy in the Netherlands. *Journal of Cleaner Production, 128*, 142–155. DOI: 10.1016/j.jclepro.2015.06.028

Vaz, J., & Brown, K. (2020). Sustainable development and cryptocurrencies as private money. *Economia e Politica Industriale, 47*(1), 163–184. DOI: 10.1007/s40812-019-00139-5

Vermicelli, S., Cricelli, L., & Grimaldi, M. (2021). How can crowdsourcing help tackle the COVID-19 pandemic? An explorative overview of innovative collaborative practices. *R & D Management, 51*(2), 183–194. DOI: 10.1111/radm.12443

Vermicelli, S., Cricelli, L., Grimaldi, M., Mignacca, B., & Strazzullo, S. (2022). Crowdsourcing initiatives during the COVID-19 pandemic: Empirical evidence from the Italian context. *European Journal of Innovation Management, 27*(3), 1042–1055. DOI: 10.1108/EJIM-06-2022-0341

Vigna, P., & Casey, M. J. (2015). *The Age of Cryptocurrency: How Bitcoin and Digital Money Are Challenging the Global Economic Order*. St. Martin's Press, Inc.

Vismara, S. (2019). Sustainability in equity crowdfunding. *Technological Forecasting and Social Change, 141*, 98–106. DOI: 10.1016/j.techfore.2018.07.014

Vizcaíno, C. F. O., Valle, C. T., & Puig, P. G. (2024). Spillover effects of microcredit on the GDP of surrounding cantons in Ecuador. *Journal of Strategy and Management, ahead-of-print*(ahead-of-print). https://doi.org/DOI: 10.1108/JSMA-07-2023-0199

Watson, R., Nielsen, K. R., Wilson, H. N., Macdonald, E. K., Mera, C., & Reisch, L. (2023). Policy for sustainable entrepreneurship: A crowdsourced framework. *Journal of Cleaner Production, 383*, 135234. DOI: 10.1016/j.jclepro.2022.135234

Weber, O. (2019). Sustainable finance and the SDGs: The role of the banking sector. In *Achieving the Sustainable Development Goals: Global Governance Challenges* (pp. 226–239). Scopus. https://doi.org/DOI: 10.4324/9780429029622

Widiarto, I., & Emrouznejad, A. (2015). Social and financial efficiency of Islamic microfinance institutions: A Data Envelopment Analysis application. *Socio-Economic Planning Sciences*, *50*, 1–17. DOI: 10.1016/j.seps.2014.12.001

World Bank. (Director). (2020). Reversing the Inequality Pandemic: Speech by World Bank Group President David Malpass [Broadcast]. In *World Bank Live*. https://www.worldbank.org/en/news/speech/2020/10/05/reversing-the-inequality-pandemic-speech-by-world-bank-group-president-david-malpass

World Bank. (2022). *Financial Inclusion* [Text/HTML]. World Bank. https://www.worldbank.org/en/topic/financialinclusion/overview

Yi, X., Bai, C., Lyu, S., & Dai, L. (2021). The impacts of the COVID-19 pandemic on China's green bond market. *Finance Research Letters*, *42*, 101948. DOI: 10.1016/j.frl.2021.101948 PMID: 34566534

Zanotto, E. D., & Carvalho, V. (2021). Article age- and field-normalized tools to evaluate scientific impact and momentum. *Scientometrics*, *126*(4), 2865–2883. DOI: 10.1007/s11192-021-03877-3

Zauro, N. A., Saad, R. A. J., Ahmi, A., & Hussin, M. Y. M. (2020). Integration of Waqf towards enhancing financial inclusion and socio-economic justice in Nigeria. *International Journal of Ethics and Systems*, *36*(4), 491–505. DOI: 10.1108/IJOES-04-2020-0054

Zhang, D. (2023). Fiscal policy benefits and green recovery of firms: An experimental exploration of Chinese listed firms in post-Covid-19. *Economic Change and Restructuring*, *56*(5), 2921–2942. DOI: 10.1007/s10644-021-09344-6

Zhao, X. (2022). How Blockchain Can Empower the Growth in Green Finance. In Y. Jiang et al. (Eds.), Proceedings of the 2022 International Conference on E-Business and Digital Commerce (ICEDBC 2022), AEBMR 225 (pp. 412-416). Atlantis Press. https://doi.org/DOI: 10.2991/978-94-6463-036-7_60

Zupic, I., & Čater, T. (2015). Bibliometric Methods in Management and Organization. *Organizational Research Methods*, *18*(3), 429–472.

ENDNOTES

1 until September 30, 2024

2 Source: Scopus. As of September 30, 2024

Chapter 3
Mapping the Intersection of Fintech and Social and Sustainable Finance:
A Bibliometric Review

Rabia Fatima
https://orcid.org/0000-0002-3471-9756
HAN University of Applied Sciences, The Netherlands

Simone Taddeo
https://orcid.org/0000-0002-1656-1588
University of Cà Foscari Venice, Italy

ABSTRACT

The growing challenge of limited capital, resources, and technology in maintaining sustainable production has underscored the need for integrating environmental, social, and governance (ESG) principles into financial decision-making. This has driven the rise of sustainable finance, channeling investments toward projects that align with long-term societal goals. At the same time, the FinTech sector has become a key player in addressing global issues such as financial inclusion, poverty reduction, gender equity, and environmental sustainability. Despite increasing recognition of FinTech's role in promoting social and sustainable finance, research on the intersection of these domains remains in its early stages. This chapter seeks to bridge this gap by providing a comprehensive bibliometric analysis of FinTech's contribution to advancing social and sustainable finance. It will examine the evolution of this field, highlight influential contributors, and explore key research trends, offering valuable insights into emerging opportunities for further development in this critical area.

DOI: 10.4018/979-8-3693-9551-6.ch003

1. INTRODUCTION

The pressing challenge for many countries today is the lack of sufficient capital, resources, and technology to maintain sustainable production processes, therefore sustainable finance has become essential for integrating environmental, social, and governance (ESG) principles into financial decision-making (Bayram et al., 2022). This need has also spurred growth in the FinTech sector across numerous countries (Bayram et al., 2022). According to Ren et al. (2023), the concept of sustainable finance has emerged as a critical framework at the crossroads of financial development and sustainable goals, with the objective of meeting today's societal needs while safeguarding the ability of future generations to meet theirs. More precisely, sustainable finance is defined as incorporating ESG factors into investment decisions, encouraging long-term investments in sustainable economic projects (European Commission, 2024). Whereas, financial technologies (or FinTech), which refer to technological innovations in financial activities, are having a significant impact on core financial services that have traditionally been provided by banks. Many recent studies indicate that FinTech plays a pivotal role in addressing complex challenges related to financial inclusion, poverty reduction, gender equity, healthcare access, educational advancement, and environmental sustainability (e.g., see Arner et al., 2020; Moro-Visconti et al., 2020). By utilizing digital platforms, mobile technology, and innovative financial solutions, FinTech firms are enhancing access to financial resources, driving economic growth, and empowering underserved communities (Moro-Visconti et al., 2020; Siano et al., 2020; Bayar et al., 2021; Singh & Stakic, 2021).

Moreover, many research studies have increasingly focused on the interplay between ESG principles and FinTech innovations within the sustainable finance framework, particularly in green finance (e.g., see, Dadabada, 2024; Kashif et al. 2024; Trotta et al., 2024; Yang & Jung, 2024). However, research on the relationship between ESG and FinTech is still in its early stages (Trotta et al., 2024), and the literature on social and sustainable finance and FinTech remains fragmented. Therefore, this chapter aims to bridge this gap through a comprehensive bibliometric analysis of FinTech's intersection with social and sustainable finance. This chapter addresses the following research questions:

RQ1: How has research on the role of FinTech in advancing social and sustainable finance evolved over time?

RQ 2: What are the key articles, journals, and authors that have significantly contributed to the field of FinTech and social and sustainable finance?

RQ 3: What are the most prominent research streams identified in the literature concerning the intersection of FinTech and social and sustainable finance?

RQ 4: What are the main research fronts in the field of FinTech related to social and sustainable finance, and what opportunities exist for further advancement in this area?

More in detail, this chapter employ a comprehensive bibliometric analysis using the Scopus database, focusing on English-language literature within the disciplines of Economics (ECON), Business (BUSI), and Sociology (SOCI). The methodology incorporates three core techniques: performance analysis, science mapping, and content analysis. Performance analysis assesses the productivity and impact of key authors, institutions, and publications within the field (Donthu et al., 2021), while science mapping visualizes and interprets the structure of relationships among research topics, authors, and institutions, providing a structured view of major themes and scholarly networks (van Eck & Waltman, 2010, 2014). Content analysis further deepens insights by identifying specific themes, patterns, and gaps in the literature on FinTech's role in social and sustainable finance. By combining these approaches, this chapter aims to provide a detailed overview of research trends and highlight significant yet underexplored areas within the intersection of FinTech and social and sustainable finance. Ultimately, the findings enhance academic understanding and offer valuable insights for researchers, policymakers, and practitioners looking to navigate and contribute to this dynamic and evolving field.

The chapter is divided into five main sections. Section 2 provides a detailed description of the bibliometric methodology. Section 3 focuses on bibliometric analysis, addressing both performance and science mapping. Section 4 presents the main thematic clusters identified, while Section 5 discusses the results, conclusions, and limitations. Finally, Section 6 outlines open issues and future research directions.

2. METHODOLOGICAL NOTES

2.1 Applied Techniques

Bibliometric analysis has become increasingly popular in recent years due to several factors, such as the availability of software tools and the improved capacity to handle large volumes of data (Donthu et al., 2021). One of the advantages of the bibliometric approach is its objective quantitativeness, which helps eliminate sample selection bias often found in systematic reviews. Bibliometric methods are also useful for identifying trends in classic research topics, co-authorships, co-citations, and journal performance within a specific field (Baker et al., 2020). It is not surprising that bibliometric research in finance has gained significant attention (Bahoo, 2020;

Baker et al., 2020; Naeem et al., 2023; Carè et al., 2023; Carè & Cumming, 2024; Fatima & Carè, 2024b, 2024a).

To address RQ1 and RQ2, which focus on identifying publication trends, key journals, authors, and articles within FinTech and social and sustainable finance research fields, we employed a performance analysis approach. In contrast, RQ3 and RQ4 were approached using science mapping and content analysis techniques. Performance analysis focuses on identifying developmental trends as well as prolific authors and journals, whereas science mapping, as defined by Cobo et al. (2011), explores the conceptual structure of a specific research topic. Science mapping primarily aims to reveal how various academic specialties, materials, fields, and authors are interconnected and evolve (Zupic & Čater, 2015). It provides a visual representation of the relationships between different research domains. To facilitate science mapping analysis, we adopted the visualization of similarities technique, introduced by van Eck and Waltman (2010, 2014). Knowledge maps were created using the open-access bibliometric network analysis tool, VOSviewer, developed by van Eck and Waltman (2010). Additionally, a content analysis was conducted to uncover cognitive structures, often recognized as emerging research themes or categories.

2.2 Data Selection and Standardization

A multi-step approach was used to identify the initial set of keywords for the analysis. The process began by formulating a list of relevant search terms for extracting data from the Scopus database. Scopus, known for its comprehensive coverage of peer-reviewed research from reputable journals, was selected for this study (Alshater et al., 2020; Baker et al., 2020; Donthu et al., 2021). Strict selection criteria were applied to ensure that only relevant and high-quality articles were included in our bibliometric and content analysis, enhancing the reliability of our results. We included studies from all time periods, with a focus on English-language and peer-reviewed journal articles.

Using the selection criteria and search strings, we compiled a database of 107 documents, which were saved in CSV format for detailed bibliometric analysis. Any typographical errors or bibliographic inconsistencies, as noted by Ruiz-Parrado et al. (2022), were corrected. This was in line with the caution raised by Franceschini et al. (2016) about potential inaccuracies in bibliometric data, including author names, titles, journal names, publication years, and keywords. The dataset was manually verified to ensure accuracy. To address the variability in keyword usage among journals and authors, a bibliometric technique for keyword standardization was employed. A standardized set of terms is not always used (e.g., acronyms, singular/plural forms), and thus, a thesaurus (.csv) file was created following the rules outlined in Table 1 to standardize keywords before conducting the science mapping analysis. After completing the keyword standardization, the articles were exported to VOSviewer, a freely available software designed for constructing and visualizing bibliometric maps (van Eck and Waltman, 2010). Figure 1 provides an overview of the four-step methodology employed.

Table 1. Key terms Standardization rules

#	Standardization procedure
1.	Acronyms have been replaced with their full forms for better clarity and understanding (Palshikar, 2007; Choi et al., 2011; Castriotta et al., 2021). For instance, replaced "FinTech" into "financial technologies".
2.	Singular and plural key terms have been unified to maintain consistency and clarity throughout the dataset (Choi et al., 2011; Dehdarirad et al., 2014; Castriotta et al., 2021). For instance, "SDG" and "SDGs" were merged into "SDG", and "Bank" and " Banks" were merged into "Banks".
3.	Hyphens have been removed from keywords where the meaning remains unchanged to ensure consistency and simplicity (Choi et al., 2011), for instance, "corporate social-responsibility" into "corporate social responsibility, and "corporate-governance" into "corporate governance".
4.	All irrelevant keywords unrelated to the context of FinTech and sustainable finance and/or social finance have been excluded to maintain focus and relevance. (Ding et al., 2022; Dehdarirad et al., 2014; Castriotta et al., 2021). For instance, JEL classification codes, countries' names, and general meaning key terms.
5.	Synonyms and closely related terms have been combined or replaced with a more general term, ensuring consistency and clarity in the context. (Choi et al., 2011).

Source: Author's elaboration

Figure 1. Research methodology workflow

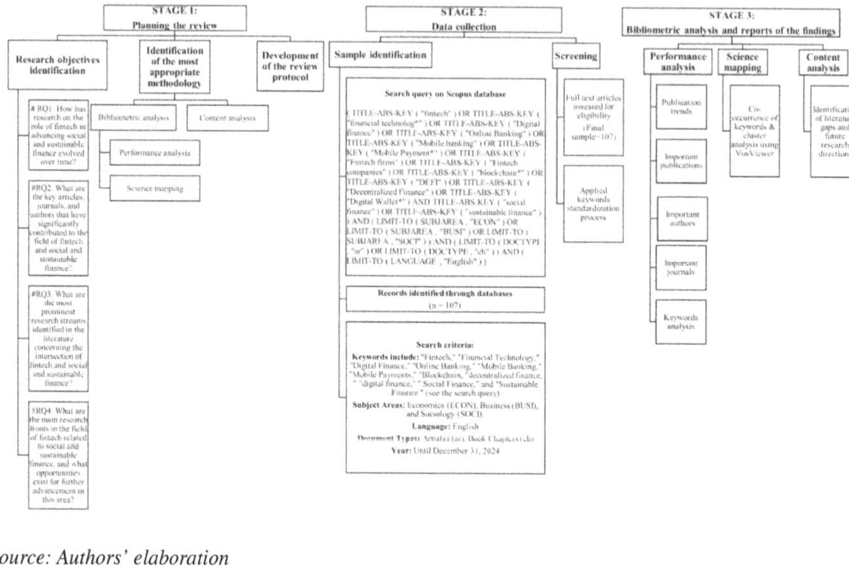

Source: Authors' elaboration

3. BIBLIOMETRIC ANALYSIS

3.1 Performance Analysis

3.1.1 Publication trends

The graph in figure 2 illustrates the publication trends in the field of FinTech and social and sustainable finance. From 2010 to 2018, there was minimal research output, with only a handful of publications and negligible citations, indicating limited academic interest in the topic during this period. However, starting in 2019, there was a noticeable increase in publications, which grew steadily through 2020. Citations also rose significantly in 2020, reaching 241, suggesting that research in this area began to gain wider recognition.

The years 2021 and 2022 marked the peak of research activity, with the number of publications increasing to 16 and 19, respectively, accompanied by the highest citation counts of 250 and 288. This indicates that these years were pivotal for the development and impact of FinTech and social and sustainable finance research. In 2023, there was a slight decline in both publications and citations, with 15 publications and 86 citations. However, 2024 saw a significant rise in the number of publications to 49, while citation counts slightly decreased to 78. Overall, the data highlights the growing academic interest and influence of research in FinTech and social and sustainable finance, particularly in recent years.

Figure 2. Total publications and total citations

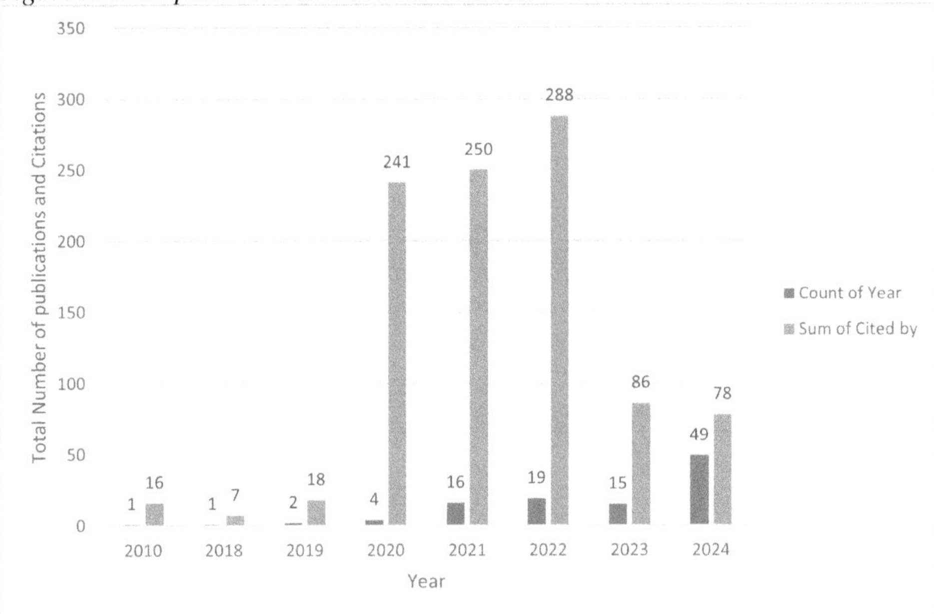

3.1.2 Important publications

Citation counts served as a measure to pinpoint key articles (Liu, 1993; Carè et al., 2024). Table 2 highlights the most important articles in the field of FinTech and social and sustainable finance, published between 2010 and 2024.

Hasan et al. (2020) discuss the role of Islamic finance and banking in the post-COVID era, receiving the highest citation count among the listed articles with 112, which underscores its significant impact. Similarly, Rabani et al. (2021) explored Islamic FinTech's role in mitigating the economic and social effects of the pandemic, received total 91 citations. Moro-Visconti et al. (2020) investigate sustainability in FinTechs, focusing on how business model scalability and market valuation contribute to sustainable outcomes. Another prominent area of focus is sustainable finance, as explored by Macchiavelli et al. (2022), who examine how FinTech can contribute to achieving environmental goals. Ren et al. (2022) explained the integration of sustainable finance and blockchain, adding a technological perspective. Mejia-

Escobar et al. (2020) examine the adoption and development of sustainable financial products in the Latin American banking industry, providing valuable insights into current practices and challenges. Ascarya (2022) explores the role of Islamic social finance during the COVID-19 pandemic in Indonesia, particularly its contribution to economic recovery. Meoli and Vismara (2021) investigate information manipulation in equity crowdfunding markets. Metawa et al. (2022) analyze the interplay between the green economy, clean technology, and FinTech. Lastly, Bayram et al. (2022) explore the potential of FinTech to promote sustainable finance, offering policy lessons from Turkey.

Thus, the articles collectively demonstrate the rising academic interest in leveraging FinTech for sustainability, with topics ranging from Islamic finance to environmental and regional concerns, reflecting the field's diversity and growing relevance. The emphasis on green finance and its presence in finance and economics journals further highlight its centrality to the discourse in sustainable finance research.

Table 2. Most important articles

Authors	Publication Year	Title	Source Title	Total citation
Hassan M.K.; Rabbani M.R.; Mohd. Ali M.A.	2020	Challenges for the Islamic finance and banking in post COVID era and the role of FinTech	Journal of Economic Cooperation and Development	112
Rabbani M.R.; Bashar A.; Nawaz N.; Karim S.; Ali M.A.M.; Rahiman H.U.; Alam M.S.	2021	Exploring the role of Islamic FinTech in combating the aftershocks of covid-19: The open social innovation of the Islamic financial system	Journal of Open Innovation: Technology, Market, and Complexity	91
Moro-Visconti R.; Rambaud S.C.; Pascual J.L.	2020	Sustainability in FinTechs: An explanation through business model scalability and market valuation	Sustainability (Switzerland)	82
Macchiavello E.; Siri M.	2022	Sustainable Finance and FinTech: Can Technology Contribute to Achieving Environmental Goals? A Preliminary Assessment of 'Green FinTech' and 'Sustainable Digital Finance'	European Company and Financial Law Review	74
Ren Y.-S.; Ma C.-Q.; Chen X.-Q.; Lei Y.-T.; Wang Y.-R.	2023	Sustainable finance and blockchain: A systematic review and research agenda	Research in International Business and Finance	46
Mejia-Escobar J.C.; González-Ruiz J.D.; Duque-Grisales E.	2020	Sustainable financial products in the Latin America banking industry: Current status and insights	Sustainability (Switzerland)	45
Ascarya A.	2022	The role of Islamic social finance during Covid-19 pandemic in Indonesia's economic recovery	International Journal of Islamic and Middle Eastern Finance and Management	44
Meoli M.; Vismara S.	2021	Information manipulation in equity crowdfunding markets	Journal of Corporate Finance	38
Metawa N.; Dogan E.; Taskin D.	2022	Analyzing the nexus of green economy, clean and financial technology	Economic Analysis and Policy	36
Bayram O.; Talay I.; Feridun M.	2022	Can FinTech Promote Sustainable Finance? Policy Lessons from the Case of Turkey	Sustainability (Switzerland)	35

Source: Authors' elaboration

3.1.3 Important Authors

The total publication count was used as a proxy to find the most contributing authors (Carè et al., 2024). In the areas of FinTech, social and sustainable finance, several authors have made key contributions. Rabbani, M.R. stands out with 3 publications and 203 citations, focusing on FinTech, Islamic banking, and social finance. Following closely is Hassan, M.K., who has 2 publications and 112 citations, with similar research interests. Other important contributors include Sergi, B.S. and Zetzsche, D.A., each with 2 publications, addressing peer-to-peer lending and sustainable finance, respectively. Sergi has 10 citations, while Zetzsche has 28. Anker-Sørensen, L. and Abdul-Majid, M. also have 2 publications each, focusing on sustainable finance and blockchain technology. Finally, Kassim, S. and Bashar, A. contribute in areas like microfinance and Islamic banking, with varying levels of impact. Table 3 scholars who have published 3 or more than 3 articles since 2010.

Table 3. Most contributing author

Authors	Total Publications (n≥2)	Research Areas	Citations*	Country	Affiliation	H-Index (h)
Rabbani, M.R.	3	FinTech, Islamic banking, social finance, Islamic economics	203	United Arab Emirates	University of Khorfakkan	25
Abdul-Majid, M.	2	Blockchain technology; FinTech; Islamic social finance	36	Malaysia	Universiti Kebangsaan Malaysia	8
Abdullah Othman, A.H.	2	FinTech; Islamic social finance	6	United Arab Emirates	Institute of Islamic Banking and Finance	9
Anker-Sørensen, L.	2	EU Green Deal; Sustainable Finance	28	Norway	Universitetet i Oslo	4
Ashurov, S.	2	FinTech; Islamic social finance	6	Malaysia	International Islamic University Malaysia	5
Bashar, A.	2	COVID-19; Islamic banking; Islamic economics; Open innovation	91	Bahrain	University of Bahrain	13

continued on following page

Table 3. Continued

Authors	Total Publications (n≥2)	Research Areas	Citations*	Country	Affiliation	H-Index (h)
Ben Jabeur, S.	2	Islamic digital currency; Blockchain; Cryptocurrency; Distributed ledger technology	0	France	ESDES Business School	23
Bulut, M.	2	Islamic finance; Islamic social finance; Waqf	12	Turkey	Sabahattin Zaim Üniversitesi	6
Ghaemi Asl, M.	2	Green investment; Islamic digital currency; Blockchain; Cryptocurrency; Inclusive banking; Sustainability	0	Iran	Kharazmi University	12
Habibullah, M.	2	Islamic social finance; Artificial intelligence; FinTech	6	Malaysia	International Islamic University Malaysia	2
Hassan, M.K.	2	FinTech, Islamic banking, social finance, Islamic economics	112	United States	University of New Orleans	53
Kassim, S.	2	FinTech; Microfinance; sustainable finance	1	Malaysia	International Islamic University Malaysia	20
Kharisma, D.B.	2	Islamic cryptocurrency; Shariah compliance	7	Indonesia	Universitas Sebelas Maret	6
Muhamad Yusof, M.S.	2	Islamic social finance; FinTech; blockchain; artificial intelligence	6	Malaysia	Techtrade Defence Sdn Bhd	2
Muneeza, A.	2	Islamic FinTech; Social finance; Blockchain technology	10	Malaysia	INCEIF University	12
Sergi, B.S.	2	Peer-to-peer lending; Sustainable finance; FinTech	10	United States	Harvard University	37

continued on following page

Table 3. Continued

Authors	Total Publications (n≥2)	Research Areas	Citations*	Country	Affiliation	H-Index (h)
Venegas, P.	2	FinTech; Green finance; sustainable finance	8	United Kingdom	King's College London	2
Zetzsche, D.A.	2	EU Green Deal; Sustainable finance	28	Luxembourg	University of Luxembourg	11

*Source: Scopus. As of December 2024
Source: Authors' elaboration

3.1.3 Important Journals

The journal Sustainability contains 7 published papers starting from 2010. Regarding the variety of journals that have published papers on FinTech, social and sustainable finance, it can be concluded that research in this area is multidisciplinary, ranging from Economics, Econometrics, and Finance to Environmental Science. However, many of the journals found are from the categories of Economics and Business Management. Table 4 ranked the most contributing journals.

Table 4. Most contributing journals

Publication Titles	No. (n≥2)	IF**	Subject areas*	H-Index
Sustainability Switzerland	7	3.3	A; B; C; D	169
Research In International Business and Finance	4	6.3	E; F	73
Contemporary Studies In Economic and Financial Analysis	2	n.a.	E; F	11
European Business Law Review	2	n.a.	D	8
Isra International Journal Of Islamic Finance	2	n.a.	D; E	19
Journal Of Financial Crime	2	n.a.	D; E	33
Journal Of Financial Economics	2	10.4	E; F	311
Managerial Finance	2	1.90	E; F	48

*Categories assigned b SCImago (Source: https://www.scimagojr.com/): "Computer Science" = **A**; "Energy" = **B**; "Environmental Science" = **C**; "Social Sciences" = **D**; "Economics, Econometrics, and Finance" = **E** ; "Business, Management, and Accounting" = **F**

**Impact factor values added from Journal official webpages.

n.a.: Not available

Source: Authors' elaboration

3.2 Science Mapping

3.2.1 Keyword Analysis

To gain a deeper understanding of the research landscape in FinTech and social and sustainable finance, this section provides a visual representation of keyword co-occurrence. Co-occurrence refers to how frequently two keywords appear together across different publications (Farrukh et al., 2020). Using co-word analysis, this study examined the relationship between keywords in articles, helping to identify the framework of knowledge in this research area. This method analyzes the frequency and connection between co-occurring terms within the content of publications. In this case, the analysis was based on the "all author keywords."

Co-word analysis specifically looks at the simultaneous appearance of two terms within a text to reveal the conceptual structure of a field of study (Bautista-Bernal et al., 2021). In addition, clustering analysis was performed using the co-occurrence of keywords to identify research trends, with VOSviewer being used to create a network map. At the threshold level of three and the minimum cluster size of four, three distinct clusters were identified, each marked by key terms, as shown in Section 3.2.2. These clusters vary not only in the number of keywords but also in the research topics they cover. The VOSviewer software displays these clusters in different colors, where each cluster represents a group of closely related keywords, with lines indicating their connections (van Eck et al., 2006; van Eck & Waltman, 2010) (see Figure 3). The size of each circle corresponds to the significance of the keywords, and a smaller distance between items signifies a stronger relationship (van Eck & Waltman, 2014).

Figure 3. Network visualization map

This analysis identified 26 keywords divided into three distinct research clusters, detailed in Figure 3 and Table 5.

Table 5. Keyword Analysis and clusters' composition

Cluster Colour	Keywords
Red	Banks (6), decentralized finance (9), ESG (7), financial market (4), financial system (5), green digital finance (3), green economy (4), green finance (7), SDGs (12), sustainable development (19), sustainable finance (31).
Green	COVID-19 (9), digital finance (3), financial inclusion (5), financial technologies (31), Islamic finance (3), Islamic social finance (8), poverty (3), shariah compliance (3), social finance (10), waqf (4), zakah (3).
Blue	blockchain (16), cryptocurrencies (5), developing countries (3), investment (3),

Source: Authors' elaboration

In the overlay visualization map, the color of the nodes (keywords) represents a specific characteristic of the node (van Eck & Waltman, 2014). This map highlights emerging research directions for researchers, decision-makers and analysts. Specifically, the color of the nodes in the overlay visualization map (see Figure 4) corresponds to the publication year of the research articles from which the authors' keywords are derived. For example, the yellow-colored nodes represent recently emerging key themes or research areas, such as sustainable finance, ESG, green finance, decentralized finance, green economy, cryptocurrencies, and the financial system.

Figure 4. Overlay visualization map

3.2.2 Cluster Analysis

To identify the key research areas within the FinTech, social finance, and sustainable finance literature, the keyword analysis was followed by a comprehensive content analysis of 107 papers, categorized into three clusters. A detailed examination of the papers within each cluster revealed recurring themes. The following subsections provide a thorough overview of the primary research domains within these clusters, shedding light on the critical areas of focus in these evolving fields.

3.2.2.1 Cluster 1 (Red): Sustainable Finance and Its Role in Driving Global Sustainability Objectives

The red cluster centers around themes of sustainable finance (31), emphasizing its pivotal role in driving global sustainability objectives. Key areas of focus include sustainable development (19), SDGs (sustainable development goals) (12), and ESG (environmental, social, and governance) frameworks (7), which integrate environmental and social considerations into financial decision-making. The cluster also highlights innovative approaches such as decentralized finance (9) and green digital finance (3), showcasing the intersection of technological advancements and sustainable practices. Additional themes include green finance (7) and the green economy (4), which promote environmentally conscious financial strategies, and the role of financial institutions, markets, and systems in fostering sustainability. Together, these interconnected themes underline the importance of sustainable finance in addressing global challenges and advancing environmental and social priorities.

The World Bank and International Monetary Fund (IMF) reported that the achievement of the SDGs needs an escalation of development finance (Ziolo et al., 2021; Arora & Sarker, 2023). Sustainable finance is an emerging concept and new paradigm of finance. Sustainable finance has developed as a key concept bridging finance and the objectives of sustainable development (Ren et al., 2023), which ultimately helps in achieving the SDGs (Ziolo et al., 2021). More precisely, sustainable finance encompasses a broad range of practices aimed at aligning financial and investment decisions with environmental, social, and economic priorities (Kumar et al., 2022). This approach recognizes the interdependence of capital allocation, investments, and broader societal and environmental considerations (Ren et al., 2023). According to the European Commission (2025), sustainable finance involves integrating ESG criteria into financial and investment decision-making processes in this financial sector (Clarke & Boersma, 2016). In this, environmental factors may involve actions to mitigate and adapt to climate change, along with broader environmental concerns such as protecting biodiversity, preventing pollution, and supporting the circular economy. Social factors could address issues such as inclusiveness, inequality, labor relations, investing in people and their skills, community development, and human rights. The governance of both public and private institutions—including executive compensation, employee relations, and management structures—plays a key role in ensuring that social and environmental factors are incorporated into decision-making (European Commission, 2025). Even though, in the current financial market, banks can gain valuable expertise by developing sustainable financial products (SFP), which not only benefits their corporate image and reputation (Dell'Atti et al., 2017; Ibe-enwo et al., 2019) but also leads to improved customer loyalty (Ferreira et al., 2015; Igbudu et al., 2018; Mejia-Escobar et al., 2020). According to Singhania et al., (2024), Sustainable finance instruments can be classified into ESG categories. Social instruments include Social Impact Bonds (SIBs), microfinance, and social bonds. Environmental instruments encompass Green bonds, green credit, emission trading, green banks, sustainable banks, sustainability-linked bonds, green loans, green sukuk, climate bonds, blue bonds, and transition bonds. Instruments covering ESG dimensions include sustainability-linked bonds, SDG bonds, and ESG bonds (for details, see Kish & Leroy, 2015; Fatima et al., 2022; Carè et al., 2023). However, various studies suggest that FinTech has the potential to play a significant role in advancing sustainable finance. For example, a 2017 report by the United Nations

Environment Programme (UNEP) on sustainable financial systems highlighted FinTech's ability to improve access to sustainable finance and support the achievement of SDGs encompassing economic, social, and environmental dimensions (Kashif et al., 2024). Similarly, a 2019 report from the World Economic Forum emphasized that FinTech can increase transparency in sustainable finance by facilitating improved access to data and insights on sustainable investments (Rupeika-Apoga & Thalassinos 2020). Additionally, Ding et al. (2022) conducted a survey across FinTech companies in 49 countries, revealing that 27% of the respondents were actively engaged in providing sustainable finance products and services.

To achieve the 2030 agenda for sustainable development, within the sustainable finance paradigm, the concept of green finance has emerged to address these essential environmental issues. Moreover, in the financial system, technology has emerged as a driving force, stimulating global economic growth through eco-friendly financial products (Metawa et al., 2022). In regards, the green digital finance uses advanced cutting-edge digital technologies to support the recovery of green economy. As the green economy is considered to have a strong correlation with the progress toward achieving the SDGs (Metawa et al., 2022). As noted by Metawa et al. (2022), FinTech (also known as Digital financial technologies or financial technologies) plays an important role in promoting the green economy by lowering financing costs for companies and supporting investments in environmentally driven innovations, thereby helping to bridge the financing gap for the development of green sustainable technologies. However, Morgan (2022) highlights that while digital financial technologies, especially the new generation of FinTech, can foster green finance, but it may also bring about new risks and unintended consequences for both the environment and users, which could restrict the potential for scaling sustainable finance.

While research on FinTech is still in a nascent stage, decentralized finance (DeFi) raises the associated opportunities and challenges to a new level. DeFI is defined as a "financial ecosystem built on technology that does not require a central organization to operate and that has no safety net" (Auer et al., 2024; Wójcik & Bratton, 2024, p. 16). It consists of protocols—known as "smart contracts"—that run on a network of computers to automatically handle financial transactions. As it is built on top of distributed ledger technology (DLT), it eliminates the need for banks or other traditional centralized financial intermediaries (Popescu, 2020; Auer et al., 2024). Several studies within this cluster indicate widespread interest in DeFi, not only due to its potential to eliminate traditional financial intermediaries, but also because it improves access to financial services, enhances financial inclusion, accelerates transaction speeds, increases flexibility in smart contracts, improves transparency and privacy, strengthens security, fosters trust, and enhances efficiency by reducing overhead costs for banks (e.g., see Popescu, 2020; Chohan, 2021; Katona, 2021; Ozcan, 2021; Ozili, 2022; Schär, 2021; Auer et al., 2024)

3.2.2.2 Cluster 2 (Green): The Intersection of FinTech, Social Finance, and COVID-19

The cluster centers around themes of FinTech (31), highlighting their transformative impact on global financial systems and inclusion. Central to this cluster is the role of digital finance (3) in enabling broader access to financial services, especially in the context of promoting financial inclusion (5) for underserved populations. The intersection of Islamic finance (3) and Islamic social finance (8) introduces unique mechanisms like zakah (3) and waqf (4), which adhere to shariah compliance (3) and contribute to poverty alleviation (3) through socially responsible financial practices. Additionally, the implications of COVID-19 (9) are examined, emphasizing the pandemic's influence on accelerating digital financial adoption and reshaping social finance (10) priorities. Together, these interconnected themes underscore the critical role of financial innovation and inclusivity in addressing societal challenges and advancing equitable economic development.

FinTech and digital finance are revolutionizing the financial sector by introducing innovative technologies, software, business models, and practices that extend beyond traditional financial services, offering innovative and alternative financial solutions (Suryono et al., 2020; Firmansyah et al., 2023; Trotta et al., 2024). FinTech is a novel financial industry that applies technology to provide better financial activities (Suryono et al., 2020). Very limited studies in the finance literature examine the interplay between digital and social finance(see Ozili, 2021). According to Rizzi et al. (2018), social finance is defined as "the set of alternative lending and investment approaches for financing projects and ventures, requiring to generate both positive impacts on society, the environment, or sustainable development, along with financial returns" (p. 805). In simple words, social finance can be viewed as an approach to manage money, that combines economic/financial profits with social dividends (Ozili, 2021). In recent years, 'traditional finance' has been overtaken by 'digital finance', as it acts as an enabler of social finance and green finance (Ozili, 2021). Digital finance thrives through financial innovations such as the use of artificial intelligence in finance, the Internet of Things (IoT), mobile phone platforms, web-based FinTech platforms, and blockchain or distributed ledger technology (Ozili, 2021). However, many research studies in this cluster explained the interplay between FinTech and Islamic social finance, emphasizing the significant role of COVID-19 in accelerating digital finance adoption (e.g.. see Ascarya, 2021; Atif et al., 2021; Ozili, 2021; Bin-Nashwan et al., 2023). According to Ascarya (2021), Islamic social finance tools like zakat, infaq, and waqf can play a vital role in helping the government and economy recover from the Covid-19 financial crisis through the following solutions: i) saving lives by providing medical assistance via zakat-infaq and healthcare waqf; ii) supporting households with a social safety net and graduation programs using zakat-infaq; iii) assisting businesses, particularly micro-small enterprises (MSEs), with financial and business support, including digital marketing, through zakat-infaq-waqf; and iv) helping financial institutions, especially micro-small scale, by developing cash waqf and integrating FinTech and Islamic commercial and social finance (IICSF), particularly in Islamic financial institutions catering to MSEs. FinTech is an innovation that has transformed the entire financial landscape and got acceptance in the Islamic finance sector (Atif et al., 2021). According to Rabbani et al. (2021), during the pandemic, Islamic finance has the capacity and potential to offer alternative finance, and social finance tools in combination with FinTech to help fight the economic consequences of COVID-19. More precisely, developing a strategy that involves FinTech in the zakat management system. The use of FinTech in providing Islamic financial services such as crowdfunding, waqf, and zakah etc. will make it more efficient, innovative, transparent, user-friendly, and attractive to deliver financial services to users (Todorof, 2018), as it showed significant evidence in post-Covid recovery (e.g., see Ascarya, 2021; Rabbani et al., 2021; Bin-Nashwan et al., 2023;Ghaouri et al., 2023). Many scholars in this cluster also explained the concept of Islamic FinTech (Hassan et al., 2020; Atif et al., 2021). According to Hassan et al. (2020), Islamic FinTech can be defined as the "delivery of Islamic finance products with the use of technology" (p. 95). Islamic FinTech can revolutionize the Islamic finance industry in order to achieve financial inclusion (Jouti, 2021), which is a key enabler to mitigate poverty and contribute towards achieving SDGs (Shaikh, 2020).

3.2.2.3 Cluster 3 (Blue): Interconnections Between Blockchain, Cryptocurrencies, and Financial Innovations in Developing Countries

This cluster visualizes the interconnections between key themes in finance and technology, including developing countries (3), investment (3), blockchain (16), cryptocurrencies (5), and their relationships. The focus suggests an emphasis on how these technologies and financial strategies interact, particularly in the context of emerging markets and innovations like blockchain and cryptocurrencies.

In recent years, blockchain has been utilized extensively in the sustainable finance field as one of the developing technologies (Ren et al., 2023). Blockchain technology has the potential to address key challenges faced by developing countries, both domestically and in international trade (Kshetri & Voas, 2018; Gillpatrick et al., 2022). By enhancing transparency, security, and efficiency, it enables these economies to become more competitive in the global market (Gillpatrick et al., 2022). Karakas et al. (2021) highlighted the fact that the adoption of blockchain in the logistics industry and supply chain can mitigate resource waste and improve labor efficiency. Thakor (2020) demonstrated that blockchain can reduce market-matching transaction costs, gather and store large data, improve the efficiency of information management, and reduce verification costs. A review of existing literature by Patel et al. (2022)

explores the impact of blockchain technology on financial intermediaries, financial applications, and regulatory oversight. Their study also assesses both the advantages and limitations of blockchain in the context of sustainable finance. However, currently, blockchain technology is used to provide semi-formal financial services to financially excluded or unbanked individuals (Larios-Hernández, 2017). Moreover, blockchain is the distributed ledger system (or distributed ledger technology) that underpins cryptocurrencies, currently reshaping the foundation of financial services. It enables multiple applications, such as reduced settlement times, value transfer, financing, real-time tracking of transactions, asset acknowledgment, information protection, ledger databases, and smart contracts (Larios-Hernández, 2017). Also, blockchain-based project bonds provide a means of raising funds through digital crowdfunding platforms, offering transparency and verification of fund allocation, sustainability impact, and project revenue streams. By integrating timestamping, public and private key encryption, and smart contract technology, these platforms enhance security, accountability, and efficiency in financial transactions (Chen & Volz, 2022). Thus, blockchain supports sustainable development by driving a technological revolution in finance, enhancing security, and improving governance. As a distributed and decentralized ledger, it promotes transparency, reduces reliance on intermediaries, and increases efficiency in financial transactions (Sharma et al., 2024). Additionally, blockchain aligns with the principles of a sustainable cyclical environment, ensuring long-term economic, social, and environmental sustainability (Adams et al., 2017; Clohessy et al., 2020; Esmaeilian et al., 2020; Sharma et al., 2024).

4. DISCUSSION OF RESULT, CONCLUSIONS AND LIMITATIONS

The findings of this bibliometric analysis highlight the increasing academic and industry focus on the intersection of FinTech and sustainable finance, emphasizing its potential in driving financial inclusion, ESG integration, and impact investing. The results indicate a growing body of research exploring how digital financial technologies—such as blockchain, AI, and mobile banking—facilitate access to capital, enhance transparency, and promote sustainable investment practices. Key contributors to this field include scholars from finance, technology, and sustainability disciplines, reflecting its multidisciplinary nature. However, despite the progress, significant gaps remain, particularly in empirical studies evaluating the real-world impact of FinTech-driven sustainability initiatives. Moreover, regional disparities in research output suggest the need for greater focus on developing economies, where FinTech adoption could play a transformative role. The study is limited by its reliance on bibliometric data, which may not fully capture qualitative advancements in the field. Future research should explore longitudinal case studies, regulatory challenges, and the ethical implications of FinTech in sustainable finance to provide a more holistic understanding of its long-term viability and societal impact.

5. OPEN ISSUES AND FUTURE RESEARCH DIRECTIONS

Despite the growing interest in the intersection of FinTech, social and sustainable finance, several open issues remain that require further exploration. One key challenge is the regulatory uncertainty surrounding FinTech innovations, particularly in areas such as decentralized finance (DeFi), digital assets, and AI-driven investment strategies, which may pose risks to financial stability and ESG compliance. Additionally, while FinTech has the potential to enhance financial inclusion, research is needed to assess whether it effectively reduces inequalities or inadvertently exacerbates the digital divide, particularly in low-income and underserved regions. Another critical area for future investigation is the standardization of ESG data and metrics, as the lack of consistent frameworks limits the ability of FinTech solutions to provide accurate and transparent sustainability assessments. Furthermore, the ethical implications of algorithm-driven decision-making in sustainable finance, including biases in AI models and the accountability of automated systems, remain largely unexplored. Future research should focus on developing robust regulatory frameworks, assessing the real-world impact of FinTech on ESG objectives, and exploring how emerging technologies can further enhance sustainability-driven financial solutions. Addressing these challenges will be crucial in ensuring that FinTech serves as an effective enabler of long-term sustainable development.

REFERENCES

Adams, R., Parry, G., Godsiff, P., & Ward, P. (2017). The future of money and further applications of the blockchain. *Strategic Change*, *26*(5), 417–422. DOI: 10.1002/jsc.2141

Alshater, M. M., Hassan, M. K., Khan, A., & Saba, I. (2020). Influential and intellectual structure of Islamic finance: A bibliometric review. *International Journal of Islamic and Middle Eastern Finance and Management*.

Arner, D. W., Buckley, R. P., Zetzsche, D. A., & Veidt, R. (2020). Sustainability, FinTech and financial inclusion. *European Business Organization Law Review*, *21*(1), 7–35. DOI: 10.1007/s40804-020-00183-y

Arora, R. U., & Sarker, T. (2023). Financing for Sustainable Development Goals (SDGs) in the Era of COVID-19 and Beyond. *European Journal of Development Research*, *35*(1), 1–19. DOI: 10.1057/s41287-022-00571-9 PMID: 36620200

Ascarya, A. (2021). The role of Islamic social finance during Covid-19 pandemic in Indonesia's economic recovery. *International Journal of Islamic and Middle Eastern Finance and Management*, *15*(2), 386–405. DOI: 10.1108/IMEFM-07-2020-0351

Atif, M., Hassan, M. K., Rabbani, M. R., & Khan, S. (2021). Islamic FinTech: The digital transformation bringing sustainability to Islamic finance. In *COVID-19 and Islamic Social Finance*. Routledge.

Auer, R., Haslhofer, B., Kitzler, S., Saggese, P., & Victor, F. (2024). The technology of decentralized finance (DeFi). *Digital Finance*, *6*(1), 55–95. DOI: 10.1007/s42521-023-00088-8

Bahoo, S., Alon, I., & Paltrinieri, A. (2020). Corruption in international business: A review and research agenda. *International Business Review*, *29*(4), 101660. DOI: 10.1016/j.ibusrev.2019.101660

Baker, H. K., Kumar, S., & Pandey, N. (2020). A bibliometric analysis of European Financial Management's first 25 years. *European Financial Management*, *26*(5), 1224–1260.

Bautista-Bernal, I., Quintana-García, C., & Marchante-Lara, M. (2021). Research trends in occupational health and social responsibility: A bibliometric analysis. *Safety Science*, *137*, 105167. DOI: 10.1016/j.ssci.2021.105167

Bayar, Y., Gavriletea, M. D., & Păun, D. (2021). Impact of mobile phones and internet use on financial inclusion: Empirical evidence from the EU post-communist countries. *Technological and Economic Development of Economy*, *27*(3), 722–741. DOI: 10.3846/tede.2021.14508

Bayram, O., Talay, I., & Feridun, M. (2022). Can Fintech Promote Sustainable Finance? Policy Lessons from the Case of Turkey. *Sustainability*, *14*(19), 19. Advance online publication. DOI: 10.3390/su141912414

Bin-Nashwan, S. A., Ismaiel, A. E. A., Muneeza, A., & Isa, M. Y. (2023). Adoption of ZakaTech in the time of COVID-19: Cross-country and gender differences. *Journal of Islamic Marketing*, *14*(11), 2949–2979. DOI: 10.1108/JIMA-08-2021-0278

Carè, R., Carè, S., Lévy, N., & Fatima, R. (2023). Missing finance in social impact bond research? A bibliometric overview between past and future research. *Corporate Social Responsibility and Environmental Management*, *30*(5), 2101–2120. DOI: 10.1002/csr.2496

Carè, R., & Cumming, D. (2024). Technology and automation in financial trading: A bibliometric review. *Research in International Business and Finance*, *71*, 102471. DOI: 10.1016/j.ribaf.2024.102471

Carè, R., Fatima, R., & Boitan, I. A. (2024). Central banks and climate risks: Where we are and where we are going? *International Review of Economics & Finance*, *92*, 1200–1229. DOI: 10.1016/j.iref.2024.01.057

Castriotta, M., Loi, M., Marku, E., & Moi, L. (2021). Disentangling the corporate entrepreneurship construct: Conceptualizing through co-words. *Scientometrics*, *126*(4), 2821–2863.

Chen, Y., & Volz, U. (2022). Scaling up sustainable investment through blockchain-based project bonds. *Development Policy Review*, *40*(3). https://www.econstor.eu/bitstream/10419/287886/1/DPR_DPR12582.pdf

Chohan, U. W. (2021). *Decentralized Finance (DeFi): An Emergent Alternative Financial Architecture* (SSRN Scholarly Paper 3791921). Social Science Research Network. https://doi.org/DOI: 10.2139/ssrn.3791921

Choi, J., Yi, S., & Lee, K. C. (2011). Analysis of keyword networks in MIS research and implications for predicting knowledge evolution. *Information & Management*, *48*(8), 371–381. DOI: 10.1016/j.im.2011.09.004

Clarke, T., & Boersma, M. (2016). *Sustainable Finance? A Critical Analysis of the Regulation, Policies, Strategies, Implementation and Reporting on Sustainability in International Finance*. https://opus.lib.uts.edu.au/handle/10453/42043

Clohessy, T., Treiblmaier, H., Acton, T., & Rogers, N. (2020). Antecedents of blockchain adoption: An integrative framework. *Strategic Change*, *29*(5), 501–515. DOI: 10.1002/jsc.2360

Cobo, M. j., López-Herrera, A. g., Herrera-Viedma, E., & Herrera, F. (2011). Science mapping software tools: Review, analysis, and cooperative study among tools. *Journal of the American Society for Information Science and Technology*, *62*(7), 1382–1402. DOI: 10.1002/asi.21525

Dadabada, P. K. (2024). Analyzing the Impact of ESG Integration and FinTech Innovations on Green Finance: A Comparative Case Studies Approach. *Journal of the Knowledge Economy*. Advance online publication. DOI: 10.1007/s13132-024-02197-0

Dehdarirad, T., Villarroya, A., & Barrios, M. (2014). Research trends in gender differences in higher education and science: A co-word analysis. *Scientometrics*, *101*(1), 273–290. DOI: 10.1007/s11192-014-1327-2

Dell'Atti, S., Trotta, A., Iannuzzi, A. P., & Demaria, F. (2017). Corporate Social Responsibility Engagement as a Determinant of Bank Reputation: An Empirical Analysis. *Corporate Social Responsibility and Environmental Management*, *24*(6), 589–605. DOI: 10.1002/csr.1430

Ding, X., Li, W., Huang, D., & Qin, X. (2022). Does Innovation Climate Help to Effectiveness of Green Finance Product R&D Team? The Mediating Role of Knowledge Sharing and Moderating Effect of Knowledge Heterogeneity. *Sustainability*, *14*(7), 7. Advance online publication. DOI: 10.3390/su14073926

Donthu, N., Kumar, S., Mukherjee, D., Pandey, N., & Lim, W. M. (2021). How to conduct a bibliometric analysis: An overview and guidelines. *Journal of Business Research*, *133*, 285–296. DOI: 10.1016/j.jbusres.2021.04.070

Esmaeilian, B., Sarkis, J., Lewis, K., & Behdad, S. (2020). Blockchain for the future of sustainable supply chain management in Industry 4.0. *Resources, Conservation and Recycling*, *163*, 105064. DOI: 10.1016/j.resconrec.2020.105064

European Commission. (2024). *Overview of sustainable finance*. Available at https://finance.ec.europa.eu/sustainable-finance/overview-sustainable-finance_en

European Commission. (2025). *Overview of sustainable finance*. https://finance.ec.europa.eu/sustainable-finance/overview-sustainable-finance_en

Farrukh, M., Meng, F., Raza, A., & Tahir, M. S. (2020). Twenty-seven years of Sustainable Development Journal: A bibliometric analysis. *Sustainable Development*, *28*(6), 1725–1737. DOI: 10.1002/sd.2120

Fatima, R., Boitan, I. A., & Carè, R. (2022). How Many Shades Are There in Sustainable Finance?: A Bibliometric Review. In Gok, I. Y. (Ed.), *Handbook of Research on Global Aspects of Sustainable Finance in Times of Crises* (pp. 1–26). IGI Global., DOI: 10.4018/978-1-7998-8501-6.ch001

Fatima, R., & Carè, R. (2024a). Navigating the landscape of nature-inspired finance approaches: A bibliometric analysis. In *Reference Module in Social Sciences*. Elsevier., DOI: 10.1016/B978-0-44-313776-1.00278-6

Fatima, R., & Carè, R. (2024b). The Role of FinTech and DeFi for Sustainable Development Goals and Sustainable Development: A Comprehensive Bibliometric Review. In *Decentralized Finance and Tokenization in FinTech* (pp. 238–270). IGI Global., DOI: 10.4018/979-8-3693-3346-4.ch014

Ferreira, F. A. F., Jalali, M. S., Meidutė-Kavaliauskienė, I., & Viana, B. A. C. P. (2015). A metacognitive decision making based-framework for bank customer loyalty measurement and management. *Technological and Economic Development of Economy*, *21*(2), 280–300. DOI: 10.3846/20294913.2014.981764

Firmansyah, E. A., Masri, M., Anshari, M., & Besar, M. H. A. (2023). Factors Affecting Fintech Adoption: A Systematic Literature Review. *FinTech*, *2*(1), 1. Advance online publication. DOI: 10.3390/fintech2010002

Franceschini, F., Maisano, D., & Mastrogiacomo, L. (2016). Empirical analysis and classification of database errors in Scopus and Web of Science. *Journal of Informetrics*, *10*(4), 933–953.

Ghaouri, M. H., Kassim, S., & Rashid, H. (2023). Waqf-Linked Islamic Fintech Microfinance as a Business Enabler in Post-pandemic Economy: The Experience of Hal Microfinance, Kenya. In Hamdan, A., Harraf, A., Buallay, A., Arora, P., & Alsabatin, H. (Eds.), *From Industry 4.0 to Industry 5.0: Mapping the Transitions* (pp. 357–370). Springer Nature Switzerland., DOI: 10.1007/978-3-031-28314-7_30

Gillpatrick, T., Boğa, S., & Aldanmaz, O. (2022). How Can Blockchain Contribute to Developing Country Economies? A Literature Review on Application Areas. *ECONOMICS*, *10*(1), 105–128. DOI: 10.2478/eoik-2022-0009

Hassan, M. K., Rabbani, M. R., & Ali, M. A. M. (2020). Challenges for the Islamic Finance and banking in post COVID era and the role of Fintech. *Journal of Economic Cooperation & Development*, *41*(3), 93–116.

Ibe-enwo, G., Igbudu, N., Garanti, Z., & Popoola, T. (2019). Assessing the Relevance of Green Banking Practice on Bank Loyalty: The Mediating Effect of Green Image and Bank Trust. *Sustainability, 11*(17), 17. Advance online publication. DOI: 10.3390/su11174651

Igbudu, N., Garanti, Z., & Popoola, T. (2018). Enhancing Bank Loyalty through Sustainable Banking Practices: The Mediating Effect of Corporate Image. *Sustainability, 10*(11), 11. Advance online publication. DOI: 10.3390/su10114050

Jouti, A. T. (2021). Islamic FinTech and Financial Inclusion. In Billah, M. M. (Ed.), *Islamic FinTech: Insights and Solutions* (pp. 209–229). Springer International Publishing., DOI: 10.1007/978-3-030-45827-0_12

Karakas, S., Acar, A. Z., & Kucukaltan, B. (2021). Blockchain adoption in logistics and supply chain: A literature review and research agenda. *International Journal of Production Research, 62*(22), 8193–8216. DOI: 10.1080/00207543.2021.2012613

Kashif, M., Pinglu, C., Ullah, S., & Zaman, M. (2024). Evaluating the influence of financial technology (FinTech) on sustainable finance: A comprehensive global analysis. *Financial Markets and Portfolio Management, 38*(1), 123–155. DOI: 10.1007/s11408-023-00439-w

Katona, T. (2021). Decentralized Finance—The Possibilities of a Blockchain "Money Lego" System. *Financial and Economic Review, 20*(1), 74–102.

Kish, Z., & Leroy, J. (2015). Bonded Life: Technologies of racial finance from slave insurance to philanthrocapital. *Cultural Studies, 29*(5–6), 630–651. DOI: 10.1080/09502386.2015.1017137

Kshetri, N., & Voas, J. (2018). Blockchain in Developing Countries. *IT Professional, 20*(2), 11–14. *IT Professional*. Advance online publication. DOI: 10.1109/MITP.2018.021921645

Kumar, S., Sharma, D., Rao, S., Lim, W. M., & Mangla, S. K. (2022). Past, present, and future of sustainable finance: Insights from big data analytics through machine learning of scholarly research. *Annals of Operations Research*. Advance online publication. DOI: 10.1007/s10479-021-04410-8 PMID: 35002001

Larios-Hernández, G. J. (2017). Blockchain entrepreneurship opportunity in the practices of the unbanked. *Business Horizons, 60*(6), 865–874. DOI: 10.1016/j.bushor.2017.07.012

LIU, M. (1993). Progress in documentation the complexities of citation practice: A review of citation studies. *The Journal of Documentation, 49*(4), 370–408. DOI: 10.1108/eb026920

Macchiavello, E., & Siri, M. (2022). Sustainable Finance and Fintech: Can Technology Contribute to Achieving Environmental Goals? A Preliminary Assessment of 'Green Fintech' and 'Sustainable Digital Finance.'. *European Company and Financial Law Review*, *19*(1), 128–174. DOI: 10.1515/ecfr-2022-0005

Mejia-Escobar, J. C., González-Ruiz, J. D., & Duque-Grisales, E. (2020). Sustainable Financial Products in the Latin America Banking Industry: Current Status and Insights. *Sustainability*, *12*(14), 14. Advance online publication. DOI: 10.3390/su12145648

Mejia-Escobar, J. C., González-Ruiz, J. D., & Duque-Grisales, E. (2020). Sustainable Financial Products in the Latin America Banking Industry: Current Status and Insights. *Sustainability*, *12*(14), 14. Advance online publication. DOI: 10.3390/su12145648

Meoli, M., & Vismara, S. (2021). Information manipulation in equity crowdfunding markets. *Journal of Corporate Finance*, *67*, 101866. DOI: 10.1016/j.jcorpfin.2020.101866

Metawa, N., Dogan, E., & Taskin, D. (2022). Analyzing the nexus of green economy, clean and financial technology. *Economic Analysis and Policy*, *76*, 385–396. DOI: 10.1016/j.eap.2022.08.023

Morgan, P. J. (2022). Assessing the Risks Associated with Green Digital Finance and Policies for Coping with Them. In Taghizadeh-Hesary, F., & Hyun, S. (Eds.), *Green Digital Finance and Sustainable Development Goals* (pp. 51–68). Springer Nature., DOI: 10.1007/978-981-19-2662-4_3

Moro-Visconti, R., Cruz Rambaud, S., & López Pascual, J. (2020). Sustainability in FinTechs: An Explanation through Business Model Scalability and Market Valuation. *Sustainability*, *12*(24), 24. Advance online publication. DOI: 10.3390/su122410316

Naeem, M. A., Karim, S., Rabbani, M. R., Bashar, A., & Kumar, S. (2023). Current state and future directions of green and sustainable finance: A bibliometric analysis. *Qualitative Research in Financial Markets*, *15*(4), 608–629. DOI: 10.1108/QRFM-10-2021-0174

Ozcan, R. (2021). Decentralized Finance. In Hacioglu, U., & Aksoy, T. (Eds.), *Financial Ecosystem and Strategy in the Digital Era: Global Approaches and New Opportunities* (pp. 57–75). Springer International Publishing., DOI: 10.1007/978-3-030-72624-9_4

Ozili, P. K. (2021). Digital Finance, Green Finance and Social Finance: Is there a Link? *Financial Internet Quarterly*, *17*(1), 1–7. DOI: 10.2478/fiqf-2021-0001

Ozili, P. K. (2022). Assessing global interest in decentralized finance, embedded finance, open finance, ocean finance and sustainable finance. *Asian Journal of Economics and Banking*, *7*(2), 197–216. DOI: 10.1108/AJEB-03-2022-0029

Palshikar, G. K. (2007). Keyword Extraction from a Single Document Using Centrality Measures. In Ghosh, A., De, R. K., & Pal, S. K. (Eds.), *Pattern Recognition and Machine Intelligence* (pp. 503–510). Springer., DOI: 10.1007/978-3-540-77046-6_62

Patel, R., Migliavacca, M., & Oriani, M. E. (2022). Blockchain in banking and finance: A bibliometric review. *Research in International Business and Finance*, *62*, 101718. DOI: 10.1016/j.ribaf.2022.101718

Popescu, A.-D. (2020). Decentralized finance (defi) – The lego of finance. *Social Sciences and Education Research Review*, *7*(1), 321–349.

Rabbani, M. R., Bashar, A., Nawaz, N., Karim, S., & Ali, M. A. Mohd., Rahiman, H. U., & Alam, Md. S. (2021). Exploring the Role of Islamic Fintech in Combating the Aftershocks of COVID-19: The Open Social Innovation of the Islamic Financial System. *Journal of Open Innovation*, *7*(2), 136. DOI: 10.3390/joitmc7020136

Ren, Y.-S., Ma, C.-Q., Chen, X.-Q., Lei, Y.-T., & Wang, Y.-R. (2023). Sustainable finance and blockchain: A systematic review and research agenda. *Research in International Business and Finance*, *64*, 101871. DOI: 10.1016/j.ribaf.2022.101871

Rizzi, F., Pellegrini, C., & Battaglia, M. (2018). The structuring of social finance: Emerging approaches for supporting environmentally and socially impactful projects. *Journal of Cleaner Production*, *170*, 805–817. DOI: 10.1016/j.jclepro.2017.09.167

Ruiz-Parrado, V., Heradio, R., Aranda-Escolastico, E., Sánchez, Á., & Vélez, J. F. (2022). A bibliometric analysis of off-line handwritten document analysis literature (1990–2020). *Pattern Recognition*, *125*, 108513.

Rupeika-Apoga, R., & Thalassinos, E. I. (2020). *Ideas for a regulatory definition of FinTech*. https://www.um.edu.mt/library/oar/handle/123456789/55195

Schär, F. (2021). *Decentralized Finance: On Blockchain- and Smart Contract-Based Financial Markets* (SSRN Scholarly Paper 3843844). Social Science Research Network. https://doi.org/DOI: 10.20955/r.103.153-74

Shaikh, S. A. (2020). Using Fintech in scaling up Islamic microfinance. *Journal of Islamic Accounting and Business Research*, *12*(2), 186–203. DOI: 10.1108/JIABR-10-2019-0198

Sharma, G. D., Tiwari, A. K., Chopra, R., & Dev, D. (2024). Past, present, and future of block-chain in finance. *Journal of Business Research, 177*, 114640. DOI: 10.1016/j.jbusres.2024.114640

Siano, A., Raimi, L., Palazzo, M., & Panait, M. C. (2020). Mobile Banking: An Innovative Solution for Increasing Financial Inclusion in Sub-Saharan African Countries: Evidence from Nigeria. *Sustainability, 12*(23), 10130. DOI: 10.3390/su122310130

Singh, D., & Stakic, N. (2021). Financial inclusion and economic growth nexus: Evidence from SAARC countries. *South Asia Research, 41*(2), 238–258. DOI: 10.1177/0262728020964605

Singhania, M., Chadha, G., & Prasad, R. (2024). Sustainable finance research: Review and agenda. *International Journal of Finance & Economics, 29*(4), 4010–4045. DOI: 10.1002/ijfe.2854

Suryono, R. R., Budi, I., & Purwandari, B. (2020). Challenges and Trends of Financial Technology (Fintech): A Systematic Literature Review. *Information (Basel), 11*(12), 12. Advance online publication. DOI: 10.3390/info11120590

Thakor, A. V. (2020). Fintech and banking: What do we know? *Journal of Financial Intermediation, 41*, 100833. DOI: 10.1016/j.jfi.2019.100833

Todorof, M. (2018). Shariah-compliant FinTech in the banking industry. *ERA Forum, 19*(1), 1–17. https://doi.org/DOI: 10.1007/s12027-018-0505-8

Trotta, A., Rania, F., & Strano, E. (2024). Exploring the linkages between FinTech and ESG: A bibliometric perspective. *Research in International Business and Finance, 69*, 102200. DOI: 10.1016/j.ribaf.2023.102200

van Eck, N., & Waltman, L. (2009). Software survey: VOSviewer, a computer program for bibliometric mapping. *Scientometrics, 84*(2), 523–538. DOI: 10.1007/s11192-009-0146-3 PMID: 20585380

van Eck, N., & Waltman, L. (2010). Software survey: VOSviewer, a computer program for bibliometric mapping. *Scientometrics, 84*(2), 523–538. DOI: 10.1007/s11192-009-0146-3 PMID: 20585380

van Eck, N. J., & Waltman, L. (2014). Visualizing Bibliometric Networks. In Ding, Y., Rousseau, R., & Wolfram, D. (Eds.), *Measuring Scholarly Impact: Methods and Practice* (pp. 285–320). Springer International Publishing., DOI: 10.1007/978-3-319-10377-8_13 van Eck, N. J., Waltman, L., van den Berg, J., & Kaymak, U. (2006). Visualizing the computational intelligence field [Application Notes]. *IEEE Computational Intelligence Magazine, 1*(4), 6–10. *IEEE Computational Intelligence Magazine*. Advance online publication. DOI: 10.1109/MCI.2006.329702

Wójcik, D., & Bratton, W. (2024). Theory, explanation, and economics in financial geographies. *Dialogues in Human Geography, 20438206241280659*. Advance online publication. DOI: 10.1177/20438206241280659

Yang, J., & Jung, S. U. (2024). Harnessing FinTech for Sustainable Finance in Developing Countries: An Integrated SWOT–Multi-Level Perspective Analysis of Mongolia. *Sustainability*, *16*(10), 4102. DOI: 10.3390/su16104102

Ziolo, M., Bak, I., & Cheba, K. (2021). The role of sustainable finance in achieving Sustainable Development Goals: Does it work? *Technological and Economic Development of Economy*, *27*(1), 1. Advance online publication. DOI: 10.3846/tede.2020.13863

Zupic, I., & Čater, T. (2015). Bibliometric Methods in Management and Organization. *Organizational Research Methods*, *18*(3), 429–472. DOI: 10.1177/1094428114562629

Chapter 4
Redefining Sustainable Energy Financing:
The Disruptive Influence of Decentralised Finance (DeFi)

Gagandeep Singh
https://orcid.org/0000-0001-8644-4064
Lovely Professional University, India

Jasdeep Singh Walia
https://orcid.org/0000-0001-9010-082X
Lovely Professional University, India

ABSTRACT

The challenges imposed by the convention financing (high initial outlay, long gestation periods, absence of standard legislation and non-availability of hedge risk tools) have emerged as barriers in the extensive implementation of sustainable energy projects. The advent of blockchain technologies has empowered to discover unconventional financing systems and efficiently tap the opportunities embraced by Decentralised finance (DeFi). This contemporary source of finance is evolving as an assuring protocol, built on a robust ecosystem encompassing disruptive approaches built on blockchain technology. The present book chapter intends to explore the transformative perspective of DeFi in revolutionizing sustainable energy financing. It outlines a model that underscores the association among various challenges impeding DeFi adoption. It bestows a comprehensive model that focuses on adhering to strategic steps for effectual DeFi integration. The outcomes of this study emphasize insights for policymakers to facilitate informed decision-making for promising sustainable energy projects.

DOI: 10.4018/979-8-3693-9551-6.ch004

1. INTRODUCTION

Traditional financing and its mechanics have played a substantial role in developing sufficient infrastructure towards sustainable energy projects. However, the cumulative energy demands and acceleration in the pace of the sustainable development prerequisites have put traditional financing on its back foot (González & Rendon, 2022). This financing type failed to adequately recognise the growing challenges of climate change and sustain the augmented transitional needs towards green financial products. It faced serious challenges regarding its centralised financial system wherein major mediators controlled the capital flow and enforced several constraints on its lending systems (Misra et al., 2024). The rigorous lending conditions created multi-level barriers to small-scale and clean energy-driven environmental initiatives leading to various difficulties in accessing secure funding among various business firms. The mechanisms governing traditional financing and its overall processes failed to secure appropriate funding due to prolonged due diligence practices, lengthy bookkeeping procedures and excessive transaction costs. Such factors led to a diminishing in the feasibility and viability of the different projects governing sustainable energy and its progressions (Brown et al., 2020). The elements of non-transparency and non-traceability created momentous obstructions for the stakeholders and discouraged their significant partaking in sustainable energy funding thereby creating distrust in the development of the overall financing system (Popescu, 2020; Pereira et al., 2022). The decentralised financing (DeFi), in contrast, outlined a welcome change by suitably including the significant elements of transparency, composability, programmability and offering suitable yield opportunities. The decentralised governance enables constructing its protocols on unrestricted blockchain linkages, which aims to prevent frauds and any kind of manoeuvrings (Harvey & Rabetti, 2024).

The traditional sources of financing relied mainly on climate bonds, grants-in-aid, and socially responsible investing to accumulate capital. The traditional fixed income instruments were instituted in the past decade, and they served as asset-backed securities for financing the renewable energy programs (González & Rendon, 2022). The government authorities across various nations facilitated energy financing, which reduced the restrictions for low-carbon transitions. Historically, it is noted that traditional financing options faced limitations related to centralisation, administrative delays, government setbacks and administrative hold-ups. In such a scenario, blockchain finance and peer-to-peer finance (DeFi) materialised in the recent past as a paradigm-shifting source of finance. Such a financing option provided configurable, unambiguous, and unrestricted financial services, which adequately handled the issues pertaining to traditional financing options. It enables broadened access to funding for renewable energy by marking a paradigm shift in sustainable financing.

The basic building block of DeFi is built on improving accessibility wherein the traditional financing lags. It tends to provide banking services to the underbanked and unbanked population with low access to finance by providing them with an adequate cryptocurrency wallet (Patel & Wang, 2020; Goda, 2021). It is inferred that the open-source structure of the DeFi system promotes the unassailable landscape of the blockchain networks thereby upholding dependence and answerability. It is further delineated that DeFi procedures are constructed using an interoperable design, which duly acknowledges the operators to syndicate various protocols to develop innovative financial services (González & Rendon, 2022). The element of composability further stimulates high-end innovation and enables the formation of complex financial instruments that were not accessible in traditional finance. The investors in the DeFi ecosystem can make adequate investments without requesting any endorsement from third parties, and in this case, their transactions are not blocked or annulled by any centralised agencies (Pereira et al., 2022; Amuzu-Sefordzi et al., 2018). The DeFi protocols are adequate to provide efficient allocation of capital by allowing its investors to advance, borrow, and trade in financial assets without involving any mediators. The DeFi process tends to lessen the costs of inadequacies connected with traditional financial systems (Wieczorek et al., 2024). Furthermore, it is outlined that DeFi procedures mainly rely on smart contracts reflecting the robust blockchain ecosystem. Such encoding permits the development of mechanized financial instruments, in the structure of decentralised exchanges and various lending stages (Pereira et al., 2022). The governance of the DeFi domains is done by decentralised autonomous bodies, which suitably enables the investors to actively contribute to decision-making activities and contour the future advancement of the procedures (Brisbois, 2019). DeFi runs on the model of decentralised governance which upholds investor ownership and brings into line enticements among them.

The current book chapter intends to explore the transformative perspective of DeFi in revolutionizing sustainable energy financing. It outlines a model highlighting the interconnectivity among various current challenges impeding mainstream DeFi adoption, such as regulatory uncertainties, security concerns, and technical complexities. Additionally, it presents a comprehensive model highlighting strategic steps for effectual DeFi integration, focusing on strategic barriers and advancing its' widespread adoption. Moreover, it accentuates valuable insights for policymakers and regulatory authorities, emphasizing the implications of DeFi on sustainable energy policies and regulatory frameworks to facilitate informed decision-making for a sustainable energy future.

2. REVIEW OF LITERATURE

Decentralised finance (DeFi) can revolutionize the financing of sustainable energy for the investors to access different, flexible and open honest structures of funding of on sustainable energy. DeFi dismantled financing for its users so they could attend the global market without intermediaries and high costs. Consequently, decentralised lending, crowdfunding, and tokenization open up DeFi prospects for the development of new types of financing for messages on the creation of sustainable energy. Nevertheless, there are still several problems with regulation and security, as well as the lack of scalability and adoption key for DeFi's further evolution as a means of utilizing the shifts to greener energy sources. The present study considers *five realms* of literature concerning (1). The disruptive potential of Decentralised finance (2). Funding prototypes in sustainable energy financing (3). DeFi's impact on sustainable energy financing (4). Challenges and Considerations for DeFi Adoption in Sustainable Energy (5). Best use cases – DeFi application in sustainable energy financing.

2.1. Disruptive Potential of Decentralised Finance

Decentralised Finance, or DeFi is a relatively experiencing a massive expansion that threatens to eliminate traditional centralised financial systems with the help of blockchain and various decentralised applications. The research work of Harvey & Rabetti, (2024); Berka & Dreyfus (2021); Popescu (2020) outlined that the DeFi protocols have the latent ability to integrate portrayals, based on decentralisation and open-sourced contractual systems. It effectively retains smart contracts and decentralised protocols through which various investors can enter various financing transactions. It was highlighted by the studies of Amuzu-Sefordzi et al. (2018) and Goda, (2021) that the DeFi model shall be pronounced as the 'paradigm shift' as it has the superior ability to augment accessibility and effectively reduce the associated costs. The DeFi protocols are open-sourced and anyone with an internet connection can participate in DeFi regardless of their location or income level.

According to Ahuja & Khandelwal (2023), González & Rendon (2022), Misra et al., (2024) the liberalization of the financial services sector may contribute to the improvement of financial inclusion and positive change for underprivileged societies on a global scale. These studies described that the concept of DeFi protocol is that every action and every transaction that happens within the protocol occurs on the blockchain which is a decentralised system that cannot be altered. It was pointed out that a well-established financial system shall suitably enhance the reliability of the system and also ensure that accountability is well enhanced. Additionally, it was enumerated that the participants in the DeFi system would be in a position to ascertain the validity of the system besides being able to trace the movement of their funds. The overall new financial system works on several protocols and applications that can be stacked together and sequentially to create new DeFi products and services. Thus, modularity and interoperability open the door to innovation and the development of new and original financial products suitable for different uses (Mäkinen, 2021).

2.2. Funding Prototypes in Sustainable Energy Financing

Various funding prototypes, such as decentralised crowdfunding platforms, DAO-led initiatives, and tokenisation mechanisms in sustainable energy financing, serve as an important element in fostering innovation and thus contribute to the creation of a sustainable energy culture. It was delineated that conventional financing structures have inherent drawbacks in terms of riskier technology setups and uncertain early-stage propositions but DeFi can suitably open up new possibilities for investing in prototypes and contributing to the creation of efficient solutions in the sphere of renewable energy (Zhuk, A., 2025; Ahuja & Khandelwal, 2023; Pereira et al., 2022; Brown et al., 2020; Popescu, 2020). The prototype of decentralised crowdfunding presents one of the most viable solutions as it is based on superior blockchain technology thereby, allowing direct funding from investors across the world. The DAOs serve as a major source of funding for prototypes in the new financing ecosystem (Harvey & Rabetti, 2024; González & Rendon, 2022; Pereira et al., 2022 and Mäkinen, 2021). These decentralised entities managed by P2P relations that follow the open-source rules of smart contracts can follow the principles of collective pool funding to support green energy projects. It was stressed that DAOs maintain decision-making structures that decentralize funding decisions, thus promoting the funding decisions of all the stakeholders. Additionally, their research work underscored the noteworthy presence of the tokenization process which holds its potential in the pre-funding of prototypes in ecological energy financing. It was described that tokenization possesses the superior ability to create digital tokens designated ownership or rights in the sustainable energy project within the blockchain framework, thereby fostering developers to attract more investors in this new financing system as well as its upcoming prototypes (Zhuk, A., 2025; Wieczorek et al., 2024; Harvey & Rabetti, 2024; Pereira et al., 2022; Brown et al., 2020; Berka & Dreyfus, 2021; Goda, 2021)

2.3. DeFi's Impact on Sustainable Energy Financing

The adoption of DeFi is particularly anticipated to transform the financing of sustainable energy because of its capability to provide solutions to the issues and challenges posed by traditional financing strategies. The research outcomes of Wieczorek et al. (2024), Alamsyah et al. (2024), Piñeiro-Chousa et al. (2022), Brisbois (2019), Popescu (2020); and Richter (2013) revealed that blockchain and decentralised applications by DeFi have the greater ability to revolutionise the ways for raising, deploying and utilizing capital for sustainable energy projects. It was delineated that traditional financing models place significant restrictions in terms of multiple policy and terrestrial barriers thereby hindering the smooth flow of capital across the globe. The DeFi protocols operate on sophisticated decentralised platforms, thereby allowing different financial bodies to manage their fund flows in the most appropriate manner for green energy financing. Additionally, it was furthered in the studies by Misra et al. (2024), Brown et al. (2020), Berka & Dreyfus (2021) and Amuzu-Sefordzi et al. (2018) that platforms on which DeFi operates tend to considerably increases the transparency and accountability of financing ecological energy projects. It is outlined that blockchain ledgers are permanent and can be viewed by all the investors thereby guaranteeing that every action and transaction that happens in DeFi protocols is well documented. It increases credibility because investors can adequately verify the correct dispensing and application of funds hence ensuring accountability in the handling of sustainable energy projects.

2.4. Challenges and Considerations for DeFi Adoption in Sustainable Energy

The protocols on which the decentralised financing system operates have multiple jurisdictions and there is non-clarity on the governance models through which it is regulated (Zhou, 2024). A lack of a unified and cohesive governance framework for DeFi models makes it challenging for the operators and investors to engage with its protocols adequately (Santiago et al., 2025; Alamsyah et al., 2024; Vinoth & Srivastava, 2024; Kayani & Hasan, 2024; Rios & Zhang, 2021). The regulatory opacity for this innovative financing option may not efficiently address the distinctive characteristics of the decentralised financing systems. Additionally, it is fostered that several jurisdictional differences tend to undermine the overall reliability of the DeFi ecosystem and discourage its adoption across the widespread unbanked population (Zhuk, A., 2025; Zumbansen, 2023; Alamsyah et al., 2024; Singh & Singh, 2023 and Bielenberg et al., 2016). The early adopters tend to manipulate jurisdictional dissimilarities and also engage in regulatory havens to bypass rules and their oversight (Richter, 2013). The protocols on which DeFi functions do not carry any adequate oversight and protection mechanisms which further tends to expose its investors to various types of financial abnormalities as well as rip-offs

(Zhuk, 2025; Wieczorek et al., 2024; Piñeiro-Chousa et al., 2022; Chavez & Gupta, 2021; Brisbois, 2019).

Suitable financial safeguards must be adequately enforced to endorse their widespread acceptability and uphold investor protection rights at all levels. It was outlined that by converging on the financial regulatory uncertainties shall be the chief priority and efforts must be made to develop consistent and adaptive regulatory frameworks to encourage their pervasive acceptance and assimilation into the conventional financial structure (Alamsyah et al., 2024; Zumbansen, 2023; Berka & Dreyfus, 2021; Brown et al., 2020 and Amuzu-Sefordzi et al., 2018). The dearth of well-defined and inclusive financial regulatory frameworks involving the DeFi protocols leads to the creation of a void in adequate financial knowledge among investors. There exist no proper and well-defined protocols about preeminent practices, compliance necessities, and financial operational standards (Santiago et al., 2025; Chavez & Gupta, 2021; Brisbois, 2019). This knowledge gap results in misperceptions, contradictions, and prospective hazards for contractors, investors, and establishments engaging their transactions on DeFi platforms (Zhuk, 2025; Amuzu-Sefordzi et al., 2018). It was, therefore, accentuated in previous research works that regulatory uncertainties of the DeFi ecosystem tend to result in a knowledge gap and simultaneously tend to cause various interoperability challenges (Wieczorek et al., 2024; Popescu, 2020).

2.5. Best Use Cases: DeFi Applications in Sustainable Energy Financing

The upsurge of application of DeFi in sustainable energy financing in recent years has presented some best use cases. Past literature in this area outlined more on the theoretical foundations of the capabilities of decentralised financing, while contemporary investigations have laid out some best use cases focusing on its practical applications and efficacy. A profound empirical investigation was conducted by Nguyen et al. (2023) wherein a cross-country comparative analysis on distributed ledger-enabled renewable energy subsidising was conducted. The outcomes highlighted those investors across Asian countries exhibited an increased interest in resorting to these new-age financing options, as it significantly reduced their transaction costs. Additionally, the study by Wang and Zeng (2024) demonstrated that data fragmentation and blockchain-based agreements ensured new investor integration. This study reviewed various DeFi-enabled ongoing green energy projects at various locations. The research outcomes of this research work praised the benefits of advanced financing ensures clarity in fund management, and significantly lessens funding timelines compared to green use of proceeds bonds. It was stressed that an immutable digital ledger could effectively implement capital accumulation. Furthermore, an empirical analysis by Smith et al. (2023) outlined that adequate dispersal of energy transmission in various localities involves suitable integration of DeFi projects with decentralised energy financing. The findings of the study matched with the broader implications outlined in the study by Ahmed & Liu (2023). His funded project conducted in various African nations illustrated that smart contracts enabled upfront pricing, ensured building of assurance and credibility among the participatory stakeholders. (Ahmed & Liu, 2023). A noteworthy case study by Garcia & Lopez (2022) illustrated the effect of DeFi on encouraging and promoting sustainable actions. It presented an integrated project information which can be applied in community-based funding in sustainable energy initiatives. This experiential knowledge corroborates the assumptions of DeFi as an impactful domain in clean energy financing.

3. IMPEDIMENTS TO MAINSTREAM DeFi ADOPTION

The DeFi system is constructed as an open-source system that ensures the disabling of the decentralised blockchain network, making it dependable and accountable (Chavez & Gupta, 2021; Patel & Wang, 2020). However, such a new financing system is subject to several challenges threatening its broad adoption worldwide. The underpinning of impediments to mainstream adoption of DeFi is the innovation diffusion and technology acceptance paradigms (Auer et al. 2024). The model outlined in this section aims to transcend the challenges by incorporating various disputes and challenges that strengthen and constrain DeFi adoption (Olutimehin, 2025). The model conceptualisation is built on the barriers-to-adoption Framework and insights from the technology acceptance model. Such a model is based upon a multi-dimensional process that is determined by both individual-level and system-level dimensions. The model is eminent and establishes the correlation between four essential sectors i.e., regulatory uncertainty, technical complexity, access barriers, and knowledge gaps (Santiago et al., 2025). The legal issues and regulatory concerns persist because the legal status of DeFi projects is still uncertain, thereby leading to a proliferation of legal grey areas that define what is allowed and which therefore constitutes a low risk for participants and investors to undertake (Pereira et al., 2022; Brown et al., 2020; Berka & Dreyfus, 2021 and Amuzu-Sefordzi et al., 2018). Some of the underlying networks for scaling have poor scalability and this is because they are not efficient in handling large traffic hence, they experience traffic jams; they are costly, they limit the number of transactions they can handle per day and most importantly they affect the user experience. It is furthered that the present technological solutions of DeFi protocols and smart contracts in progress with the involvement of blockchain technology are subjected to fraud and other hacking attacks by bad actors, making them skeptical or producing concerns over the safety of such systems, and leaving original and complex inherent smart users or financial institutions out.

Additionally, it is outlined that issues surrounding the awareness of governance proposal can be traced from DeFi is dependence on smart contracts, cryptographic algorithms, and financial instruments making it difficult for the investors to comprehend the protocols properly. Strict prerequisites to adopting the MCCs such as technical competency, availability of broadband, and the user interface make up for the low usage rates, which inevitably decentralises the power of decision-making and locks out many people in the chain (Rios & Zhang, 2021; Zumbansen, 2023; Bongini et al., 2025). These debates will be most crucial in the future growth and innovation of decentralised finance, as there was a response to the mentioned challenges by developing and enforcing legal provisions concerning decentralised finance services, finding a solution to the scalability question, creating effective security protocol, building an educational framework, and raising access to decentralised finance services (Santiago et al., 2025; Olutimehin, 2025; Singh & Singh, 2023; Berka & Dreyfus, 2021; Alamsyah et al., 2024). The interlinkage among various factors causing hindrances in the effective DeFi adoption is outlined in Figure 1.

3.1. Regulatory Uncertainty Leads to the Knowledge Gap

The overall concept of decentralised finance has been developed and endorsed to encourage financial inclusion among the widespread population. However, it is determined that the technology on which Defi works is based on complex blockchain protocols and cryptographical models which becomes challenging for all the investors possessing non-technical knowledge to comprehend the channels governing the decentralised finance. It is underlined that technical impediments significantly create knowledge gaps among its users. The investors making the transactions using the blockchain protocols may find it arduous to adequately use its platforms, determine the risk factors and make cognizant decisions related to their investments. Additionally, it is fostered that the non-availability of all-inclusive educational materials also leads to the widening of the knowledge gap, making it tougher for investors to absorb the DeFi protocols the appraise its potential. The rapidly evolving innovative procedures in the DeFi ecosystem also suggestively contribute to the knowledge gap (Bongini et al., 2025; Kumar & Sharma, 2022). It required considerable efforts on the part of investors to comprehend and acknowledge the evolving FinTech protocols, systems and technological developments. It is, therefore, accentuated that policymakers and enforcement agencies shall be involved in fabricating adaptable resources, constituting innovative financial literacy lectures and ensuring inclusive admittance to digital technological resources governing the new financing systems based on sophisticated expertise.

3.2. Regulatory Uncertainty Leads to Interoperability Challenges

The various regulatory uncertainties pose several trials in attaining interoperability among different stages of the new financial ecosystem. The mechanism of interoperability in decentralised finance is imperative for ensuring the continuous exchange of information in the entire ecosystem. The lack of unified and clear guidelines and regulations poses abstruseness and ambiguity in the interoperability of the DeFi systems. The decentralised financial ecosystem is operating worldwide and its regulatory authorities are scattered and hugely vary across multiple jurisdictions which makes it perplexing to ascertain common protocols that would support its adequate interoperability. The present protocols on the DeFi ecosystem are required to conform with multiple regulatory regimes, which results in contradictions and compatibility questions. Additionally, it is advanced that various regulatory uncertainties governing data privacy pose difficulties for interoperability in the DeFi ecosystem. The jurisdictions vary across multiple locations and dissimilarities in regulations make it extremely difficult to establish conjoint benchmarks for data sharing across platforms. Such an approach tends to disintegrate the data organization, thereby, encumbering the continuous flow of financial information (Bongini et al., 2025; Zhuk, 2025; Kumar & Sharma, 2022; Pereira et al., 2022). Lack of precision on regulatory obligations may lead to dejection in making adequate innovations and results in the creation of various opposing approaches among DeFi platforms and protocols. This results in various compatibility disputes and impedes the progress of industry-wide benchmarks for interoperability. Regulatory improbability significantly affects the technological improvement and adoption of interoperability resolutions.

Figure 1. Model outlining the key inter-linkages in impediments of the DeFi ecosystem

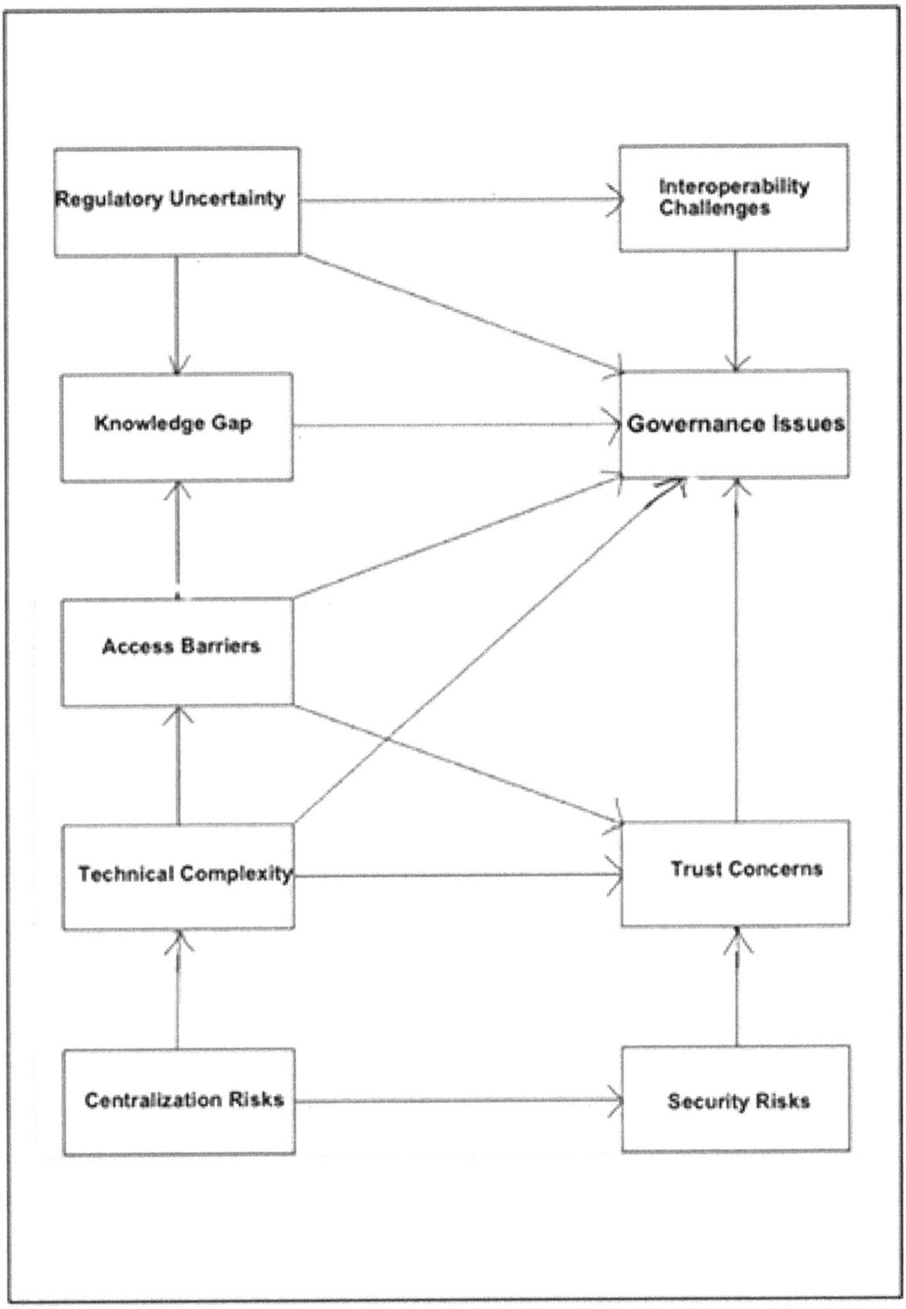

Source: Authors creation

3.3. Access Barriers Lead to the Knowledge Gap

The access barriers hamper the extensive acceptance and comprehension of the blockchain-based financial ecosystem leading to the widening of the knowledge gaps. The platforms on which DeFi works require sophisticated work with complex technical mechanisms, such as smart contracts, decentralised connections, and borrowing-lending platforms. The system's complexity poses multiple barriers to knowledge acquisition among existing and new investors. These technical complications lead to a knowledge gap, furthering to widening of the learning curve and theoretically dissuading its widespread embracing. Attainment of practical and hands-on experience in the working of the DeFi platforms is domineering for mounting a fair comprehension of this new financial ecosystem. However, access barriers in context with the requirement for initial capital, crypto wallets working, asset management and familiarity with user interfaces can prevent individuals from engaging with DeFi platforms, limiting their ability to learn through hands-on experience. Furthermore, it is outlined that knowledge access in the DeFi ecosystem often requires permission to digital devices, unswerving internet connectivity, and the ability to navigate various online programs and supplies. Investors coming up from the areas of underprivileged backgrounds with limited digital infrastructure may face noteworthy impediments in retrieving and obtaining cognizance about DeFi, further aggravating the knowledge gap.

3.4. Technical Complexity Leads to Access Barriers

The different technicalities therefore present a noteworthy challenge that has the potential of slowing down the proper uptake of the decentralised system of new forms of financing. The foundations of DeFi are highly sophisticated blockchain technologies, which inevitably result in vast gaps in comprehension and, consequently, limit the seamless implementation of DeFi by investors who possess no or negligible levels of technical expertise in this sphere (Uzougbo et. al., 2024). As for the technical background, it is mentioned that DeFi procedures and applications are archetypally built with particular encoding languages and development tools, including Solidity, Rust, and others, along with various blockchain development frameworks. Understanding these coding features and tools requires a vast amount of knowledge, thus presenting barriers for the newcomers and the existing investors, implementing the newly developed financing models. This is further emphasized on the premise that the underlying mechanisms of decentralised financing require the delegation of confidence in the unanimity devices like the Proof-of-Work (PoW) or Proof-of-Stake (PoS) to maintain the reliability and reassurance of the protocols. A lot of time, energy, and resources are required to be expended on analyzing the dynamics of such P2P networks, distributed structures and consensus instruments (Olutimehin, 2025). Additionally, it is pointed out that the main focus of decentralised finance aims to develop simple UIs for users that can interact with the DeFi applications, the technical part of DeFi applications and protocols become quite complex for upcoming investors. Navigating through decentralised applications, handling blockchain wallets, and engaging with sensible contracts gets quite complicated for investors thereby further widening the access barriers in the DeFi system.

3.5. Centralization Risks Lead to Technical Complexity

The ecosystem of decentralised finance (DeFi), which entails relying on extreme decentralisation is inextricably linked with the question of avoiding tendencies towards centralization. On the contrary, the technical nature of the DeFi protocols and applications poses definite possibilities of centralization that in turn raise the circumstantial technicality levels. Decentralised Finance is a concept that seeks to have a decentralised system, but the majority of them integrate several components that involve the use of centralised structures like cloud services, nodes that are hosted or centralised oracles among others. However, this reliance on centralised infrastructure can create new weaknesses including censorship or downtime for large segments of the system and the potential for external manipulation by powerful centralised actors. It is emphasized that mitigating these centralization risks typically entails the application of technical solutions that are both intricate and disrupt the status quo, including decentralised storage, the peer-to-peer network, and decentralised oracle solutions, which boost the technical difficulty of the DeFi realm. Moreover, it is highlighted that as DeFi protocols get more accepted, the scalability and performance shall turn out to be essential factors as DeFi protocols gradually integrate into investor's lives, and the question of scalability and velocity rises. It is a major technical endeavour to ensure both high bandwidth and low delay while at the same time adopting a decentralised model that is also secure.

It is pointed out that concerns such as rollup non-scalability, centralization of validators, and general DeFi application slowness can be removed by Sharding, Layer-2 scaling solutions like rollups and state channels, and cross-chain communication strategies imply additional technical challenges to mitigate these most alarming risks (Olutimehin, 2025; Uzougbo et. al., 2024; Popescu, 2020). Additionally, it is stated that the anonymity and data privacy of the users remains a core directing principle of decentralised finance. Nevertheless, a simultaneous guarantee of privacy and openness with the possibility of further investigation on pretty public blockchains is somewhat of a challenging task technically. The use of privacy-enhancing blockchain technologies, including zero-knowledge proofs, ring signatures, or confidential transactions affects not only the overall design of a single DeFi application but also raises the technical complexity of the process due to the specific properties of the mentioned cryptographic tools.

3.6. Centralization Risks Lead to Security Risks

The centralization risks inherent in the decentralised finance ecosystem pose serious security threats, which inevitably involve the probable opening of new and systemically dangerous threats thereby defeating the basic axiomatic safety of decentralised solutions. It is fostered that the concentration of functions and assets in DeFi can lead to developing specific points of weak links whenever a specific subject or a specific component becomes crucial for the entire network. The various centralised oracles, custodial services, or centralised governance points could render the system susceptible to premeditated attack, censorship, or doping by antagonistic players or nation-states. It is highlighted that the decentralisation process allows having single points of failure that may lead to the violation of the security and integrity of the entire DeFi. The centralised facility can be the cloud service or hosted nodes or servers and that requires noteworthy protection against DDoS attacks, hacking, or data breaches. Large projects employing centralised governance structures or development teams can also be vulnerable to social engineering, insider threat/coercion or may compromise governance protocols or insert code. Because of this, a centralised part of the DeFi realm, or the infrastructure within it, risks being targeted by governments, censored, or pressured in some way. This can result in funds being frozen; transactions being blocked or certain censorship mechanisms being introduced, which is against the fundamental belief of decentralised finance such as financial freedom and censorship. Centralised components in the DeFi ecosystem can lead to the obscurity of the computing steps and therefore become hard to trace and ensure that the system is pure. It is pointed out that with no or low transparency and built-in audit mechanism, various flaws could operate without control exposing a huge security risk to users and the ecosystem.

3.7. Technical Complexity Leads to Trust Concerns

It is imperative to recognize that technical complexity often creates substantial trust issues in DeFi, which may reduce the amount of adoption of such systems and challenge the principles of transparency and trustless systems on which this emerging financial model relies. Concerning the DeFi industry, the technical aspect of the defi protocols and applications like smart contracts, DEXs, yield farming, and others may sometimes be a little hard to apprehend by investors who are not so technically sound in this arena. This ignorance can lead to suspicions and doubts among new investors as they cannot significantly establish whether the systems, they engage in are reliable and efficient, especially when handling financial transactions. Moreover, it is outlined that DeFi protocols have many moving parts in terms of smart contracts' code and interconnectivity, implying that verifying all of them would be rather challenging (Berka & Dreyfus, 2021; Popescu, 2020 and Harvey & Rabetti, 2024). Despite having an open-source code audited by the community, the technicality presents a challenge for new investors to verify, hence decreasing the levels of trust in the security and reliability of such systems. However, although DeFi strives to maximize the transparency of transactions and interactions between protocols' components, the technical side of the interactions might be rather convoluted at times. It is not easy for investors to ascertain the key dependencies, processes, and threats in ensemble protocols, which may cause trust issues and doubts. It is further, stressed that cryptocurrencies and blockchain technology are not invulnerable as various attacks, such as scams, exploits, and rug pulls, impact the financial transactions occurring in the DeFi environment, thereby increasing the technology's complexity with financial risks.

3.8. Access Barriers Lead to Trust Concerns

Various restrictions and limitations in the DeFi ecosystem can cause trust issues, which can negatively affect the further development of this innovative finance system. It is accentuated that the DeFi protocols set up barriers to access which makes for the exclusion of some investors and this could lead to a lack of trust in the system in the long run. Various barriers such as technical constraints, inequitable distribution of assets, and low literacy levels regarding technology, tend to create various access barriers thereby further creating various trust issues in the DeFi ecosystem. It was highlighted that when a large investor's group cannot engage with the ecosystem or cognize its entirety a certain homogeneity is introduced, which can reduce decentralisation and bring into question the trustless nature of DeFi. It outlines that if access to DeFi is granted only to a few selected investors, or financial organizations with technical background, financial capital, or necessary IT support, knowledge and control over DeFi will be centralised in the system. There is a risk of entity control, where investors might feel that the system is being controlled, or manipulated, by certain dominant entities, which goes against the principles of decentralisation and trustlessness. It is further pointed out that significant access barriers can potentially lead to a lack of transparency or flexibility which is evident in the DeFi ecosystem. When investors cannot easily comprehend or authenticate the protocols, smart contracts, and governance structures because of technology or other impediments, then they will be sceptical and wary of engaging in crypto asset handling, possibly discouraging the broad uptake. Moreover, the lack of accreditation resources, technical skills, and community protection can make users of the platform or even investors more susceptible to fraudsters, scams, or negative influence within the DeFi environment. This vulnerability can drastically affect trust since the investor feels that the system is unsafe, easily hacked or is managed by individuals who benefit from the investor's ignorance or incompetence.

3.9. Security Risks Lead to Trust Concerns

The security issues in the DeFi ecosystem can significantly affect trust issues or agendas in this innovative ecosystem, which may limit the development and adoption in the financial sector. It is highlighted that DeFi protocols are based upon intricate technologies such as blockchain and cryptography as its foundation and having sophisticated security features is one of the foundational key features of any blockchain-based protocol. In this regard, it is argued that one of the primary security concerns of DeFi is when illicit users tend to exploit smart contracts, dApps, or other structural aspects of the ecosystem. It is underscored that three major events including the DAO hack, Poly Network exploit, and multiple flash lager attacks have already damaged the credibility of the ecosystem, and future investors shall perceive that developing a weak chain can be influenced by fraudsters (Mäkinen, 2021; Brown et al., 2020). The infrastructures within DeFi are generally pseudonymous and the barriers to entry for creating new projects are relatively low, there is the risk of scams or fraud and getting away with a rug pull or exit scam defrauding investors of their money. These actions can severely damage the overall financial ecosystem, as investors will have no trust in the system and feel like they have no recourse for protecting their investments, as the participants and developers of DeFi projects remain anonymous (Harvey & Rabetti, 2024). Although most DeFi protocols declare primary objectives of transparency through being open source, few are subjected to full code review and, even fewer, go through proper formal verification. Open or unaudited code can further engender mistrust as investors never are quite sure of the protocol's validity that they are interfacing with particularly when handling valuable person and/or corporate assets such as money. It is outlined that this kind of centralization or single points of failure creates new risks and vulnerabilities in systems that are supposed to be decentralised. Pseudonymity, anonymity, and any kind of reliance on centralised infrastructure, oracles, or other centralised institutions can become a problem if they raise trust issues for the users who focus on decentralisation and trustlessness (Kirişci, 2025).

3.10. Governance Issues in the DeFi Ecosystem

The DeFi ecosystem is currently facing significant concerns such as a lack of clarity about the regulation, integration problems, lack of information, entry hurdles, trust and issues related to governance arising out of technical characteristics. Since DeFi protocols do not follow strict and uncompromising rules, there is a lot of discrepancy and confusion in financial operations. This lack of a clear regulatory environment is likely to disrupt the growth and use of DeFi solutions because investors are rather hesitant to invest in a system where investment rules are not well established and legal frameworks are enormous. It is further emphasized that various governance structures within the DeFi financing system scuffle to make decisions and follow various guidelines and laws without adequate regulation. Each of the various platforms within the DeFi ecosystem operates on different complex blockchains, these have their own operating protocols, procedures, and mechanisms of decision. This difference makes it difficult to achieve interoperability between these protocols and can result in further fragmentation and conflicts over governance (Harvey & Rabetti, 2024; Amuzu-Sefordzi et al., 2018).

It is highlighted that DeFi is a vast and developing sector and it involves a momentous understanding of blockchain technology, cryptography and economic tools; investors do not have all the knowledge and competence to become players in the new financial system given its problematic nature in governance. It is important to note that despite DeFi's sound goal of being open to anyone, there are limitations such as technical know-how, reliable internet connection and inability to scheme through seemingly complex interfaces. These access barriers often result in the marginalization of certain investor groups from either participating in corporate governance or the concentration of this power in the hands of other select groups. However, it is pointed out that the decentralised and anonymous system of the DeFi protocols raises questions of trust specifically about the integrative management of the DeFi. Major issues that are of particular interest to investors include issues to do with the level of transparency and accountability of decisions made and the possibility of an oligopolistic manoeuvre by the key players in the systems. Most of the DeFi platforms have intricate smart contracts, cryptographic procedures, and even other financial instruments. These protocol features argue that technical complexity hinders investors from understanding and relying on governance proposals leading to financially unaware decision-making.

4. ROADMAP FOR SEAMLESS DeFi ADOPTION

DeFi is a stacked procedure wherein each kind of procedure contributes to the movement to the subsequent degree of offering decentralised financial services. It is indicated as a ten-step process and the elements highlighted here can be seen as interconnected because all the fragments take their obligatory part in the functioning of the DeFi ecosystem and the implementation of the goals set by the participants

(Kirişci, 2025; Harvey & Rabetti, 2024; Amuzu-Sefordzi et al., 2018; Mäkinen, 2021; Brown et al., 2020). Thus, the issues from the sphere of awareness, integration and scalability, governance and regulation, technological infrastructures, security and transparency in the solutions of such problems that took place establish the essential factors defining the further rise of the DeFi ecosystem. Several steps in the process of DeFi have been outlined in Figure 2 which can lead to the engagement, incorporation, and ultimately, the adoption of a new financing system.

The initial process is essentially a learning phase wherein investors initiate their engagement and participation in this new financial ecosystem. The first phase here pertains to awareness creation and sensitization of investors to the DeFi concept as well as the benefits possible to accrue from its implementation. The subsequent step pertains to integration and scalability. It is highlighted that as awareness and interest of the investors in DeFi is created, the next stage is to refine the integration issues and its scaling to the highest levels of engagement. This involves creating connection standards by which Dapp platforms and blockchains in the established ecosystem can interface with other DeFi structures. Besides, it significantly commands deploying scalability features for fixing various issues that arise due to a surge in the transaction throughput and the increasing demand and usage of DeFi networks among investors. Subsequently, policymakers and regulators are required to stabilize the regulatory policies to provide legal security for legal regulation of DeFi endeavours and other involved parties. It also involves embracing the creation of credible social architectures that work for decentralisation together with rightful and just decision-making systems. Furthermore, it is imperative to construct robust models and protocols in the DeFi systems set-up. This consists of developing interfaces which are user-friendly, complex and security-oriented smart contracts platforms as well as creating bridges between DeFi protocols and platforms.

The two main pillars of DeFi's ecosystem are transparency and security which serves as the fundamental principles harnessing its protocols (Kirişci, 2025; Mäkinen, 2021; González & Rendon, 2022 and Misra et al., 2024). This step entails guaranteeing that the system & applications expended strictly follow securitized protocols that protect coins & data belonging to the investors besides embracing decentralisation in the DeFi projects. DeFi platforms are familiar with security experience and contract transparency of contract, which will lay a foundation for confidence among potential investors. Leveraging a well-developed and growing confidence in the technological foundation of DeFi, the sixth stage is marked as adoption. This adequately involves the creation of multiple investor set-ups starting from single investors up to institutional ones by creating a clearly defined value proposition, active and visually attractive interfaces and the benefit of using that platform rather than traditional financial services.

The consequent stage involves developing a set of calls and interfaces to be targeted to a gigantic number of the populace starting from individual investors, to institutions to help in presenting a certain level of convenience together with the high utility compared to the traditional financial system. As adoption upsurges, it further involves integrating various DeFi protocols and platforms (Kirişci, 2025; Berka & Dreyfus, 2021; Popescu, 2020). This integration nurtures interoperability and composability, enabling investors to seamlessly navigate and leverage various DeFi services. An efficacious integration emphasizes trust in the ecosystem by exhibiting its ability to provide an organized and user-friendly experience. The subsequent stage involves building achieved outcomes of trust to, lead to higher engagement and participation with the designed DeFi solutions. This is because the more accredited the investors and stakeholders are with the decentralised finance application in terms of security, transparency, and reliability, the more up they will be in governance and the development of more application use of the protocol.

Figure 2. An exemplar summarizing a strategic blueprint for an effective DeFi adoption

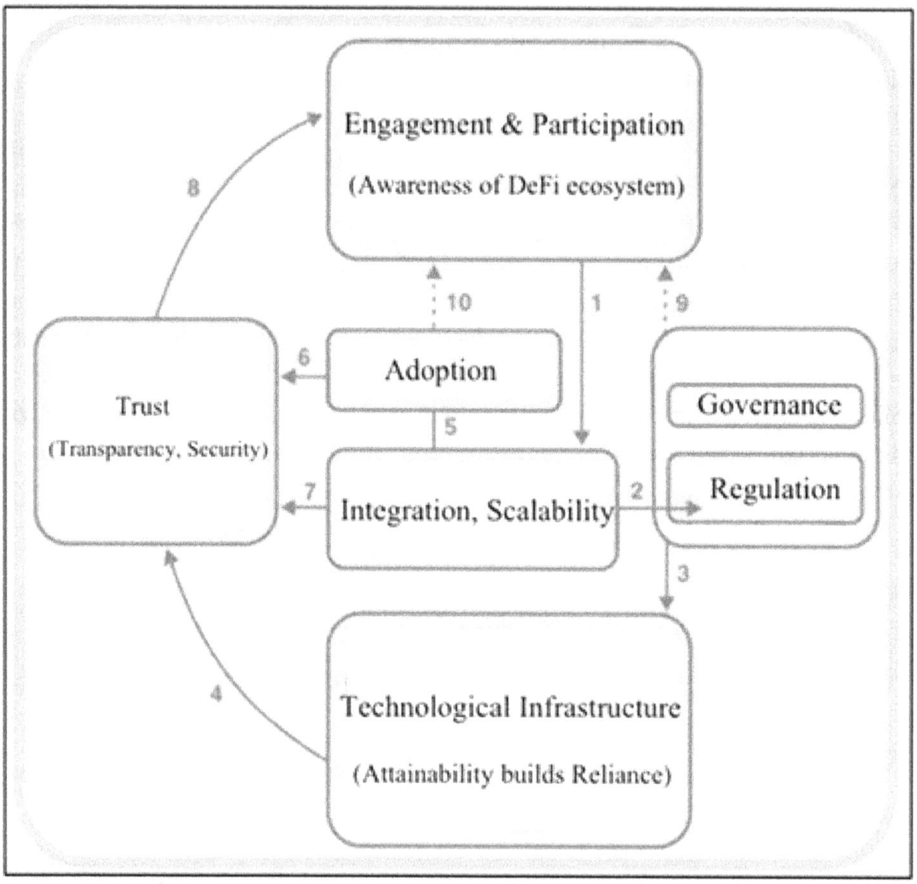

Source: Authors creation

Good governance built on the principles of decentralisation, openness, accountability, and involvement of investors will also ensure that users and all the relevant stakeholders are more involved in the process of the DeFi ecosystem. It also leads to better participation by the adopting parties besides guaranteeing the production of ownership within the DeFi ecosystem commensurate with their adoption. This, in turn, promotes the thought that adoption results in positive feedback that fuels engagement and participation levels even further (Harvey & Rabetti, 2024; Alamsyah et al., 2024; Amuzu-Sefordzi et al., 2018; Goda, 2021). This results in a greater number of users and investors in the ecosystem involved in contributing to its growth, management, and enhancement in alignment with the original goals of decentralisation and collaborative development.

5. IMPLICATIONS OF THE STUDY

The disruptive influence of decentralised finance (DeFi) on sustainable energy financing has noteworthy implications for policymakers and regulatory authorities. It is imperative for decision-makers to proactively address the challenges and opportunities presented by DeFi to foster a conducive environment for innovation while ensuring consumer protection and financial stability. The implications of the present study are outlined as follows:

5.1. Establishment of Comprehensive Regulatory Framework

It is imperative to institute a clear regulatory framework for the financial transactions governing sustainable projects in the DeFi ecosystem. The decentralised and global nature of DeFi poses challenges to traditional regulatory approaches, requiring policymakers to equalize between assisting innovation and mitigating potential risks. Constructing a robust regulatory framework shall permit the secure testing and experimentation of DeFi applications, enabling regulators to better comprehend the technology and its implications.

5.2. Addressing Uncertainties Governing DeFi Platforms

The policymakers shall suitably address the legal uncertainties surrounding the tokenization of assets, smart contracts, and decentralised autonomous organizations. Their legal status and associated rights are presently unclear and ambiguous. Policymakers must adequately simplify their legal status and its connected rights to enable adequate clarity for DeFi projects and its investors. This shall suitably foster trust, mitigate unsystematic risks and enable wider adoption of projects in the sustainable energy sector.

5.3. Fostering Inclusive Sustainability and Reliability

The policymakers shall suitably investigate the possibility of DeFi as a tool for enabling the underbanked population affordable funding for sustainable energy solutions. It is imperative to integrate the elements of decentralisation and transparency to ensure greater participation in sustainability projects at all levels. Moreover, the regulators shall give due accord to developing robust security measures, control checks, and management procedures that shall protect it's investors from risks of cybercrimes and fraud.

5.4. Creating an Adaptive Approach to DeFi Regulations

The policymakers must intend to adopt a policy of agility in their approach governing DeFi regulation. It is outlined that DeFi platforms are recognised by continuous technological innovation and therefore, continuous scrutinizing and appraisal of existing policies, rules and regulations must be fostered appropriately. Embracing a collaborative and consultative approach involving industry stakeholders, academia, and investor groups shall ensure that regulatory frameworks remain relevant and responsive to the evolving DeFi ecosystem.

5.5. Supporting Long-Term Viability of DeFi Projects

The policymakers shall duly focus on supporting the long-term viability of these projects and ensure that DeFi projects in the sustainable energy space are not short-lived or speculative. This involves fostering an ecosystem that incentivizes sound financial practices, encourages responsible risk-taking, and emphasizes the development of scalable, sustainable solutions. Regulatory frameworks should help mitigate the challenges interlinked with liquidity and token volatility, and ensure the creation of sustainable business models that prioritize long-term value creation over short-term profits.

5.6. Balancing Decentralization with Accountability

The policymakers must find a balance between maintaining decentralisation and ensuring accountability. In the absence of clear accountability, DeFi platforms shall become vulnerable to unethical practices, such as market manipulation and financial misreporting. To address this, regulatory authorities should consider implementing mechanisms that promote transparency and responsibility within decentralised projects, without hindering innovation. This could include enforcing governance standards, such as requiring transparent reporting of project finances or establishing independent auditing processes.

5.7. Facilitating Sustainable Investment Opportunities

Decentralised finance shall duly democratize access to sustainable energy investments, enabling individuals and smaller investors to participate in high-impact projects that were previously restricted to large institutional players. Policymakers could play a pivotal role in facilitating this democratization by ensuring that regulatory frameworks support fractionalized and tokenized investment opportunities in sustainable energy. This would lower the entry barrier for investors, diversify the sources of funding for green projects, and contribute to long-term sustainability goals.

6. CONCLUSION

Decentralized finance (DeFi) has emerged as a transformative tool for financing sustainable energy projects, offering innovative opportunities that leverage blockchain technology to reduce intermediaries, enhance transparency, and lower transaction costs. Through mechanisms such as tokenization and fractionalized ownership, DeFi enables more inclusive access to capital, allowing a broader range of investors—both retail and institutional—to participate in funding energy initiatives that were previously restricted to large financial players. The decentralized nature of DeFi eliminates the need for traditional intermediaries like banks or venture capitalists, making financial transactions faster and more cost-efficient while ensuring transparency through immutable, publicly accessible blockchain records. However, despite these advantages, the adoption of DeFi in energy financing remains contingent on overcoming several challenges. Regulatory uncertainty is a major hurdle, as the global and borderless nature of DeFi platforms complicates the application of existing financial regulations. This creates legal ambiguities that could undermine investor confidence and hinder widespread adoption. Therefore, it is essential for policymakers to develop clear, adaptable frameworks that accommodate the decentralized nature of these platforms while ensuring sufficient investor protection and market integrity. Security concerns also pose significant risks, as DeFi platforms are often vulnerable to cyberattacks, fraud, and smart contract failures. The lack of centralized oversight in DeFi can make it difficult to enforce consistent security standards, putting both investor funds and project integrity at risk. Addressing these vulnerabilities through robust security protocols, audits, and risk management practices is crucial for the long-term viability of DeFi in energy finance. Additionally, technical complexities such as scalability issues and interoperability between different DeFi platforms need to be addressed for these systems to function efficiently on a global scale. Future research should focus on optimizing decentralized autonomous organizations (DAOs), which are integral to DeFi governance, and exploring solutions to enhance data connectivity and verification mechanisms, ensuring the accuracy and reliability of transactions. Collaborative efforts between regulators, energy stakeholders, and DeFi developers will be key to unlocking the full potential of DeFi in sustainable energy financing. It is outlined that DeFi can drive financial inclusion, accelerate the transition to renewable energy, and contribute to a more sustainable, transparent, and efficient global energy market by addressing these challenges.

REFERENCES

Ahmed, S., & Liu, H. (2023). Decentralized finance and governance in low-trust economies: Evidence from Sub-Saharan Africa. *Journal of Emerging Financial Markets*, *12*(1), 45–61.

Ahuja, R., & Khandelwal, J. (2023). Challenges, Opportunities And Risk Analysis Of Adoption Of Decentralised Finance Applications. ICTACT Journal on Soft Computing, 14(1).

Alamsyah, A., Kusuma, G. N. W., & Ramadhani, D. P. (2024). A *Review on Decentralised Finance Ecosystems. Future Internet*, *16*(3), 76.

Alamsyah, A., Kusuma, G. N. W., & Ramadhani, D. P. (2024). A review on decentralized finance ecosystems. *Future Internet*, *16*(3), 76.

Amuzu-Sefordzi, B., Martinus, K., Tschakert, P., & Wills, R. (2018). Disruptive innovations and decentralised renewable energy systems in Africa: *A socio-technical review. Energy Research & Social Science*, *46*, 140–154.

Auer, R., Haslhofer, B., Kitzler, S., Saggese, P., & Victor, F. (2024). The technology of decentralized finance (DeFi). *Digital Finance*, *6*(1), 55–95.

Berka, A., & Dreyfus, M. (2021). Decentralisation and inclusivity in the energy sector: Preconditions, impacts and avenues for further research. *Renewable & Sustainable Energy Reviews*, *138*, 110663.

Bielenberg, A., Kerlin, M., Oppenheim, J., & Roberts, M. (2016). Financing change: How to mobilize private-sector financing for sustainable infrastructure. *McKinsey Center for Business and Environment*, 24-25.

Bongini, P. A., Mattassoglio, F., Pedrazzoli, A., & Vismara, S. (2025). Crypto ecosystem: Navigating the past, present, and future of decentralized finance. *The Journal of Technology Transfer*, •••, 1–22.

Brisbois, M. C. (2019). Powershifts: A framework for assessing the growing impact of decentralised ownership of energy transitions on political decision-making. *Energy Research & Social Science*, *50*, 151–161.

Brown, D., Hall, S., & Davis, M. E. (2020). What is prosumerism for? Exploring the normative dimensions of decentralised energy transitions. *Energy Research & Social Science*, *66*, 101475.

Chavez, F. J., & Gupta, R. (2021). Decentralized finance: A comprehensive review of technologies, applications, and challenges. *Journal of Blockchain Research, 10*(3), 56–72.

Garcia, J., & Lopez, M. (2022). Tokenized incentives for sustainable energy behavior: Evidence from Argentina. *Renewable Energy Review, 45*(3), 223–234.

Goda, D. R. (2021). The Evolution of Business Models in the Digital Age: Implications for Energy, Environment, and Finance. *Digitalization & Sustainability Review, 1*(1), 41–56.

González, D. M. L., & Rendon, J. G. (2022). Opportunities and challenges of mainstreaming distributed energy resources towards the transition to more efficient and resilient energy markets. *Renewable & Sustainable Energy Reviews, 157*, 112018.

Harvey, C. R., & Rabetti, D. (2024). International business and decentralised finance. *Journal of International Business Studies*, •••, 1–24.

Kayani, U., & Hasan, F. (2024). Unveiling Cryptocurrency Impact on Financial Markets and Traditional Banking Systems: Lessons for Sustainable Blockchain and Interdisciplinary Collaborations. *Journal of Risk and Financial Management, 17*(2), 58.

Kirişci, M. (2025). An integrated decision-making process for risk analysis of decentralized finance. *Neural Computing & Applications*, •••, 1–31.

Kumar, S., & Sharma, M. (2022). The role of DeFi in sustainable energy financing: Opportunities and risks. *International Journal of Renewable Energy, 45*(4), 231–249.

Mäkinen, S. J. (2021). Sustainable Disruptive Innovation (SDI): Initiating Systemic Changes by Reconfiguring User Preferences. In *Affordable and Clean Energy* (pp. 1205–1213). Springer International Publishing.

Misra, N., Gupta, S., & Rao, T. J. (2024). Fintech's role in green finance: Procuring funds for sustainable energy. *International Research Journal of Multidisciplinary Scope, 5*(02), 290–312.

Nguyen, T., Choudhury, M., & Okafor, N. (2023). Blockchain-enabled crowdfunding for sustainable energy: An empirical analysis. *Energy Finance Journal, 18*(2), 112–130.

Olutimehin, A. T. (2025). Assessing the effectiveness of cybersecurity frameworks in mitigating cyberattacks in the banking sector and its applicability to decentralized finance (DeFi). Available at *SSRN* 5133050.

Patel, N., & Wang, L. (2020). Blockchain and decentralized finance: Transforming energy markets and investment structures. *Energy Economics*, *42*(6), 102–118.

Pereira, G. I., Niesten, E., & Pinkse, J. (2022). Sustainable energy systems in the making: A study on business model adaptation in incumbent utilities. *Technological Forecasting and Social Change*, *174*, 121207.

Piñeiro-Chousa, J., López-Cabarcos, M. Á., Sevic, A., & González-López, I. (2022). A preliminary assessment of the performance of DeFi cryptocurrencies in relation to other financial assets, volatility, and user-generated content. *Technological Forecasting and Social Change*, *181*, 121740.

Popescu, A. D. (2020). Decentralised finance (defi)–the lego of finance. *Social Sciences and Education Research Review*, *7*(1), 321–349.

Richter, M. (2013). Business model innovation for sustainable energy: German utilities and renewable energy. *Energy Policy*, *62*, 1226–1237.

Rios, J., & Zhang, X. (2021). Blockchain technology and decentralized finance: A critical review of its implications for investment and energy markets. *Journal of Financial Innovation*, *8*(2), 1–19.

Santiago, V., Charifzadeh, M., & Herberger, T. A. (2025). Risks of decentralized finance and their potential negative effects on capital markets: The Terra-Luna case. *Studies in Economics and Finance*, *42*(3), 427–448.

Singh, A., & Singh, S. (2023). Regulatory frameworks for decentralized finance in energy investments: Challenges and opportunities. *Journal of Energy Regulation and Policy*, *12*(1), 89–101.

Smith, L., Kim, D., & Mwangi, J. (2023). Decentralized finance and peer-to-peer energy systems: A case study from Kenya. *International Journal of Green Finance*, *9*(4), 178–196.

Uzougbo, N. S., Ikegwu, C. G., & Adewusi, A. O. (2024). Regulatory frameworks for decentralized finance (DEFI): Challenges and opportunities. *GSC Advanced Research and Reviews*, *19*(02), 116–129.

Vinoth, S., & Srivastava, N. (2024). Disruptive Business Models and the Shift Towards Decentralised Marketplaces. In *Digital Technologies, Ethics, and Decentralisation in the Digital Era* (pp. 34–58). IGI Global.

Wang, Y., & Zeng, Q. (2024). Smart contracts and tokenization in green energy: A quantitative review of DeFi platforms. *Journal of Sustainable Finance & Investment*, *14*(1), 55–78.

Wieczorek, A. J., Rohracher, H., Bauknecht, D., Kubeczko, K., Bolwig, S., Valkering, P., & Maggiore, S. (2024). Citizen-led decentralised energy futures: Emerging rationales of energy system organisation. *Energy Research & Social Science*, *113*, 103557.

Zhou, S. (2024). Financial Innovation and Market Transformation in the Age of Digital Finance. Transactions on Economics. *Business and Management Research*, *6*, 118–127.

Zhuk, A. (2025). From Cypherpunks to Decentralized Finance: How Crypto-Anarchy is Redefining Legal and Economic Systems. Markets, *Globalization &. Developmental Review*, *9*(3).

Zumbansen, P. (2023). Runaway train? Decentralised finance and the myth of the private platform economy. *Transnational Legal Theory*, *14*(4), 413–452.

Chapter 5
The Evolution of Social Finance:
From Social Impact Bonds to Technological Innovation for Social Good

Rosella Carè
https://orcid.org/0000-0003-3222-0510
University of Waterloo, Canada & University Magna Graecia of Catanzaro, Italy

ABSTRACT

This chapter examines the evolution of social finance as a transformative approach that reorients financial practices toward measurable social and environmental goals. In response to the limits of traditional finance—focused on shareholder value and short-term profit—social finance has emerged as a multidimensional field encompassing microfinance, social impact bonds, impact investing, and equity crowdfunding. It highlights the strategic role of equity crowdfunding, the impact of digital innovation on scaling inclusive finance, and the emergence of sustainability-oriented FinTech. Key challenges—such as accountability, impact measurement, data governance, and financialization—are also discussed. The chapter concludes by outlining priorities for research and policy, emphasizing the need for conceptual clarity, robust evaluation tools, supportive regulation, and cross-sector collaboration. Social finance is framed not just as an alternative mechanism, but as a redefinition of finance's role in advancing inclusive and sustainable societies.

DOI: 10.4018/979-8-3693-9551-6.ch005

1. INTRODUCTION

In recent years, the financial system has been increasingly called upon to play a transformative role in addressing some of the most pressing challenges of our time, including rising social inequalities, climate change, and systemic exclusion. These challenges have exposed the limitations of traditional financial paradigms centered on shareholder value maximization and short-term profitability, prompting a growing interest in alternative models that embed social and environmental considerations into financial decision-making (Nicholls & Emerson, 2015; Lagoarde-Segot, 2016). Within this context, social finance (SF) has emerged as a multidimensional and evolving field that seeks to align capital allocation with the pursuit of measurable societal outcomes (Carè & Weber, 2023).

Social finance encompasses a wide array of financial mechanisms—such as microfinance, social impact bonds (SIBs), impact investing, and crowdfunding—designed to generate social value alongside economic returns (Carè & Weber, 2023). Unlike mainstream financial practices, which often treat social impact as ancillary, social finance explicitly prioritizes the creation of public good through innovative funding models and collaborative governance structures. At the same time, the growing convergence of social finance with technological innovation has further expanded its reach, introducing new forms of digital intermediation and enabling broader participation in impact-driven initiatives.

This chapter aims to provide a comprehensive and critical overview of the current landscape of social finance and its evolving intersection with technology and entrepreneurship. By examining key domains such as social innovation, equity crowdfunding, public–private partnerships, and the rise of Impact-Oriented FinTech, the chapter highlights both the opportunities and tensions embedded in the reconfiguration of finance as a social institution.

The remainder of the chapter is structured as follows. Section 2 reviews the foundations of social finance and its role in fostering social innovation, with particular attention to definitional challenges and emerging research streams. Section 3 focuses on the integration of equity crowdfunding as a strategic component of the social finance ecosystem. Section 4 examines how digital technologies are reshaping financial inclusion, accountability, and scalability within social finance. Section 5 delves into the consolidation of a new FinTech paradigm oriented toward social and environmental impact, discussing emerging models, challenges in impact measurement, and implications for policy and research. Section 6 provides concluding reflections, while Section 7 offers a synthesis of key messages and outlines future directions for advancing this dynamic field.

2. SOCIAL FINANCE AND ITS ROLE IN PROMOTING SOCIAL INNOVATION

In recent decades, the concept of Social Finance has gained significant attention within academic and policy circles, driven largely by the global financial crisis of 2007–2009. This crisis acted as a catalyst, prompting both scholars and practitioners to critically reexamine the fundamental assumptions and paradigms underlying mainstream finance (Lagoarde-Segot, 2016; Carè et al., 2018). The limitations and failures of traditional financial mechanisms in addressing societal inequalities and environmental challenges have led to an increased interest in more inclusive financial approaches, capable of mobilizing resources specifically toward achieving tangible and measurable social impacts (Geobey et al., 2012; Carè et al., 2018; Rizzi et al., 2018; Carè & Weber, 2023).

Despite its growing prominence, SF still faces terminological ambiguity and conceptual fragmentation (Carè & Weber, 2023). The academic discourse continues to exhibit significant heterogeneity, often conflating social finance with related but distinct concepts such as socially responsible investing (SRI), impact investing, ethical banking, and sustainable finance (Weber, 2016; Connaker & Madsbjerg, 2019; Langley, 2020). For instance, Laing et al. (2012) characterize SF as one of the three principal domains of impact investing, alongside clean technology and microfinance. Conversely, Weber and Duan (2012) suggest a distinct tripartite classification, categorizing SF into impact investing, social banking, and microfinance. Such conceptual divergence underscores the complexity inherent in defining SF, highlighting the need for greater clarity and theoretical integration in this evolving research area.

At its core, SF involves capital allocation strategies explicitly designed to generate positive societal and environmental outcomes, typically without compromising, and in some cases intentionally moderating, traditional financial returns (Nicholls & Emerson, 2015). This approach directly challenges the conventional finance paradigm, as it incorporates ethical priorities, ecological considerations, and long-term public welfare into investment decisions, effectively aligning finance with broader societal objectives (Emerson, 2003; Vandemeulebroucke et al., 2010). This repositioning of finance as a socially constructed means of achieving common goals significantly differentiates SF from mainstream finance, emphasizing values such as solidarity, responsibility, and social justice (Snick, 2021).

Social finance operates through a diverse range of financial instruments, including microfinance, crowdfunding, social impact bonds (SIBs), venture philanthropy, and mission-related investments (Nicholls & Emerson, 2015; Andrikopoulos, 2020). Among these, social impact bonds have gained particular recognition as innovative financial mechanisms capable of fostering collaboration between public entities and private investors by aligning financial incentives with social outcomes (Carè & De Lisa, 2019). By incorporating a pay-for-success model, SIBs effectively transfer project risks from the public to the private sector, potentially increasing the efficiency and accountability of social service delivery (Broccardo & Mazzuca, 2019; Edmiston & Nicholls, 2018).

Crucially, SF is closely linked to the notion of social innovation, which refers to novel solutions, strategies, or processes that effectively address persistent social and environmental problems, creating value for society as a whole (Moore et al., 2012). Social enterprises (SEs), characterized by their dual commitment to social missions and entrepreneurial innovation, have emerged as essential actors driving social innovation. However, SEs frequently encounter significant financial barriers due to their hybrid nature, which blends non-profit objectives with market-driven strategies, thereby complicating traditional assessments of financial risk and return (Nicholls, 2010; Defourny & Nyssens, 2010; Lehner & Kansikas, 2012). Consequently, SF serves as a critical source of financing for social enterprises, offering tailored financial solutions that accommodate their unique operational models and missions (Geobey et al., 2012; Moore et al., 2012).

The European Union has actively encouraged the integration of SF into broader strategies aimed at promoting social entrepreneurship, recognizing the importance of these initiatives for sustainable economic growth and local community development. For instance, various European countries have leveraged financial resources such as the European Social Fund (ESF) to create supportive ecosystems that facilitate access to social finance for SEs, thereby fostering innovative social projects capable of addressing pressing societal challenges (European Commission, 2016).

Despite this growing momentum, scholarly literature on social finance remains comparatively underdeveloped, with academic contributions primarily concentrated in niche journals or specialized conferences rather than mainstream finance outlets. This indicates an ongoing gap between the potential impact of SF practices and their recognition within traditional financial scholarship. A recent bibliometric analysis of the SF literature identified distinct clusters of research, particularly focusing on impact investing, social entrepreneurship, social impact bonds, and social innovation (Carè et al., 2023). While these clusters highlight significant developments within the field, they also reflect a fragmented scholarly landscape lacking cohesive theoretical frameworks or universally accepted definitions.

Furthermore, the small size of the scholarly community actively engaged in SF research suggests the field remains relatively nascent, despite its practical relevance and policy importance (Carè et al., 2023). Prominent academic contributors have provided foundational insights, yet broader integration of SF within mainstream financial theory and practice remains limited (Carè & Weber, 2023). This could be attributed partly to the inherent interdisciplinary nature of SF, which intersects economics, finance, management, ethics, and public policy, making theoretical and empirical consensus challenging (Nicholls & Emerson, 2015; Lagoarde-Segot & Paranque, 2017).

Addressing these limitations requires further conceptual clarity, rigorous empirical studies, and greater integration between SF and mainstream financial theories. Specifically, future research should aim to develop more robust methodologies for evaluating the social impacts and financial sustainability of SF initiatives. Moreover, enhancing dialogue between finance scholars and practitioners can foster mutual understanding and promote the broader recognition of SF as a legitimate and essential component of contemporary financial systems (Carè et al., 2018).

Overall, social finance represents a critical advancement in aligning financial practices with societal and environmental objectives, offering a promising pathway for fostering impactful social innovations. Although the field has experienced considerable growth, significant theoretical and empirical gaps remain, presenting ample opportunities for future scholarly exploration aimed at advancing SF as a cohesive, recognized, and integrated domain within the broader discipline of finance.

2.1. Emerging Trends and Issues in Social Finance

Recent research by Carè and Weber (2025), employing bibliometric and co-word analysis, has provided an extensive overview of the social finance research landscape. Their findings indicate that the field of social finance encompasses distinct yet interconnected research streams, each highlighting different aspects of how finance can serve broader social purposes and contribute positively to societal change. The following subsections explore and expand upon the major research areas identified in their study, discussing their key concepts, developments, and implications for both theory and practice.

2.2 Religious and Ethical Dimensions in Social Finance

The intersection of ethical, moral, and religious principles with financial practices has emerged as a relevant research area within social finance (Carè & Weber, 2023). In particular, social banking and Islamic finance exemplify financial models deeply rooted in ethical commitments, transparency, and moral responsibility. Social banks explicitly aim to achieve positive social outcomes and reject speculative transactions, thereby redefining traditional banking practices. Similarly, Islamic finance integrates ethical investment principles guided by Shariah law, emphasizing economic justice, equitable wealth distribution, and societal welfare (Jouti, 2019; Andrikopoulos, 2020). This ethical orientation challenges conventional finance by promoting financial inclusion, social cohesion, and sustainable development.

2.3 Impact Investing and Social Entrepreneurship

Impact investing has gained significant attention as a mechanism to mobilize private capital toward enterprises that generate measurable social or environmental impact alongside financial returns (Carè & Weber, 2023). This financial approach directly supports social entrepreneurship by providing resources necessary for innovation in addressing societal challenges (Phillips et al., 2015). Impact investors, driven by both profit and purpose, are increasingly influential in shaping the landscape of sustainable business, offering tailored financing solutions such as venture philanthropy and equity crowdfunding, thereby enabling social enterprises to scale their impact effectively (Nicholls & Emerson, 2015).

2.4 Social Finance, Public Policies, and the Third Sector

Another significant research area explores how social finance interacts with public policies, reshaping welfare strategies and public-sector funding through mechanisms inspired by New Public Management paradigms (Carè & Weber, 2023). Governments increasingly view social finance as a strategic approach to managing welfare budgets more effectively, adopting outcome-based financing tools such as Social Impact Bonds (SIBs) to leverage private investments and enhance service delivery efficiency (Edmiston & Nicholls, 2018; Fraser et al., 2018). However, this integration has also sparked debates about potential financialization and marketization of social policy, raising concerns regarding accountability, transaction costs, and the alignment of incentives among diverse stakeholders (Joy & Shields, 2013; Cooper et al., 2016).

2.5 Social Impact Bonds: Innovative Instruments for Public Good

SIBs represent a specialized area of social finance research identified as crucial for facilitating public-private collaboration to address complex societal issues (Carè & Weber, 2023). By linking investor returns directly to measurable social outcomes, SIBs incentivize performance and shift financial risks from public bodies to private investors, fostering innovative approaches to social service provision. Despite their theoretical appeal and practical experimentation, the global diffusion of SIBs remains limited due to their inherent complexity, evaluation challenges, and high transaction costs (Sinclair et al., 2021; Albertson & Fox, 2019). Nonetheless, SIBs are increasingly seen as instrumental tools aligned with broader global objectives, such as the United Nations' Sustainable Development Goals (SDGs).

2.6 Crowdfunding and Technological Innovation in Sustainable Entrepreneurship

Finally, technological innovation, notably crowdfunding and Fintech has emerged as a powerful enabler within social finance, significantly reshaping the dynamics of capital accessibility for sustainable entrepreneurs (Carè & Weber, 2023). Crowdfunding platforms democratize access to funding, allowing entrepreneurs to tap into resources from diverse retail investors who share a commitment to sustainability and social impact. Simultaneously, fintech innovations support financial inclusion and enable more efficient alignment of private capital with sustainable and socially responsible initiatives. These technological advancements not only bridge traditional financing gaps but also promote more inclusive economic growth aligned with sustainability and social equity principles (Arner et al., 2020).

3. INTEGRATING EQUITY CROWDFUNDING INTO SOCIAL FINANCE: A STRATEGIC AVENUE FOR SUSTAINABLE IMPACT

In addressing the persistent funding challenges faced by initiatives with a social or environmental mission, equity crowdfunding emerges as a pivotal financial mechanism embedded within the broader realm of social finance. Social finance encompasses a range of financial activities explicitly designed to achieve measurable social and environmental impacts alongside economic returns (Spiess-Knafl & Jansen, 2014). Within this innovative financing ecosystem, equity crowdfunding represents a strategic solution uniquely suited to bridge the funding gap typically encountered by social enterprises (SEs), entities that often face difficulties attracting traditional forms of investment due to their unconventional risk-return profiles and hybrid organizational structures (Austin et al., 2006; Doherty et al., 2014; Ometto et al., 2019).

Distinct from traditional funding channels such as banks, venture capital, and private equity—which typically prioritize financial returns over societal impact (Lyons & Kickul, 2013)—equity crowdfunding mobilizes the collective financial contributions of numerous socially motivated investors via digital platforms. These investors acquire equity stakes in SEs, effectively aligning their long-term financial interests with the mission-driven objectives of the enterprises they support. By holding equity, investors not only provide vital capital but also become committed stakeholders in the enterprise's growth trajectory, creating a sustained partnership that extends beyond mere transactional interactions and enhances organizational resilience (Carè et al., 2018; Cosma et al., 2019).

The integration of equity crowdfunding into the social finance landscape is particularly impactful due to its intrinsic promotion of transparency and rigorous impact measurement—core tenets of social finance (Tenner & Hörisch, 2021). SEs utilizing equity crowdfunding are compelled to clearly articulate their social and environmental objectives, thereby increasing accountability to investors. This heightened transparency is instrumental in attracting and maintaining investor confidence, offering potential to significantly expand the investor base beyond conventional capital providers (Hussain et al., 2023; Mollick, 2012). Thus, equity crowdfunding acts as a facilitator of enhanced governance and impact accountability within social entrepreneurship.

Furthermore, specialized equity crowdfunding platforms dedicated to social and environmental impact—such as La Bolsa Social and Lita.Co—or more generalist platforms with clear social mandates like FrontFundr and WeFunder, play a crucial intermediary role by effectively matching SEs with impact-oriented investors (Rey-Martí et al., 2019; FrontFundr, n.d.; Wefunder, 2021). These platforms operate not merely as financial intermediaries but as catalysts for social innovation, providing critical infrastructure that supports SEs across various developmental stages, from early seed funding through growth and maturity phases (Carè et al., 2018; Vecchi et al., 2017). The resulting long-term financial and strategic partnerships cultivated through these platforms significantly bolster the capacity of SEs to achieve sustained societal impact.

Overall, equity crowdfunding occupies a vital and increasingly influential role within social finance, distinctively blending financial investment with explicit societal impact objectives. This equity-based approach not only addresses immediate capital needs but also fosters durable relationships between SEs and their investors, thereby promoting long-term stability, growth, and measurable social and environmental outcomes. Given the transformative potential demonstrated by this innovative financing model, further research, policy development, and practical refinement of equity crowdfunding strategies hold significant promise for advancing the effectiveness and scalability of social entrepreneurship initiatives globally.

4. TECHNOLOGY AND THE EVOLUTION OF SOCIAL FINANCE

The progressive evolution of social finance has been significantly influenced by technological innovation, which has reshaped not only the mechanisms of financial intermediation but also the ways in which social and environmental goals are pursued and achieved. In particular, digital technologies have played a catalytic role in expanding access to finance for social enterprises (SEs), scaling impact-driven investments, and enhancing transparency and accountability within the sector (Carè et al., 2023).

Traditionally, social finance has suffered from informational asymmetries, high transaction costs, and limited scalability (Nicholls & Tomkinson, 2015). Technological advancements, notably in FinTech, have addressed these structural inefficiencies by introducing digital platforms that facilitate more inclusive, efficient, and democratized access to capital. Platforms dedicated to equity crowdfunding, peer-to-peer lending, and impact investing represent a paradigm shift, offering SEs alternative routes to mobilize financial resources while simultaneously fostering communities of socially motivated investors (Carè et al., 2023).

One of the most profound transformations enabled by technology is the emergence of crowdfunding platforms tailored to social and environmental objectives. These platforms reduce reliance on traditional financial intermediaries, which historically prioritized financial returns over societal impact, and instead allow a broader base of small investors to directly support projects aligned with their personal values (Carè et al., 2023). By leveraging technologies such as online portals, real-time data analytics, and blockchain solutions for traceability, crowdfunding platforms not only improve the efficiency of fund allocation but also enhance trust through increased transparency and verifiability of social impact claims.

Furthermore, technology has been instrumental in promoting financial inclusion within social finance ecosystems. Digital infrastructures lower entry barriers for underserved and marginalized groups, allowing SEs operating in remote or economically disadvantaged regions to access funding opportunities that were previously unattainable (Carè et al., 2023). This democratization of finance contributes to a more equitable distribution of resources and amplifies the potential for achieving SDGs by facilitating the scaling of social innovation initiatives beyond local contexts.

Importantly, technological innovations also redefine how impact is measured, communicated, and verified. Traditional impact assessment practices—often static, costly, and opaque—are increasingly supplemented or replaced by dynamic, technology-driven tools capable of real-time impact monitoring. Digital dashboards, AI-powered data analytics, and blockchain-based impact tracking systems empower SEs to provide investors with continuous updates on the social and environmental outcomes achieved, thus fostering a culture of accountability and evidence-based reporting (Carè et al., 2023).

Nevertheless, the integration of technology into social finance is not devoid of challenges. Concerns persist regarding the digital divide, data privacy, cybersecurity, and the potential depersonalization of investor-SE relationships (Carè et al., 2023). Moreover, while technological solutions can enhance the efficiency and scalability of social finance, they do not automatically guarantee inclusivity or impact integrity; deliberate governance mechanisms and regulatory frameworks are needed to ensure that technological advancements align with the fundamental mission of social finance to prioritize social and environmental value over purely financial metrics.

In conclusion, technology constitutes a transformative force within social finance, facilitating broader participation, enhancing operational efficiency, improving transparency, and enabling scalable impact measurement. However, the responsible governance of these technological innovations remains critical to ensuring that the ultimate goal of social finance—the pursuit of measurable, long-term social and environmental impact—is preserved and strengthened rather than diluted in the digital age.

5. TOWARDS A NEW PARADIGM OF IMPACT-ORIENTED FINTECH

Recent developments in the FinTech sector suggest the consolidation of a new paradigm in which financial innovation is increasingly mobilized to generate measurable social and environmental value. While early generations of FinTech focused primarily on improving efficiency, speed, and cost-effectiveness in the delivery of financial services, a growing number of enterprises are now explicitly integrating sustainability objectives into their core business strategies. This evolution reflects a broader transformation in the purpose of financial technologies, from tools of disruption and convenience to vehicles for social change and development.

Rather than treating impact as a peripheral or secondary concern, a subset of FinTech firms—commonly referred to as "Impact FinTechs"—places the achievement of the SDGs at the center of their mission. These companies challenge the notion that financial and impact objectives are necessarily in conflict, adopting business models that seek to balance profitability with the delivery of social value. As documented by Carè et al. (2023), this shift is not merely rhetorical, but operational: it involves reconfiguring technological infrastructures, value chains, and stakeholder relationships to ensure that financial services contribute directly to inclusive growth, environmental sustainability, and the well-being of underserved populations.

5.1 From Financial Innovation to Impact Intentionality

The evolving FinTech landscape is increasingly defined by a shift from financial efficiency toward intentional contributions to the SDGs. As Carè et al. (2023) observe, an emerging class of "Impact FinTech" ventures combines the delivery of financial services with the explicit aim of addressing social and environmental needs. These firms operate under the assumption that financial value and positive impact are not mutually exclusive, but mutually reinforcing (Carè et al., 2023, p. 6). This reconceptualization echoes broader calls for finance to be reoriented toward the public good (Rizzello & Kabli, 2020), and responds to critical development challenges such as financial exclusion and lack of access to capital for underserved groups.

5.2 Business Model Innovation and the Delivery of Impact

Impact-oriented FinTech firms are distinguished by their hybrid business models, which embed sustainability within core operations and extend value creation across both economic and non-economic dimensions. As highlighted in Carè et al. (2023), these firms often adopt structures—such as B2B2C models—that allow them to serve vulnerable populations while leveraging partnerships with larger institutions (Carè et al., 2023, p. 9). This aligns with the broader literature on sustainable business model innovation, which emphasizes integrated value propositions and stakeholder collaboration (Bocken et al., 2014; Joyce & Paquin, 2016). Moreover, the SDG alignment pursued by these firms is not limited to philanthropy or peripheral CSR activities: it is embedded in the digital architecture of their services and platforms (Puschmann et al., 2020; Ayala, 2021).

5.3 Challenges of Impact Measurement and Future Integration

Despite their promise, Impact FinTechs face substantial challenges in demonstrating and communicating their non-financial performance. Standardized metrics for impact measurement remain underdeveloped, limiting comparability and investor confidence. As discussed by Van der Waal & Thijssens (2020) and Calabrese et al. (2021), current ESG frameworks are often insufficient to capture the full scope of FinTech contributions to SDGs. Some firms are experimenting with proprietary tools to track user-level environmental outcomes, such as carbon tracking, but this raises questions about data transparency, accountability, and integration with mainstream financial reporting standards (Szennay et al., 2019; Rosati & Faria, 2019; Pizzi et al., 2021). Addressing these gaps requires collaborative efforts among regulators, technology providers, and researchers to co-develop standards that reflect the unique nature of digital and impact-driven finance.

5.4 Implications for Research, Policy, and Practice

The emergence of Impact-Oriented FinTech calls for a rethinking of traditional regulatory, academic, and investment frameworks. From a policy perspective, there is a need for regulatory environments that are both enabling and protective: enabling, in the sense of fostering innovation and experimentation through regulatory sandboxes and open banking regimes; and protective, in ensuring that firms claiming social impact are subject to transparency, accountability, and proper certification mechanisms. Given the current lack of harmonized metrics, policymakers should prioritize the development of impact reporting standards tailored to digital finance, building on the limitations observed in current ESG disclosure regimes (Van der Waal & Thijssens, 2020; Calabrese et al., 2021).

In terms of practice, financial institutions and investors need to adopt due diligence processes that incorporate social and environmental criteria into risk–return analyses, particularly for partnerships involving early-stage Impact FinTech ventures. This may involve the refinement of hybrid performance indicators or the use of real-time data platforms for monitoring impact outcomes. Platforms enabling user-level sustainability choices—such as carbon tracking and SDG-linked wallets—should be supported through collaborative ecosystems that include financial incumbents, technology firms, and civil society actors (Carè et al., 2023; Rosati & Faria, 2019).

From a research perspective, the conceptualization of Impact FinTech as a distinct paradigm opens several avenues for theoretical development and empirical inquiry. Scholars should explore how digital infrastructures influence the governance of social value, and how technological innovation affects the alignment—or misalignment—between financial and societal incentives. Moreover, further work is needed to clarify the boundaries between Impact FinTech, sustainable finance, and social finance, particularly in terms of institutional configurations, business model typologies, and stakeholder networks (Ayala, 2021; Puschmann et al., 2020). A robust research agenda should aim to integrate insights from development studies, innovation management, and critical finance to advance a deeper understanding of how FinTech can contribute meaningfully to inclusive and sustainable development.

6. CONCLUSION

This chapter examined the evolution of social finance as a multidimensional response to the limitations of traditional financial paradigms, particularly in the wake of recurring economic crises and persistent social inequalities. Drawing on a wide array of financial instruments - including SIBs, equity crowdfunding, and emerging FinTech applications - the analysis has shown how social finance operates as both a practical mechanism for funding socially beneficial initiatives and a conceptual challenge to dominant market-based logics.

At its core, social finance represents a paradigmatic shift: it redefines the purpose of capital allocation by placing social and environmental objectives at the center of financial decision-making. Rather than pursuing profit maximization in isolation, the instruments and models discussed throughout this chapter emphasize outcome-orientation, stakeholder engagement, and long-term value creation. This has important implications for the role of finance in democratic societies, as it positions financial innovation as a tool not merely for efficiency, but for inclusion, accountability, and systemic change.

Yet, as this chapter has argued, the transformative potential of social finance is not without tensions. The integration of private capital into public service delivery, for example, raises questions about financialization, risk transfer, and the erosion of public accountability. Similarly, while FinTech-driven models offer new opportunities for scalability and impact transparency, they also introduce novel risks related to data governance, algorithmic exclusion, and impact-washing.

Future research must grapple with these contradictions by adopting more critical, interdisciplinary, and context-sensitive approaches. In particular, scholars and practitioners must work together to refine measurement frameworks, clarify the boundaries and definitions within the field, and assess the real-world outcomes of social finance initiatives across different institutional and geographical settings. From a policy standpoint, enabling regulatory environments, outcome-oriented public procurement strategies, and hybrid financing structures will be crucial to unlock the full potential of social finance in achieving the SDGs.

In sum, social finance should not be seen merely as an alternative funding mechanism, but as part of a broader rethinking of how financial systems can—and should—contribute to social progress. Its success will ultimately depend on our collective ability to balance innovation with equity, efficiency with justice, and financial performance with lasting societal value.

KEY MESSAGES AND FUTURE PERSPECTIVES

This chapter has underscored the growing relevance of social finance as a framework for aligning financial mechanisms with social and environmental goals. Several forward-looking insights can be drawn from the current evolution of this field:

- Finance is undergoing a purpose shift, with impact-oriented models—such as SIBs, equity crowdfunding, and FinTech for sustainability—redefining the role of capital in addressing societal challenges.
- Hybrid financial architectures are becoming central to bridging public, private, and community interests, yet they require appropriate governance frameworks and accountability mechanisms to avoid mission drift or capture.
- Technology plays a dual role: as an enabler of financial inclusion and scalable impact, and as a potential source of new exclusion risks, measurement distortions, and ethical dilemmas in data governance.

- Standardization and evaluation remain open challenges, particularly in measuring impact across heterogeneous contexts and aligning incentives among diverse actors.

Looking forward, future progress in this field depends on three key pillars:

(1) advancing interdisciplinary research to clarify conceptual boundaries and impact pathways;
(2) designing enabling policy environments that balance innovation with regulation;
(3) fostering collaborative ecosystems involving social enterprises, institutional investors, regulators, and digital innovators.

Social finance is no longer a niche but a critical component of the transition toward more inclusive and sustainable financial systems. Its consolidation will depend on our collective ability to rethink how financial tools are designed, governed, and evaluated.

ACKNOWLEDGEMENT

This project has received funding from the European Union's Horizon 2020 research and innovation program under the Marie Skłodowska-Curie grant agreement number 892293.

REFERENCES

Albertson, K., & Fox, C. (2019). The marketisation of rehabilitation: Some economic considerations. *Probation Journal*, *66*(1), 25–42.

Andrikopoulos, A. (2020). Delineating social finance. *International Review of Financial Analysis*, *70*, 101519. DOI: 10.1016/j.irfa.2020.101519

Arner, D. W., Buckley, R. P., Zetzsche, D. A., & Robin, V. (2020). Sustainability, FinTech and financial inclusion. *European Business Organization Law Review*, *21*(1), 7–35. DOI: 10.1007/s40804-020-00183-y

Austin, J., Stevenson, H., & Wei–Skillern, J. (2006). Social and commercial entrepreneurship: Same, different, or both? *Entrepreneurship Theory and Practice*, *30*(1), 1–22.

Ayala, T. 2021. Financial technology and social impact: socialfintech sector. Soc. FinTech. https://socialfintech.org/social-fintech-sector

Bocken, N. M., Short, S. W., Rana, P., & Evans, S. (2014). A literature and practice review to develop sustainable business model archetypes. *Journal of Cleaner Production*, *65*, 42–56.

Broccardo, E., & Mazzuca, M. (2019). Social impact bonds: The evolution of research and a review of the academic literature. *Corporate Social Responsibility and Environmental Management*, *27*(3), 1316–1332. DOI: 10.1002/csr.1886

Calabrese, A., Costa, R., Gastaldi, M., Ghiron, N. L., & Montalvan, R. A. V. (2021). Implications for sustainable development goals: A framework to assess company disclosure in sustainability reporting. *Journal of Cleaner Production*, *319*, 128624. DOI: 10.1016/j.jclepro.2021.128624

Carè, R., & De Lisa, R. (2019). Social impact bonds: A new tool to finance social services. *Journal of Cleaner Production*, *210*, 1434–1447.

Carè, R., Trotta, A., & Rizzello, A. (2018). An alternative finance approach for a more sustainable financial system. In Walker, T., Kibsey, S. D., & Crichton, R. (Eds.), *Designing a Sustainable Financial System: Development Goals and Socio-Ecological Responsibility* (pp. 17–63). Springer., DOI: 10.1007/978-3-319-66387-6_2

Carè, R., & Weber, O. (2023). What's in a name? Exploring the intellectual structure of social finance. *International Journal of Emerging Markets*, *20*(4), 1617–1640.

Carè, S., Trotta, A., Carè, R., & Rizzello, A. (2018). Crowdfunding for the development of smart cities. *Business Horizons*, *61*(4), 501–509.

Connaker, A., & Madsbjerg, S. (2019). The state of socially responsible investing. *Harvard Business Review*, *17*, •••. https://hbr.org/2019/01/the-state-of-socially-responsible-investing

Cooper, C., Graham, C., & Hinick, D. (2016). Social impact bonds: The securitization of the homeless. *Accounting, Organizations and Society*, *55*, 63–82. DOI: 10.1016/j.aos.2016.10.003

Cosma, S., Grasso, A. G., Pagliacci, F., & Pedrazzoli, A. (2019). Is Equity Crowdfunding a Good Tool for Social Enterprises?. *Socially Responsible Investments: The Crossroads Between Institutional and Retail Investors*, 149-170.

Defourny, J., & Nyssens, M. (2010). Conceptions of social enterprise and social entrepreneurship in Europe and the United States: Convergences and divergences. *Journal of Social Entrepreneurship*, *1*(1), 32–53. DOI: 10.1080/19420670903442053

Doherty, B., Haugh, H., & Lyon, F. (2014). Social enterprises as hybrid organizations: A review and research agenda. *International Journal of Management Reviews*, *16*(4), 417–436.

Edmiston, D., & Nicholls, A. (2018). Social impact bonds: The role of private capital in outcome-based commissioning. *Journal of Social Policy*, *47*(1), 57–76.

Emerson, J. (2003). The blended value proposition: Integrating social and financial returns. *California Management Review*, *45*(4), 35–51. DOI: 10.2307/41166187

European Commission. (2016). *A recipe book for social finance*.

Fraser, A., Tan, S., Lagarde, M., & Mays, N. (2018). Narratives of promise, narratives of caution: A review of the literature on Social Impact Bonds. *Social Policy and Administration*, *52*(1), 4–28. DOI: 10.1111/spol.12260

FrontFundr. (n.d.). About Us. Retrieved from http://www.frontfundr.com/

Geobey, S., Westley, F. R., & Weber, O. (2012). Enabling social innovation through developmental social finance. *Journal of Social Entrepreneurship*, *3*(2), 151–165. DOI: 10.1080/19420676.2012.726006

Hussain, N., Di Pietro, F., & Rosati, P. (2023). Crowdfunding for Social Entrepreneurship: A systematic review of the literature. *Journal of Social Entrepreneurship*, •••, 1–24.

Jouti, A. T. (2019). An integrated approach for building sustainable Islamic social finance ecosystems. *ISRA International Journal of Islamic Finance*, *11*(2), 246–266. DOI: 10.1108/IJIF-10-2018-0118

Joy, M., & Shields, J. (2013). Social impact bonds: The next phase of third sector marketization? *Canadian Journal of Nonprofit and Social Economy Research*, *4*(2), 39–55. DOI: 10.22230/cjnser.2013v4n2a148

Joyce, A., & Paquin, R. L. (2016). The triple layered business model canvas: A tool to design more sustainable business models. *Journal of Cleaner Production*, *135*, 1474–1486.

Lagoarde-Segot, T. (2016). Prolegomena to an alternative study of finance. In Paranque, B., & Pérez, R. (Eds.), *Finance Reconsidered: New Perspectives for a Responsible and Sustainable Finance* (Vol. 10, pp. 89–110). Emerald Group Publishing., DOI: 10.1108/S2043-/905920160000010024

Lagoarde-Segot, T., & Paranque, B. (2017). Sustainability and the reconstruction of academic finance. *Research in International Business and Finance*, *39*, 657–662. DOI: 10.1016/j.ribaf.2016.03.002

Laing, N., Long, C., Marcandalli, A., Matthews, J., Grahovac, A., & Featherby, J. (2012). *The UK Social Investment Market: The Current Landscape and a Framework for Investor Decision Making*. Cambridge Associates.

Langley, P. (2020). "The folds of social finance: Making markets, remaking the social." Environment and Planning A. *Economy and Space*, *52*(1), 130–147. DOI: 10.1177/0308518X17752682

Lehner, O. M., & Kansikas, J. (2012). Opportunity recognition in social entrepreneurship: A thematic meta-analysis. *The Journal of Entrepreneurship*, *21*(1), 25–58. DOI: 10.1177/097135571102100102

Lyons, T. S., & Kickul, J. R. (2013). The social enterprise financing landscape: The lay of the land and new research on the horizon. *Entrepreneurship Research Journal*, *3*(2), 147–159.

Mollick, E. (2012). The dynamics of crowdfunding: Determinants of success and failure. *Journal of Business Venturing*, *29*(1), 1–16.

Moore, M. L., Westley, F. R., & Nicholls, A. (2012). The social finance and social innovation nexus. *Journal of Social Entrepreneurship*, *3*(2), 115–132. DOI: 10.1080/19420676.2012.725824

Nicholls, A. (2010). The legitimacy of social entrepreneurship: Reflexive isomorphism in a pre-paradigmatic field. *Entrepreneurship Theory and Practice*, *34*(4), 611–633. DOI: 10.1111/j.1540-6520.2010.00397.x

Nicholls, A., & Emerson, J. (2015). Social finance: Capitalizing social impact. In Nicholls, A., Paton, R., & Emerson, J. (Eds.), *Social Finance* (pp. 1–41). Oxford University Press., DOI: 10.1093/acprof:oso/9780198703761.003.0001

Nicholls, A., & Tomkinson, E. (2015). Risk and return in social. *Social Finance*, 282.

Ometto, M. P., Gegenhuber, T., Winter, J., & Greenwood, R. (2019). From balancing missions to mission drift: The role of the institutional context, spaces, and compartmentalization in the scaling of social enterprises. *Business & Society*, *58*(5), 1003–1046.

Phillips, W., Lee, H., Ghobadian, A., O'Regan, N., & James, P. (2015). Social innovation and social entrepreneurship: A systematic review. *Group & Organization Management*, *40*(3), 428–461. DOI: 10.1177/1059601114560063

Pizzi, S., Rosati, F., & Venturelli, A. (2021). The determinants of business contribution to the 2030 Agenda: Introducing the SDG reporting score. *Business Strategy and the Environment*, *30*(1), 404–421. DOI: 10.1002/bse.2628

Puschmann, T., Hoffmann, C. H., & Khmarskyi, V. (2020). How green FinTech can alleviate the impact of climate change—The case of Switzerland. *Sustainability*, *12*(24), 10691.

Rey-Martí, A., Mohedano-Suanes, A., & Simón-Moya, V. (2019). Crowdfunding and social entrepreneurship: Spotlight on intermediaries. *Sustainability*, *11*(4), 1175.

Rizzello, A., & Kabli, A. (2020). Social finance and sustainable development goals: A literature synthesis, current approaches and research agenda. *ACRN Journal of Finance and Risk Perspectives, 9.*

Rizzi, F., Pellegrini, C., & Battaglia, M. (2018). The structuring of social finance: Emerging approaches for supporting environmentally and socially impactful projects. *Journal of Cleaner Production*, *170*, 805–817. DOI: 10.1016/j.jclepro.2017.09.167

Rosati, F., & Faria, L. G. D. (2019). Addressing the SDGs in sustainability reports: The relationship with institutional factors. *Journal of Cleaner Production, 215*, 1312–1326. DOI: 10.1016/j.jclepro.2018.12.107

Sinclair, S., McHugh, N., & Roy, M. J. (2021). Social innovation, financialisation and commodification: A critique of social impact bonds. *Journal of Economic Policy Reform*, *24*(1), 11–27.

Snick, A. (2021). Social finance in the Anthropocene. In Walker, T., McGaughey, J., Goubran, S., & Wagdy, N. (Eds.), *Innovations in Social Finance* (pp. 13–34). Palgrave Macmillan., DOI: 10.1007/978-3-030-72535-8_2

Spiess-Knafl, W., & Jansen, S. A. (2014). Social enterprises and the financing of different scaling strategies. *Emerging research directions in social entrepreneurship*, 67-83.

Szennay, Á., Szigeti, C., Kovács, N., & Szabó, D. R. (2019). Through the blurry looking glass—SDGs in the GRI reports. *Resources*, *8*(2), 101.

Tenner, I., & Hörisch, J. (2021). Crowdfunding sustainable entrepreneurship: What are the characteristics of crowdfunding investors? *Journal of Cleaner Production*, *290*, 125667.

Van der Waal, J. W., & Thijssens, T. (2020). Corporate involvement in sustainable development goals: Exploring the territory. *Journal of Cleaner Production*, *252*, 119625.

Vandemeulebroucke, V., Beck, K., & Kauefer, K. (2010). *Networking Social Finance*. INAISE.

Vecchi, V., Casalini, F., & Caselli, S. (2017). Impact investing as a societal refocus of venture capital: The perspective of mature economies. In *Principles and Practice of Impact Investing* (pp. 62–80). Routledge.

Weber, O. (2016). Impact investing. In Lehner, O. M. (Ed.), *Routledge Handbook of Social and Sustainable Finance* (pp. 85–101). Routledge.

Weber, O., & Duan, Y. (2012). Social finance and banking. *Socially responsible finance and investing: Financial institutions, corporations, investors, and activists*, 161-180.

Wefunder. (2021). Impact Report. Retrieved from https://wefunder.com/pbc

Chapter 6
Social Impact Bonds: Evolution, Challenges, and Future Directions in Outcome-Based Financing

Rosella Carè
https://orcid.org/0000-0003-3222-0510
University of Waterloo, Canada & University Magna Graecia of Catanzaro, Italy

ABSTRACT

This chapter analyzes Social Impact Bonds (SIBs) as innovative, outcome-based financing tools that unite public, private, and third-sector actors to tackle complex social issues. Rooted in New Public Management, SIBs tie investor returns to independently verified social outcomes, promoting collaboration, risk-sharing, and performance-based service delivery. Despite global interest, adoption has lagged due to structural, contractual, and evaluation challenges. The chapter traces the development of SIBs, examines stakeholder motivations, contractual models, key success factors, and risks. It emphasizes the evolution of SIBs into complex partnerships needing strong institutional backing, smart incentives, and rigorous evaluations. Special focus is given to high transaction costs, principal–agent problems, and measuring outcomes. Drawing on recent data and policy trends, the chapter identifies enabling conditions for scaling and replicating SIBs and concludes with future paths for embedding them into wider social finance frameworks, including blended finance and ESG-aligned models.

DOI: 10.4018/979-8-3693-9551-6.ch006

1. INTRODUCTION

In recent years, Social Impact Bonds (SIBs) have attracted significant attention from researchers, policymakers, and practitioners in the fields of sustainable finance and public service innovation. SIBs represent a financial and contractual innovation, evolving from the traditional pay-for-results (PbR) framework by actively involving private investors to fund social programs (Edmiston & Nicholls, 2018). Compared to conventional PbR schemes, SIBs offer several distinctive advantages. They redirect private resources toward social interventions critical for community development, enhance efficiency in the allocation of public and private funds, and transfer project implementation risks from public sector bodies to private actors better equipped to manage them (Fox & Morris, 2019).

Conceived as a collaborative model bridging the public and private sectors, SIBs aim to improve the design, funding, and delivery of social services through innovative governance structures and risk-sharing mechanisms (Broccardo et al., 2019; Carè, 2018; Carè & De Lisa, 2019; Carè et al., 2023). From a contractual perspective, SIBs differ from traditional PbR models by incorporating impact investors who provide the working capital necessary for service provision and receive a financial return only if the pre-defined outcomes are independently verified (Carè, 2019; Rizzello & Carè, 2016). Outcome evaluation, typically conducted by independent assessors, plays a central role in the success of SIB projects (Nazari Chamaki et al., 2019; Carè & De Lisa, 2019; Carè, 2022).

Although SIBs have progressively expanded at the international level, the number of operational projects remains limited relative to their theoretical potential. As of 2025, more than 300 SIBs have been launched across 34 countries, targeting a variety of social challenges, including criminal justice, homelessness, health and wellbeing, and workforce development (Government Outcomes Lab, 2025). However, the slow pace of adoption highlights the presence of structural barriers and practical constraints (Carè & De Lisa, 2019; FitzGerald et al., 2020).

The academic debate on SIBs remains polarized. While several studies emphasize their ability to mobilize private resources and foster social innovation (Schinckus, 2017; Schinckus, 2018), others draw attention to significant challenges related to high transaction costs, governance complexity, accountability issues, and the financialization of welfare services (McHugh et al., 2013; FitzGerald et al., 2020; Sinclair et al., 2021). The COVID-19 pandemic has further accentuated the need for innovative financial instruments capable of supporting vulnerable populations and strengthening social protection systems.

Given these considerations, a deeper understanding of the motivations, critical success factors, and risks associated with SIB projects appears essential to advancing their effective implementation. Strengthening the knowledge base surrounding SIBs can contribute to improving project design, mitigating potential sources of failure, and fostering the development of appropriate guidelines and risk management strategies (Carè & De Lisa, 2019; Balboa, 2016; Pandey et al., 2018).

The objective of this chapter is to provide a comprehensive analysis of the SIB model by examining its origins, structure, stakeholder motivations, market trends, and challenges. Particular attention is devoted to identifying the conditions that enable successful SIB implementation and to outlining perspectives on the future evolution of these instruments as tools for sustainable and innovative public service delivery.

2. ABOUT THE ORIGINS OF SIBs

In the 1970s, a radically different consensus emerged regarding the role of the state in the economy and the optimal approach to managing economic activity, marking a shift towards neoliberalism and austerity (Alonso et al., 2015). Originating in the UK (Vickers & Yarrow, 1988) and spreading across Europe in the following decades, this shift led to significant reforms in the public sector, including large-scale privatization, liberalization, and deregulation efforts (Clifton et al., 2006). The core belief behind these policies was that private companies, operating in a fully competitive market, are more efficient than the government, a viewpoint that informed the rise of New Public Management (NPM) (Harvey, 2006; Robison, 2006). NPM emerged as a response to the growing perception that the public sector was inefficient and becoming increasingly unmanageable (Alonso et al., 2015). In the post-COVID-19 era, many governments are once again considering measures to cut public spending in order to reduce deficits and public debt. SIBs - seen as intellectual descendants of NPM's focus on markets and performance management - have emerged as instruments that "introduce the rigors of private sector investors, the standards of positivistic scientific evaluation, and the discipline of market mechanisms to determine payment and the allocation of risk" (Warner, 2012, p. 12). SIBs are rooted in three key NPM elements: contracting, performance measurement, and public-private partnerships (PPPs) (Warner, 2012; Carè & De Lisa, 2019). They combine contracting with private finance capital and payment by results (PbR), used in the delivery of publicly funded social services in areas such as health, education, housing, and criminal justice (Hajer, 2020). Trotta et al. (2021) suggest that SIBs could offer concrete responses to the socioeconomic challenges posed by the COVID-19 pandemic in Italy and Europe, emphasizing that "the challenges posed by COVID-19 should be considered as the starting point for the reconsideration of public policies and for the development of a new era of welfare services provision" (Trotta et al., 2021, p. 74).

The term 'Social Impact Bond' is widely used in the UK, while other names, such as 'social impact contracts' in France and Spain, 'Pay for Success' in the USA, and 'Social Benefit Bond' in Australia, have been adopted elsewhere (Maier & Meyer, 2017; European Investment Advisory Hub, 2021). Despite the growing debate around these instruments, a limited number of SIBs have been launched globally (Sinclair et al., 2021; Trotta et al., 2021). Some critics argue that SIBs commodify citizens, viewing them as problems or potential sources of revenue, promoting an ideology of marketization and financialization in social policy (Dowling, 2017; Tse & Warner, 2020; Carter, 2021; Sinclair et al., 2021). Conversely, proponents consider SIBs a "win-win" model capable of fostering social innovation, particularly when applied to more traditional welfare service delivery models.

3. THE SOCIAL IMPACT BOND (SIB) MODEL: STRUCTURE AND MOTIVATIONS

SIBs have emerged as a novel financing mechanism designed to foster cross-sector collaboration, encourage innovation in social service delivery, and promote outcome-based funding approaches (Carè, 2022). Their structure is characterized by the interaction of multiple stakeholders—public commissioners, private investors, service providers, and intermediaries—who work together to achieve predefined social outcomes (Carè, 2018; Carè, 2022). This section explores the architecture of SIBs, focusing on how the interests of different actors are integrated within the contractual framework (Section 3.1), and discusses the motivations that drive the participation of diverse stakeholders in SIB projects (Section 3.2).

3.1 SIB Architecture and the Role of Different Actors' Interests

The SIB model was first launched in the United Kingdom with the HMP Peterborough project in 2010, and it has since expanded internationally across multiple sectors (Clifford & Jung, 2016). SIBs represent an innovative financing model built on public–private collaboration, aimed at enhancing service quality and social outcomes by leveraging private rather than public funds (Nazari Chamaki et al., 2019).

In this model, the public sector commits to paying only for the achievement of agreed-upon outcomes, effectively transferring the financial risk associated with project failure to private investors (Nazari Chamaki et al., 2019). Proponents argue that SIBs can mobilize new financial resources for social innovation, ultimately producing both improved social outcomes and cost savings for public authorities (Edmiston & Nicholls, 2018).

The academic literature on SIBs reflects two main perspectives. One depicts SIBs as a "win–win" model capable of uniting public benefit and private profit, while the other adopts a more cautious view, questioning their ability to genuinely deliver better outcomes, highlighting concerns about cost structures, administrative complexity, and marketization of welfare services (Fraser et al., 2016; Edmiston & Nicholls, 2018; Albertson & Fox, 2019; Nazari Chamaki et al., 2019; FitzGerald et al., 2020; Ormiston et al., 2020).

SIBs are widely considered an evolution of the traditional public–private partnership (PPP) model, structured through a series of contracts formalizing the principal–multi-agent relationship between commissioners, service providers, investors, and intermediaries (Del Giudice & Migliavacca, 2019).

This arrangement allows public authorities to introduce innovative services while sharing financial risks with private investors, who provide upfront capital and seek both financial and social returns (Carè, 2019; Del Giudice & Migliavacca, 2019).

Moreover, depending on the specific design of a SIB, additional actors such as subordinate investors, guarantors, and legal or technical advisors may also play a role (Carè & De Lisa, 2019).

3.2 Review of Motivations for Implementing SIB Projects

A core strength of the SIB model lies in its ability to align the interests of multiple stakeholders, each with different motivations for participation (Gustafsson-Wright et al., 2015). Across all actors—public commissioners, private investors, and service providers—the shared goal is to achieve measurable social outcomes capable of generating sufficient cost savings to deliver a return on investment (Schinckus, 2017). Private-sector actors, particularly impact investors, are drawn to SIBs by the opportunity to achieve both financial returns and measurable social impact (Joy & Shields, 2013). SIBs provide a mechanism for channeling investments into entrepreneurial initiatives that may otherwise fall outside conventional impact investment portfolios (Roundy et al., 2017). Goodall (2014) emphasized that SIBs offer a unique investment opportunity for socially motivated investors seeking entrepreneurial solutions aligned with their values. Foundations participating in SIBs are motivated by a range of factors, from the opportunity to earn back invested capital through program-related investments to the strategic recycling of grants into future social ventures (Goodall, 2014). Corporations, in turn, often see SIBs as an effective CSR strategy, combining reputational benefits with tangible social outcomes (Gustafsson-Wright et al., 2015). Service providers—usually social enterprises—are motivated by the access to stable, performance-based funding. This structure encourages innovation, minimizes bureaucratic constraints, and allows service providers to focus on achieving the agreed social outcomes (Goodall, 2014; Gustafsson-Wright et al., 2015). For public commissioners, SIBs represent an opportunity to deliver cost savings, reduce fiscal risks associated with service failure, and achieve measurable improvements in public service delivery (Goodall, 2014; Gustafsson-Wright et al., 2015). Finally, the visibility and reputational gains associated with participation in high-profile SIB projects should not be underestimated as a motivating factor (Gustafsson-Wright et al., 2015).

4. CRITICAL SUCCESS FACTORS AND RISKS IN SIB PROJECTS

SIBs have attracted significant academic and policy attention as innovative financial mechanisms for addressing social challenges through cross-sector collaboration. However, their effective implementation and scaling depend heavily on a set of critical success factors, while at the same time they remain exposed to a complex set of risks. This section outlines the enabling conditions that foster the success of SIBs and offers a comprehensive overview of the main risks that can undermine their performance.

4.1 Critical Success Factors in SIB Projects

The successful implementation of SIBs relies on several interconnected factors, particularly the establishment of clear contractual arrangements, alignment of stakeholder interests, strong institutional support, and access to technical expertise throughout the project's life cycle (Gustafsson-Wright et al., 2015; Carè & De Lisa, 2019). A well-structured SIB contract plays a fundamental role in ensuring project stability. As emphasized by Carè and De Lisa (2019), it is crucial to create "certainty where possible, and bounded flexibility where needed," thereby limiting uncertainty for both public commissioners and private investors. A robust contractual framework should define clear outcome metrics, risk-sharing mechanisms, and dispute resolution procedures to prevent opportunistic behaviors and foster collaboration among parties.

From a theoretical standpoint, the alignment of stakeholder interests—particularly between commissioners, service providers, and investors—is a central condition for SIB success (Maier & Meyer, 2017). Drawing on agency theory, aligned incentives are essential to reduce moral hazard and adverse selection risks that typically arise in principal–agent relationships (Pandey et al., 2018). Nonetheless, despite outcome-based incentives, SIBs remain susceptible to agency problems, including the potential for service providers to "cherry-pick" beneficiaries who are most likely to achieve the desired outcomes (Edmiston & Nicholls, 2018).

Governance structures must also address the accountability challenges inherent in SIBs. As Balboa (2016) highlights, different actors may prioritize different goals during the implementation process, reflecting divergent public and private sector normative priorities. Moreover, the absence of a direct contractual link between public commissioners and service providers can exacerbate information asymmetries and diminish public oversight capacity (Carè & De Lisa, 2019).

Beyond contractual design and incentive alignment, additional critical success factors include strong governmental and institutional support, the credibility and experience of intermediaries, and the availability of specialized technical and legal advisory services (Carè & De Lisa, 2019; Ravi et al., 2019). Intermediaries, in particular, play a pivotal role by structuring the financial deal, managing stakeholder relationships, and monitoring performance throughout the project's duration.

Ultimately, achieving a balance between innovation and risk mitigation, and ensuring transparent evaluation mechanisms, are key determinants for maximizing the effectiveness and scalability of SIBs in addressing complex social problems.

4.2 Risks Affecting SIB Projects

Despite their innovative appeal, SIBs are subject to a wide range of risks that can compromise both financial and social returns. The literature identifies two main perspectives in analyzing these risks: one viewing SIBs within the broader field of impact investing, and the other emphasizing risks specific to public–private partnerships (Emerson, 2012; Schinckus, 2017).

From an impact investment standpoint, SIBs are exposed to conventional financial risks, including the risk of loss of principal and uncertain financial returns for investors (Schinckus, 2017). Emerson (2012) further identifies risks specific to the impact investing domain, such as liquidity risk, impact risk, measurement and reporting risk, thematic area risk, and exit risk. Investors must therefore manage a combination of traditional financial uncertainties and sector-specific challenges linked to social outcomes.

In the context of public-private collaborations, SIBs face additional contractual and operational risks. As highlighted by Ng et al. (2015), coordination risk, funding risk, implementation risk, outcome measurement risk, and counterparty risk are all critical concerns. These risks reflect the complexity of managing multi-stakeholder projects with diverse interests, objectives, and accountability structures.

Carè (2019) proposes a useful classification of risks affecting SIBs into three interconnected levels:

- Macro-level risks, which include political and policy risks beyond the control of project actors. These risks relate to changes in government priorities, regulatory environments, or political support that can destabilize projects.
- Micro-level risks, encompassing partnership risks and agency problems arising from relationships between stakeholders.
- Meso-level risks, focusing on risks internal to the project, such as operational risks (delays or failures in program implementation), programmatic risks (ineffectiveness of interventions), and evaluation risks (failure to accurately assess outcomes) (Tekolste et al., 2016; Carè, 2019).

Several specific categories of risk deserve particular attention:

- Execution risk, concerning the feasibility and realistic design of the social intervention (Brandstetter & Lehner, 2015; Schinckus, 2017).
- Financial risk, relating to the uncertainty of investor repayments based on achieved outcomes (Schinckus, 2017).
- Intermediary risk, arising if intermediaries fail to perform their roles adequately, compromising both social and financial returns (Burand, 2012).
- Political risk, referring to potential government actions that may undermine contractual agreements, such as legislative changes or funding interruptions (Burand, 2012).
- Reputational risk, affecting all actors if the project fails to deliver expected outcomes (Burand, 2012; Ng et al., 2015).
- Impact risk, linked to the possibility that the intervention does not produce the intended social benefits (Scognamiglio et al., 2019).
- Liquidity risk, particularly relevant given the extended timelines often associated with SIB projects (Bergfeld et al., 2019).

Macroeconomic factors, such as inflation or interest rate volatility, may also affect the project's viability, compounding financial risks and undermining the stability of expected cash flows (World Bank, 2019).

Given these multiple layers of uncertainty, robust risk assessment and mitigation strategies are essential from the early stages of SIB project design. These strategies should include clear risk-sharing agreements, contingency planning, and flexible governance frameworks capable of adapting to unforeseen challenges throughout the project's lifecycle.

5. THE EVOLUTION AND GLOBAL DIFFUSION OF THE SOCIAL IMPACT BOND MARKET

Since their inception in 2010, SIBs have become a widely discussed and increasingly adopted financial mechanism to address complex social challenges. They represent an innovative partnership model in which private investors provide upfront capital to fund social programmes, with repayments and returns linked to the achievement of measurable outcomes, typically evaluated by an independent assessor.

According to data retrieved from the GO Lab's INDIGO database, a total of 315 SIBs had been launched worldwide as of April 2025. These initiatives span a broad range of sectors—from education and employment to homelessness and criminal justice—demonstrating the versatility of SIBs in addressing diverse policy issues. The United Kingdom continues to lead globally, followed by the United States, Australia, the Netherlands, and Portugal.

The temporal evolution of SIBs shows a marked increase between 2015 and 2019, reaching a peak in 2018 with over 40 new initiatives launched in a single year. While recent years have seen a slight deceleration, the continued deployment of SIBs—even during the pandemic—underscores their perceived potential for leveraging private finance for public good.

Despite the growth, the SIB model remains subject to ongoing debate. Key concerns include the high transaction costs associated with structuring the contracts, challenges in outcome measurement, and the risk of financializing public services. Yet, SIBs have also demonstrated the capacity to bring together stakeholders from public, private, and non-profit sectors, fostering experimentation and innovation in social service delivery.

As the global policy landscape increasingly emphasizes evidence-based interventions and results-oriented financing, SIBs may continue to evolve as part of a broader toolbox of outcome-based contracting strategies. They also serve as a foundation for further models—such as Development Impact Bonds and ESG-linked social financing tools—that integrate performance metrics into capital markets.

6. ISSUES AND CHALLENGES

Although SIBs have emerged as a promising innovation in the field of public–private partnerships, their practical implementation has encountered several critical challenges that limit their broader diffusion and scalability. While SIBs are designed to align the interests of governments, investors, and service providers toward achieving social outcomes, numerous structural and operational difficulties complicate this ideal alignment.

First, the complexity of SIB arrangements—due to the involvement of multiple stakeholders and the need for formalized contractual relationships—raises transaction costs substantially compared to traditional public sector contracting. The process of designing, negotiating, and managing these complex, outcome-based contracts often requires specialized intermediaries, adding additional layers of governance and cost.

Second, while the SIB model is theoretically structured to achieve an alignment of interests, in practice, it often reproduces principal–agent problems familiar to public procurement. Governments must rely on private actors to deliver public services while retaining only indirect oversight, thereby increasing the risk of information asymmetries, misaligned incentives, and reduced public accountability.

Third, evaluating the success of SIB projects remains a substantial hurdle. Robust evaluation frameworks are essential not only for determining whether the promised social outcomes have been achieved but also for calculating investor returns. However, the lack of standardized metrics and methodologies complicates the verification of impact, undermines transparency, and makes scaling successful models more difficult.

Finally, the high costs associated with structuring and implementing SIBs, coupled with the uncertain realization of public savings, challenge the sustainability of the model itself. In many cases, SIBs have not conclusively demonstrated superior cost-effectiveness compared to traditional service delivery models, raising important questions about their broader replicability.

6.1 Cross-Sector Partnerships and Contractual Models

SIBs represent an innovative form of cross-sector collaboration aimed at sustainability, built upon public–private partnerships structured through outcome-based contracts that integrate impact finance logics (La Torre et al., 2019). The SIB model is essentially a new variant of public-private partnership (PPP) contracts, structured through a series of formal agreements between the commissioning body, service providers, investors, and intermediaries. The complexity of SIBs is reflected in the heterogeneity of contractual models developed internationally. As Clifford and Jung (2016) classify, three primary contractual frameworks have emerged: (i) an SPV model where the Special Purpose Vehicle centralizes funding and service contracting; (ii) a model where the SPV acts mainly as a contract manager while the commissioner contracts directly with service providers; and (iii) a managed network configuration with a project manager coordinating the network of stakeholders. Similarly, Fraser et al. (2016) distinguish between (i) direct provider models, (ii) SPV-based models, and (iii) Social Investment Partnership (SIP) models, in which multiple initiatives are launched under a unified SPV structure (Warner, 2013). So and Jagelewski (2013) further clarify the advantages of the SPV structure in mitigating risks: the SPV contracts with the commissioner and service providers, secures direct investments from investors, and is governed by a board representing investors' interests, ensuring robust oversight over the achievement of outcomes.

6.2 Incentive Structures and Principal–Agent Challenges

SIBs typically finance additional, non-core social services and promote innovation in tackling entrenched social problems by generating economies through scaling and more effective performance management practices (Morley, 2019).

This model is particularly suited for interventions requiring significant upfront investments, targeting large populations, and supported by strong empirical evidence.

From a governmental perspective, SIBs offer an attractive framework by combining risk transfer to the private sector with improved performance management and incentivized outcome achievement (Fitzgerald et al., 2019).

The alignment of interests between governments, investors, and service providers is a key strength of SIBs (Social Finance UK, 2016; Giacomantonio, 2017; Maier et al., 2018). Nevertheless, Maier and Meyer (2017) observe that despite this incentive structure, a complete alignment of interests is rarely achieved, as each actor retains distinct and sometimes diverging objectives. Moreover, SIBs may exacerbate the principal–agent problem traditionally present in public sector contracts: governments, acting as principals, must rely on intermediaries and service providers to appropriately manage public funds, while facing challenges related to monitoring and ensuring accountability from a distance (Stid, 2013).

6.3 Evaluation, Transaction Costs, and Public Value for Money

Despite the potential advantages, achieving savings through SIBs compared to traditional contracting mechanisms is not guaranteed. Transaction costs - including negotiation, structuring, monitoring, and evaluation costs - are substantially higher for SIBs (Azemati et al., 2013; Social Finance UK, 2016; Giacomantonio, 2018; Morley, 2019).

Applying Spiller's Transaction Cost Regulation (TCR) theory (Spiller, 2008), Pandey et al. (2018) underline that SIBs are vulnerable to governmental and third-party opportunism, exacerbating contractual hazards typical of complex public–private arrangements. The governance structure of SIBs, which introduces intermediaries between commissioners and service providers, can further aggravate information asymmetries and dilute governmental oversight capacities (McHugh et al., 2013; Stid, 2013).

Evaluation remains a critical bottleneck: while investors' returns depend on independent assessment of outcome achievements, discrepancies in outcome definitions and measurements between stakeholders can jeopardize trust and transparency (Flynn et al., 2015; Wilson et al., 2015; Fraser et al., 2016).

To address these issues, frameworks like Value for Money (VFM) assessments—originally developed in the UK's PPP context—have been proposed (Glynn & Murphy, 1996; Siemiatycki & Farooqi, 2012), although calculating VFM is complicated by the challenges of estimating public sector comparators (PSC) and risk-adjusted cash flows (Grimsey & Lewis, 2005; Carè, 2018).

Furthermore, Fraser et al. (2016) highlight that the lack of standardized evaluation practices complicates both the setup and scaling of SIB initiatives.

Ultimately, aligning cost-benefit analysis across public and private perspectives remains a major challenge, as public sector value considerations prioritize quality and access, while private sector stakeholders focus on risk-return optimization (Carè, 2018; Schinckus, 2018).

7. KEY DRIVERS FOR THE DEVELOPMENT OF SOCIAL IMPACT BONDS

Although SIBs have gained increasing visibility in the past decade, their diffusion and scalability remain constrained by several challenges, including limited market size, high transaction costs, and concerns about effectiveness and evaluation frameworks. Nonetheless, both academic and professional communities have identified a range of enabling factors that could foster the broader adoption and success of SIB initiatives.

Understanding these drivers is crucial for moving beyond the experimental phase and toward a more structured integration of SIBs within public service delivery systems. This section outlines the critical conditions and mechanisms that can support the development, replication, and scaling of SIBs, emphasizing the importance of policy frameworks, robust contractual arrangements, institutional commitment, and a rethinking of evaluation practices.

Recognizing and strengthening these enablers is essential for maximizing the potential of SIBs as innovative tools for addressing complex social challenges through cross-sector collaboration and outcome-based financing.

7.1. The Role of Public Policies and Market Infrastructure

Despite growing attention, SIBs remain relatively small in scale in terms of both capital mobilized and number of beneficiaries reached (Cooper et al., 2016; Sinclair et al., 2019). They have faced criticisms regarding their actual effectiveness (Sinclair et al., 2019) and the sometimes overly optimistic "win–win" narratives promoted in many countries (Fitzgerald et al., 2019).

Nonetheless, several enabling conditions have been identified that could foster their development. A critical factor is the proactive role of public policies in creating an ecosystem supportive of social finance. Evidence from countries with a strong SIB presence underscores the importance of governmental action through initiatives such as the creation of independent social investment institutions, social outcomes funds, and targeted market-building policies. These actions, launched at central and local levels, signal a commitment to exploring innovative funding models for social impact.

Moreover, the presence of specialized intermediaries and outcome funds has been instrumental in supporting the structuring and financing of SIBs, by offering technical assistance and helping overcome early-stage financial barriers (Albertson & Fox, 2018).

7.2. Enhancing Scalability Through Robust Contractual Frameworks

A core factor influencing the replicability and scaling of SIBs lies in the design of contractual frameworks. Academic literature has clarified that SIBs are not traditional bonds but rather a series of outcome-contingent contracts among multiple stakeholders (Clifford & Jung, 2016; Cooper et al., 2016; Child et al., 2016; Carè & Ferraro, 2019).

Careful risk allocation, bounded flexibility, and clearly defined roles and responsibilities are essential to balancing the interests of public and private actors. Improving the standardization and modularity of contracts could enhance scalability by reducing complexity and transaction costs.

However, SIBs also present inherent governance challenges: given the multiparty structure, misaligned interests and costly oversight mechanisms can limit efficiency. A well-designed contractual environment, supported by a favorable legislative framework, can help to mitigate these risks by promoting transparency, accountability, and alignment of objectives between stakeholders.

7.3. Institutional Commitment and Cross-Sector Partnerships

The development and diffusion of SIBs are closely linked to the broader institutional environment. Key institutional variables include the willingness of public authorities across different levels of government to collaborate, the prioritization of efficiency and accountability in service delivery, and a proactive stance toward fiscal sustainability and innovative finance mechanisms.

When institutional support is strong, SIBs are more likely to gain traction, as public sector openness reduces perceived risks for private investors. Furthermore, the emergence of dedicated financial intermediaries and outcome funds reflects a growing institutionalization of social finance ecosystems, thus facilitating the expansion of SIB initiatives beyond pilot projects.

7.4. Rethinking the Role of Evaluation and Outcome Measurement

The effectiveness of SIBs heavily depends on the ability to design credible, transparent, and feasible evaluation frameworks. Yet, to date, evaluation practices remain underdeveloped, and cost–benefit analyses or Value for Money (VFM) assessments often face methodological challenges (Grimsey & Lewis, 2005; Glynn & Murphy, 1996; Siemiatycki & Farooqi, 2012; Azemati et al., 2013; Flynn et al., 2015; Wilson et al., 2015; Social Finance UK, 2016; Center for Disease Control Prevention, 2017; Giacomantonio, 2018; Carè, 2018; Morley, 2019).

SIBs require the identification of measurable and achievable outcomes, which is not always possible across all social sectors. Moreover, placing excessive emphasis on immediate public savings could risk narrowing the scope of eligible projects to only those with easily quantifiable fiscal returns.

Emerging perspectives suggest decoupling outcome payments from short-term public savings calculations, instead recognizing broader and longer-term social value creation. Such an approach could foster greater flexibility in project design and align SIBs more closely with preventive and wellbeing-enhancing interventions.

8. REFLECTIONS ON SOCIAL IMPACT BONDS IN THE CONTEXT OF NEOLIBERAL GOVERNANCE

Over the past decade, SIBs have gained international attention as innovative financial mechanisms for enhancing the efficiency and effectiveness of social service delivery. While much of the literature focuses on their structure, potential benefits, and implementation challenges, it is equally important to situate SIBs within the broader political and economic transformations that have shaped their emergence. In particular, SIBs must be understood in relation to the rise of neoliberal governance models that redefined the role of the state, reshaped public accountability, and expanded the influence of market-based instruments in the social domain.

The logic underpinning SIBs reflects a significant departure from traditional conceptions of public welfare. Rather than financing services directly through taxation and public budgets, SIBs invite private investors to assume the financial risk of program delivery in exchange for outcome-contingent returns. This model does not emerge in a vacuum: it builds upon decades of public sector reform driven by New Public Management (NPM) principles, which emphasize performance metrics, contractualization, decentralization, and market discipline (Harvey, 2006; Warner, 2012). As a result, SIBs have come to symbolize a broader shift toward the financialization of social policy, in which social value is increasingly defined by return on investment, cost savings, and measurable outputs (Sinclair et al., 2021).

Yet, the very features that make SIBs appealing to policymakers—such as risk-sharing, cross-sector collaboration, and outcome-based payment—also raise fundamental questions about equity, transparency, democratic accountability, and the long-term role of private finance in the welfare state. These concerns are particularly relevant in contexts where austerity, public sector retrenchment, and fiscal consolidation have eroded universal access to social rights. Rather than merely evaluating the operational dynamics of SIBs, this final section offers a critical reflection on their normative foundations and political implications, drawing attention to the tensions between innovation and marketization, and between financial performance and public value.

8.1 Neoliberal Rationality and the Financialization of Social Policy

SIBs exemplify the neoliberal shift in welfare governance whereby social problems are reframed as investment opportunities. Rooted in the broader logics of New Public Management (NPM), SIBs extend the belief that market mechanisms can efficiently solve social challenges traditionally addressed by public provision (Harvey, 2006; Warner, 2012). By tying public payments to outcomes rather than inputs or processes, these instruments privatize not only financial risk but also the epistemology of policy success (Carè & De Lisa, 2019). This commodification of welfare aligns with what Sinclair et al. (2021) critique as the financialization of the social sector, wherein citizens are reframed as data points or cost-saving targets rather than rights-bearing individuals.

8.2 From New Public Management to New Public Value?

Some scholars argue that SIBs represent a shift from classic NPM toward a "new public governance" paradigm, emphasizing social impact and multi-stakeholder collaboration (Rijpens et al., 2020; Vecchi & Casalini, 2019). However, this optimistic interpretation is contested by those who stress that SIBs often entrench, rather than disrupt, neoliberal norms. While enabling innovation and private investment in public goods, SIBs also institutionalize rigid performance metrics and contractual complexity that may marginalize community voices and reproduce existing inequities (Dowling, 2017; Carter, 2021). The paradox is that in seeking to improve public outcomes, SIBs may further displace democratic control over social priorities.

8.3 Transaction Costs, Risk Allocation, and Democratic Accountability

The promise of SIBs as efficiency-enhancing tools is also challenged by their often underacknowledged transaction costs and opaque governance structures (Fitzgerald et al., 2019; Fox & Morris, 2019). Contractual arrangements in SIBs introduce new intermediaries and shift risks from the state to private actors, yet without sufficient transparency or evidence that such shifts generate better outcomes or long-term savings (Pandey et al., 2018). Furthermore, the logic of "pay for success" may favor interventions that are easily quantifiable, crowding out complex or preventative services that resist standard evaluation models (Fraser et al., 2016).

8.4 Toward a Critical Appraisal of SIBs as Policy Tools

Rather than viewing SIBs as neutral instruments, it is crucial to assess them as policy tools embedded in a neoliberal governmentality that values calculability, investment logics, and managerial rationality (Chiapello & Knoll, 2020). While SIBs may offer flexibility and innovation in targeted areas, they also risk reinforcing the fragmentation of welfare systems and the subordination of public goals to financial viability. A more democratic approach would require reimagining accountability beyond investor return, incorporating the lived experiences of service users, and critically reflecting on the kinds of knowledge and value that SIBs privilege.

9. ADVANCING A FINANCIAL LENS IN SIB RESEARCH AND PRACTICE

Despite the growing literature on SIBs, a notable gap persists in the integration of finance-centered perspectives within their conceptualization, design, and evaluation. Most academic discussions still tend to frame SIBs predominantly as public service innovations or tools of social policy reform, often neglecting their nature as hybrid financial instruments requiring rigorous financial modeling, risk assessment, and investor engagement (Carè et al., 2023).

9.1 The Absence of Financial Standardization and Evaluation Frameworks

Scholars have increasingly pointed out the lack of standardized financial evaluation frameworks as a key obstacle to both theoretical understanding and practical uptake of SIBs by mainstream finance actors. As Schinckus (2018) argued, SIBs often fail to attract private investors not because of inherent flaws in their purpose, but due to the absence of a "unified framework for the evaluation of these assets" that would present opportunities using the language and tools familiar to financiers . Without such frameworks, the risk–return profiles of SIBs remain opaque and unattractive for institutional investors and finance scholars alike.

9.2 Methodological Fragmentation and the Lack of Financial Rigor

The bibliometric overview by Carè et al. (2023) highlighted that SIB research is dominated by theoretical reflections and commentary pieces, with limited use of empirical data or financial modeling approaches. This pattern contributes to the continued marginalization of finance as a discipline within the SIB research domain. Financial research is typically valued only when it adopts methodologically rigorous and quantitatively robust designs, a standard rarely met in current SIB literature.

9.3 Future Directions: From Conceptual Framing to Policy Translation

To fill this methodological and disciplinary gap, future research should aim at embedding financial logics more explicitly into the design and evaluation of SIBs. This includes: (i) the development of risk-adjusted valuation models; (ii) scenario-based simulations of investor returns; and (iii) standardized outcome pricing mechanisms across jurisdictions. Doing so would not only improve the academic robustness of the field but also enhance the credibility and scalability of SIBs in real-world financial markets. As Carè et al. (2023) suggest, expanding the scope beyond the UK-centric welfare finance framing may offer promising avenues for cross-national learning and policy experimentation.

10. CONCLUSION AND PERSPECTIVES ON THE EVOLUTION OF SIBs

SIBs have emerged over the past decade as a distinctive innovation in the field of outcome-based financing, offering a mechanism to align public, private, and non-profit sector interests toward achieving measurable social outcomes. Throughout this work, we have critically examined the origins, structural features, success factors, and main challenges associated with SIBs.

While the early years of SIB implementation—particularly between 2015 and 2019—were characterized by growing enthusiasm and a relatively rapid proliferation of initiatives across multiple countries and policy domains, recent trends suggest a noticeable shift. Data from the most recent years (2022–2025) indicate a slowdown in the launch of new SIB projects globally. This deceleration raises important questions about the sustainability and scalability of the model beyond its initial experimental phase.

A key observation is that, to date, only the United Kingdom's model has demonstrated consistent effectiveness in fostering a robust and dynamic SIB market. Several factors explain this relative success:

- the early establishment of enabling policy frameworks;
- the proactive role of dedicated social investment institutions;
- the development of standardized outcome-based contracting practices;
- and the creation of financial and technical support mechanisms through intermediaries and social outcomes funds. In contrast, in many other jurisdictions, the lack of such a comprehensive enabling ecosystem has limited the diffusion and sustainability of SIBs, often relegating them to pilot initiatives rather than mainstream policy tools.

The future evolution of SIBs will likely depend on several critical dimensions. First, addressing transaction costs and contractual complexity remains essential for achieving broader scalability. Simplified and standardized models, combined with more flexible and transparent outcome measurement frameworks, could enhance feasibility and attractiveness for both investors and commissioners.

Second, a broader vision of success beyond immediate public cost savings is needed. Emerging perspectives advocate for recognizing longer-term and systemic social value creation, aligning SIBs more closely with preventive interventions and wellbeing-oriented public policies.

Third, the evolution of SIBs must be contextualized within the growing landscape of impact investing and blended finance. Hybrid models that integrate SIB principles with ESG-linked investment strategies, Development Impact Bonds (DIBs), and performance-based grants offer promising pathways for enhancing both financial sustainability and social impact.

Finally, greater institutional learning and international cooperation will be crucial. The accumulation of best practices, the establishment of shared standards for outcome validation, and the mobilization of catalytic public and philanthropic funding could help SIBs transition from niche instruments to more systemic components of social finance ecosystems.

In conclusion, while the initial promises of SIBs have not been fully realized on a global scale, their potential as catalysts for innovation in social service delivery remains significant. Their continued relevance will depend on the ability of policymakers, investors, and service providers to adapt the model to evolving societal needs, financial ecosystems, and governance challenges.

ACKNOWLEDGEMENT

This project has received funding from the European Union's Horizon 2020 research and innovation program under the Marie Skłodowska-Curie grant agreement number 892293.

REFERENCES

Albertson, K., & Fox, C. (2018). *Payment by results and social impact bonds: Outcome-based payment systems in the UK and US*. Policy Press.

Albertson, K., & Fox, C. (2019). The marketisation of rehabilitation: Some economic considerations. *Probation Journal*, *66*(1), 25–42.

Alonso, J. M., Clifton, J., & Diaz-Fuentes, D. (2015). Did new public management matter? An empirical analysis of the outsourcing and decentralization effects on public sector size. *Public Management Review*, *17*, 643–660.

Azemati, H., Belinsky, M., Gillette, R., Liebman, J., Sellman, A., & Wyse, A. (2013). Social impact bonds: Lessons learned so far. *Community Development Investment Review*, *9*(1), 23–34.

Balboa, C. M. (2016). Accountability of environmental impact bonds: The future of global environmental governance? *Global Environmental Politics*, *16*(1), 33–41.

Bergfeld, N., Klausner, D., & Samel, M. (2019). Improving Social Impact Bonds: Assessing Alternative Financial Models to Scale Pay-for-Success. *Annual Review of Policy Design*, *7*, 1–20.

Brandstetter, L., & Lehner, O. M. (2015). Opening the market for impact investments: The need for adapted portfolio tools. *Entrepreneurship Research Journal*, *5*(2), 87–107.

Broccardo, E., Mazzuca, M., & Frigotto, M. L. (2019). Social impact bonds: The evolution of research and a review of the academic literature. *Corporate Social Responsibility and Environmental Management*, *27*(3), 1316–1332.

Burand, D. (2012). Globalizing social finance: How social impact bonds and social impact performance guarantees can scale development. *NYU Journal of Law & Business*, *9*, 447.

Carè, R. (2018). Social Impact Bond: Beyond financial innovation. In Wendt, K. (Ed.), *Sustainable Financial Innovation* (pp. xx–xx). Taylor & Francis.

Carè, R. (2019). Social Impact Bond: Beyond financial innovation. In *Sustainable Financial Innovation* (pp. 149–171). CRC Press.

Carè, R. (2022). From New Public Management to Social Impact Bonds: The European Experience. In *The Anglo-American Model of Neoliberalism of the 1980s: Construction, Development and Dissemination* (pp. 293–317). Springer International Publishing.

Carè, R., Carè, S., Lévy, N., & Fatima, R. (2023). Missing finance in social impact bond research? A bibliometric overview between past and future research. *Corporate Social Responsibility and Environmental Management*, *30*(5), 2101–2120.

Carè, R., & De Lisa, R. (2019). Social Impact Bonds for a Sustainable Welfare State: The Role of Enabling Factors. *Sustainability*, *11*(10), 2884.

Carè, R., & Ferraro, G. (2019). Funding innovative healthcare programs through social impact bonds: Issues and challenges. *China-USA Business Review*, *18*(1), 1–15.

Carter, E. (2021). More than marketised? Exploring the governance and accountability mechanisms at play in social impact bonds. *Journal of Economic Policy Reform*, *24*(1), 78–94.

Center for Disease Control and Prevention (CDC). (2017). *Pay for success: How-to guide for local government focused on lead-safe homes*. Retrieved from https://www.cdc.gov/nceh/lead/docs/pay_for_success_guide.pdf

Chiapello, E., & Knoll, L. (2020). The welfare conventions approach: A comparative perspective on social impact bonds. *Journal of Comparative Policy Analysis*, *22*(2), 100–115.

Child, C., Gibbs, B. G., & Rowley, K. J. (2016). Paying for success: An appraisal of social impact bonds. *Global Economics and Management Review*, *21*(1), 36–45.

Clifford, J., & Jung, T. (2016). Social Impact Bonds: Exploring and understanding an emerging funding approach. In Lehner, O. (Ed.), *Routledge Handbook of Social and Sustainable Finance* (pp. 161–176). Routledge.

Clifton, J., Comin, F., & Diaz-Fuentes, D. (2006). Privatization in the European Union: Pragmatic, ideological, inevitable? *Journal of European Public Policy*, *13*(5), 736–756.

Cooper, C., Graham, C., & Himick, D. (2016). Social impact bonds: The securitization of the homeless. *Accounting, Organizations and Society*, *55*, 63–82.

Del Giudice, A., & Migliavacca, M. (2019). Social impact bonds and institutional investors: An empirical analysis of a complicated relationship. *Nonprofit and Voluntary Sector Quarterly*, *48*(1), 50–70.

Dowling, E. (2017). In the wake of austerity: Social impact bonds and the financialisation of the welfare state in Britain. *New Political Economy*, *22*(3), 294–310.

Edmiston, D., & Nicholls, A. (2018). Social Impact Bonds: The role of private capital in outcome-based commissioning. *Journal of Social Policy*, *47*(1), 57–76.

Emerson, J. (2012). Risk, return and impact: Understanding diversification and performance within an impact investing portfolio. *ImpactAssets*, *2*, 1–15.

European Investment Advisory Hub. (2021). *Social outcomes contracting in Europe: An introductory guide to social outcomes contracting in European Union Member States*. https://eiah.eib.org/publications/attachments/socialoutcomes-contracting-in-Europe-10052021.pdf

Fitzgerald, C., Carter, E., Dixon, R., & Airoldi, M. (2019). Walking the contractual tightrope: A transaction cost economics perspective on social impact bonds. *Public Money & Management*, *39*(5), 327–336.

FitzGerald, C., Fraser, A., & Kimmitt, J. (2020). Tackling the Big Questions in Social Impact Bond Research through Comparative Approaches. *Journal of Comparative Policy Analysis*, •••, 1–15.

Flynn, J., Young, J., & Barnett, C. (2015). *Impact Investments: A literature Review*. Centre for Development Impact.

Fox, C., & Morris, S. (2019). Evaluating outcome-based payment programmes: Challenges for evidence-based policy. *Journal of Economic Policy Reform*. Advance online publication. DOI: 10.1080/17487870.2019.1575217

Fraser, A., Tan, S., Lagarde, M., & Mays, N. (2016). Narratives of promise, narratives of caution: A review of the literature on Social Impact Bonds. *Social Policy and Administration*, *52*(1), 4–28.

Giacomantonio, C. (2017). Grant-Maximizing but not Money-Making: A Simple Decision-Tree Analysis for Social Impact Bonds. *Journal of Social Entrepreneurship*, *8*(1), 47–66.

Giacomantonio, C. (2018). Setting realistic expectations: The narrow use-case for Social Impact Bonds. *Journal of Community Safety & Well-being*, *3*(3), 93–95.

Glynn, J. J., & Murphy, M. P. (1996). Public management: Failing accountabilities and failing performance review. *International Journal of Public Sector Management, 9*(5/6/7), 125–137.

Goodall, E. (2014). *Choosing Social Impact Bonds: A Practitioner's Guide*. Bridges Ventures.

Government Outcomes Lab. (2025.). *INDIGO impact bond dataset*. https://golab.bsg.ox.ac.uk/knowledge-bank/indigo/

Grimsey, D., & Lewis, M. K. (2005). Are public private partnerships value for money? Evaluating alternative approaches and comparing academic and practitioner views. *Accounting Forum, 29*(4), 345–378.

Gustafsson-Wright, E., Gardiner, S., & Putcha, V. (2015). *The Potential and Limitations of Impact Bonds: Lessons from the First Five Years of Experience Worldwide*. Global Economy and Development at Brookings.

Hajer, J. (2020). The national governance and policy context of social impact bond emergence: A comparative analysis of leaders and skeptics. *Journal of Comparative Policy Analysis, 22*(2), 116–133.

Harvey, D. (2006). Neo-liberalism as creative destruction. *Geografiska Annaler, 88*(2), 145–158.

Joy, M., & Shields, J. (2013). Social impact bonds: The next phase of third sector marketization? *Canadian Journal of Nonprofit and Social Economy Research, 4*(2).

La Torre, M., Trotta, A., Chiappini, H., & Rizzello, A. (2019). Business models for sustainable finance: The case study of Social Impact Bonds. *Sustainability, 11*(7), 1887.

Maier, F., Barbetta, G. P., & Godina, F. (2018). Paradoxes of social impact bonds. *Social Policy and Administration, 52*(7), 1332–1353.

Maier, F., & Meyer, M. (2017). Social Impact Bonds and the Perils of Aligned Interests. *Administrative Sciences, 7*(3), 24.

McHugh, N., Sinclair, S., Roy, M., Huckfield, L., & Donaldson, C. (2013). Social impact bonds: A wolf in sheep's clothing? *The Journal of Poverty and Social Justice : Research, Policy, Practice, 21*(3), 247–257.

Morley, J. (2019). The ethical status of social impact bonds. *Journal of Economic Policy Reform, 22*(3), 231–246.

Nazari Chamaki, F., Jenkins, G. P., & Hashemi, M. (2019). Social Impact Bonds: Implementation, Evaluation, and Monitoring. *International Journal of Public Administration, 42*(4), 289–297.

Ng, A., Mirakhor, A., & Ibrahim, M. H. (2015). Risk sharing and social impact partnerships. In *Social Capital and Risk Sharing* (pp. 133–156). Palgrave Macmillan.

Ormiston, J., Moran, M., Castellas, E. I., & Tomkinson, E. (2020). Everybody wins? A discourse analysis of competing stakeholder expectations in social impact bonds. *Public Money & Management, 40*(3), 237–246.

Pandey, S., Cordes, J. J., Pandey, S. K., & Winfrey, W. F. (2018). Use of social impact bonds to address social problems: Understanding contractual risks and transaction costs. *Nonprofit Management & Leadership, 28*(4), 511–528.

Ravi, S., Gustafsson-Wright, E., Sharma, P., & Boggild-Jones, I. (2019). *The Promise of Impact Investing in India*. Brookings India Research Paper No. 062019. Brookings Institution India Center: New Delhi, India.

Rijpens, J., Bouchard, M. J., Gruet, E., & Salathe-Beaulieu, G. (2020). *Social impact bonds: Promises versus facts. What does the recent scientific literature tell us?* (Working Paper, CIREC 2020/15) Liege University.

Rizzello, A., & Carè, R. (2016). Insight into the social impact bond market: An analysis of investors. *ACRN Oxford Journal of Finance and Risk Perspectives, 5*(3), 145–171.

Robison, R. (2006). *Neo-liberalism and the market state: What is the ideal shell?* Palgrave Macmillan.

Roundy, P., Holzhauer, H., & Dai, Y. (2017). Finance or philanthropy? Exploring the motivations and criteria of impact investors. *Social Responsibility Journal, 13*(3), 491–512.

Schinckus, C. (2017). Financial innovation as a potential force for a positive social change: The challenging future of social impact bonds. *Research in International Business and Finance, 39*, 727–736.

Schinckus, C. (2018). The valuation of social impact bonds: An introductory perspective with the Peterborough SIB. *International Review of Financial Analysis, 59*, 1–6.

Scognamiglio, E., Di Lorenzo, E., Sibillo, M., & Trotta, A. (2019). Social uncertainty evaluation in Social Impact Bonds: Review and framework. *Research in International Business and Finance, 47*, 40–56.

Siemiatycki, M., & Farooqi, N. (2012). Value for money and risk in public–private partnerships: Evaluating the evidence. *Journal of the American Planning Association, 78*(3), 286–299.

Sinclair, S., McHugh, N., & Roy, M. J. (2019). Social innovation, financialisation and commodification: A critique of social impact bonds. *Journal of Economic Policy Reform*, •••, 1–17.

Sinclair, S., McHugh, N., & Roy, M. J. (2021). Social innovation, financialization and commodification: A critique of social impact bonds. *Journal of Economic Policy Reform, 24*(1), 11–27.

So, I., & Jagelewski, A. (2013). *Social Impact Bond: Technical Guide for Service Providers*. MaRS Centre for Impact Investing.

Social Finance, U. K. (2016). *Social Impact Bond. The Early Years*. Retrieved from https://www.socialfinance.org.uk/sites/default/files/publications/sibs-early-years_social_finance_2016_final.pdf

Spiller, P. T. (2008). *An Institutional Theory of Public Contracts: Regulatory Implications (No. w14152)*. National Bureau of Economic Research.

Stid, D. (2013). Pay for success is not a panacea. *Community Development Investment Review, 9*(1), 13–18.

Tekolste, R., Eldridge, M., & Hawkins, R. (2016). *Managing Investors' Risk in Pay for Success Projects*. Urban Institute.

Trotta, A., Care, R., Carida, R., & Migliazza, M. C. (2021). Fighting poverty and inequalities through social impact bonds: Learning from case studies to support the Covid-19 response. In *Contemporary Issues in Sustainable Finance: Financial Products and Financial Institutions* (p. 37). Springer.

Tse, A. E., & Warner, M. E. (2020). The razor's edge: Social impact bonds and the financialization of early childhood services. *Journal of Urban Affairs, 42*(6), 816–832.

Vecchi, V., & Casalini, F. (2019). Is a social empowerment of PPP for infrastructure delivery possible? Lessons from social impact bonds. *Annals of Public and Cooperative Economics, 90*(2), 353–369.

Vickers, J., & Yarrow, G. (1988). *Privatization: An economic analysis*. MIT Press.

Warner, M. (2012, September). Profiting from public value? The case of social impact bonds. Draft paper prepared for *Creating Public Value Conference*. University of Minnesota.

Warner, M. E. (2013). Private finance for public goods: Social impact bonds. *Journal of Economic Policy Reform*, *16*(4), 303–319.

Wilson, K. E., Silva, F., & Richardson, D. (2015). *Social Impact Investment: Building the Evidence Base*. OECD Reports World Bank. (2019). *The Global Partnership for Results-Based Approaches. Impact Bonds: Considerations for Investment Returns and Pricing of Outcomes.*

Chapter 7
Results-Based Funding via Development Impact Bonds:
Stakeholder Perceptions on Benefits and Costs

Hilary Olson
https://orcid.org/0009-0009-6803-4753
Price School of Public Policy, University of Southern California, USA

ABSTRACT

In response to growing social challenges compounded by stretched public and philanthropic resources, the international development sector has become increasingly interested in results-based funding mechanisms such as Development Impact Bonds (DIBs). This study contributes to the growing field of research on DIBs in low- and middle-income counties (LMICs) by exploring stakeholder perceptions on the model's benefits and costs thus far. Drawing on stakeholder interviews from 7 recent DIBs, the study finds that stakeholders wanted to test the effectiveness of DIBs, and that the DIB's provision of outcomes-focused risk capital helped enable a collaborative and adaptive approach to service delivery. This approach then generated evidence of blended returns and increased organizational capacity, as well as spurred cultural shifts towards more sustainable outcomes-based working. Stakeholders also experienced costs and challenges in implementation – especially around garnering institutional buy-in, negotiating contract terms, and managing changing relationships.

DOI: 10.4018/979-8-3693-9551-6.ch007

INTRODUCTION

Reflecting the urgency of pressing social, economic, and environmental issues, in 2015 the United Nations (UN) launched 17 Sustainable Development Goals (SDGs) to be met by 2030 (Halkos & Gkampoura, 2021). With only 5 years remaining, there is a sizeable funding gap with which to meet these complex global problems (Jackson, 2013). Not only do governments face limited public budgets with which to improve service delivery, service providers are often unable to offer sufficient financial returns to attract private capital (Alenda-Demoutiez, 2020; Gallucci et al., 2019; Clarke et al., 2018). Meanwhile, development funding has become more competitive as humanitarian crises grow (Oroxom et al., 2018). To overcome these financial constraints, the international community is increasingly turning to social finance tools such as Development Impact Bonds (DIBs) to improve both access to capital and the effectiveness of aid (Rizzello & Kabli, 2020).

DIBs are a type of results-based funding contract in which principals agree to pay agents based on the achievement of specified outcomes (Pearson, 2011; Grittner, 2013). By making payment contingent on measurable results, results-based funding aims to incentivize better performance than traditional input-based funding (Grittner, 2013, p. 3). Through the DIB model, investors give service providers up-front funding for development programs; outcome funders repay this investment according to program success; and intermediaries provide support ranging from contract negotiations to monitoring and evaluation (Gallucci et al., 2019; Williams, 2020; de Gruyter et al., 2020; Rizzello & Kabli, 2020). Unlike Social Impact Bonds (SIBs) in which a (domestic) government entity serves as outcome funder, in DIBs investment is repaid by donor organizations like foundations, NGOs, and aid agencies (Loraque, 2018).

Figure 1. Timeline of Impact Bond Growth

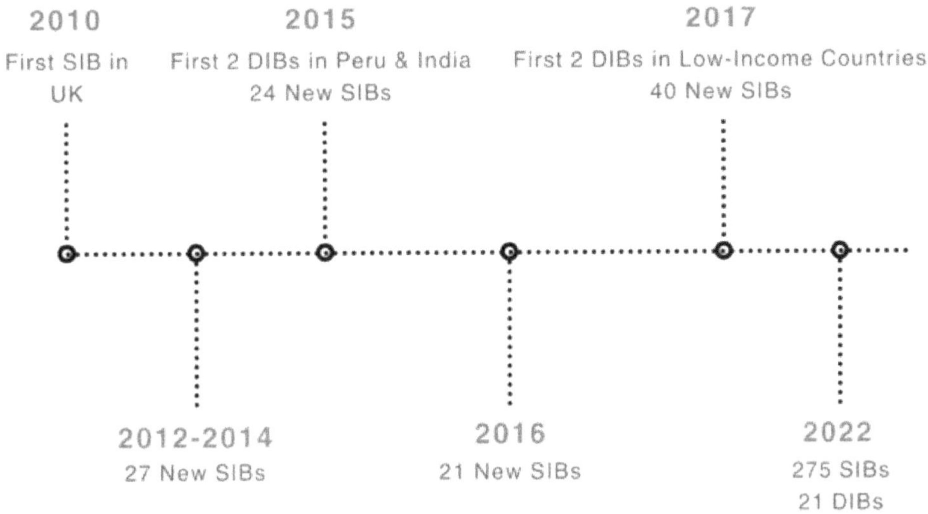

Note: Author's calculations based on data from Indigo (2023).

Throughout the literature, articles tend to differentiate SIBs from DIBs based on the nature of their outcome funders without discussing larger contextual differences (Gallucci et al., 2019; Mishra & Dash, 2022). Some authors, however, have begun to offer more nuance, explaining that "DIBs leverage private capital to address market failures which traditional funders… cannot because of political, financial, or operational constraints" (Clarke et al., 2018, p. 3). Further, while SIBs fit within public service reform efforts following the 2008 financial crisis (e.g. Fox & Morris, 2021), DIBs align with efforts to improve the professionalism, transparency, and accountability of international development organizations (e.g. Alenda-Demoutiez, 2020). As SIBs have also proliferated much more quickly than DIBs (see figures 1, 2, and 3), impact bond research has largely centered on SIBs in High-Income Countries (HICs) (Alenda-Demoutiez, 2020; Velez-Valencia et al., 2025) as opposed to DIBs supporting development initiatives in Low- and Middle-Income Countries (LMICs)[1].

Figure 2. Regional Comparisons of DIBs and SIBs

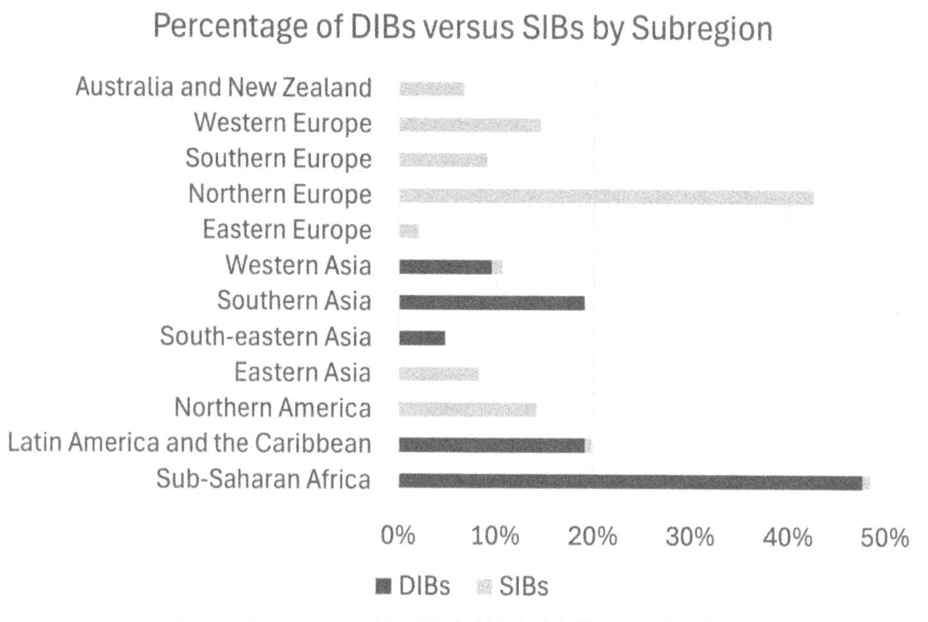

Figure 3. Income Comparisons of DIBs and SIBs

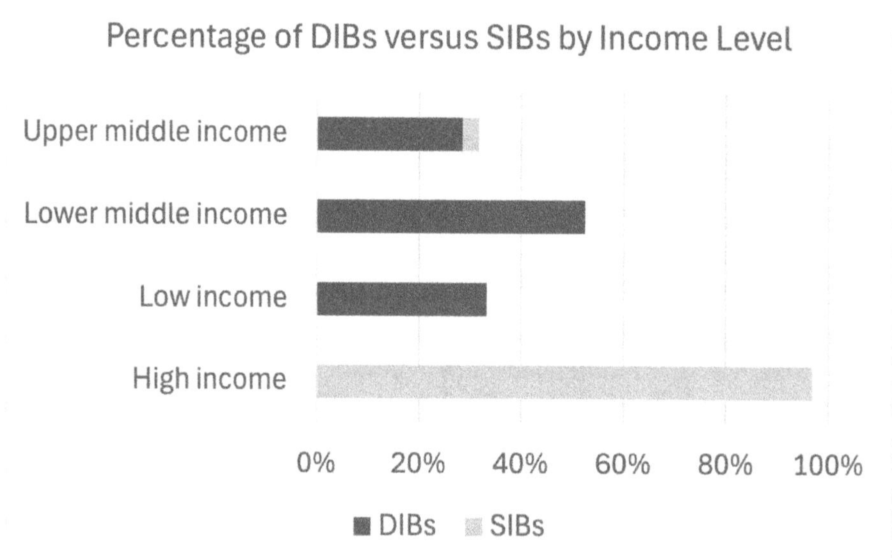

Note: Author's calculations based on data from Indigo (2023).

To address this gap, this study offers novel evidence on stakeholder perceptions on the DIB model's primary benefits and costs.[2] The paper begins with a review of the current DIB literature and an outline of the study's conceptual framework. Next, it describes the study's methodological approach, drawing largely on primary interviews. The paper then provides the study's results and concludes by offering insights for practice and research.

LITERATURE REVIEW

Although interest in DIBs is growing globally, DIB-specific literature remains limited (Gustafsson-Wright et al., 2017; Gallucci et al., 2019; Mishra & Dash, 2022). Research has most often involved single case studies (e.g. Belt et al., 2017; Loraque, 2018; Gallucci et al., 2019; Oroxom et al., 2018; Gustafsson-Wright et al., 2022) or final reports for completed DIBs (e.g. Kitzmuller et al., 2018; O'Neil et al., 2021; Savell & Eddleston, 2021; Hera, 2022). Only a few studies have conducted more comprehensive literature reviews (e.g. Alenda-Demoutiez, 2020; Mishra & Dash, 2022) or larger cross-case empirical analyses (e.g. Gallucci et al., 2022; Gustafsson-Wright et al., 2021; Gustafsson-Wright et al., 2017). Nonetheless, this nascent literature identifies a range of potential DIB benefits and costs to date (summarized in table 1).

Expected DIB Benefits

To address budget limitations and service gaps, international development stakeholders may be motivated to try the DIB model for various reasons (Alenda-Demoutiez, 2020). Service providers may join to access flexible up-front capital with which to innovate and scale up their services (Oroxom et al., 2018; Gallucci et al., 2019; Belt et al., 2017; Alenda-Demoutiez, 2020). Service providers could further aim to attract future funding by building performance management capacity and demonstrating (successful) program outcomes (Gallucci et al., 2019; Muñoz & Kimmitt, 2019; Alenda-Demoutiez, 2020; Belt et al., 2017; Oroxom et al., 2018; Loraque, 2018; Clarke et al., 2018). Investors may participate to generate blended social and financial returns to boost their reputations and recycle capital into other social programs (Gallucci et al., 2019; Belt et al., 2017; Loraque, 2018; Alenda-Demoutiez, 2020). Outcome funders may participate to transfer financial risk and improve resource efficiency by only paying for successful program outcomes (Alenda-Demoutiez, 2020; Belt et al., 2017; Loraque, 2018; Clarke et al., 2018). Funders could additionally seek to improve accountability and transparency through monitoring and evaluation activities (Alenda-Demoutiez, 2020). Finally, to overcome potential challenges related to low institutional capacity, political constraints, or corruption, funders could use DIBs to intentionally avoid involving government actors in development initiatives (Alenda-Demoutiez, 2020).[3]

Potential DIB Costs

In addition to these anticipated benefits, the literature notes numerous possible costs of DIB implementation. Perhaps most common are the start-up costs of hiring intermediaries, lawyers, and technical advisors, as well as establishing effective data management systems (Muñoz & Kimmitt, 2019; Belt et al., 2017; Alenda-Demoutiez, 2020; Loraque, 2018). There are also often high transaction costs due to regulatory and legal issues alongside low data availability (Muñoz & Kimmitt, 2019). Moreover, negotiations around risk transfer, outcome targets, payments, and verification methods can be time-consuming (Clarke et al., 2018; Oroxom et al., 2018). For instance, investors could push for higher interest rates and capital protections, or prefer scaling proven rather than experimental interventions (Alenda-Demoutiez, 2020; Loraque, 2018). Meanwhile, outcome funders could struggle to obtain institutional buy-in due to concerns around paying private sector returns and taking a more hands-off approach to project oversight (Clarke et al., 2018; Belt et al., 2017; Gustafsson-Wright et al., 2017). Another challenge is the susceptibility of LMICs to political and economic shocks which could disrupt DIB operations (Gustafsson-Wright et al., 2017). One such shock was the COVID-19 pandemic.

COVID Impacts

Although COVID impacts were felt globally, vulnerable populations in LMICs were disproportionately impacted by the ensuing health and economic crises (Gustafsson-Wright et al., 2021). To understand the ability for impact bonds to adapt to such crises, Gustafsson-Wright et al. (2021) surveyed 12 impact bonds[4] in LMICs. With lockdowns and other safety concerns causing major operational disruptions, many programs transitioned from in-person to remote services. While this change caused programming delays, only one program shut down. In addition, eight programs augmented their monitoring and evaluation strategies, such as switching to virtual data collection methods like phone interviews and digital assessments. To account for these adjustments, five programs updated their contractual payment structures, such as by shifting "outcomes measurement and payment to the following year, giving service providers sufficient time to adapt their programs" (Gustafsson-Wright et al., 2021, p. 12). However, amending contracts also took time (in one case seven months), due to complexities in coordinating among different stakeholders. Nonetheless, most stakeholders surveyed felt that the impact bond structure offered more flexibility than traditional funding arrangements in making necessary program adjustments. Based on these findings, Gustafsson-Wright et al. (2021) conclude that while it can be hard to change impact bond outcome metrics, even during crises, the model's flexible outcomes-oriented approach allows for considerable adaptability when responding to external shocks. Moreover, many of the new approaches to remote and hybrid service delivery and evaluation were expected to continue after the pandemic ended.

Table 1. Existing Themes from the DIB Literature

Motivations and Expected Benefits	• Limited resources and service gaps • Up-front capital, innovation, and scaled impact • Performance management capacity and monitoring/evaluation • Blended returns, reputational gains, and future funding • Financial risk transfer, resource efficiency, and accountability • Reduced reliance on governments
Potential Costs and Challenges	• Start-up and transaction costs • Protracted negotiations and institutional-buy-in • Changing roles and relationships • External shocks (EX: COVID)

Note: Based on author's analysis of literature.

CONCEPTUAL FRAMING

To offer new insights into the DIB model's benefits and costs, this study turns to two conceptual frameworks from the SIB literature. Drawing on research by Ormiston et al. (2020), this study analyzes DIB benefits according to broader stakeholder objectives around social finance, collaboration, and social impact. To analyze DIB costs, the study follows Agusti Strid and Ronicle's (2021) model of SIB market development barriers around government demand, regulatory frameworks, economic and political contexts, data availability, and market capacity.

Stakeholder Expectations

In analyzing press releases from 29 SIBs in the UK, US, and Australia, Ormiston et al. (2020) identify three broad discourses reflecting stakeholder objectives: social finance, collaboration, and impact. Within the social finance discourse (46%), stakeholder expectations relate to testing a new financial model (36%), building the social finance market (8%), and attracting private capital (2%). Meanwhile, within the collaboration discourse (26%), expectations include intersectoral partnership

(14%), financial returns for investors (6%), government savings (5%), and flexible funding for service providers (1%). Finally, within the impact discourse (28%), expectations correspond to improved social outcomes (22%), measurement and accountability (4%), and innovation (2%).

In addition, their analysis finds that outcome funders and investors tend to emphasize the role of SIBs "as an innovative funding mechanism targeted at catalysing social finance markets" (Ormiston et al., 2020, p. 240). Meanwhile, intermediaries focus more on collaborative efforts to build the social finance sector, and service providers focus more on SIB impacts for service users. The authors also note that while the social finance discourse is most prevalent during SIB launch, the discursive focus shifts to impact during implementation. The study finds slight discursive differences between the three countries as well, suggesting that stakeholders should adapt SIB implementation based on local conditions.

In situating these results within the wider SIB literature, Ormiston et al. (2020) view the social finance discourse as aligning with New Public Management (NPM), which stresses the importance of incentives, performance management, and evaluation in achieving measurable outcomes and improving public sector efficiency (Fitzgerald et al., 2020; Osborne, 2006; Chandra et al., 2021). They align the collaboration discourse with New Public Governance (NPG), which underscores the role of collaborative relationships in delivering effective public services and generating positive social outcomes (Osborne, 2006). Moreover, they see the collaborative discourse as supporting the social finance discourse by prioritizing private sector investors as non-traditional partners in social service delivery. They further posit that "the marginalization of service providers and the impact discourse" (Ormiston et al., 2020, p. 244) supports a cautionary narrative around SIBs, in which financialization prioritizes financial sector interests over social needs (Fraser et al., 2018).

Market Development Factors

In their study of Latin American SIBs, Agusti Strid and Ronicle (2021) identify three SIB market development phases: 1) developing first time SIBs, 2) establishing the SIB mechanism, and 3) growing the SIB ecosystem. Within the first phase, the main objectives are to generate learnings about the model, to demonstrate the model's viability, and to gain stakeholder buy-in. During the second phase, the focus shifts to building on the lessons learned from first-time SIBs, demonstrating the model's cost-effectiveness, and capacity building for external stakeholders to participate in future SIBs. In the third phase, the aim becomes better understanding how SIBs can best be applied in different contexts, while also addressing structural barriers.

To advance phases, Agusti Strid and Ronicle (2021, p. 57) identify five 'DREAM' factors which can act as barriers (or enablers): Demand from government, Regulatory framework, Economic and political context, Availability of data, and Market capacity. Government demand refers to whether there are potential public sector outcome funders with sufficient understanding of the model and organizational buy-in to contribute to SIB design and implementation. Supportive regulatory frameworks include legal contexts in which governments (or other funders) can commission SIBs over multiple years; investors can legally earn a return on their investments; and payments can be tied to outcomes. Data availability relates to whether stakeholders have access to robust and reliable socio-economic data with which to establish baselines as well as price and validate outcomes. Economic and political context is dependent on the stability of public institutions and market conditions, and is affected by factors such as elections and recessions. Lastly, market capacity refers to whether there is sufficient investor interest and service provider capabilities to participate in SIBs. Capacity also includes whether stakeholders have access to technical expertise in designing and managing SIBs.

Agusti Strid and Ronicle (2021) further report that stakeholders can overcome issues posed by unsupportive regulatory frameworks, unstable economic and political contexts, and low data availability on a case-by-case basis as long as stakeholders remain committed and flexible. To do so, "it is essential to work with a coalition of like-minded, purpose-driven organizations" during the early stages of market development, as well as have champions within organizations who are willing to drive the cause forward (Agusti Strid & Ronicle, 2021, p. 69). However, as the SIB market matures, stakeholders will need to more seriously and systematically resolve such structural barriers; otherwise, transaction costs will remain high as stakeholders navigate legal and political obstacles one project at a time. Meanwhile, relational challenges around government demand and market capacity should diminish (to a certain extent) as stakeholders embed institutional knowledge and share lessons learned with broader networks which should encourage future SIB participation.

Research Questions

Based on the literature review and the conceptual frameworks above, this study's research questions are:

1) What are the contextual factors and anticipated model benefits that are motivating stakeholders to use DIBs?
    a. How do these motivations and benefits align with broader objectives around social finance, collaboration, and social impact?
2) What costs and challenges do stakeholders experience in implementing DIBs?
    a. How do these costs and challenges relate to impact bond market development barriers?

In answering these questions, this research aims to address some critical gaps in DIB scholarship. First, there is a growing call from academics and policymakers to specify SIB effects, or the effects of using impact bonds compared to alternative financial arrangements (Gallucci et al., 2019). However, as it is hard to find valid counterfactuals, it could be beneficial to develop an alternative frame through which to evaluate whether DIBs are meeting stakeholders' longer-term expectations. Second, SIB market development has thus far been slower than expected – with DIB market growth even slower (Williams, 2020). To avoid market collapse, which could limit financing options for addressing pressing social issues, it is vital understand potential barriers to continued DIB development (Williams, 2020; de Gruyter et al., 2020). Third, by using SIB frameworks to analyze DIBs, this study will situate DIBs within larger narratives around the costs and benefits of the impact bond model – offering novel evidence outside the Western, Anglo-Saxon context predominant in existing SIB scholarship (Dahbi et al., 2024).

DATA AND METHODS

To answer the study's research questions, the analysis drew on primary data from DIB stakeholder interviews and secondary data from program-related documents. By conducting semi-structured interviews, this study sought to collect in-depth insights from a relatively small set of participants (Leech, 2002). Data collection involved 16 interviews with 18 individuals from outcome funder (8), investor (3), service provider (3), and intermediary (2) organizations. During the interviews, questions asked individuals about their decisions to participate in DIBs and their views on the model's benefits and costs thus far. Interviews lasted approximately 60 minutes, were conducted virtually, and were recorded with participant consent. All interview quotes have been anonymized due to the potentially sensitive or political nature of responses. In addition, the analysis collected evidence from press releases, news articles, and program reports.

Analysis entailed thematically coding interview transcripts corresponding to 'motivations', 'benefits', 'costs,' and 'challenges.' 'Motivations' included contextual factors and incentivizing model design elements ('inputs'), while 'benefits' captured immediate 'outputs', short-term 'outcomes', and longer-term 'impacts.' 'Costs' were divided into 'transaction costs' pertaining to DIB design and development and 'management challenges' relating to DIB implementation and administration (Fitzgerald et al., 2020; Gustafsson-Wright & Osborne, 2020b). The analysis then classified motivations and benefits as aligning with Ormiston et al.'s (2020) stakeholder objectives and classified costs and challenges using Agusti Strid and Ronicle's (2021) DREAM framework.[5] These classifications are summarized in figures 4 and 5.

Figure 4. Stakeholder Objective Classifications

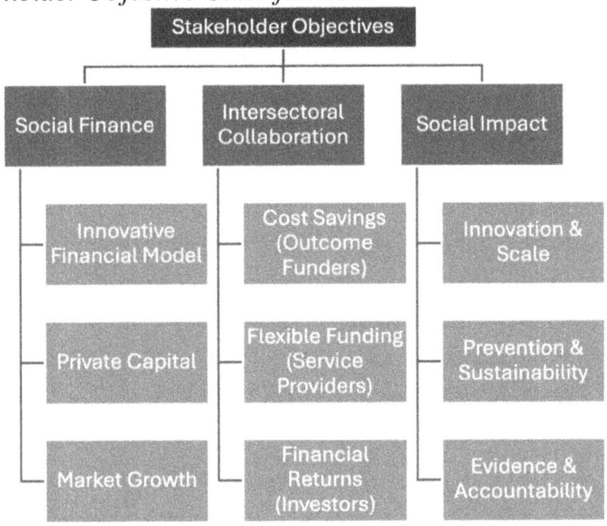

Figure 5. Market Barrier Classifications

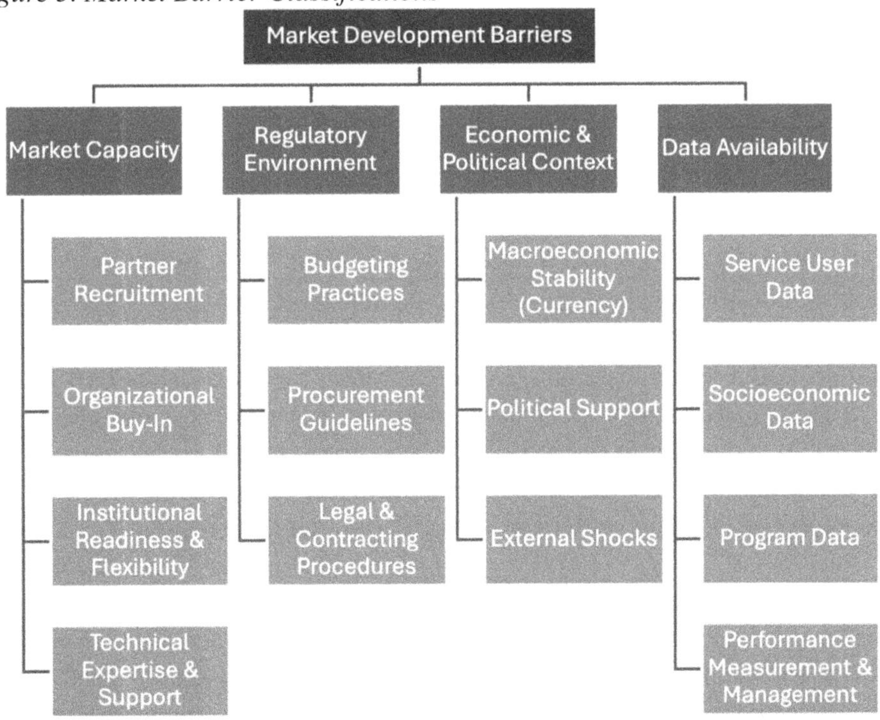

Note: Classifications adapted from Ormiston et al. (2020) and Agusti Strid & Ronicle (2021).

Sample

The study selected the sample from the 21 DIBs in LMICs included in the Government Outcomes Lab's Impact Bond Dataset as of 2023 (Indigo, 2023). The sample was restricted to DIBs that launched before 2022 and that concluded (or were projected to conclude) after 2021. Due to language limitations, one DIB was excluded from the sample. This selection criteria gave the study a final sample size of 7 DIBs. As shown in table 2, these DIBs ranged in size, location, and sector. Countries and stakeholders also had varying levels of experience with impact bonds, although most DIBs were the first impact bonds to be launched in a country. The three exceptions were the Quality Education in India (QEI) and Skill India DIBs in India and the In Their Hands DIB[6] in Kenya.[7]

Table 2. DIB Characteristics

DIB	Country	Start Year	End Year	Sector	Beneficiaries	Max Outcome Funding (USD)
ICRC	Mali DRC Nigeria	2017	2022	Health	3,600 individuals with physical disabilities	$26.6 M
QEI	India	2018	2022	Education	300,000 primary school-aged children	$9.2 M
Cameroon Cataract	Cameroon	2018	2023	Health	18,000 low/middle-income patients	$2.2 M
Cambodia Rural Sanitation	Cambodia	2019	2023	Poverty reduction	1,600 rural villages	$10.0 M
F4J	Palestine	2019	2023	Employment and training	1,500 job seekers (18-29 years old)	$5.0 M
In Their Hands	Kenya	2020	2022	Health	193,000 girls (15-19 years old)	$6.6 M
Skill India	India	2021	2025	Employment and training	50,000 unemployed youth	$14.4 M

Source: Based on data from Indigo (2023) and author's analysis of secondary sources.

In fact, India represents a unique context within this study as its DIB market was more advanced than other countries. India was the site of the world's first DIB, Educate Girls, which ran from 2015 to 2018. When Skill India launched as the fourth DIB in India, it involved a number of stakeholders with prior DIB experience. Such stakeholders included two of QEI's intermediaries: the British Asian Trust (BAT) and Dalberg Associates. Another common stakeholder was the Michael and Susan Dell Foundation, which served as an outcome funder in the QEI DIB and an investor in the Skill India DIB. In addition, Skill India's outcome funder, CIFF, previously served as an outcome funder and investor in the Educate Girls and In Their Hands DIBs, respectively. Two of Skill India's intermediaries, USAID and FCDO, served as outcome funders for three prior DIBs as well. Consequently, India's DIBs were able to build off of learnings from one another, including in some cases by sharing stakeholders with institutional knowledge on DIBs. For instance, an FCDO evaluation found that "learning had been taken forwards from the Educate Girls DIB [into QEI] to improve design and increase efficiency in transactions," including "involving an outcome evaluator earlier in the project and allowing flexibility within the contracting process" (Erskine, 2021, p. 29, p. 2).

RESULTS

Corresponding to the study's research questions, findings related to four main topics. First, results include contextual factors and model design elements incentivizing DIB use, along with the (positive) outputs, outcomes, and impacts of the DIB model. Second, findings demonstrate how these motivations and benefits align with social finance, collaboration, and social impact objectives (Ormiston et al., 2020). Third, evidence shows the various transaction costs and management difficulties stakeholders experienced by participating in DIBs. Results further outline how such costs and challenges relate to market capacity, data, regulatory, and economic and political barriers (Agusti Strid & Ronicle, 2021).

Motivations and Model Benefits

The top motivation driving DIB participation was the opportunity to test a *new financial model* (69%), with stakeholders "genuinely interested in proof of concept here… for others in the space to learn what this looks like" (Service Provider). Stakeholders sought to gain first-hand experience with results-based funding and to obtain evidence on DIBs for the development sector as a whole. The importance of testing the DIB model was reflected in stakeholder and program press releases and websites, which frequently emphasized how DIBs were the first within a country or sector, or novel in terms of target population or budget size (visualized in figure 6). For instance, Kanthan Shankar, the World Bank Country Director, highlighted the importance of the F4J DIB in Palestine as "the first time to be applied by the World Bank in a fragile environment" (FMO, 2019).

Figure 6. Word Cloud Visualizing Statements on DIB Novelty

Note: Based on author's analysis of secondary sources.

Another frequent motivation was overcoming *limited resources* (31%) from local governmental agencies and international aid organizations by diversifying or pooling capital. This need became even more acute following the onset of COVID when considerable funding was diverted to relief efforts. Addressing persistent *service gaps* (38%), such as by targeting marginalized groups, expanding programs to larger populations, and improving the quality of existing services, was also a common objective. A less frequent goal was addressing a *lack of evidence* (19%) on development programs, for instance on the (cost) effectiveness of different interventions. Interestingly, even when service providers had sufficient access to donor funding, it was often difficult to link inputs to program outcomes. Thus, stakeholders wanted more evidence tying impacts to funding as this would facilitate future decision-making. For example, "if they can demonstrate how outcomes under DIBs are better, cost price discovery is better... Some of this will start influencing the national, the federal and the state government schemes… So mainstreaming of outcome-based financing principles was a key motivation" (Intermediary).

In terms of model design elements (or inputs), the most common motivation was the *transfer of risk* (75%) from both outcome funders and service providers to investors. For outcome funders, this risk transfer centered on the provision of only paying for successful program results. In turn, the potential to use scarce resources more efficiently helped generate institutional buy-in, as "it's a marketing point to be able to say the risk elements are more suitable for institutions like ours" (Outcome Funder). While DIBs helped shift some financial risk from outcome funders to investors, the operational risk of delivering services in volatile areas was not explicitly covered by the DIB contracts, because "What happens if there's a war? What happens if… there's a run on banks and they shut down?" (Outcome Funder). The amount of financial risk transfer also varied considerably among the DIBs. In the Cameroon Cataract DIB, although the loan's interest rate depends on outcome achievement, investors have complete capital protection and financial risks are shared between outcome funders and service providers (Indigo, 2022a). Conversely, while all investor capital is at risk in the Cambodia Sanitation DIB, the service provider has also invested and will receive a portion of the profits if certain targets are met (Stone Family Foundation & iDE, n.d.).

Meanwhile, DIBs gave service providers access to *up-front flexible funding* (56%), transferring financial risk to investors during program implementation. By focusing on outcomes targets rather than input specifications, DIBs afforded service providers much more flexibility in how they spent money and designed interventions. This flexibility empowered service providers by changing the traditional donor-grantee relationships, as "It didn't seem the power was with the donor… it felt like [the funder] was saying, here's the outcome, however you are able to achieve it is your problem… [and] there's someone there to pay for your risk taking" (Intermediary). Although such risk transfer encouraged some services providers to innovate with less fear of failure, risk capital seemed primarily intended to scale proven interventions, with one Outcome Funder sharing, "[We] don't see DIBs as an innovation instrument, we really see it as a scaling instrument."

Additionally, investors were incentivized to take on delivery risk through potential *financial returns* (25%). Investors viewed taking such financial risks as part of their institutional mandates, with many pursuing blended social and financial returns. Generating financial returns also facilitated reinvestment in future social projects, because, "if we can recycle our capital, then we can go and do more things with it, have more social impact, invest in other good things" (Investor). These various inputs were unanimously considered important incentives for encouraging *intersectoral collaboration*, with private sector partners playing a crucial role.

Although DIBs do not usually include governments as contractual parties, the degree to which stakeholders strategically engaged with government actors varied by program. In most DIBs, *government engagement* was limited; although stakeholders worked to gain government buy-in by aligning on policy priorities, government actors were not involved in day-to-day DIB operations. However, some DIBs required government coordination when interventions were run through public facilities or when the government was involved in outcome verification or reporting. In other DIBs, government interaction was intentionally minimal, for instance due to a focus on building local private sector capacity instead. In these cases, engagement primarily entailed informing government officials of the DIB's activities and progress. However, government involvement was more formalized in a couple of the DIBs. For example, the ICRC DIB was "implemented by DAI Global on behalf of the Palestinian Ministry of Finance, and… funded by the World Bank" (FMO, 2019), while one of Skill India's investors is the National Skill Development Corporation (NSDC), "a public-private partnership set up by the Ministry of Skill Development and Entrepreneurship" (Gustafsson-Wright et al., 2022, p. 15). Table 3 summarizes these motivations and model incentives.

Table 3. Motivating Contextual Factors and Model Inputs

Contextual factors	• New financial model (11, 69%) • Service gaps (6, 38%) • Limited resources (5, 31%) • Lack of evidence (3, 19%)
Design elements (inputs)	• Incentives for collaboration o Risk transfer (12, 75%) o Up-front flexible funding (9, 56%) o Potential financial returns (4, 25%) • Strategic government engagement (varied)

Note: Based on author's analysis of primary interview data.

In addition to these motivations, DIB model benefits included a range of immediate outputs, intermediate outcomes, and longer-term impacts (summarized in table 4). The principal output was the use of *adaptive performance management* (63%), through which stakeholders use insights from real-time data to continuously improve program design. Triggerise (now Tiko), the service provider for the In Their Hands DIB, used a digital platform to monitor data in real time, explaining that "if the data showed a decline in uptake for a certain service, the platform would alert us and we would dig into potential factors driving the decline" (Tiko, 2023). This responsive, data-driven approach enabled the DIB to surpass its targets for total and repeat health visits by 148% and 262%, respectively. Adaptive management additionally required innovation when designing and testing new services. DIB stakeholders also had to pivot service delivery when experiencing shocks in local political, economic, and social conditions – such as the crises following the outbreak of COVID. Another prominent output was *monitoring and evaluation* (63%). Evaluation not only included internal verification processes and third-party assessments, but sometimes included learning-oriented components not tied to investor repayments, like measuring longer-term impacts and DIB effects.

Another common output was *capacity building* (38%), often to support the public sector. One facet of this capacity building was helping governments better understand results-based funding models. DIB stakeholders also supported governments in overcoming implementation barriers and improving outreach strategies, because "when you get down to the provincial and local government level... we rely really heavily on those government partners, and in turn do a lot of capacity building... [around] mapping communities, understanding what the barriers are" (Service Provider). While some DIBs worked to build service provider capacity, for instance around data collection and reporting, service providers were generally chosen as DIB partners for having strong preexisting performance management and monitoring capabilities. As an example, QEI's service providers were all well-established and high-performing organizations with "over 10 years' experience providing education interventions, experience operating at scale and ... independent evaluations to measure their effectiveness" (Erskine, 2021, p. 5).

Turning to DIB outcomes, key benefits were evidence generation, accountability, financial returns, and scaled impact (63%). *Evidence generation* included data on program outcomes and cost-efficiency, with an Intermediary sharing: "I cannot emphasize how important that is... evidence on costs, price efficiency... [I] know of donors who would do a DIB just because of the quality and level of evidence generation that would happen." Evidence also related to increased *accountability*, especially for investors and outcome funders seeking to demonstrate responsible use of resources. Meanwhile, *financial returns* related to investment repayment plus any profits from interest or return rates. Cost recovery enabled re-investment into other social programs, while financial returns signaled the model's viability to attract more private investors in the future. As one Investor explained, "The optics around the return were important in the sense that... we needed to make a sort of 5% return to make it credible to achieve that secondary impact that we were looking for, which is really about changing the way finance flows in the sector." The DIBs also generated considerable *social impacts*– at a faster pace, greater scale, and higher quality. Additionally, participating in a DIB, particularly when launched in a new context, brought high visibility to program partners, providing them with *reputational gains* (38%) and greater credibility as leaders in their respective sectors.

In addition, the DIBs had numerous impacts (or anticipated impact) beyond the individual contracts themselves. The primary impact was *growth of the social finance market* (88%). This growth included opportunities for follow-on DIBs (e.g. same programs), other DIBs (e.g. different programs), and potential future SIBs, with "very, very strong interest from the donor community to say, what is the next version of it? Can we participate? Will you scale this up?" (Intermediary). In fact, after the successful completion of the In Their Hands DIB in Kenya, the UN Joint SDG Fund scaled the DIB by investing $7 million (Indigo, 2022b). Incorporating learnings from the first DIB, "this new phase of the DIB will also have more engagement from the public sector as the national government will be a member of the project committee" (Indigo, 2022b). Another benefit was helping service providers attract more private (non-DIB) funding in the future.

The DIBs also catalyzed *cultural shifts* (31%) towards outcome-based working more broadly, especially among service providers where "the culture shift that's happening… is really out of this world" (Outcome Funder). Such promising changes were not limited to service providers but seen within donor and even government organizations as well. Given the increased focus on monitoring, evaluation, and learning within the DIBs, this cultural shift was sometimes correlated with the more general trend toward professionalization within the international development sector. Evidence generated by the DIBs was further expected to enable service providers to continue improving and growing their programs, for instance by producing helpful *programmatic learnings* (19%) which aid and public sector organizations could also use to scale effective approaches. The DIBs also contributed to greater impact *sustainability* (31%), through increased local capacity, private sector stimulation, and a focus on prevention.

Overall, stakeholders were impressed with how effectively the DIB model performed in practice. As one Intermediary expressed, "I was really surprised that it worked. And worked well. The ethics of it worked… the data, the flexible funding, the power dynamics, the focus on MEL [monitoring, evaluation, and learning], those things work." Moreover, while other funding arrangements could potentially offer similar benefits as DIBs – like high levels of collaboration and flexible service delivery – DIBs offer a convenient package which stakeholders can adapt to meet their needs. In addition to offering greater convenience compared to less flexible models, one Outcome Funder shared that the DIBs has "been functioning like clockwork in a way that I've not seen many other traditional [Institutional] projects actually operate as smoothly."

Table 4. Beneficial Model Outputs, Outcomes, and Impacts

Immediate benefits (outputs)	• Adaptive performance management (10, 63%) • Monitoring and evaluation (10, 63%) • Capacity building (for governments) (6, 38%)
Intermediate benefits (outcomes)	• Evidence/Accountability (10, 63%) • Financial returns (10, 63%) • (Scaled) social impact (10, 63%) • Reputational gains (6, 38%)
Longer-term benefits (impacts)	• Social finance market growth (14, 88%) • Cultural shifts (outcome-based working) (5, 31%) • Sustainability (5, 31%) • Programmatic learnings (3, 19%)

Note: Based on author's analysis of primary interview data.

Broader Objectives

In categorizing these motivations and benefits around wider objectives (Ormiston et al., 2020), evidence suggests a strong focus on social finance. As with Ormiston et al. (2020), DIB stakeholders frequently wanted to test DIBs as an innovative financial tool, with broader goals of growing the social finance market. For instance, by demonstrating the potential of earning financial returns, investors hoped to attract additional investments to the DIB or results-based finance space in the future. Unlike the marginalization of the social impact discourse found by Ormiston et al. (2020), this study's results also highlighted prominent social impact objectives. The DIBs allowed stakeholders to more rigorously measure and manage performance as well as improve accountability and scale social impact. The DIBs further promoted longer-term social change by offering programmatic learnings for the sector, producing more sustainable outcomes for beneficiaries, and spurring broader cultural effects around monitoring and evaluation. In contrast, collaboration objectives were largely limited to model inputs, which tended to offer incentives for intersectoral partnership. Table 5 summarizes these categorizations.

Table 5. Motivations and Benefits Categorizations

	Social Finance	Collaboration	Social Impact
Contextual Factors	-Limited resources (5, 31%) -New financial model (11, 69%)		-Lack of evidence (3, 19%) -Service gaps (6, 38%)
Model Inputs		-Up-front, flexible funding (9, 56%) -Potential financial returns (4, 25%) -Risk transfer (12, 75%) -Strategic government engagement (varied)	
Model Outputs		-Capacity building (6, 38%)	-Adaptive management (10, 63%) -Monitoring and evaluation (10, 63%)
Model Outcomes	-Financial returns (10, 63%) - Reputational gains (6, 38%)		-Evidence/ Accountability (10, 63%) -(Scaled) social impact (10, 63%)
Model Impacts	- Social finance market growth (14, 88%)		- Cultural shifts (towards outcomes) (5, 31%) -Sustainability (5, 31%) -Programmatic learnings (3, 19%)

Note: Based on author's analysis of primary interview data.

In situating these findings within the wider SIB literature, the interest in testing and demonstrating DIB effectiveness reflects trends within early SIB development (Gustafsson-Wright et al., 2015). This motivation will likely become less relevant as evidence is accumulated on DIB viability and the focus shifts to establishing the model's suitability in various contexts (Agusti Strid & Ronicle, 2021). This shift has already begun to occur within the SIB landscape, with academics and policymakers increasingly calling for evaluations into SIB effects to examine whether the financing mechanism itself or the funded interventions are driving outcome achievement (Carter et al., 2018; Hevenstone et al., 2023).

Conversely, a unique consideration for DIB stakeholders in growing the social finance market is strategic government engagement. While DIBs theoretically exclude (domestic) governments as contractual partners, some DIBs had explicit goals to build local public capacity while others even formally contracted with government actors outside of traditional outcome funder roles. Such engagement diverges from prior findings that "the presence of local or national government is very limited" in DIBs (Alenda-Demoutiez, 2020, p. 898), and demonstrates that an objective for many DIB stakeholders was to encourage governments to serve as outcome funders for future SIBs (Agusti Strid & Ronicle, 2021).

Additionally, the greater emphasis on social impact in DIBs compared to SIBs could reflect challenges that LMICs can face around data availability. As governments and NGOs often lack funding for large-scale data collection and impact evaluations, development organizations may struggle to establish baselines or outcome targets due to a scarcity of publicly available data (Clarke et al., 2018; Muñoz & Kimmitt, 2019). Such data limitations could help explain why DIB stakeholder motivations include building up the evidence base on social indicators. The larger focus on social impact could also be because LMICs face bigger gaps in social services in terms of breadth and depth, thus requiring larger-scale solutions (Gustafsson-Wright et al., 2015). For instance, while DIBs account for just 9% of all impact bonds worldwide, they represent 47% of beneficiaries (Gustafsson-Wright & Osborne, 2020a).

Costs and Challenges

In addition to these various benefits, implementing DIBs posed a number of transaction costs and management challenges (see table 6). Transaction costs corresponded to the time, effort, and money it took to *set-up the DIBs* (25%). These start-up costs included fees for hiring intermediary services and conducting feasibility studies. Further, it was often difficult to *find partner organizations* (25%) to fill the investor and outcome funder roles, partly due to the limited evidence on DIBs at the time. Potential outcome funders also faced difficulties such as earmarking funding for DIBs in future years' budgets. Moreover, outcome funders were sometimes skeptical about paying returns to private investors, as this could inflate the cost of funding the same programs. A Service Provider even felt that, "the most challenging part of the impact bond model… [is] the ability to secure outcome funding." Meanwhile, potential investors ranged from wanting no returns due to their corporate social responsibility mandates to wanting higher returns (or more capital guarantees) due to the perceived risks of investing in DIBs for the first time or in un-tested contexts. Francoise de Borchgrave, the founder and Managing Director of ICRC, expressed: "The challenge was to develop a product that would make investors comfortable with the idea to invest in a very volatile and fragile context: post-conflict zones" (Bollag, 2017, para. 7). For these reasons, individual staff members of investor or outcome funder organizations often worked hard to garner sufficient support and *organizational buy-in* (25%) to enter into DIB contracts.

Another high cost was the considerable time it took to *negotiate contracts* (31%). While financial terms like return rates and capital protections took time to negotiate, it proved more challenging for DIB parties to agree on outcome definition. One Service Provider recalled, "when it comes to figuring out what the outcome metric is, that was a big and difficult and long-term conversation… there were some who thought that longer-term… outcomes should be something that we look at… which ultimately [you] hope you're contributing to but in terms of defining outcomes didn't make sense." Selecting metrics and achievement targets that were both measurable and appropriately ambitious often posed a difficulty – especially when existing evidence was limited.

Once such negotiations were settled, stakeholders also had trouble with the contracting itself. Partners frequently had their own procedures and guidelines, as when the DIBs involved parties from different jurisdictions subject to their own separate laws. Larger organizations also tended to be more bureaucratic and inflexible, further complicating contracting incompatibilities. As one Outcome Funder explained, it can be difficult to "convince these folks to get on board and think outside the box of the traditional [Institutional] processes and convince them that they're not breaking rules." Another hurdle arose when stakeholders had a difference in currencies. Illustrating this point, the QEI DIB had a "difference in the exchange rates between the currencies in the DIB (US Dollars, British Pounds and Indian Rupees)… [so outcome] partners have agreed to take on the risk… [and] if the value of the India rupee appreciates against the US Dollar, BAT will be liable to cover the funding gap" (Erskine, 2021, p. 15).

With regards to management challenges, most common was adjusting to *new roles and organizational practices* (44%). For instance, DIB participation prompted investors to have a greater role in management, outcome funders to participate less in monitoring, and service providers to become more flexible in their approach to service delivery. This proved challenging for outcome funders in the Cameroon Cataract DIB, who were previously "used to a hands-on management approach from their grants and acknowledged that allowing the bond manager to take on the intermediary role between them and the service provider was a steep learning curve" (Strid, 2021, p. 23). Moreover, adapting to new ways of working often required organizational change, which was again hard to orchestrate in more established organizations which "have strict rules that we have to follow to ensure transparency and competition in procuring services… [that] seems to pivot us back into the traditional way of doing things" (Outcome Funder). Additionally, as organizations adopted new collaborative roles, inter-organizational relationships had to adjust, occasionally causing tension among DIB partners – particularly those who had worked together previously through more traditional funding models. One Service Provider expressed, "I think one of the valuable learnings for us… was learning how to work with a trusted partner… but with a slightly different relationship."

Another common theme was insufficient *institutional readiness* (19%) when DIB partners lacked prior experience working in a results-based way. As one Intermediary explained, "I think also a little bit of a challenge is just to see how different stakeholders who have not been part of a DIB get used to the workings of a DIB… it has required extensive hand holding and capacity building for them to realize why the data matters, why the data quality matters, and for them to actually incentivize different rank and file of the organization to do this well.. [including] frontline staff." To overcome low in-house capacity, DIB partners turned to intermediaries specialized in results-based funding, given that "the kinds of expertise that I think you need to pull something like this off… Having outside support is really important. And that was surprising to me… I would call it even a shock." DIB partners also experienced *evaluation challenges* (19%), stemming from data access, evaluator technical expertise, and political risks around outcome reporting. To overcome such difficulties, DIB partners had to adapt, as seen in the In Their Hands DIB, where "because of unforeseen delays in the procurement process, the impact evaluation… and data collection for the baseline started after 10 months after the intervention… [so funders] decided to pay 100% of outcome payments according to service delivery" rather than including a portion of payments on contraceptive uptake (Indigo, 2022b).

An external shock collectively felt among the DIBs was *COVID*. As the pandemic grew, the DIBs were at various stages of implementation, with some preparing to launch with others already underway. However, while COVID represented a challenge to all DIBs, most partners remained committed to supporting program delivery, recognizing the growing need for urgent social services at this time. In fact, one of the service providers in Cambodia's Rural Sanitation DIB "integrated COVID-19 safety campaigns into the project's existing work, training over 400 local government officials on COVID-19 prevention" (Gustafsson-Wright et al., 2021, p. 11). Nonetheless, although some stakeholders felt that the DIB's flexibility allowed them to update their outcome targets and investment terms relatively quickly and easily, others cited an existing ability to operating in difficult and changing environments, enabling them to adapt operations regardless of the DIB structure. As one Outcome Funder explained: "I think that [COVID response] has to do with… the impact bond but … also the fact that it's… ups and downs all the time. And having to… be able to adapt quickly and adjust to the worst-case scenario, I think also plays a huge factor… there was definitely already an adaptability factor there."

Table 6. Start-Up Costs and Management Challenges

Transaction costs	• Start-up costs (4, 25%) • Partner recruitment (4, 25%) • Institutional buy-in (4, 25%) • Contract negotiations (5, 31%)
Management challenges	• Changing roles and relationships (7, 44%) • Evaluation difficulties (3, 19%) • Institutional readiness (3, 19%) • COVID (varied)

Note: Based on author's analysis of primary interview data.

Market Development Barriers

In classifying these costs and challenges using Agusti Strid and Ronicle's (2021) (D)REAM framework (summarized in Table 7), the majority fall within market capacity considerations; these include high start-up fees along with difficulties recruiting partner organizations and adjusting to new ways of working. DIB stakeholders should experience fewer market capacity problems as they gain experience using this model and generate institutional knowledge for use in future DIBs (Agusti Strid & Ronicle, 2021). Further, by sharing lessons learned with their networks, stakeholders should help encourage future DIB participation by external stakeholders (Agusti Strid & Ronicle, 2021). India has already exhibited such market capacity growth as its DIB ecosystem matures.

To some degree, the challenges around data availability should also decrease with DIB market growth. As more DIBs come to an end and results are shared through evaluation reports, new evidence on cohort characteristics and effective program strategies should facilitate easier DIB design processes (Maier et al., 2018). Particularly when implementing DIBs in similar geographic and policy areas, stakeholders should face fewer hurdles in selecting appropriate outcome metrics, targets, and costs (Agusti Strid & Ronicle, 2021). However, a more persistent problem will probably be access to socioeconomic data, most notably when service providers deliver services through public institutions and evaluations use government-enforced standards to validate DIB outcomes (Agusti Strid & Ronicle, 2021).

Although posing less frequent challenges, unsupportive regulatory environments and unstable economic and political conditions will likely present more structural barriers. Regulatory issues primarily related to the rigid procurement policies within larger outcome funder organizations as well as jurisdictional differences in legal regulations and contracting procedures. To date, DIB partners have mostly addressed such obstacles on an ad hoc basis; for example, by having different outcome funders pay investors in separate years to overcome annual budgeting restrictions (Agusti Strid & Ronicle, 2021). If organizations do not work to create more supportive procedures moving forward, DIB development costs will remain high. However, such changes require policy or organizational change, involving considerable time and advocacy efforts (Agusti Strid & Ronicle, 2021).

Even harder to surmount are economic and political obstacles, such as uncertainties around currency values, political sensitivities when validating and reporting outcomes, and external shocks like the COVID pandemic. Some DIBs even faced threats of violent outbreaks, with the F4J DIB in Palestine and the ICRC DIB in Nigeria, Mali, and the DRC operating in areas experiencing high levels of fragility and conflict, respectively (FMO, 2019; ICRC, 2022). When facing such insecurity and instability, intermediaries could face additional costs in reestablishing stakeholder confidence and counteracting low trust in markets and institutions (Agusti Strid & Ronicle, 2021). To reduce such potential disruptions, stakeholders should take strategic measures, such as designing DIBs to account for upcoming election cycles, as turnover in public servants or leadership could affect government priorities and support for DIB initiatives (Agusti Strid & Ronicle, 2021). Nonetheless, these types of conditional factors are likely to remain uncertain and unstable, as they depend on political systems bureaucratic institutions which are resistant to change (Agusti Strid & Ronicle, 2021).

Table 7. Costs and Challenges Categorizations

		Market Capacity	**Regulatory Framework**	**Economic and Political Context**	**Data Availability**
Transaction Costs	Start-up costs (4, 25%)	x			x
	Partner recruitment (4, 25%)	x	x		
	Institutional buy-in (4, 25%)	x			
	Contract negotiations (5, 31%)		x	x	x

continued on following page

Table 7. Continued

		Market Capacity	Regulatory Framework	Economic and Political Context	Data Availability
Management Challenges	Changing roles and relationships (7, 44%)	x	x		
	Evaluation difficulties (3, 19%)	x		x	x
	Institutional readiness (3, 19%)	x			
	COVID (varied)			x	

Note: Based on author's analysis of primary interview data.

DISCUSSION

These results make some notable contributions to the growing DIB literature. To begin with, evidence on the short- and long-term DIB benefits suggests an emergent theory of change. Next, the ability for DIBs to promote broader objectives around social finance and social impact demonstrates considerable theoretical alignment with social innovation. Social innovation theory further offers insights into important ethical considerations when developing and evaluating DIBs. Lastly, findings on the costs and challenges of using the DIB model have implications for future DIB design and model applicability.

Emergent Theory of Change

In providing evidence on the DIB model's most prominent design features and anticipated benefits, this study offers new insights into an emergent DIB theory of change (Gugiu & Rodríguez-Campos, 2007). A theory of change explains the relationships between a policy tool's inputs, outputs, outcomes, impacts, and contexts (White & Phillips, 2012; NSF, 2010; GAO, 2012). Such models help make stakeholder assumptions explicit, allowing stakeholders to better collaborate in achieving common objectives (Rogers, 2000; Rush & Ogborne, 1991). As visualized in figure 7 (and expanded upon in Appendix A), this study's findings suggest that the DIB's provision of outcomes-focused risk capital enables partners to take an adaptive data-driven approach to service delivery. This approach builds evidence of blended returns and organizational capacity, helping spur cultural shifts towards more outcomes-based working (and funding) in the future. This model is similar to the impact bond theories of change proposed by Oroxom et al. (2018) and Gustafsson-Wright and Osborne (2020b), which both posit that the model's outcomes focus, up-front funding, risk incentives (financial and reputational), and private sector engagement fosters greater innovation, performance management, capacity building, and collaboration. Notably, though, the present study includes potential longer-term DIB outcomes and impacts, while the other models focus more on inputs and outputs. The new theory of change further views innovation as pertaining more to adaptive management's role in scaling proven interventions as opposed to the creation of wholly new services (Gustafsson-Wright et al., 2015).

Figure 7. Possible DIB Theory of Change

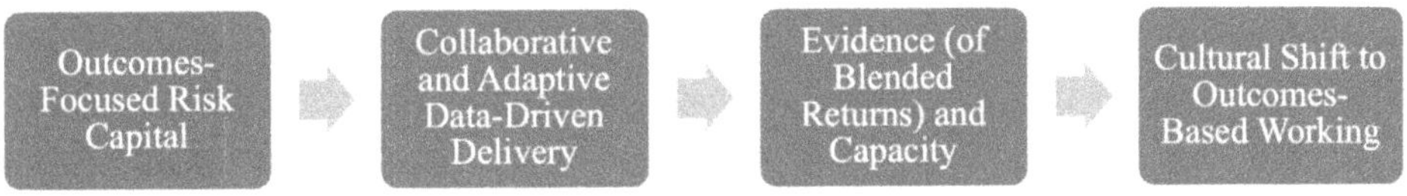

Note: Based on author's original analysis.

DIB Alignment with Social Innovation

With a strong focus on social finance and social impact objectives, DIBs also align with prominent concepts within social innovation theory. Social innovation is "a novel process or product that intends to generate more effective and just solutions to address complex social problems for collective gain" (Beckman et al., 2023, p. 4). As a social finance tool which generates both social and financial returns, DIBs have the potential to serve as social innovation products which increase access to private capital for social purposes (de Gruyter et al., 2020; Ormiston et al., 2020; Olson et al., 2022). Although this study found evidence that DIBs advance many social finance objectives, questions remain whether impact bonds as a whole will be able to attract more mainstream (e.g. commercial rather than philanthropic) investors in the future – crucial to scaling the model (Agusti Strid & Ronicle, 2021; Williams, 2024; Velez-Valencia et al., 2025).

With a flexible funding structure and a focus on outcomes, DIBs also have considerable potential in facilitating the social innovation process by enabling greater experimentation within service delivery (e.g. Muñoz & Kimmitt, 2019; Loraque, 2018; Gustafsson-Wright et al., 2015). In practice, SIBs have thus far primarily been used to scale proven interventions as opposed to pilot test novel interventions (Gustafsson-Wright et al., 2015; Olson et al., 2022). This study finds similar results for DIBs. Additionally, many scholars are critical of the potential for SIBs to engage in co-production and systems change (Sinclair et al., 2021; Andreu, 2018; Broccardo et al., 2020), other key stages of the social innovation process (Beckman et al., 2023; Olson et al., 2022). Although this study's findings suggest that DIBs can promote longer-term impacts such as cultural changes, there remains little evidence to date on the ability for impact bonds to co-produce and diffuse social solutions (Alenda-Demoutiez, 2023). However, Agusti Strid and Ronicle (2021, p. 47) predict that "once the mechanism has been tested and further established… more complex and innovative interventions can be developed through SIBs."

Ethical Considerations

Social innovation theory additionally offers helpful insights into potential ethical considerations of using the DIB model. Within the field of social innovation, there are two competing paradigms: an instrumental and a democratic perspective (Beckman et al., 2023). The instrumental (or utilitarian) perspective promotes market-oriented goals such as efficiency and effectiveness, while the democratic (or radical) perspective promotes justice-oriented goals such as equity (Ayob et al., 2016; Beckman et al., 2023). SIB analyses have tended to situate the model within the instrumental school of thought, highlighting the importance of private capital in scaling innovations (Olson et al., 2022). In turn, SIB research has paid less attention to more democratic concepts like inclusive participation, which underscores the value of engaging local and marginalized communities in decision-making processes (Beckman et al., 2023). In fact, critics argue that SIBs view service users "as potential revenue sources rather than as conscious agents and citizens" (Sinclair et al., 2021, p. 13). Such views are reflected in Fraser et al.'s (2018) 'cautionary' SIB narrative, in which critical scholars align SIBs with the financialization of service delivery. Similar concerns have been echoed in DIB scholarship, as monetizing development outcomes has notable implications for (unequal) power dynamics between international, national, and local development actors (Alenda-Demoutiez, 2023; Bärnreuther, 2025). However, recent studies show some promising advancements in SIB design, as newer SIBs in the UK are placing a greater focus on co-production as a means of facilitating early-stage innovation (e.g. Fox et al., 2022). Nonetheless, there remains considerable opportunity to more strongly incorporate democratic social innovation principles into both DIB design and evaluation.

Recommendations for Future DIBs

As shown throughout this paper, stakeholders face a range of possible benefits and costs in funding development programs through DIBs. As such, organizations should weigh whether funding an intervention is best done through a DIB or a more traditional mechanism and whether local conditions are supportive to the DIB model. When deciding if the DIB approach is appropriate, potential DIB partners should ask themselves: Have results-based funding initiatives been launched in the country or region before? Is there a strong and active impact investing sector? Does the civil society have a history of being involved in social innovation initiatives? (Agusti Strid & Ronicle, 2021).

Organizations should also assess their own organizational fit for DIB partnerships. Investors should be mission-driven, risk-taking organizations and outcome funders and service providers should be flexible, learning-oriented organizations. Donor organizations should further reflect on if they are better suited to serve as investors or outcome funders, depending on their comfort over having more or less control and oversight. As seen in this study, DIB partners chose to fill different roles in various impact bonds based on their objectives for each program. As one Intermediary shared, "if they [the Investor] had come in as outcome funders, they would have been distanced from the day to day. So the learnings, the best practices… would not be institutionalized the same way."

Finally, stakeholders should consider if the intended program is suitable for the DIB model. As establishing DIBs involves relatively high transaction costs, the model appears most appropriate for larger projects and larger investments. To further reduce transaction costs, stakeholders could launch DIBs using a relatively newer approach: outcome funds (Gustafsson-Wright & Osborne, 2020b). Outcome funds "pool several different impact bond agreements through streamlined and shared contract templates, metrics, and evaluation systems," thereby spreading costs among a wider number of projects (Gustafsson-Wright & Osborne, 2020b, p. 25). For example, the Sierra Leone Education Innovation Fund simultaneously launched three DIBs which share the same five outcome funders (including FCDO), a common intermediary (Bridges) (Indigo, 2023).

Another possible way to reduce DIB costs is by harnessing emergent technological innovations such as blockchain. Blockchain is a decentralized digital ledger for securely recording and verifying transactions (Sharma et al., 2024). Blockchain technology can be used to create smart contracts that "automate lending agreements and execute transactions via self-executing contracts, enhancing transparency, security, and efficiency in the lending process" (Yang & Jung, 2024, p. 4). Demonstrating the potential of incorporating blockchain technology into the DIB model is a green finance project from the BIS Innovation Hub which supports environmental efforts through green bonds. This project, called Genesis, uses blockchain technologies to streamline workflows and enable real-time data sharing across project stakeholders (BIS Innovation Hub & HKMA, 2023). Using smart contracts which define stakeholder roles and responsibilities as well as automate contract settlement, the project sought to improve the efficiency and transparency of green bond processes (BIS Innovation Hub & HKMA, 2023). Future DIB design could thus test whether incorporating such smart contract concepts similarly benefits international development initiatives. Regardless of the exact specifications, successful DIB implementation requires carefully adapting model design to account for each project's specific needs – be they related to stakeholder objectives or contextual constraints.

CONCLUSION

Overall, this study identified several important considerations of funding development interventions through DIB contracts, drawing on stakeholder views of DIB costs and benefits. DIB benefits primarily corresponded to objectives around social finance and social impact (Ormiston et al., 2020), while costs and challenges related to DIB market development. For instance, difficulties around market capacity and data availability are expected to decrease with DIB growth, while challenges around unsupportive regulatory frameworks and unstable economic and political environments are more likely to persistent.

This study's findings have notable implications for practice as well. Crucially, stakeholders should establish solid reasoning for why a DIB would be the most appropriate financial arrangement for the project under consideration. Evidence suggests that DIBs are most suitable to scaling evidence-based interventions with room for improvement, especially when the DIB is being launched in untested contexts. Stakeholders should also recruit partners that are a strong cultural match for the DIB, such as mission-driven, flexible, and learning-oriented organizations with expertise in social finance or specific geographies and policy sectors. Lastly, potential DIB partners must take market factors into account when designing and adapting DIBs to fit the model to each project's specific needs and constraints.

This study also suggests fruitful areas for further inquiry. First, additional studies should include a diverse range of both DIBs and SIBs in LMICs, as comparisons could help shed greater light on the impact of involving the government as a direct versus indirect actor in the model. Research could also delve deeper into the impact of the local political economy on impact bond design and purpose. Second, as the DIB market is still relatively new, studies should track how DIB features change over time as the model evolves. In fact, SIB scholarship shows that recent SIBs already look considerably different from early-wave SIBs (Fox et al., 2022; Olson et al., 2022). Third, future research should consider analyzing DIBs through the lens of social innovation. An alternative framework advanced by recent SIB papers (e.g. Albertson et al., 2020; Fox et al., 2022; Olson et al., 2022), social innovation appears to "capture many of the features of SIBs, particularly the opportunity for stakeholders in different sectors… to work collaboratively to address pressing social challenges and deliver social outcomes in new ways" (Olson et al., 2022, p. 7). Evaluating DIBs as aligning with more market-based versus more democratic conceptions of social innovation could thus offer more nuanced insights into the pros and cons of the DIB approach (Ayob et al., 2016; Beckman et al., 2023).

REFERENCES

Agusti Strid, A., & Ronicle, J. (2021). *Social Impact Bonds in Latin America-IDB Lab's pioneering work in the region: lessons learnt*. Technical Note No. IDB-TN-2087. Inter-American Development Bank.

Albertson, K., Fox, C., O'Leary, C., & Painter, G. (2020). 'Towards a Theoretical Framework for Social Impact Bonds'. *Nonprofit Policy Forum, 11*(2).

Alenda-Demoutiez, J. (2020). 'A fictitious commodification of local development through development impact bonds?'. *Journal of Urban Affairs, 42*(6), 892–906.

Alenda-Demoutiez, J. (2023). Financialization in development projects and new modes of governance: the case of development impact bonds. In Chiapello, E., Engles, A., & Gresse, E. G. (Eds.), *Financializations of Development: Global Games and Local Experiments* (1st ed., pp. 123–138). Routledge.

Andreu, M. (2018). 'A Responsibility to Profit? Social Impact Bonds as a Form of "Humanitarian Finance"'. *New Political Science, 40*(4), 708–726.

Ayob, N., Teasdale, S., & Fagan, K. (2016). 'How social innovation 'came to be': Tracing the evolution of a contested concept'. *Journal of Social Policy, 45*(4), 635–653.

Bärnreuther, S. (2025). Financializing Maternal and Newborn Care: Temporal Tensions within a Development Impact Bond in India. *Development and Change, 56*(1), 31–55.

Beckman, C., Rosen, J., Estrada-Miller, J., & Painter, G. (2023). 'The Social Innovation Trap: Critical Insights into an Emerging Field'. *The Academy of Management Annals, 17*(2), 684–709.

Belt, J., Kuleshov, A., & Minneboo, E. (2017). 'Development impact bonds: Learning from the Asháninka cocoa and coffee case in Peru'. *Enterprise Development & Microfinance, 28*(1-2), 130–144.

BIS Innovation Hub & Hong Kong Monetary Authority (HKMA). (2023). *A prototype for green bond tokenisation by Digital Asset and GFT*. Retrieved March 15, 2025 from https://www.bis.org/publ/othp43_report3.pdf

Bollag, B. (2017, September 8). ICRC launches World's first Humanitarian Impact Bond. Retrieved April 27, 2023, from https://www.devex.com/news/icrc-launches-world-s-first-humanitarian-impact-bond-90981

Broccardo, E., Mazzuca, M., & Frigotto, M. L. (2020). 'Social impact bonds: The evolution of research and a review of the academic literature'. *Corporate Social Responsibility and Environmental Management*, *27*(3), 1316–1332.

Carter, E., FitzGerald, C., Dixon, R., Economy, C., Hameed, T., & Airoldi, M. (2018). *Building the tools for public services to secure better outcomes: Collaboration, Prevention, Innovation.* Government Outcomes Lab, University of Oxford, Blavatnik School of Government.

Chandra, Y., Shang, L., & Roy, M. J. (2021). 'Understanding Healthcare Social Enterprises: A New Public Governance Perspective'. *Journal of Social Policy*, •••, 1–22.

Clarke, L., Chalkidou, K., & Nemzoff, C. (2018). 'Development impact bonds targeting health outcomes'. *CGD Policy Paper, 133.*

Dahbi, F., Carrasco, I., & Petracci, B. (2024). A systematic literature review on social impact bonds. *Finance Research Letters*, *62*, 105063.

de Gruyter, E., Petrie, D., Black, N., & Gharghori, P. (2020). 'Attracting investors for public health programmes with Social Impact Bonds'. *Public Money & Management*, *40*(3), 225–236.

Erskine, C. (2021). *Quality Education India Development Impact Bond: A case study produced as part of the FCDO DIBs Evaluation.* Ecorys. Retrieved April 27, 2023, from https://golab.bsg.ox.ac.uk/knowledge-bank/resource-library/quality-education-india-report/

FitzGerald, C., Fraser, A., & Kimmitt, J. (2020). 'Tackling the Big Questions in Social Impact Bond Research through Comparative Approaches'. *Journal of Comparative Policy Analysis*, *22*(2), 85–99.

FMO. (2019, November 15). FMO supports the first Palestinian Employment Development Impact Bond (DIB). Retrieved April 27, 2023, from https://www.fmo.nl/news-detail/4f39ef8e-d43f-44c6-9d8f-47c0a8fb4ca4/fmo-supports-the-first-palestinian-employment-development-impact-bond-(dib)

Fox, C., & Morris, S. (2021). 'Evaluating outcome-based payment programmes: Challenges for evidence-based policy'. *Journal of Economic Policy Reform*, *24*(1), 61–77.

Fox, C., Olson, H., Armitage, H., Baines, S., & Painter, G. (2022). Can a Focus on Co-Created, Strengths-Based Services Facilitate Early-Stage Innovation within SIBs? *International Public Management Journal*, •••, 1–17.

Fraser, A., Tan, S., Lagarde, M., & Mays, N. (2018). 'Narratives of Promise, Narratives of Caution: A review of the literature on Social Impact Bonds'. *Social Policy and Administration*, *52*(1), 4–28.

Gallucci, C., Del Giudice, A., & Santulli, R. (2022). 'How to attract professional investors in developing countries? An evidence-based structure for development impact bonds'. *Finance Research Letters*, *46*, 102816.

Gallucci, C., Rosalia, S., & Riccardo, T. (2019). 'Development impact bonds to overcome investors-services providers agency problems: Insights from a case study analysis'. *African Journal of Business Management*, *13*(13), 415–427.

GAO [Government Accountability Office]. (2012). *Designing Evaluations, 2012 Revision.*

Grittner, A. M. (2013). *Results-based Financing: Evidence from performance-based financing in the health sector*. Discussion Paper No. 6/2013. Deutsches Institut für Entwicklungspolitik.

Gugiu, P. C., & Rodríguez-Campos, L. (2007). 'Semi-structured interview protocol for constructing logic models'. *Evaluation and Program Planning*, *30*(4), 339–350. PMID: 17905433

Gustafsson-Wright, E., Boggild-Jones, I., Segell, D., & Durland, J. (2017). *Impact Bonds in Developing Countries: Early Learning from the Field.* Global Economy and Development at Brookings, Brookings Institution.

Gustafsson-Wright, E., Gardiner, S., & Putcha, V. (2015). *The potential and limitations of impact bonds: Lessons from the first five years of experience worldwide.* Global Economy and Development at Brookings, Brookings Institution.

Gustafsson-Wright, E., & Osborne, S. (2020a). *Are Impact Bonds Reaching the Intended Populations?* Global Economy and Development at Brookings, Brookings Institution.

Gustafsson-Wright, E., & Osborne, S. (2020b). *Do the Benefits Outweigh the Costs of Impact Bonds?* Global Economy and Development at Brookings, Brookings Institution.

Gustafsson-Wright, E., Osborne, S., & Crane, E. (2021). *How have impact bond-funded projects in low-and middle-income countries fared in COVID-19?* Working Paper No. 164. Global Economy and Development at Brookings, Brookings Institution: Washington, DC.

Gustafsson-Wright, E., Osborne, S., & Shankar, A. (2022). *From Evidence to Scale: Lessons Learned from the Quality Education India Development Impact Bond.* Center for Universal Education, Brookings Institution: Washington, DC.

Halkos, G., & Gkampoura, E. C. (2021). 'Where do we stand on the 17 Sustainable Development Goals? An overview on progress'. *Economic Analysis and Policy, 70*, 94–122.

Hamadeh, N., Van Rompaey, C., Metreau, E., & Eapen, S. G. (2022, July 1). *New World Bank country classifications by income level: 2022-2023.* World Bank Blogs. Retrieved April 27, 2023, from https://blogs.worldbank.org/opendata/new-world-bank-country-classifications-income-level-2022-2023

Hera. (2022). *A Development Impact Bond to Finance the In Their Hands Project: Third Party Monitoring Final Report.* UK Foreign, Commonwealth & Development Office. Retrieved April 27, 2023, from https://iati.fcdo.gov.uk/iati_documents/D0001335.pdf

Hevenstone, D., Fraser, A., Hobi, L., Przepiorka, W., & Geuke, G. G. (2023). The impact of social impact bond financing. *Public Administration Review, 83*(4), 930–946.

Indigo. (2022a, February 22). Cameroon Cataract Bond. Retrieved April 27, 2023, from https://golab.bsg.ox.ac.uk/knowledge-bank/case-studies/cameroon-cataract-bond/

Indigo. (2022b, September 4). In Their Hands. Retrieved April 27, 2023, from https://golab.bsg.ox.ac.uk/knowledge-bank/case-studies/in-their-hands/

Indigo. (2023). Impact Bond Dataset. Retrieved April 27, 2023, from https://golab.bsg.ox.ac.uk/knowledge-bank/indigo/impact-bond-dataset-v2/

International Committee of the Red Cross (ICRC). (2022, June 28). First Humanitarian Impact Bond successfully brings physical rehabilitation services to conflict-affected communities. Retrieved April 27, 2023, from https://www.icrc.org/en/document/humanitarian-impact-bond-brings-physical-rehabilitation-services

Jackson, E. T. (2013). 'Interrogating the theory of change: Evaluating impact investing where it matters most'. *Journal of Sustainable Finance & Investment, 3*(2), 95–110.

Kitzmuller, L., McManus, J., Shah, N. B., & Starla, K. (2018). *Educate Girls Development Impact Bond: Final Evaluation Report.* IDinsight. Retrieved April 27, 2023, from https://golab.bsg.ox.ac.uk/documents/ID_Insight_2018_Educate_Girls_Development_Impact_Bond_-_Final_Evaluation_Report.pdf

Leech, B. (2002). 'Asking Questions: Techniques for Semistructured Interviews'. *PS, Political Science & Politics*, *35*(4), 665–668.

Loraque, J. (2018). 'Development Impact Bonds: Bringing innovation to education development financing and delivery'. *Childhood Education*, *94*(4), 64–68.

Maier, F., Barbetta, G. P., & Godina, F. (2018). 'Paradoxes of social impact bonds'. *Social Policy and Administration*, *52*(7), 1332–1353.

Mishra, A. K., & Dash, A. K. (2022). 'Development impact bonds in developing countries: An emerging innovation for achieving social outcomes'. *Journal of Social and Economic Development*, •••, 1–27. PMID: 36532830

Muñoz, P., & Kimmitt, J. (2019). 'A diagnostic framework for social impact bonds in emerging economies'. *Journal of Business Venturing Insights*, *12*, e00141.

NSF [National Science Foundation]. (2010). *The 2010 User-Friendly Handbook for Project Evaluation*.

O'Neil, S., Vohra, D., Spitzer, M., Kalyanwala, S., & Rotz, D. (2021). *Maternal Health Care Quality Improvement in Rajasthan, India: A Series of Insights from a Development Impact Bond Verification Agent*. Mathematica.

Olson, H., Painter, G., Albertson, K., Fox, C., & O'Leary, C. (2022). 'Are Social Impact Bonds an innovation in finance or do they help finance social innovation?'. *Journal of Social Policy*, •••, 1–25.

Ormiston, J., Moran, M., Castellas, E. I., & Tomkinson, E. (2020). 'Everybody wins? A discourse analysis of competing stakeholder expectations in Social Impact Bonds'. *Public Money & Management*, *40*(3), 237–246.

Oroxom, R., Glassman, A., & McDonald, L. (2018). *Structuring and funding development impact bonds for health: nine lessons from Cameroon and beyond*. Center for Global Development.

Osborne, S. P. (2006). 'The New Public Governance?'. *Public Management Review*, *8*(3), 377–387.

Pearson, M. (2011). *Results based aid and results based financing: What are they? Have they delivered results*. HLSP Institute.

Rizzello, A., & Kabli, A. (2020). 'Sustainable Financial Partnerships for the SDGs: The Case of Social Impact Bonds'. *Sustainability (Basel, Switzerland)*, *12*(13), 5362.

Rogers, P. J. (2000). 'Causal models in program theory evaluation'. *New Directions for Evaluation*, *2000*(87), 47–55.

Rush, B., & Ogborne, A. (1991). 'Program logic models: Expanding their role and structure for program planning and evaluation'. *The Canadian Journal of Program Evaluation*, *6*(2), 95.

Savell, L., & Eddleston, C. (2021). Cameroon Kangaroo Mother Care Development Impact Bond 2018- 2021: End of programme report. Social Finance. Retrieved April 27, 2023, from https://www.socialfinance.org.uk/sites/default/files/publications/cameroon_kmc_development_impact_bond_report_-_en.pdf

Sharma, G. D., Tiwari, A. K., Chopra, R., & Dev, D. (2024). 'Past, present, and future of block-chain in finance'. *Journal of Business Research*, *177*, 114640.

Sinclair, S., McHugh, N., & Roy, M. J. (2021). 'Social innovation, financialisation and commodification: A critique of social impact bonds'. *Journal of Economic Policy Reform*, *24*(1), 11–27.

Stone Family Foundation, & iDE. (n.d.). The Cambodia Rural Sanitation Development Impact Bond: Two Years of Delivering Results through Innovative Finance. Retrieved April 27, 2023, from https://www.thesff.com/wp-content/uploads/2022/05/Cambodia-Rural-Sanitation-Development-Impact-Bond-Year-2-Report.pdf

Strid, A. A. (2021). *Cameroon Cataract Bond: A case study produced as part of the Cameroon Cataract Bond Evaluation*. The Government Outcomes Lab. Retrieved April 27, 2023, from https://golab.bsg.ox.ac.uk/knowledge-bank/resource-library/cameroon-cataract-bond-eval/

Tiko. (2023, November 20). How Real-Time Data Spurred Success in World-First Adolescent Sexual Reproductive Health Development Impact Bond. Retrieved January 16, 2025, from tiko.org/2023/11/20/how-real-time-data-spurred-success-in-world-first-adolescent-sexual-reproductive-health-development-impact-bond/

Velez-Valencia, C., Herrera-Cano, C., Gonzalez-Perez, M., Alvarez, P., & Vergara Garavito, J. (2025). *'Aligning Investment with Impact: Exploring Social Impact Bonds in Emerging Markets for Sustainable Development.' Corporate Social Responsibility and Environmental Management*. EarlyView.

White, H., & Phillips, D. (2012). *Addressing attribution of cause and effect in small n impact evaluations: towards an integrated framework*. International Initiative for Impact Evaluation.

Williams, J. W. (2020). 'Surveying the SIB economy: Social impact bonds, "local" challenges, and shifting markets in urban social problems'. *Journal of Urban Affairs*, *42*(6), 907–919.

Williams, J. W. (2024). 'Finance interrupted: Social impact bonds, spatial politics, and the limits of financial innovation in the social sector.' *Environment and Planning A. Economy and Space*, *56*(1), 42–58.

Yang, J., & Jung, S. U. (2024). 'Harnessing FinTech for Sustainable Finance in Developing Countries: An Integrated SWOT–Multi-Level Perspective Analysis of Mongolia'. *Sustainability*, *16*(10), 4102.

KEY TERMS AND DEFINITIONS

Results-Based Funding: A contractual arrangement in which a principal provides funding to an agent based on the achievement of specified results.

Impact Bond: A form of results-based funding in which an investor provides the up-front capital to a service provider and an outcome funder pays the investor based on the verification of measurable outcomes.

Social Finance: Capital which generates social and environmental returns, along with potential financial returns.

Social Impact: The generation of societal as opposed to economic value.

Collaborative Governance: The active participation of a network of stakeholders from various sectors in addressing social issues.

Transactions Costs: The additional expense, time, and effort incurred in establishing contractual arrangements.

Performance Management: The process of improving program efficiency and effectiveness by adapting program design and implementation based on emergent insights from data.

Monitoring and Evaluation: The collection and analysis of data to assess whether and how programs are achieving target outcomes.

ENDNOTES

1 Classified using the World Bank's 2022 income definitions, with HICs having a Gross National Income per capita of $13,205 or more (Hamadeh et al., 2022).

2 As an earlier version of this chapter was submitted as a part of my doctoral dissertation, parts of the paper may resemble original text from the dissertation, with significant revisions made for the purpose of publication.

3 Some government engagement will likely be necessary, for example to avoid duplication of services and align on policy priorities (Alenda-Demoutiez, 2020; Clarke et al., 2018; Gustafsson-Wright et al., 2017).

4 This includes 5 DIBs analyzed in this study.

5 As governmental entities do not serve as outcome funders in DIBs, the analysis eliminated government demand as a category and redefined market capacity to include outcome funder interest and capacity.

6 Kenya's first DIB, Village Enterprise (also implemented in Uganda), ran from 2017 to 2021.

7 Although partially time-dependent, the Skill India and In Their Hands DIBs also had the most stakeholders with prior DIB experience (six and three, respectively), while the rest had two or fewer.

APPENDIX A: EMERGENT DIB THEORY OF CHANGE

Figure 8. Expanded Logic Model

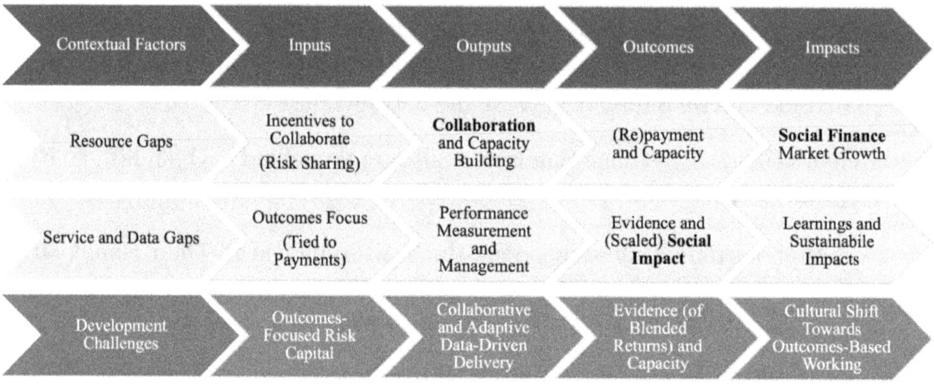

Chapter 8
Foundations of a Tailored Business Model in Climate Services for a Resilient Future

Simone Taddeo
https://orcid.org/0000-0002-1656-1588
Euro-Mediterranean Center on Climate Change, Italy

Chiara Bidoli
https://orcid.org/0009-0001-4924-0561
Euro-Mediterranean Center on Climate Change, Italy

Marina Mattera
Euro-Mediterranean Center on Climate Change, Italy & EAE Barcelona Business School, Spain

Jaroslav Mysiak
Euro-Mediterranean Center on Climate Change, Italy

ABSTRACT

Achieving a resilient, net-zero future requires a fundamental shift in how economies and societies operate. Since the early 2000s, corporations have increasingly recognized the importance of non-financial factors—particularly environmental and social ones—in shaping performance and reputation. Integrating climate knowledge, data, and insights into decision-making and market strategies is essential for driving this transformation. This study explores the growing climate services (CS) market, which has emerged in response to urgent climate-related challenges. Through a comprehensive literature review, we propose the foundations for a tailored business

DOI: 10.4018/979-8-3693-9551-6.ch008

model that supports the integration of climate services into organizational strategies. The study advances a taxonomy for climate services and examines its relevance to business model design, highlighting its role in enhancing value creation and long-term competitive advantage.

INTRODUCTION

Extreme weather and climate-related events have already caused significant damage to ecosystems, communities, and economies worldwide. According to the Centre for Research on the Epidemiology of Disasters (CRED) and the United Nations Office for Disaster Risk Reduction (UNDRR), climate-related disasters - only considering the period between 2000 and 2019 - caused a total of USD 119 billion in losses every year (Calvin et al., 2023). Heat waves, heavy precipitation, droughts, floods, and tropical cyclones have become more intense and frequent in several regions, and changes in extreme weather will continue to increase as global warming continues. In light of this, it is crucial to rapidly transition social and economic systems away from business-as-usual practices towards a new climate-neutral paradigm, to effectively and promptly address climate change impacts, and adapt accordingly.

In the evolving landscape of contemporary economies, the emphasis on sustainable practices and ethical strategies has become a central focus in both academic discourse and business practice. With growing awareness of the profound impact environmental and social factors have on all types of organizations, there has been a marked shift in how companies approach value creation for their stakeholders. This paradigm shift aligns with the principles of the Triple Bottom Line (TBL) theory, which posits that a firm's success is measured by its ability to balance economic, social, and environmental performance, moving beyond the traditional focus on profit maximization that societies had up until the end of the 20th century.

A crucial component of this shift is the growing role of climate services, which provide organizations with the data, tools, and insights necessary to navigate climate-related risks and opportunities. These services, which include climate forecasting, risk assessments, and sustainability consulting, enable institutions to make more informed decisions that align with their Environmental, Social, and Governance (ESG) strategies. Climate services also facilitate the integration of environmental factors into business models, helping firms not only mitigate climate risks but also leverage them for competitive advantage.

This paper explores the complex dimensions of sustainable business models, emphasizing the inclusion of ESG strategies and highlighting the critical role of governance in fostering sustainable competitive advantages. Teece's (2010) seminal work on the foundational characteristics of business models, alongside Osterwalder & Pigneur's (2010) strategic elements, offers a comprehensive framework for creating long-term sustainable value.

Because of the abovementioned, climate services can be valuable allies of public and private organizations. They can equip them with essential data, analytics, and insights to encode the complexity of their operating context while enabling them to take action and make informed decisions to initiate change. Climate services extend beyond the mere provision of climate data, involving the co-creation of information tailored to specific climate-related needs through user engagement and iterative dialogue (WMO, 2018). These services transform climate data into actionable knowledge bridging the gap between science, technology, and policy while supporting the transformation of societies into climate-smart communities.

Despite that, the demand for climate services - from both private and public entities - is currently deficient for several reasons, including the lack of appropriate business models. As (Lüdeke-Freund et al., 2018) point out, harnessing organizations' full potential to address environmental, social, and economic challenges requires more than introducing new products, services, processes, or organizational methods. It requires innovative frameworks for how companies create, deliver, and capture value; which does not necessarily mean devising something new but finding new ways of combining the elements to create something different (Lüdeke-Freund et al., 2018). Business models give organizations the flexibility to operate in an unpredictable context while helping them to increase their resilience and sustainability in the long term (Evans et al., 2017).

Innovative business models for climate services can serve as a reference framework for a wide range of stakeholders to rethink their mission and, at the same time, to reconfigure their activities and objectives to effectively adapt to a dynamically changing climate landscape. Further, they can contribute to systematizing knowledge facilitating cognitive, and communication processes, and co-design solutions, thereby speeding up action (Breuer & Lüdeke-Freund, 2017; Rohrbeck et al., 2013). As portrayed by (Mattera & Soto, 2023) there is a need for a theoretical model that can provide a framework for organizations to gain understanding on how to better integrate these variables into their business models.

The aim of this research is to develop a Business Model Canvas for Climate Services (BMC4CS), which allows public and private entities to methodically tackle and integrate climate-related challenges and opportunities into their strategic frameworks. This approach, in turn, enables organizations to anticipate regulatory shifts, fulfill stakeholder demands, and support sustainable development objectives effectively. By customizing the Business Model Canvas (BMC) to the climate service market, organizations ensure that climate impacts and projections are an integral part of their operating strategies and decision-making processes, thus strengthening resilience and bolstering long-term sustainability. This will be our contribution.

The present research directly addresses the gap identified by Mattera and Soto (2023) by proposing a Business Model Canvas for Climate Services (BMC4CS). First, an overview of the current studies on business models for climate services - considering both scientific and grey literature - is outlined. Then a detailed description of the key elements and the main gaps of each of the preexisting alternatives are analyzed. . Finally, the BMC4CS is presented, together with the implications and application to different types of institutions.

FROM THE TRADITIONAL BUSINESS MODEL CANVAS TO A TARGETED BM4CS

The Business Model for Climate Services (BM4CS) presented in this paper was created starting from the key elements of the Business Model Canvas (BMC) developed by Osterwalder and Pigneur (2010), which is widely acknowledged as the most prominent framework in the business sector. In addition, we have integrated key elements of business model frameworks that include sustainability elements, given their importance in the climate services market. These frameworks consist of the Eco-Canvas Business Model by Daou et al., (2020) and the Triple Layered BMC by Joyce e Paquin (2016a).

In 2005, Osterwalder et al. (2005) laid the foundations of the so-called Business Model Canvas (BMC), a visual tool for business modeling that gained popularity for its effectiveness in conceptualizing, communicating, and strategizing business concepts. Only later, in 2010, Osterwalder and Pigneur (2010) elaborated the BMC concept as a reference framework consisting of 9 building blocks that outline how an organization creates, delivers, and captures value.

The BMC has gained considerable recognition as a valuable tool in business strategy. However, Joyce and Paquin (2016) have highlighted a critical limitation in its traditional form, namely the lack of environmental and social considerations. In the context of climate services, where climate-related data are used to optimize decision-making processes and support stakeholders in adapting to climate variability and change, considering these elements becomes indispensable.

To overcome the conventional BMC limitation, Daou et al. (2020) proposed the Business Model Eco-Canvas. This innovative framework incorporates two additional components, namely the environmental and social foresight, and impacts, indispensable for developing effective CS. These extra elements make the model more comprehensive and dynamic, enabling a more in-depth examination of contextual environmental and social dimensions. The P.E.S.T.E.L framework is proposed by the authors to thoroughly characterize these key elements and include political, economic, social, technological, environmental, and legal aspects.

Joyce & Paquin (2016a) introduced similar elements by developing the Triple Layered Business Model Canvas (TLBMC), which adds environmental and social layers to the traditional BMC encouraging a holistic and sustainability-oriented innovation. The framework introduces several key elements of interest to the field of CS, including environmental and social costs and benefits, which enable businesses to internalize externalities, as well as governance, social cultures, and communities. The governance element pertains to the organizational structure and decision-making policies of an organization.

This is a pivotal aspect in the climate services market, given the multifaceted and intricate relationships that are necessary for the CS value chain to co-create pertinent and actionable climate insights. Furthermore, social cultures and community networks are crucial for considering the potential impacts that CS may have on society as a whole and the relationships that businesses should establish with local communities, who are often the primary users or beneficiaries of CS. In this context, consider early warning systems provided by public authorities that can contribute to the safety of local communities by helping them to anticipate and respond to extreme weather events (WMO, 2020).

Overall, the traditional BMC proposed by Osterwalder et al., (2005) can be considered a good starting point for defining the key elements of the BM4CS. However, elements that take into account environmental and social aspects need to be integrated. For this purpose, we added the two key elements introduced by the Eco-Canvas BM - climate and social foresight and impacts, which also comprise two of the additional aspects introduced by the tripled layer BMC, that is social culture and communities. We decided to integrate the governance element in the key partner's block, while social and environmental costs and benefits have been integrated into the blocks referred to as costs and revenue streams. It should be noted that cost structure blocks also include the costs of inaction, intended as economic and social costs linked to the business as usual trajectory (Climate Policy Initiative, 2023). *Figure 1.* provides a graphical representation of the minimum elements that a BM4CS should include.

Figure 1. BM4CS minimum elements

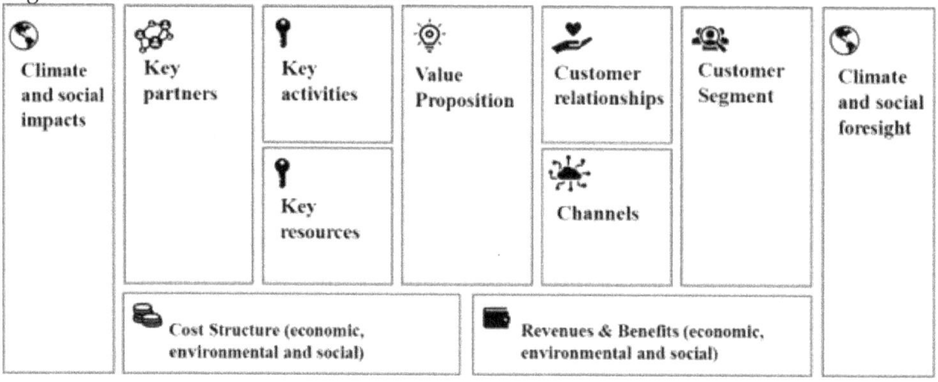

To sum up, implementing a Business Model Canvas focused on climate services enables public actors to systematically address and incorporate climate-related risks and opportunities into their strategic planning. By doing so, public and private organizations can better anticipate regulatory changes, meet stakeholder expectations, and contribute to resilience capacity-building.

Once the additional blocks have been introduced, the next step is to populate them with evidence from our literature review. This process ensures that each component of the BM4CS is based on empirical evidence and best practice. By systematically reviewing relevant literature, each block is filled with detailed, context-specific information that reflects current research and industry trends, thereby creating a robust and comprehensive business model for climate services.

METHOD

We conducted a comprehensive literature review to assess the state of the art of business model innovation for climate services and gain insight into the key elements of the CS value chain. Given the novelty of the concept of climate service business models, the present article also gathers insights from scientific literature concerning business models in more mature markets, that have similarities and synergies with climate services (e.g. data market, the public goods market, knowledge-intensive business (KIBS) market, and the weather and climate data markets).

We used the Scopus database to search for relevant scientific literature, setting the publication date limit to 2010. The keywords used in the search strings were devised through a process of desktop research, group discussions, and insights provided by experts in the field of climate services (CS). Two sets of strings (see SET A and SET B) were merged and applied using boolean operators to include the terms 'climate service' and 'business model'. In addition, we include synonyms such as 'climate knowledge' and 'climate insight', to avoid excluding relevant papers which do not use the specific term "climate services".

SET A

TITLE-ABS-KEY ("climate service?" AND business) AND (LIMIT-TO (SRCTYPE, "j") OR LIMIT-TO (SRCTYPE, "k"))

SET B

TITLE-ABS-KEY ("business innovation*" OR "business model*" OR "innovation") AND ("climate service*" OR "climate knowledge" OR "climate insight*")

A total of 108 articles were identified through the research process, however, 11 were excluded due to duplication, leaving a total of 97 articles for the following steps.

We proceeded with the title-abstract screening process to assess the relevance of the papers for the final analysis. For this purpose, we categorize them according to the following criteria:

1 = The paper is not within the scope of the review. The paper should be rejected.
2 = The research topic of the paper is of a nature that is cross-cutting with our research theme. For example, it addresses the impact of climate change on the specific economic sectors. It is recommended to consider the paper for collecting background information.
3 = The research topic of the paper is relevant from a theoretical perspective but lacks practical application. The paper is to be analyzed but with a low priority.
4 = The research topic of the paper is relevant from both a theoretical and practical point of view, but it does not present any elements of innovation. It is to be analyzed with a medium priority.
5 = The paper is within the scope of the study. The topic is relevant from both theoretical and practical points of view, and it incorporates elements of innovation. This topic is to be analyzed with the highest priority.

Out of the title-abstract screening phase, 27 papers were deemed to be irrelevant (score 1), while 12 were only tangentially relevant to the research topic (score 2). This latter group of papers focused mostly on the context in which climate services are implemented and dealt with topics such as the impacts of climate change on economic production. Sixteen of the papers analyzed addressed the research topic from a theoretical perspective (scoring 3), while a more practical approach was found in 16 papers, which reported case studies or practical experiences (score 4). None of these papers directly address the topic of business model innovation for climate services, but provide a descriptive analysis of the context in which such innovation is taking place, emphasizing existing weaknesses and barriers to overcome.

A total of 26 papers were deemed to be entirely pertinent to the research in question (score 5). Given the modest amount of scientific literature on our topic of interest, we have integrated our results with grey literature, mainly by The World Meteorological Organisation and the World Bank. In particular, since 2019 the WMO has issued an annual report on the State of climate services in response to the United Nations' request to support the adaptation endeavor of countries, by addressing climate service needs and gaps, thus fostering market expansion and investments.

Additionally, scientific literature addressing business models of markets that have synergies with CS has been reviewed. In this context, there are still not enough elements regarding the implementation of legal frameworks such as the European Climate Law, the EU Corporate Social Responsibility Directive or the EU Corporate Sustainability Due-Diligence Directive as they have been recently approved and are in phase of implementation. Due to their novelty, they are not part of the scope as this paper focuses on existing literature analyzing empirical evidence. Figure 2 below summarizes the scoping review process.

Figure 2. Summary of the scoping review process

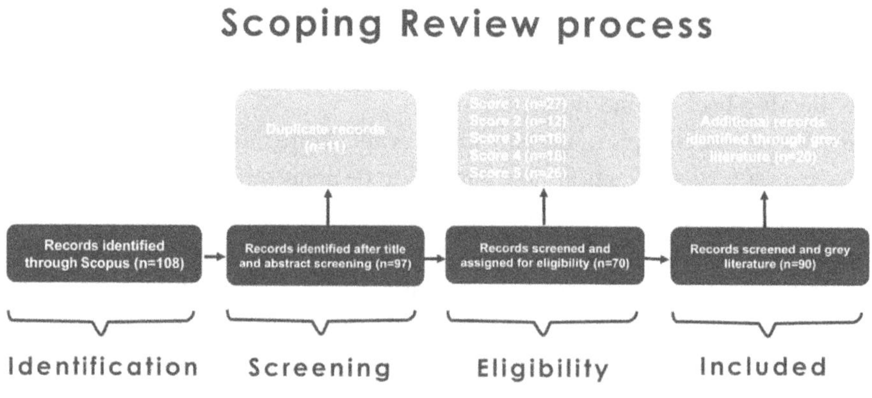

BMC4CS: Exploring Key Elements and Main Gaps

This section examines how the key elements of the BMC4CS, previously identified, may be shaped by considering the current state of the climate service market as it emerges from the literature review conducted. This includes empirical work that has observed the impact in resiliency and long-term sustainability based on different institutions' approach towards ESG strategies. In this phase, an additional element has been included (*See Figure 3 for a graphical representation of the final BM4CS*). Furthermore, the analysis identifies critical gaps that should be addressed to unlock CS innovation.

It is noteworthy that the majority of existing literature on CS addresses only 5 of the 12 elements we identified for the BMC4CS. These are data and tools (key resources), partnerships and relationship networks (key partnerships), user-centric and co-produced services (customer segment and key activities), and delivery structures (channels).

KEY RESOURCES

The primary resources for producing climate services include climate data and information, as well as tools for collecting, processing, and sharing them. Accessible, standardized, and shared data, tools, and platforms are essential for enabling decision-makers to access the insights needed to tackle climate-related challenges promptly. In this context, there is an urgent shift from traditional data collection methods to innovative approaches facilitated by advanced technologies and collaborations with partners with tailored expertises. Tools such as AI, machine learning, drones, satellites, and blockchain enhance accessibility and data sharing, revolutionizing processes and collection of data.

Indeed, these innovations not only improve the efficiency and accuracy of data but also democratize access to critical information. For example, AI and machine learning automate data analysis, making complex information more accessible and actionable. Drones provide real-time, high-resolution data from remote areas, enhancing environmental monitoring and disaster response capabilities. Satellites offer broad coverage and continuous monitoring of Earth's surface and atmosphere, which is crucial for widely accessible global- scale assessments. Blockchain ensures secure and transparent data sharing among stakeholders, fostering trust and accountability in environmental data management.

These technologies could facilitate direct access to real-time data via intuitive platforms, empowering citizens with immediate insights into environmental conditions. User-friendly interfaces and interactive tools simplify complex information, making it accessible to a wider audience. The democratization of information promotes transparency and public engagement in environmental and societal issues, fostering informed decision-making. In this way, citizens can actively participate in monitoring local ecosystems, advocating for sustainable policies, and responding promptly to emerging challenges like climate change and natural disasters.

However, data access is often restricted and not freely available for use and re-publishing due to constraints such as copyright or patents (WB, 2019). Additionally, data-sharing requirements among WMO Members tend to be conservative, limiting access to cutting-edge and aggregated data (Condon, 2023; D. Rogers et al., 2021). This adds to the fact that data generated by municipal infrastructure and corporate supply chains often require specific licenses, and the lack of standardization for data extraction and elaboration creates significant transparency issues (Condon, 2023). Therefore, common standards and rules for collecting, storing, and reporting data are crucial to ensure transparency, and consistency, and strengthen stakeholder trust, which in turn accelerates investments. However, the current policy landscape on these topics is fragmented, making it increasingly difficult to oversee the scientific rigor of the data and models used by stakeholders, leading to the so-called "black box model"(Condon, 2023). As a result, data, methods, and metrics become hard to compare, and their reliability for decision-making processes is called into question.

Key activities:

Climate services fall under the category of knowledge-intensive business services (KIBS) due to their reliance on specialized knowledge and expertise in climate science, data analysis, modeling, data manipulation, and interpretation. They involve the transformation and co-creation of information tailored to specific climate and societal-related needs and aims to empower stakeholders to take action. The high level of expertise required often presents a significant barrier to their uptake, particularly among non-expert users such as small local municipalities and businesses. In comparison to large cities and companies, these entities often lack the necessary in-house expertise and do not have sufficient resources to draw on the knowledge of external experts, such as climate scientists (Condon, 2023; Swart et al., 2021a).

The significant reliance of climate services on human capital and local knowledge makes standardization an extremely challenging endeavor (Miles et al., 1995). In light of this, it is crucial to prioritize co-production and co-design initiatives, while also taking into account the local context, encompassing factors such as the climate risk and adaptation strategies, and the specific needs of the local population (Bremer et al., 2019; Vaughan et al., 2017). Business model canvases may be used as guiding frameworks to foster collaborative activities. For example, Rubio-Martin et al. (2021) applied the traditional BMC to design a water supply system in Valencia (Spain). The approach actively engages users in the design process to fully understand their needs, integrating local knowledge and fostering a transdisciplinary outcome while preventing the rejection of the service. The approach proved to be successful, laying the ground for its replication in other sectors.

Key partners:

Collecting, storing, processing, sharing, and using climate-related data in decision-making processes requires a broad infrastructure network—such as local sensors, data collection networks, national datasets, and data manipulation tools—as well as high-skilled workers with specific competencies (Thorpe, 2023). Therefore, the production and delivery of climate services involve close collaboration among multiple organizations, pooling complementary assets and resources (Thorpe, 2022). In this perspective, formal and informal partnerships between public and private sector entities are crucial for value production, capture, and delivery.

Public entities, which are currently the primary providers of climate services, often struggle to have the necessary economic and human resources in-house (Webber & Donner, 2017). Outsourcing certain activities to either private or public stakeholders allows public organizations to focus their limited resources on core functions, among which is the final delivery of climate services to users. However, determining which activities to retain in-house is a strategic decision that requires careful evaluation to safeguard the organization's future management capacity and uphold public accountability, ensuring critical functions are not compromised by external involvement (D. Rogers et al., 2021).

In a public-private collaboration context, private businesses can work with public entities by sharing data collected through their infrastructure networks in exchange for publicly produced data. This collaboration fosters innovation and enables the public sector to leverage private sector expertise in finding data-driven solutions to various public issues, including climate change, public health, and job creation (Kazantsev et al., 2023).To ensure successful public-private partnerships (PPP), the following critical factors should be considered: (1) equitable risk distribution, (2) strong private sector involvement, (3) balanced government oversight, (4) transparent and efficient procurement procedures, (5) economic project viability, (6) the establishment of a suitable legal framework and stable political environment, and (7) access to financial markets (Frei, 2021).

Among the key partners, final users should also be included, since climate services go beyond merely providing data and information. They involve the co-creation of tailored information to meet specific climate-related needs through user engagement and iterative dialogue (WMO, 2018). Examples of this collaborative process include the MED-GOLD Dashboard (Dell'Aquila et al., 2023), a platform developed in collaboration with local vineyards in Portugal's Douro wine region, which provides wine producers with historical climate data, seasonal forecasts, and climate projections based on jointly identified Essential Climate Variables (ECVs) and bioclimatic indicators. Another example is the SHYMAT service developed in collaboration with the hydropower producers in the mountainous area of the Poqueira River basin (South Spain), to integrate climate forecasts in the decision-making process of green energy producers (Contreras et al., 2020).

Customer Segments:

The customer segment block identifies the types of clients or user who might be interested in purchasing the value proposition offered by the producers and using the service to get different benefits. However, in the realm of climate services, it's crucial to differentiate between clients and beneficiaries, since the two figures often do not overlap (Mayor et al., 2021). Clients are those who buy the service, while beneficiaries are the ones who benefit directly (users) or indirectly from the service's value. For example, if the CS is provided by a municipality, the municipality acts as the client, purchasing it or as an hybrid figure of client- user co-developing with external partners a tailored climate service for the area. The citizens then become the direct beneficiaries of the service's benefits, such as reduced climate risk. Indirect beneficiaries also include entities like private businesses that benefit from the service's positive externalities, such as avoided losses and risk reduction, even though they are not directly exposed. These effects may be included in the "climate and social impacts" block of the BMC4CS.

Climate service users may be categorized according to their level of expertise and skills in order to guarantee that the service is effectively tailored to their needs (Condon, 2023; Swart et al., 2021b). These categories are as follows: self-sufficient users, transitional climate service users, and potential climate service users (Rubio-Martin et al., 2021). Self-sufficient users can independently utilize climate information, while transitional users need external support. Potential users, on the other hand, are not yet aware of the importance of existing climate risks and the role of climate-related information in their decision-making processes.

Customer relationship

Provider - users' relationships should be defined according to the user's profile and needs. On this basis, the frequency of interaction may vary and be either continuous or occasional (like counseling) transactional, or limited to a single point of purchase (Mayor et al., 2021). In situations where there is an ongoing, close relationship between the providers and the users, opportunities for co-development and co-creation can be established (Bojovic et al., 2021). Relationships may also be automated, allowing for independence between both parties (Mayor et al., 2021).

The provider-user relationship can focus on capacity-building efforts, similar to other Knowledge Intensive Business Sectors (KIBS) like consulting (Pereira & Vence, 2021). CS providers share their expertise with users to improve their understanding of the service's potential value in their specific contexts. Providers also help users apply this knowledge and various tools to develop new skills and create tailored innovations, addressing unique challenges faced by the users. The delivery of climate services marks the start of an ongoing relationship, characterized by mutual trust and a joint commitment to continuous innovation.

Channels:

The user's profile and their relationship with the provider play a key role in selecting the distribution channel for climate services. Due to the intangible nature of climate services, e-marketplaces have become the preferred choice. These platforms facilitate communication, automate transactions, coordinate brokerage, and integrate processes. Digital channels also provide user assistance, demonstrations, and consultations. However, when face-to-face interaction is necessary, physical channels are more suitable for effective engagement.

Data management via digital channels presents unique challenges compared to physical ones. A significant issue is the lack of comprehensive legislation regarding data property rights, security, and privacy, raising concerns about the security and confidentiality of user data and affecting their trust in the service (Bergman et al., 2022). Additionally, the absence of standardized data management practices can lead to inconsistent data handling across platforms. This inconsistency can result in data fragmentation, reducing the data's usability and hindering the integration of complementary services due to compatibility issues (Guentchev et al., 2023). Infrequent data updates can also disrupt the service's continuity and reliability.

These challenges highlight the need for an innovative legal and policy framework, along with the establishment of shared standards for data access and management. Ensuring quality, transparency, security, ownership, and interoperability is essential for fostering market growth and securing financial support for climate services.

Value proposition:

The value of climate information lies in the improved outcomes that result from informed decisions. Effective decision-making depends on the ability to interpret and act on climate data, projections, and uncertainties, with the aim of minimizing impacts, optimizing response efficiency, and seizing opportunities presented by the transition to a low-carbon economy (American Meteorological Society, 2021; WMO, 2018). For instance, accurate climate forecasts enable farmers to optimize water use and improve crop yields, while renewable energy generation can be enhanced through precise weather data (Alliance for Hydromet development, 2021).

To implement ESG strategies effectively, organizations must navigate a complex legal landscape where regulatory compliance increasingly demands real-time, accurate, and verifiable data. International bodies and governments are imposing stricter disclosure requirements for environmental impact, compelling organizations to not only adopt sustainable practices but to ensure transparency in reporting (*European Commission*, 2020; SEC, 2024). Real-time data is essential for these compliance efforts as it allows stakeholders to monitor progress, adapt strategies promptly, and respond to potential risks in alignment with legal standards. This need for accuracy is amplified by the rising expectations from investors and the public, who are increasingly concerned with credible, science-backed information on environmental, social, and governance performance (OECD, 2024; TFCD, 2024) . In this context, trustworthy data is indispensable, providing the foundation for actionable insights that drive sustainable decision-making and enhance accountability across industries.

Usability is critical to ensure that climate services are aligned with users' knowledge and needs to support different decision scenarios, ranging from immediate to multi-decadal planning, such as setting insurance rates, evaluating long-term loans, or planning infrastructure projects (Condon, 2023). Co-development of climate services is therefore fundamental to the transformation of climate data into tailored knowledge services (Larosa & Mysiak, 2020; Shafer et al., 2005)

The value of climate services has been recognized as a public value by several experts (D. Rogers et al., 2021; Webber & Donner, 2017). This recognition is based on their central role in ensuring the safety of citizens from climate-related hazards, promoting the sustainable and responsible use of common natural resources, and supporting the development of a low-carbon economy. This vision is reflected in today's reality, as climate services are mostly provided by public authorities (Bocken et al., 2014). However, businesses have shown a growing interest in integrating climate risks into strategic investments and operations, as well as a growing demand for specialized climate tools and information (American Meteorological Society, 2021; Directorate-General for Research and Innovation, 2015).

COST AND REVENUE STRUCTURE (ENVIRONMENTAL, SOCIAL, AND ECONOMIC)

The majority of climate services are currently produced by public entities, especially by National Hydro-Meteorological Services (NHMS), or by small-scale enterprises founded by climate scientists and often affiliated with NHMS (Directorate-General for Research and Innovation, 2015; Thorpe, 2022)

However, public entities in developed and underdeveloped countries currently encounter difficulties in producing CS due to deficiencies in cutting-edge technologies, infrastructure, and highly skilled human resources. Their chronic underfunding affects their ability to deliver high-quality and reliable services that depend on factors such as the quality and quantity of data collected, including their temporal and spatial resolution, time horizon, and geographical coverage (Condon, 2023). Local data are particularly important when assessing climate risk for specific communities since downscaling techniques applied to global models are often not precise enough to empower local municipalities in decision-making processes. Moreover, public entities' activities are often supported by international development assistance such as short-term grants for project implementation, that do not guarantee the necessary resources for covering maintenance and operational costs, leading to frequent failures (D. P. Rogers et al., 2022)

The outsourcing of certain activities in the production of climate services and the standardization of contract conditions can assist public organizations in reducing their operational and transaction costs, thereby enabling them to direct their limited resources toward the fulfillment of their core functions (Bergman et al., 2022).

Overall, cost and revenue structures are not thoroughly analyzed in the literature and remain a critical issue to be addressed to enable the CS market to scale up. In addition, the environmental and social costs and benefits of CS implementation have not been addressed in any study.

CLIMATE AND SOCIAL IMPACTS

The evolution of BMC has allowed it to incorporate some of the aspects that relate to environmental and social impacts. Within the Eco-canvas business model for instance, the climate and social impacts are acknowledged as external factors that possess the potential to influence the overall business performance in either a positive or negative way. However, when considering climate services, these elements should be regarded as fundamental components for the development of such services, which constitutes a modification of the elements themselves, internalizing their nature, instead of adding potential external factors. The principal objective of CS is to address the climate-related and societal needs of a diverse range of stakeholders, thereby empowering them to effectively support climate adaptation, mitigation, and resilience actions (Calvin et al., 2023; United Nations Environment Programme, 2021).

Consequently, the evaluation of the present climate risk (which encompasses climatic hazards, exposure, and vulnerability of the population) and societal factors and trends (e.g. aging population) within the target community is of paramount importance to the creation of the climate service value proposition itself. An illustrative example is provided by the study of Staccione et al (2023), which modeled the pluvial flood risk (climate impact) of the Milan metropolitan area and mapped the population exposed (social impacts). This was done to assist the local municipality in identifying priority action urban areas for reducing potential damages to infrastructure and population exposure to pluvial flood risk. In this instance, a nature-based solution has been proposed for mitigating the local risk. In particular, the expansion of the city's green infrastructure network by 25% has been demonstrated to have the potential to halve the pluvial flood damages and decrease the population exposure by 40%.

CLIMATE AND SOCIAL FORESIGHT

The integration of climate and social foresight features within the BMC4CS enables the long-term projections of these impacts on stakeholders' context, allowing decision-makers to strategically plan for the future (Tang & Dessai, 2012). Indeed, businesses which integrate socio-environmental dynamics considerations into their strategies are better equipped to navigate complex environmental and social challenges while seizing opportunities for long-term success.

On the environmental side, for example, by incorporating climate projections, public actors such as government agencies, local municipalities, and regulatory bodies can anticipate and prepare for potential climate-related risks such as extreme weather events, sea-level rise, and shifts in precipitation patterns (Nilsson, 2021). For instance, the city of Rotterdam has implemented a comprehensive climate adaptation plan that includes measures such as floating homes and water plazas to manage increased flooding risks. This kind of proactive approach enables the implementation of measures to protect public infrastructure, communities, and essential services. This, in turn, helps enhance societal resilience to climate impacts, investing in sustainable and adaptive public policies (Berke & Lyles, 2013).

Moreover, climate projections help public actors anticipate future regulatory requirements related to climate change (Agrawala et al., 2011) and comply with current ones (ex. Green Deal) . This foresight allows public bodies to stay ahead of necessary regulatory changes, develop comprehensive environmental standards, and enforce compliance effectively. Furthermore, climate projections support the development of proactive strategies to mitigate transition risks while promoting innovation in sustainable public practices (Suprayitno et al., 2024.). The city of Copenhagen, for example, has integrated climate projections into its urban planning to create green roofs and enhance urban biodiversity (Xu et al., 2021).

Lastly, regarding stakeholder engagement and reputation, transparent use of climate foresight enhances engagement with citizens, builds trust in communities, and fosters collaboration with various societal actors (André et al., 2023). Public actors that demonstrate proactive efforts in climate adaptation are considered responsible and forward-thinking by the public. This strengthens institutional reputation and fosters long-term relationships with stakeholders who prioritize sustainability and ethical governance. For instance, the climate action plan of the municipality of Milan in Italy has significantly bolstered public trust and increased community participation in environmental initiatives through the Permanent Citizens' Assembly on Climate (*Municipality of Milan - Permanent Citizens' Assembly on the Climate - Milan Cambia Aria* -, s.d.)

Regarding the societal aspects, the understanding of demographic trends such as aging populations or shifts in urbanization patterns helps public actors such as government agencies, local municipalities, and policymakers plan for workforce dynamics, consumer markets, and healthcare needs (Habegger, 2010). In this view, social foresight provides not only insights into changing public preferences and values related to sustainability but also informs public actors about future trends in citizen expectations and community culture (Bain et al., 2013). Public actors can also use social foresight to foster stronger relationships with local communities by supporting initiatives that align with community values and priorities. This engagement contributes to positive social impact and enhances the reputation of public institutions as responsible and responsive entities (Doh & Guay, 2006).

Integrating both climate and social foresight into strategic planning enables public bodies to adopt a holistic approach to risk management, innovation, and sustainability. By addressing both environmental and social dimensions, public actors can better navigate uncertainties, seize opportunities, and build resilience in an increasingly complex global landscape.

Additional Element

The results of the conducted literature analysis indicate the necessity of including an additional element to the initial building blocks identified for the BMC4CS. The operational context was identified as a crucial factor in the development and scale-up of climate services, particularly in the long-term, outside pilot projects. In a recent study conducted by the International Institute for Applied Systems Analysis (IIASA)[1], the Swiss Federal Institute of Technology (ETH Zurich) and the University of Delaware have analyzed what would be the impact of not taking into consideration climate change risks and impacts in the economy. This is considered to be the cost of inaction, thus the economic impact, damages and additional expenses that will be incurred if there are no adaptation or mitigation plans. They concluded that if global warming continues to increase to 3 degree celsius, global GDP will decrease by up to 10% and developing nations will be the most impacted. Meanwhile, limiting global warming to 1.5 degree celsius, which has been the objective over the past decades, would reduce the global economic costs of climate change by half or even two thirds.

Operational Context

The operational context is here defined as the policy, legal, and technological environment in which CS providers function. Including these aspects is essential, as they have a critical impact on the production and utilization of CS.

Targeted data policies are crucial for easing data access and standardization while ensuring data quality, transparency, and interoperability. This reduces fragmentation, enhances stakeholder trust, and lowers transaction and access costs (UN environmental programme, 2024). Initiatives such as the EU's Data Space (European Commission, 2022), DestinE (EC, JRC, 2020; Nativi & Craglia, 2020), SPHERE, and the Digital Urban European Twins (Duet3) (European Commission, 2019) are aligned with these goals. The EU's Data Space aims to create a unified European data space to improve data sharing across strategic sectors, supporting the green transition. DestinE focuses on developing a highly accurate digital model of the Earth, which will monitor and simulate natural phenomena, predict environmental disasters, and aid in formulating precise adaptation and mitigation strategies (EC, 2022; EC, JRC, 2020). SPHERE and Duet3 contribute to the development of this Digital Twin by optimizing building life cycles and enhancing city management through digital replicas, facilitating better decision-making and citizen engagement (EC, 2022; EC, JRC, 2020).

The legal context is also crucial to foster CS market growth and strengthen the private sector's involvement. For instance, the establishment of a shared taxonomy and the standardization of data and methodologies for climate service production enhance transparency and efficiency throughout the value chain.

An advanced technological context is crucial for operating in the CS market. Recent technological progress, particularly in AI and machine learning, has revolutionized climate modeling and forecasting by enabling the management of big data and complex variables (Thorpe, 2022). Innovations in IoT have led to applications such as advanced smart hybrid public warning systems, which enhance the ability to warn the population of upcoming climatic disasters (Alliance for Hydromet development, 2021). Additionally, these technologies have advanced hazard modeling, geo-mapping of assets, and the creation of detailed exposure datasets, thereby expanding the role of private enterprises in the climate service production chain (American Meteorological Society, 2021).

Figure 3. Business Model Canvas For Climate Services (BM4CS)

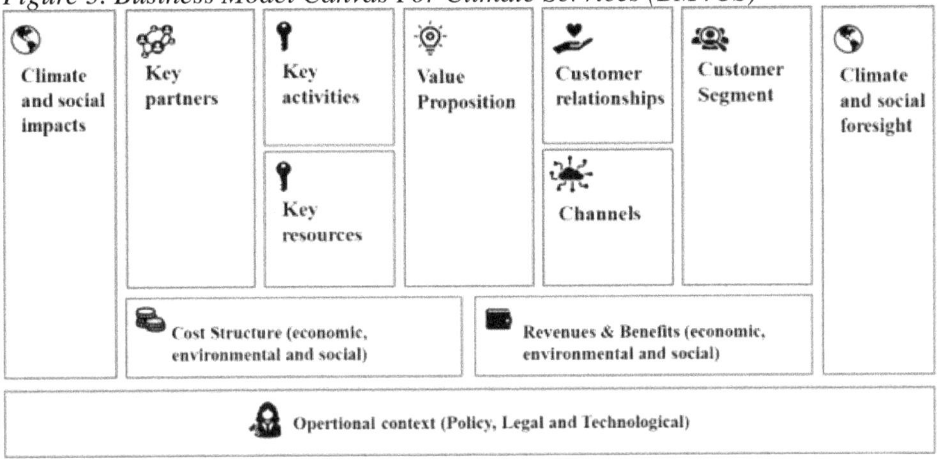

CONCLUSIONS

Integrating climate knowledge into decision-making will become increasingly important in the future, given the growing challenges that climate change poses to societies worldwide. As far as we are concerned, this is the first study that takes into account climate service considerations within a business model canvas, tring to provide a tool that can be used by multiple actors to framework the state-of-the-art and planning future action for a more resilient future.

In this context, the BM4CS should not be seen as a static and rigid operating framework, but rather as a reference framework to help stakeholders systematize their knowledge, organize their activities, communicate, and collaborate within and beyond the boundaries of their institution; a guide to creating, delivering and capturing value in an ever-changing environment.

Limitations and Recommendations for Future Research

The proposed Business Model Canvas for Climate Services sets out the key elements that should be considered to translate climate knowledge into adaptation and mitigation actions. As highlighted in the review, climate services need to be tailored to the users to be effective. Sector and user specificity is therefore fundamental to the development of these services, and specific business models should be developed accordingly.

In this vein, this study does not without several limitations. First, sectors in which climate services can be implemented, such as agriculture, health, early warning systems, and energy production, may involve different stakeholders and could be influenced by specific policies, laws, and technologies. Secondly, the geographical context in which stakeholders operate strongly influences the production of CS and the operational context in which they develop.

In particular, differences between developed and underdeveloped countries need to be taken into account to ensure not only that the service works, but also that countries most vulnerable to climate change are not left behind by the privatization of climate services.

Moreover, it should be noted that European policies on data sharing, technology development and organization sustainability had been a strong acceleration in recent years, contributing to frame an operational context quite unique compared to other countries.

Finally, future research efforts should be devoted to the development of sectoral and geographical-specific business models for climate services in order to better support stakeholders in innovating and scaling up solutions in this area in an equitable manner. This will help private and public bodies to cope with the risks associated with climate change and behave accordingly in terms of planning adaptive measures.

REFERENCES

Agrawala, S., Carraro, M., Kingsmill, N., Lanzi, E., Mullan, M., & Prudent-Richard, G. (2011). *Private Sector Engagement in Adaptation to Climate Change: Approaches to Managing Climate Risks*. OECD., DOI: 10.1787/5kg221jkf1g7-

Alliance for Hydromet developement. (2021). *Hydromet Gap Report*.

American Meteorological Society, A. (2021). *Weather-Water-Climate Value Chain(s): Giving VOICE to the Characterization of the Economic Benefits of Hydro-Met Services and Products*.

André, K., Gerger Swartling, Å., Englund, M., Petutschnig, L., Attoh, E. M. N. A. N., Milde, K., Lückerath, D., Cauchy, A., Botnen Holm, T., Hanssen Korsbrekke, M., Bour, M., & Rome, E. (2023). Improving stakeholder engagement in climate change risk assessments: Insights from six co-production initiatives in Europe. *Frontiers in Climate*, *5*. Advance online publication. DOI: 10.3389/fclim.2023.1120421

Bain, P. G., Hornsey, M. J., Bongiorno, R., Kashima, Y., & Crimston, C. R. (2013). Collective Futures: How Projections About the Future of Society Are Related to Actions and Attitudes Supporting Social Change. *Personality and Social Psychology Bulletin*, *39*(4), 523–539. DOI: 10.1177/0146167213478200 PMID: 23456559

Bergman, R., Abbas, A. E., Jung, S., Werker, C., & de Reuver, M. (2022). Business model archetypes for data marketplaces in the automotive industry. *Electronic Markets*, *32*(2), 747–765. DOI: 10.1007/s12525-022-00547-x

Berke, P., & Lyles, W. (2013). Public Risks and the Challenges to Climate-Change Adaptation: A Proposed Framework for Planning in the Age of Uncertainty. *Cityscape (Washington, D.C.)*, *15*(1), 181–208.

Bocken, N. M. P., Short, S. W., Rana, P., & Evans, S. (2014). A literature and practice review to develop sustainable business model archetypes. *Journal of Cleaner Production*, *65*, 42–56. DOI: 10.1016/j.jclepro.2013.11.039

Bojovic, D., Clair, A., Christel Jiménez, I., Terrado, M., Stanzel, P., Gonzalez, P., & Palin, E. (2021). Engagement, involvement and empowerment: Three realms of a coproduction framework for climate services. *Global Environmental Change*, *68*, 102271. DOI: 10.1016/j.gloenvcha.2021.102271

Bremer, S., Wardekker, A., Dessai, S., Sobolowski, S., Slaattelid, R., & van der Sluijs, J. (2019). Toward a multi-faceted conception of co-production of climate services. *Climate Services*, *13*, 42–50. DOI: 10.1016/j.cliser.2019.01.003

Breuer, H., & Lüdeke-Freund, F. (2017). VALUES-BASED NETWORK AND BUSINESS MODEL INNOVATION. *International Journal of Innovation Management, 21*(03), 1750028. DOI: 10.1142/S1363919617500281

Calvin, K., Dasgupta, D., Krinner, G., Mukherji, A., Thorne, P. W., Trisos, C., Romero, J., Aldunce, P., Barrett, K., Blanco, G., Cheung, W. W. L., Connors, S., Denton, F., Diongue-Niang, A., Dodman, D., Garschagen, M., Geden, O., Hayward, B., Jones, C., . . . Péan, C. (2023). *IPCC, 2023: Climate Change 2023: Synthesis Report. Contribution of Working Groups I, II and III to the Sixth Assessment Report of the Intergovernmental Panel on Climate Change [Core Writing Team, H. Lee and J. Romero (eds.)]. IPCC, Geneva, Switzerland.* (First). Intergovernmental Panel on Climate Change (IPCC). https://doi.org/DOI: 10.59327/IPCC/AR6-9789291691647

Climate Policy Initiative. (2023). *Global Landscape of Climate Finance 2023—Methodology.*

Condon, M. (2023). *Climate Services: The Business of Physical Risk* (SSRN Scholarly Paper 4396826). https://doi.org/DOI: 10.2139/ssrn.4396826

Contreras, E., Herrero, J., Crochemore, L., Pechlivanidis, I., Photiadou, C., Aguilar, C., & Polo, M. J. (2020). Advances in the Definition of Needs and Specifications for a Climate Service Tool Aimed at Small Hydropower Plants' Operation and Management. *Energies, 13*(7), 1827. DOI: 10.3390/en13071827

Daou, A., Mallat, C., Chammas, G., Cerantola, N., Kayed, S., & Saliba, N. A. (2020). The Ecocanvas as a business model canvas for a circular economy. *Journal of Cleaner Production, 258*, 120938. DOI: 10.1016/j.jclepro.2020.120938

Dell'Aquila, A., Graça, A., Teixeira, M., Fontes, N., Gonzalez-Reviriego, N., Marcos-Matamoros, R., Chou, C., Terrado, M., Giannakopoulos, C., Varotsos, K. V., Caboni, F., Locci, R., Nanu, M., Porru, S., Argiolas, G., Bruno Soares, M., & Sanderson, M. (2023). Monitoring climate related risk and opportunities for the wine sector: The MED-GOLD pilot service. *Climate Services, 30*, 100346. DOI: 10.1016/j.cliser.2023.100346

Directorate-General for Research and Innovation. (2015). *A European Research innovation _ Roadmap for Climate Services.*

Doh, J. P., & Guay, T. R. (2006). Corporate Social Responsibility, Public Policy, and NGO Activism in Europe and the United States: An Institutional-Stakeholder Perspective. *Journal of Management Studies, 43*(1), 47–73. DOI: 10.1111/j.1467-6486.2006.00582.x

EC. JRC. (2020). *Destination Earth: Survey on "Digital Twins" technologies and activities, in the Green Deal area.* Publications Office. https://data.europa.eu/doi/10.2760/430025

EC. (2022). *COMMISSION STAFF WORKING DOCUMENT on Common European Data Spaces.*

European Commission. (2019). *Digital Urban European Twins for smarter decision making | DUET Project | Fact Sheet | H2020.* CORDIS | European Commission. https://cordis.europa.eu/project/id/870697

European Commission. (2022). *A European strategy for data | Shaping Europe's digital future.* https://digital-strategy.ec.europa.eu/en/policies/strategy-data

European Commission. (2020). https://commission.europa.eu/index_it

Evans, S., Vladimirova, D., Holgado, M., Van Fossen, K., Yang, M., Silva, E., & Barlow, C. (2017). Business Model Innovation for Sustainability. *Business Strategy and the Environment, 26.* Advance online publication. DOI: 10.1002/bse.1939

Frei, T. (2021). Public–private engagement (PPE) in hydromet services and the role of the academic sector. *Meteorological Applications, 28*(5), e2025. DOI: 10.1002/met.2025

Guentchev, G., Palin, E. J., Lowe, J. A., & Harrison, M. (2023). Upscaling of climate services – What is it? A literature review. *Climate Services, 30*, 100352. DOI: 10.1016/j.cliser.2023.100352

Habegger, B. (2010). Strategic foresight in public policy: Reviewing the experiences of the UK, Singapore, and the Netherlands. *Futures, 42*(1), 49–58. DOI: 10.1016/j.futures.2009.08.002

Joyce, A., & Paquin, R. L. (2016a). The triple layered business model canvas: A tool to design more sustainable business models. *Journal of Cleaner Production, 135*, 1474–1486. DOI: 10.1016/j.jclepro.2016.06.067

Joyce, A., & Paquin, R. L. (2016b). The triple layered business model canvas: A tool to design more sustainable business models. *Journal of Cleaner Production, 135*, 1474–1486. DOI: 10.1016/j.jclepro.2016.06.067

Kazantsev, N., Islam, N., Zwiegelaar, J., Brown, A., & Maull, R. (2023). Data sharing for business model innovation in platform ecosystems: From private data to public good. *Technological Forecasting and Social Change, 192*, 122515. DOI: 10.1016/j.techfore.2023.122515

Larosa, F., & Mysiak, J. (2020). Business models for climate services: An analysis. *Climate Services*, *17*, 100111. DOI: 10.1016/j.cliser.2019.100111

Lüdeke-Freund, F., Carroux, S., Joyce, A., Massa, L., & Breuer, H. (2018). The sustainable business model pattern taxonomy—45 patterns to support sustainability-oriented business model innovation. *Sustainable Production and Consumption*, *15*, 145–162. DOI: 10.1016/j.spc.2018.06.004

Mattera, M., & Soto, F. (2023). Dodging the bullet: Overcoming the financial impact of Ukraine armed conflict with sustainable business strategies and environmental approaches. *The Journal of Risk Finance*, *24*(1), 122–142. DOI: 10.1108/JRF-04-2022-0092

Mayor, B., Zorrilla-Miras, P., Coent, P. L., Biffin, T., Dartée, K., Peña, K., Graveline, N., Marchal, R., Nanu, F., Scrieciu, A., Calatrava, J., Manzano, M., & López Gunn, E. (2021). Natural Assurance Schemes Canvas: A Framework to Develop Business Models for Nature-Based Solutions Aimed at Disaster Risk Reduction. *Sustainability, 13*(3). *Articolo, 3*. Advance online publication. DOI: 10.3390/su13031291

Miles, I., Kastrinos, N., Bilderbeek, R., den Hertog, P., Flanagan, K., Huntink, W., & Bouman, M. (1995). *Knowledge-intensive business services: Users, carriers and sources of innovation*. https://research.manchester.ac.uk/en/publications/knowledge-intensive-business-services-users-carriers-and-sources-

Municipality of Milan—Permanent citizens' assembly on the climate—Milan Cambia Aria -. (s.d.). Milan Municipality. Recuperato 9 luglio 2024, da https://www.comune.milano.it/en/web/milano-cambia-aria/cosa-puoi-fare-tu/sei-una-cittadina-o-un-cittadino/assemblea-permanente-dei-cittadini-sul-clima

Nativi, S., & Craglia, M. (2020, novembre 10). *Destination Earth: Use Cases Analysis*. JRC Publications Repository. https://doi.org/DOI: 10.2760/17457

Nilsson, F. (2021). *Anticipating Environmental Change in Local Climate Governance: A Case Study of Gothenburg, Sweden* [B]. https://campus-fryslan.studenttheses.ub.rug.nl/70/

OECD. (2024). *Better policies for better lives*. OECD. https://www.oecd.org/en.html

Osterwalder, A., & Pigneur, Y. (2010). *Business Model Generation: A Handbook for Visionaries, Game Changers, and Challengers*. John Wiley & Sons.

Osterwalder, A., Pigneur, Y., & Tucci, C. L. (2005a). Clarifying Business Models: Origins, Present, and Future of the Concept. *Communications of the Association for Information Systems*, *16*. Advance online publication. DOI: 10.17705/1CAIS.01601

Osterwalder, A., Pigneur, Y., & Tucci, C. L. (2005b). Clarifying Business Models: Origins, Present, and Future of the Concept. *Communications of the Association for Information Systems, 16*(1). Advance online publication. DOI: 10.17705/1CAIS.01601

Pereira, Á., & Vence, X. (2021). The role of KIBS and consultancy in the emergence of Circular Oriented Innovation. *Journal of Cleaner Production, 302*, 127000. DOI: 10.1016/j.jclepro.2021.127000

Rogers, D., Bogdanova, A.-M., Tsirkunov, V., & Suwa, M. (2021). *Public and Private Engagement in Hydromet Services: From Rivalry to Coproduction in Meteorological and Hydrological Service Delivery*. GFDRR.

Rogers, D. P., Staudinger, M., Tsirkunov, V., Suwa, M., & Kootval, H. (2022). *Affordability of National Meteorological and Hydrological Services*. GFDRR.

Rohrbeck, R., Konnertz, L., & Knab, S. (2013). Collaborative business modelling for systemic and sustainability innovations. *International Journal of Technology Management*. https://www.inderscienceonline.com/doi/10.1504/IJTM.2013.055577

Rubio-Martin, A., Mañez Costa, M., Pulido-Velazquez, M., Garcia-Prats, A., Celliers, L., Llario, F., & Macian, J. (2021). Structuring Climate Service Co-Creation Using a Business Model Approach. *Earth's Future, 9*(10), e2021EF002181. https://doi.org/DOI: 10.1029/2021EF002181

SEC. (2024). *Securities and Exchange Commission*. https://www.sec.gov/newsroom/press-releases/2022-46

Shafer, S. M., Smith, H. J., & Linder, J. C. (2005). The power of business models. *Business Horizons, 48*(3), 199–207. DOI: 10.1016/j.bushor.2004.10.014

Staccione, A., Brown, C., Arneth, A., Rounsevell, M., Hrast Essenfelder, A., Seo, B., & Mysiak, J. (2023). Exploring the effects of protected area networks on the European land system. *Journal of Environmental Management, 337*, 117741. DOI: 10.1016/j.jenvman.2023.117741 PMID: 36966632

Suprayitno, D., Iskandar, S., Dahurandi, K., Hendarto, T., & Rumambi, J. (s.d.). *Public Policy In The Era Of Climate Change: Adapting Strategies For Sustainable Futures*.

Swart, R., Celliers, L., Collard, M., Prats, A. G., Huang-Lachmann, J.-T., Sempere, F. L., de Jong, F., Máñez Costa, M., Martinez, G., Velazquez, M. P., Martín, A. R., Segretier, W., Stattner, E., & Timmermans, W. (2021a). Reframing climate services to support municipal and regional planning. *Climate Services, 22*, 100227. DOI: 10.1016/j.cliser.2021.100227

Swart, R., Celliers, L., Collard, M., Prats, A. G., Huang-Lachmann, J.-T., Sempere, F. L., de Jong, F., Máñez Costa, M., Martinez, G., Velazquez, M. P., Martín, A. R., Segretier, W., Stattner, E., & Timmermans, W. (2021b). Reframing climate services to support municipal and regional planning. *Climate Services*, *22*, 100227. DOI: 10.1016/j.cliser.2021.100227

Tang, S., & Dessai, S. (2012). *Usable Science? The U.K. Climate Projections 2009 and Decision Support for Adaptation Planning*. https://doi.org/DOI: 10.1175/WCAS-D-12-00028.1

TFCD. (2024). *Task Force on Climate-Related Financial Disclosures*. Task Force on Climate-Related Financial Disclosures. https://www.fsb-tcfd.org/

Thorpe, A. (2022). The global weather enterprise, part 1: The jigsaw pieces. *Weather*, *77*(10), 349–351. DOI: 10.1002/wea.4261

Thorpe, A. (2023). The global weather enterprise, part 3: An evolving picture. *Weather*, *78*(3), 74–78. DOI: 10.1002/wea.4347

UN environmental programme. (2024). *The climate data challenge: The critical role of open-source and neutral data platforms. Technical Supplement to the 2024 Climate Risk Landscape Report*. https://www.unepfi.org/themes/climate-change/the-climate-data-challenge-the-critical-role-of-open-source-and-neutral-data-platforms/

United Nations Environment Programme. (2021, settembre 1). *Adaptation Gap Report 2020*. UNEP - UN Environment Programme. https://www.unep.org/resources/adaptation-gap-report-2020

Vaughan, C., Dessai, S., Hewitt, C., Baethgen, W., Terra, R., & Berterretche, M. (2017). Creating an enabling environment for investment in climate services: The case of Uruguay's National Agricultural Information System. In *Climate Services* (Vol. 8, pp. 62–71). https://doi.org/DOI: 10.1016/j.cliser.2017.11.001

WB. (2019). *The Power of Partnership: Public and Private Engagement in Hydromet Services*. The World Bank.

Webber, S., & Donner, S. D. (2017). Climate service warnings: Cautions about commercializing climate science for adaptation in the developing world. *Wiley Interdisciplinary Reviews: Climate Change, 8*(1). *Scopus*. Advance online publication. DOI: 10.1002/wcc.424

WMO. (2018). *Step-by-step Guidelines for Establishing a National Framework for Climate Services. 1206*.

WMO. (2020). *2020 State of Climate Services: Risk Information and Early Warning Systems* (WMO-No. 1252; p. 25). World Meteorological Organization. https://library.wmo.int/idurl/4/57191

Xu, H., Liu, L., & Ding, P. (2021). Building Climate Resilient City through Multiple Scale Cooperative Planning: Experiences from Copenhagen. *IOP Conference Series. Materials Science and Engineering*, *1203*(3), 032063.

ENDNOTES

1 https://iiasa.ac.at/news/apr-2024/what-are-economic-costs-of-climate-inaction

Chapter 9
Integrating Double Materiality Into the Criteria of European Sustainable Finance Labels:
A Systematic Review of the Literature

Nathalie Lévy
https://orcid.org/0000-0001-5243-9953
University of Tours, France

Derick Moukoumia
https://orcid.org/0009-0008-0544-6518
Derick Patrimoine, France

ABSTRACT

The integration of double materiality—combining financial and impact perspectives—has become pivotal in the European regulatory framework for sustainable finance labels (SFDR, CSRD, Taxonomy). Yet, its operational implementation remains inconsistent due to divergent national approaches, conceptual ambiguities, and a lack of standardization. This systematic review analyses how impact measurement mechanisms—such as Principal Adverse Impacts (PAI), green share, and sectoral exclusions—are applied, and highlights risks linked to regulatory fragmentation, transparency gaps, and comparability challenges. The findings reveal significant heterogeneity affecting the credibility and effectiveness of these labels. Reinforcing

DOI: 10.4018/979-8-3693-9551-6.ch009

harmonization, standardized criteria, and oversight is recommended to ensure double materiality is meaningfully embedded in sustainable finance labeling. This study offers a valuable framework for policymakers, researchers, and practitioners working to strengthen the role of labels in supporting the transition to a sustainable economy.

I. INTRODUCTION

In the context of the climate crisis and the associated challenges of financing the energy and ecological transition, sustainable finance labels (Pappalardo, 2024) and the European regulatory framework—including the Sustainable Finance Disclosure Regulation (SFDR), the Corporate Sustainability Reporting Directive (CSRD), the Corporate Sustainability Due Diligence Directive (CSDDD), and the Taxonomy—play an important role in the European response.

Currently, the European landscape comprises approximately a dozen national sustainable finance labels. These labels serve a strategic function in measuring sustainability performance and limiting the risk of greenwashing (Kamara, 2023). However, this proliferation reflects the diversity of regulatory approaches and standards, creating uncertainty for investors and regulators alike (European Securities and Markets Authority [ESMA], 2024). The actual impact of labelled financial products depends on the comparability and credibility of the signals sent (Crifo, 2022).

To address these limitations, double materiality has become a key component of the European regulatory framework. Market participants are thus required to conduct comprehensive assessment covering "outside-in" financial risks (the impact of external factors on the company) (Coullabé, 2025) and "inside-out" societal and environmental impacts (the company's effect on its environment) (De Cristofaro & Gullu, 2023).

Although the importance of double materiality is recognized in the literature and the regulatory framework, its integration into European labelling standards and procedures remains insufficiently explored (De Merxem & Tchotourian, 2024). The coexistence of different approaches and the lack of harmonization risk accentuating information asymmetries and perpetuating greenwashing, which runs counter to the objectives of market transparency and stakeholder accountability (De Cristofaro & Gullu, 2023). In the literature and specialized press (Novethic, 2025; Weefin, 2025), attempts are made to provide an up-to-date overview of European sustainable finance labels, but the identified areas of uncertainty remain unresolved. Nicken, Zulfikar, Mulyasari, and Ismawati (2024) also emphasize the urgent need for more rigorous empirical analysis of how double materiality is operationalized in labelling systems to improve their effectiveness.

This study aims to understand the extent to which double materiality is substantially integrated into European sustainability label standards, as well as to identify the obstacles and levers for strengthening the transparency, comparability, and legitimacy of sustainable finance certification.

The research has two ambitions: (i) to clarify definitions and refocus conceptual debates (e.g., single vs. double vs. dynamic materiality), while highlighting persistent controversies by consolidating the conceptual framework proposed in the literature; and (ii) to provide a unique mapping of the requirements and criteria specific to each label, highlighting their convergences and divergences, and emphasizing the risks of regulatory fragmentation and greenwashing.

To this end, we are conducting a systematic review of literature from regulatory, scientific, and professional sources, covering the period from 2000 to 2025, based on the PRISMA (Preferred Reporting Items for Systematic reviews and Meta-Analyses) flow diagram model. This methodological approach has enabled us to compile a corpus of 40 articles that provide a critical synthesis of the approaches to integrating double materiality identified in the literature. The objective of this research is to provide a useful frame of reference for academic debate and future regulatory developments.

In Part II, we offer a systematic review of the literature on the relationship between regulatory developments (SFDR, CSRD, Taxonomy) and labeling practices (SRI, Greenfin, FNG-Siegel, LuxFLAG, Towards Sustainability, Umweltzeichen, Nordic Swan, Relance, Finansol) from the perspective of the effective integration of double materiality. Then, in Part III, we open up new perspectives for the regulation and evaluation of sustainable finance by recommending the implementation of SMART (Specific, Measurable, Achievable, Relevant, Time-bound) criteria to measure double materiality, normative alignment between labels, and strengthened control mechanisms. This set of guidelines addresses recurrent expectations identified in the academic literature and among both regulators and investors.

II. LITERATURE REVIEW METHODOLOGY

This section presents the research methodology used to analyze the actual place of double materiality in European sustainability label frameworks, as well as the obstacles and levers that could strengthen the transparency, comparability, and legitimacy of sustainable finance certification. Each step is described to ensure the comprehensiveness and robustness of the analysis, as well as transparency regarding the data collected and processed. Section 2.1 introduces the literature review methodology, and Section 2.2 describes the literature collection and processing protocol.

2.1 Typology and Relevance of Review Methods

Our literature review emphasizes comprehensiveness, rigor, and transparency in the selection, analysis, and synthesis of existing research related to our topic. To ensure methodological adequacy, we identified and compared five of the most frequently used review methodologies in the humanities and social sciences to determine their relevance to our research question. Table 1 below summarizes and contrasts the main benefits, limitations, typical uses, and specific relevance of each approach for the present study.

Table 1. Comparative relevance of literature review methodologies

Methodology	Benefits	Bounds	Typical use	Relevance for the research topic
Narrative review	Flexible and fast overview General context Access to trends	Subjectivity and selection bias Low reproducibility Risk of lack of completeness	Overview, exploration	Low to Medium (For general framing)
Systematic review	Rigour and transparency Summary and completeness Reduction of bias	Long process Not very flexible to integrate non-academic sources Very strict criteria	Decision, solid foundations	Very strong (ideal for this topic)
Scope review	Explorations of emerging fields Literature mapping Flexibility	Little critical analysis Limited depth Less selection on quality of sources	Prestudy, identification gaps	Medium to Strong (If the field is scattered)
Critical review	Indepth analysis Identification of controversies Theoretical innovation possible	More subjective Not systematic Less exhaustive	Theoretical / criticism	Medium (for conceptual discussions)
Meta narrative review	Integration of various practices Richness of interpretation Multidisciplinary view	Very time-consuming Difficult to implement in a standardized field Methodological complexity	Multidisciplinary subject	Average (if an interdisciplinary approach is needed)

Sources: Developed by the authors based on a comparative analysis of literature review methodologies and alignment with PRISMA 2020 guidelines.

As shown in Table 1, systematic review methodology provides the strongest guarantees in terms of rigor, transparency, and reduction of bias for this research topic. The relevance of this approach is confirmed by previous work, such as Touati et al. (2021), who applied the PRISMA methodology to systematically review literature on risk and protective factors associated with mental health. Similarly, the systematic review by Hafizah Hammad Ahmad Khan, Nabila Ahmad, Noorlailahusna Mohd Yusof, and Mohammad Abdul Matin Chowdhury (2024) demonstrates the applicability of this method in complex research contexts. Based on these criteria, we adopted the PRISMA framework for the present review.

Databases And Documentary Sources

The selection of publications spans the period from 2000 to 2025, offering both historical perspective and coverage of the emergence and development of the concepts of materiality, double materiality, and evolving European regulations and labels. The literature collection was carried out exhaustively, focusing first on academic sources. Articles, books, and scientific publications were retrieved using the following databases: American Economic Association, Scopus Preview, Google Scholar, Cairn.info, and ResearchGate. These databases were chosen for their rigorous peer review processes, recognized indexing standards, and their ability to provide access to research published across different regions and in multiple languages.

In addition to academic databases, specialized press sources such as Novethic and open access platforms like HAL were consulted to incorporate relevant professional publications. To further strengthen the completeness of the material collected, institutional reports and official documents from the European Commission, the European Securities and Markets Authority (ESMA), the Autorité des Marchés Financiers (AMF), and the International Energy Agency (IEA) were included. These sources enabled the integration of gray literature—defined as reports and publications produced by organizations outside traditional academic publishing channels but considered authoritative for policy and regulatory analysis.

Inclusion criteria comprised peer reviewed scientific publications (journals, conference proceedings, theses), official reports, and European institutional documents available in the public domain explicitly focusing on double materiality or its integration within labeling systems. Full text documents on sustainable finance regulation in Europe, published in French or English, were also retained.

Exclusion criteria were applied to studies outside the scope of sustainable finance or not related to materiality, publications no longer relevant due to regulatory changes or considered redundant, unverifiable documents (including partisan materials or those from noncredible sources), publications outside the field of economics or treating the topic only marginally and works lacking scientific standards such as a clear methodology or credible sources. Documents in languages other than French or English were also excluded.

Identification Of Keywords

To ensure the relevance and comprehensiveness of the literature search, keywords were identified and grouped by category based on recognized literature search strategies (Desmarais, 2014). Table 2 provides a detailed overview of the categories and associated terms used in our database and website queries.

Table 2. Keywords and related terms grouped by category

Category	Related terms
Fundamental concepts	Double materiality, impact materiality, financial materiality, outside-in, inside-out, materiality analysis, materiality assessment
European labels and certifications	European sustainable finance labels, SRI label, GreenFin, FNGSiegel, LuxFLAG, ESG/environment/climate finance, Towards Sustainability, Umweltzeichen (UZ 49), Nordic Swan Ecolabel, EU taxonomy, SFDR
Regulatory framework and associated concepts	CSRD, ESRD, NFRD, PAI, nonfinancial reporting, sustainability reporting, transparency, harmonization, greenwashing
Criteria and indicators	ESG criteria, sustainability indicators, KPI (key performance indicators), exclusions, exclusion criteria, normative exclusions, sectoral exclusions, environmental exclusions, engagement, voting, shareholder dialogue, taxonomy
Issues and challenges	Information asymmetry, inconsistencies, fragmentation, sustainable development, climate transition, transition plan, ESG performance
Stakeholders and users	Investors, savers, stakeholders
Specific aspects of reporting	Disclosure, reporting, sustainability report
Challenges and practicalities	Challenges, inconsistency, fragmentation, transposition, implementation, application, data quality, comparability, legitimation

Sources: Developed by the authors based on literature search strategies (Desmarais, 2014).

Combinations of keywords were systematically constructed using boolean operators such as "AND", "OR", and "NOT". For example, queries included combinations like "European labels OR SRI label", and trios such as "double materiality OR impact materiality OR financial materiality" or "European sustainable finance labels AND taxonomy AND double materiality", to refine and broaden the search strategies across multiple databases and specialized platforms.

2.2 Methodology for Collecting and Processing Literature

The methodological process began with the application of the previously identified and categorized keywords (see Section 2.1) to query the main academic databases and specialized search engines. Boolean operators ("AND", "OR", "NOT") were systematically employed to construct targeted search queries, ensuring comprehensive coverage of relevant literature.

The initial search yielded 3,579 publications. To limit publication bias and account for sources not indexed in major databases, additional targeted research was conducted using institutional websites and specialized press, resulting in the identification of 10 supplementary articles and reports. Duplicate and ineligible records were identified and removed using reference management software (Mendeley) and qualitative analysis tools (NVivo), reducing the number of items to 590.

A first screening, based on the inclusion and exclusion criteria defined earlier, retained 421 articles. These were further assessed through examination of their titles, abstracts, introductions, and conclusions, which allowed for the removal of documents not directly relevant to the research objectives. The final corpus was narrowed down to 40 documents. The retained resources were processed using thematic summary sheets. This facilitated systematic manual coding and in-depth analysis of key concepts, methodological approaches, principal findings, and stated limitations.

The step-by-step process for selecting, screening, and including studies in this review is summarized in Figure 1. The PRISMA flow diagram visually represents each stage, from the initial identification of records to the final qualitative synthesis, including the main reasons for exclusion and the total number of articles included for analysis.

Figure 1. PRISMA Flow Diagram

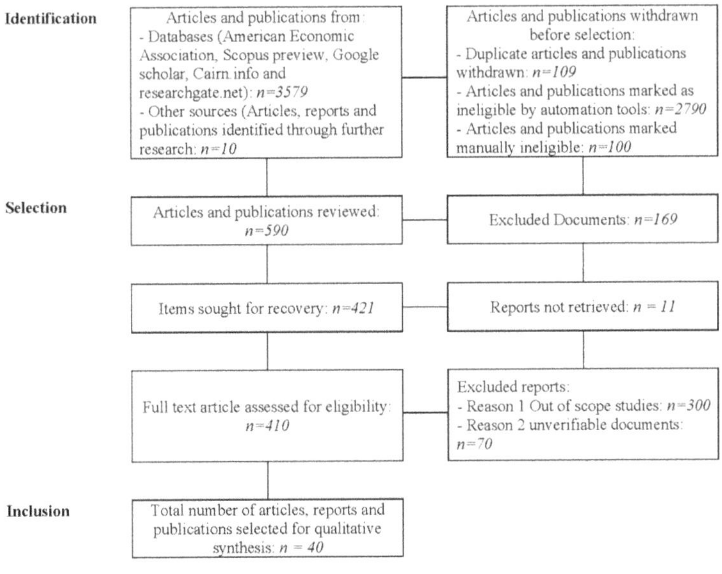

Sources: Developed by the authors based on (Touati et al., 2021)

This diagram details the number of publications retrieved and excluded at each stage, thereby documenting the systematic nature and transparency of the review protocol.

Use of artificial intelligence

The use of artificial intelligence in this study was limited to specific, minor applications that supported synthesis, literature management, and content organization. These are detailed in Table 3.

Table 3. Use of artificial intelligence

AI / Tool	Main usage	Key feature / Limitation
Perplexity (academic)	Creation of summary tables	Organizing data from summary sheets
Scispace (premium)	Search for articles by keywords	Rapid access to publications
Nvivo15 & NotebookLM	Personal virtual library, sorting and coding of the article tree	Qualitative analysis and structured management of literature data
Mymap AI (premium)	Mind map building	Most recent article updates may not be included
Quick (on demand)	Documentation, available on demand	Traceability of AI interventions

Sources: Developed by the authors based on the actual use of AI tools

Qualitative Analysis

Thematic grouping of the selected resources enabled the identification of key areas of convergence and divergence, provided a structured synthesis of definitions, approaches to double materiality integration, regulatory considerations, label types, ongoing scientific debates, and research perspectives. This analytical step also revealed persistent controversies, consensus points, and gaps in the literature needing further investigation.

Limitations

It should be noted that this systematic review is primarily based on openly accessible scientific publications and institutional reports, which may introduce a bias with respect to recent or professional contributions not yet available through the searched databases or in open access.

Transparency

Every stage of the literature review process was documented to ensure reproducibility. A comprehensive summary table of the 40 selected articles, including detailed information on the authors, year, methodology, and main results, is available in the appendix. The research protocol described above is illustrated in more detail in a schematic mind map (Figure 2). This diagram enables readers to grasp at a glance the organization of the literature review, the integration of conceptual and regulatory dimensions, and the identification of key methodological and analytical focal points informing this chapter.

Figure 2. Structure and key concepts of Double Materiality in European sustainable finance labels

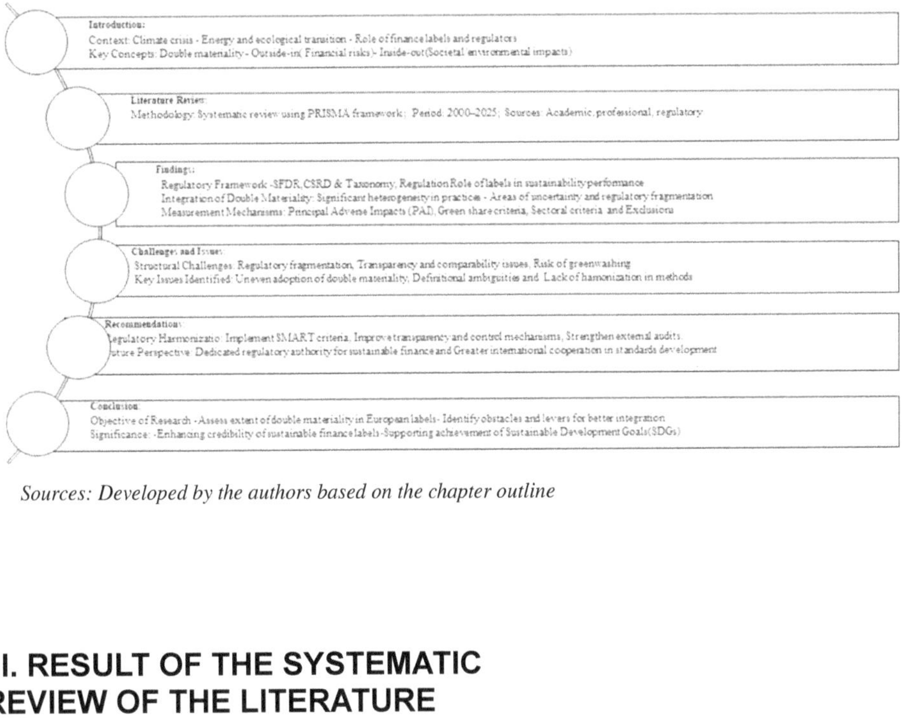

Sources: Developed by the authors based on the chapter outline

III. RESULT OF THE SYSTEMATIC REVIEW OF THE LITERATURE

This section presents the results of the systematic literature review conducted to assess the extent to which double materiality is integrated into the standards of European sustainable finance labels, and the main challenges arising from this integration. The analysis is based on the corpus established according to the methodology set out in Part II and organized around a conceptual review, evaluation of the degree of integration, examination of practical modalities and identification of main issues and challenges.

3.1 Background and Design Clarifications

Conceptual Foundations of Double Materiality

In the context of this study, double materiality is considered the joint assessment of two complementary dimensions that determine the scope and depth of sustainability-related information disclosure. Financial materiality (outside-in) refers to the analysis of sustainability-related risks and opportunities that affect organizational performance and financial outcomes. Impact materiality (inside-out) examines the positive or negative impacts of organizational activities or investment portfolios on the environment, society, and stakeholders. An overview of the double materiality framework can be found in Figure 3.

This dual analytical framework now formally enshrined in European regulations (CSRD, European Sustainability Reporting Standards [ESRS], SFDR), serves as the conceptual foundation for assessing the extent to which and the methods by which the studied labels have integrated these complementary perspectives.

Evolution Of Materiality Concepts

The concept of materiality has evolved considerably from its origins in financial accounting, where it traditionally referred to the importance or relevance of information for investment decisions. Contemporary debates on materiality definition crystallize around two primary positions, as highlighted by De Merxem and Tchotourian (2024).

The first group advocates for single (financial) materiality, emphasizing that sustainability information should primarily serve investor needs—a position supported by institutions such as the Securities and Exchange Commission (SEC) and the International Sustainability Standards Board (ISSB, 2024). Under this approach, sustainability reporting focuses on risks and opportunities that may have material financial impacts on the organization.

The second group supports double materiality, which incorporates both financial impacts and broader societal and environmental externalities. This approach addresses the information needs of both investors and stakeholders, requiring organizations to disclose not only how sustainability issues affect their financial performance, but also how their activities impact society and the environment. This position aligns closely with the European regulatory framework, which has institutionalized double materiality as a fundamental principle in the ESRS standards under the CSRD.

European Regulatory Architecture

The European regulatory framework for sustainable finance is built around three main pillars: redirecting private capital toward responsible investments, promoting transparency and long-term thinking in financial activities, and transitioning from a purely financial risk perspective to a bidirectional approach that assesses interactions between organizations, society, and the environment.

Over time, this regulatory architecture has evolved to position double materiality at the center of its disclosure framework, aiming to reduce information asymmetries and effectively combat greenwashing.

Emerging Perspectives: Dynamic Materiality

A third approach emerging in the literature focuses on dynamic materiality, based on the principle that issues deemed financially immaterial at a given point in time may become material subsequently. However, this concept remains contentious, as noted by La Chaire de la double matérialité (2025), due to its interpretive flexibility. De Cristofaro and Gullu (2023) observe similar tensions, demonstrating how dynamic materiality is sometimes perceived as reducing impact materiality to mere financial timeline considerations, potentially compromising sustainability objectives in favor of preserving existing business models.

Table 4 presents the analytical framework that structures our assessment of double materiality integration across seven key dimensions. This framework, grounded in these conceptual foundations, guides the comparative analysis in the following sections.

Table 4. Analytical framework for double materiality integration assessment

Research Dimension	Focus Area	Key Investigation Points
Background and Regulatory Evolution	Policy progression	From NFRD (2014) to CSRD (2022): gradual institutionalization
Conceptual Foundation	Double materiality definition	Financial materiality (outside-in) + impact materiality (inside-out)
Integration Modalities and Methods	Implementation approaches	PAI indicators, green share, exclusions, sectoral thresholds
Level of Integration	Heterogeneous adoption	Explicit articulation vs. Financial focused approaches
Standardization Challenges	Methodological diversity	Divergent measurement methods, criteria, and thresholds

continued on following page

Table 4. Continued

Research Dimension	Focus Area	Key Investigation Points
Transparency and Control	Disclosure and oversight	Variable external audit, reporting quality, greenwashing risks
Harmonization Perspectives	Future convergence	Alignment with Taxonomy, SFDR, CSRD requirements

Sources: Developed by the authors based on systematic literature review methodology and PRISMA 2020 guidelines; analytical dimensions derived from European regulatory framework analysis and academic literature synthesis.

3.2 Level of Integration of Double Materiality

The degree of integration of double materiality in European labels remains highly heterogeneous. Some certifications, such as Greenfin, Nordic Swan, and Towards Sustainability, clearly articulate the financial and impact dimensions, fully embracing the dual perspective imposed by the latest European regulations. In contrast, other labels, notably the French ISR label, continue to focus primarily on financial materiality.

This diversity can largely be explained by the gradual evolution of European regulatory texts. The main stages that have shaped the modalities and ambitions of the integration of double materiality into European labels are summarized in Table 5. This table presents the chronology of regulatory developments and highlights their influence on the practices adopted by the various labels.

Table 5. Regulatory milestones and impact on the integration of Double Materiality by European labels

Period / Legal text	Background and Definition	Stated Objective	Methodological progress	Observed effects on labels (data from the analysis)	References
XIXth – early 2000s	Notion of materiality from Anglo-Saxon law, focused on the protection of the investor; extension of the scope to the environment, social and governance by the Global Reporting Initiative (GRI v3, 2006).	Extend risk analysis to extra financial dimensions.	Gradual introduction of ESG indicators in voluntary benchmarks.	Conceptual preparation; Initial adoption by pioneer labels integrating extra financial transparency.	GRI (2006), Common Law Principles
Directive 2003/51/EC	Modernization of accounting and embryonic integration of ESG risks into reporting obligations.	Alignment with best accounting practices and integration of nonfinancial financial materiality.	First legal recognition of nonfinancial information in reporting.	Creation of a regulatory base encouraging certain labels to integrate financial ESG risks into their criteria.	European Parliament and Council (2003/51/ EC)
Directive 2014/95/UE (NFRD)	Lack of comparable and standardized ESG information.	Make nonfinancial reporting mandatory for large companies (>500 employees).	Implicit formalization of double materiality.	Increased inclusion of environmental and social indicators in SRI benchmarks; Significant increase in transparency.	European Parliament and Council (2014/95/ EU)
2015–2018: Paris Agreement (2015), French Energy Transition Law art.173, EU Sustainable Finance Action Plan (2018)	Climate emergency and the need to redirect financial flows towards sustainable activities.	Systematic integration of climate risks into the evaluation of investments.	Emergence of climate disclosure obligations for financial actors.	Rapid evolution of climate labels (Greenfin, etc.): integration of carbon metrics and 2°C alignment indicators.	Paris Agreement (2015); Law No. 2015992, art.173; COM (2018)97 final

continued on following page

Table 5. Continued

Period / Legal text	Background and Definition	Stated Objective	Methodological progress	Observed effects on labels (data from the analysis)	References
2019: EU Guidelines + SFDR Regulation (2019/2088)	Need for structuring of ESG information and explicit formalization of double materiality (financial impacts and environmental/ social impacts).	Increased transparency and harmonization of ESG reporting of financial products.	Two-way reporting obligation; PAI ("Principal Adverse Impacts") indicators.	Significant methodological revision; better ESG traceability in Article 8/9 SFDR labels.	European Commission (2019/C 209/01); Regulation (EU) 2019/2088
2020: Taxonomy Regulation (EU 2020/852)	Lack of harmonized definition of sustainable activities in the EU.	Create a common language and measurable technical criteria.	Introduction of standardized indicators (green share).	Gradual convergence of labels towards technical criteria Taxonomy.	Regulation (EU) 2020/852
2021: SFDR phase 2	Application of regulatory technical standards (RTS).	Obligation to publish negative impacts at product level.	Detailed structuring of product reports.	Improvement of comparability between European labels.	Delegated Regulation (EU) 2022/1288
2022: Directive CSRD (2022/2464) + normes ESRS	Gaps in the reliability and comparability of ESG data.	Impose double materiality, mandatory audit, use of ESRS standards.	Standardization and extension of the scope of entities concerned.	More robust label data, lower risk of greenwashing.	Directive (UE) 2022/2464 ; EFRAG (ESRS, 2023)
Since 2022: European harmonization of labels	Desire to align all European labels with Taxonomy, SFDR and CSRD.	Strengthen international comparability and credibility.	Cross label harmonization and common minimum criteria.	Increased credibility, easier crossborder recognition.	European Commission, 2023

Source: Developed by the authors based on European Commission, SFDR, CSRD, Taxonomy Regulation.

3.3 Integration Modalities: Criteria, Indicators, And Methods

The operational modalities used by European labels to integrate double materiality vary significantly. Eligibility criteria can range from strict sector exclusions, such as fossil fuels, to the establishment of minimum ESG thresholds. Measurement approaches, in turn, may involve alignment with the European Taxonomy, the use of Principal Adverse Impacts (PAIs) as set forth in the SFDR, internal proprietary indicators, or reference to the United Nations Sustainable Development Goals (SDGs).

Transparency and the degree of external oversight represent another major axis of differentiation among labels. Table 6 provides a comparative summary of how leading European labels operationalize double materiality, detailing their criteria, indicators, measurement methods, and control mechanisms.

Notably, the labels that are most closely aligned with the European Taxonomy and the SFDR adopt measurable and auditable indicators, which enhance comparability. Conversely, other labels rely on internal, less transparent methodologies, making impact data more difficult to compare.

Table 6. Modalities for integrating Double Materiality into major European label standards

Labels	Built in double materiality	Key criteria	Measurement methods	Indicators used	Control / Reporting	Regulatory References
SRI label (France, March 2024)	Yes, mandatory risk and impact analysis according to the MFA model	Environmental risks, governance, Principal Adverse Impacts (PII), environmental and governance exclusion criteria, consistency with the fund's objectives	AMF market model based on double materiality, performance commitment on ESG indicators chosen from PAI, integration of Taxonomy & SFDR	IAP according to SFDR, ESG indicators related to risks and extra financial impacts	Control on the consistency of objectives, AMF audits, reporting integrated with SFDR requirements	AMF (market model), SFDR, European Taxonomy
Greenfin label (France, January 2025)	Yes, full ESG integration and Taxonomy for eligible assets	Minimum "green" share of the portfolio (based on CA), thresholds excluding reinforced coal, nuclear energy now allowed	Quantitative analysis of the portfolio based on Taxonomy for the green share, environmental impact monitoring	Green share according to Taxonomy, carbon exclusion thresholds, environmental impact indicators	Third party audit and compliance with SFDR exclusion criteria, impact reporting	EU taxonomy, SFDR, Greenfin standard
FNGSiegel (Germany, Austria, Switzerland, 2024)	Yes, double materiality associated with transition risks and climate impacts	Rating by scales and stars, normative selection, exclusion, best-in-class, thematic investing	Combined ESG methodology, compliance with SBTi requirements for transition plans	Qualitative and quantitative ESG criteria, SBTi aligned transition plans	Control by certification body and continuous certification, detailed ESG reporting	Normes FNG, validation SBTi

continued on following page

Table 6. Continued

Labels	Built in double materiality	Key criteria	Measurement methods	Indicators used	Control / Reporting	Regulatory References
LuxFLAG (Luxembourg, 2025)	Partial, transparent 100% portfolio analysis, labels classified Article 8 or 9 SFDR	Classification according to ESG, Climate Finance, Environment categories with sector thresholds	Portfolio transparency statement, allocation according to climate or environmental objectives	Article 8/9 classification, specific criteria per sublabel, no strict fossil exclusion for ESG	Third party audits, enhanced transparency requirements	SFDR, LuxFLAG frame
Towards Sustainability (Belgique, 2023)	Yes, integration of risks and sustainable impacts + IAP	Minimum thresholds on carbon and gender equality IAPs, list of high impact sectors, use of SBTi standards	Rigorous portfolio IAP assessment, quantitative and qualitative criteria	Carbon intensity, council mix, specific IAP criteria, SBTi alignment	Control by external audit, regular updating of the criteria	PAI standards, SBTi, label standards
Ecolabel UZ 49 (Autriche, 2024)	Yes, strict Do No Significant Harm (DNSH) integration + transparency	Points scale, minimum threshold required, strict nuclear exclusion policy, cumulative requirements	Multicriteria points-based evaluation, future integration of the green part mandatory (11%)	ESG compliance scale, DNSH score, thresholds Taxonomy to come	Strict audit control, cumulative requirements, in-depth reporting	EU Taxonomy, Umweltzeichen Standard
Nordic Swan Ecolabel (Nordiques, 2024)	Yes, materiality imposed on critical sectors, points scale	List of critical sectors, strict thresholds for nuclear exclusion, weighting of green share by Taxonomy score	Weighted analysis of portfolios based on Taxonomy, shareholder engagement scales	Taxonomy score, ESG commitment scales, SBTi criteria	Control by independent auditors, detailed reporting, and follow-up	EU Taxonomy, Nordic Swan Standard

continued on following page

Table 6. Continued

Labels	Built in double materiality	Key criteria	Measurement methods	Indicators used	Control / Reporting	Regulatory References
Recovery (France, 2025)	Implicit, focus on local impact and shareholder engagement	Majority investment in French companies with equity participation, tobacco and arms exclusions, noncooperative countries	Evaluation of investments according to ESG criteria, exclusion from the EU list, shareholder engagement	Contextual ESG criteria for capital, sector and geographical exclusions	Regulatory control, audit, local SRI reporting	EU exclusions, Relance label reference system
Finansol (France, 2025)	Yes, prioritization of social impact, SRI management	Social impact floor rate by product, social and environmental impact indicators, mandatory exclusions	Social result and impact indicators, SRI reporting	Social and environmental indicators, quantified impact thresholds	Quality control of indicators, SRI audits	Finansol Standard

Sources: Developed by the authors from Official Label References; AMF, 2023; ESMA, 2023; Novethic, 2025; Weefin 2025

The diversity of integration methods and evaluation criteria, as outlined above, results in a range of structural challenges and persistent issues, which are explored in the following section.

3.4 Issues and Challenges Identified

The literature and institutional reports consulted highlight several structural challenges that can be systematized across the analytical dimensions examined in this review. Table 7 provides a comprehensive synthesis of the main findings and persistent challenges identified across all dimensions of this systematic review.

Table 7. Synthesis of Double Materiality integration: main findings and persistent challenges

Analytical dimension	Key findings	Structural challenges identified	Market implications
Regulatory Evolution	Progress from NFRD to CSRD / SFDR	Uneven implementation across states	Risk of fragmentation
Conceptual Understanding	Double materiality formally adopted	Often reduced to financial scope	Limits effective use
Integration Level	Heterogeneous label adoption	Explicit vs. partial implementation	Segmentation, comparability issues
Methodological Approaches	Diverse: PAI, green share, exclusion	Lack of harmonized methods	Compares poorly crosslabel
Transparency Standards	Variable disclosure quality	Persistent gaps in disclosure	Greenwashing risk, info asymmetry
Control Mechanisms	Variable audit levels	Divergent PAI methods	Credibility concerns
Harmonization Progress	Towards EU standards	On going normative fragmentation	Regulatory arbitrage risk

Sources: Authors' synthesis based on systematic literature review corpus; key references include ESMA (2023), De Cristofaro & Gullu (2023), Coullabé (2025)

The synthesis presented in Table 7 highlights several significant structural issues that hinder the effective integration of double materiality into European sustainable finance labels. Notably, there is an uneven understanding of double materiality; many frameworks reduce this dual concept to a financial perspective, undermining its transformative potential (De Cristofaro & Gullu, 2023; Coullabé, 2025). This conceptual limitation is exacerbated by a lack of harmonization in measurement methods and thresholds across different labelling systems, which creates barriers to meaningful cross-label comparisons.

Furthermore, persistent transparency issues remain problematic, particularly regarding the disclosure of adverse impacts and the application of different methodologies for Principal Adverse Impacts (PAIs). These methodological inconsistencies render rigorous comparative analysis virtually impossible, creating information asymmetries that favour less scrupulous market participants. The situation is further exacerbated by the fact that levels of external control vary greatly across different labels, amplifying the risk of greenwashing and reinforcing the regulatory fragmentation observed between European countries.

The systematic review also revealed that achieving sustainability objectives through the integration of double materiality remains highly dependent on stakeholder consensus regarding definitions of materiality, the selection of baseline references and the setting of measurable targets. The substantial latitude currently given to companies and labels to determine their own impact measurement criteria highlights the urgent need for greater transparency and standardization in this area.

In practice, the current model, which relies heavily on labels' self-adjustment of transition plans and self-monitoring, has demonstrated significant limitations. This approach has inadvertently created opportunities for regulatory arbitrage and failed to provide the robust oversight necessary to ensure a genuine sustainability impact. Furthermore, although European regulation is intended to combat greenwashing, the proliferation of national labels with different standards has caused uncertainty among investors and reduced the effectiveness of the sustainable finance ecosystem as a whole.

These findings highlight the need for a fundamental shift towards stronger regulatory harmonization, achieved by implementing SMART criteria (specific, measurable, achievable, relevant, and time-bound) at a European level. This would improve the comparability of models, strengthen regulatory governance, and reduce the current fragmentation that undermines market confidence. Furthermore, the creation and recognition of sustainable finance labels should be subject to more rigorous supranational oversight to prevent regulatory shopping and ensure the consistent application of sustainability principles.

Considering the global challenges associated with financing the ecological transition, establishing a dedicated sustainable finance regulatory authority could provide the coordinated oversight required for the effective implementation of sustainability objectives. Such an institution would mirror the governance model successfully adopted for the European Taxonomy, thereby ensuring the standardization of concepts, reference frameworks and impact calculation methodologies across participating countries. This approach would enhance the credibility and comparability of sustainable finance labels and contribute meaningfully to achieving the Sustainable Development Goals by ensuring capital is effectively directed towards genuinely impactful sustainability projects.

IV. CONCLUSION

The aim of this chapter was to answer the following question: To what extent and in what ways is double materiality effectively integrated into European sustainable finance label standards? A systematic analysis of relevant literature and institutional reports was conducted to address this question and ensure a comprehensive, rigorous, and transparent examination of the sources.

The results revealed significant variability in the integration of double materiality across labels. While some frameworks explicitly integrate both financial and impact dimensions, aligning with the latest European regulations (notably the CSRD, SFDR, and EU Taxonomy), others focus primarily on financial perspectives or apply double materiality in partial and non-standardized ways. This heterogeneity is evident in the diverse eligibility criteria, measurement methods, indicators, and control and reporting mechanisms employed.

The analysis reveals several structural issues that hinder the effective implementation of double materiality. These include definitional ambiguities, a lack of harmonized measurement and reporting methods, and inconsistent levels of external oversight. Transparency gaps, particularly regarding the disclosure of adverse impacts and the use of different methodologies for Principal Adverse Impacts (PAIs), prevent meaningful cross-label comparisons and increase the risk of greenwashing. Furthermore, regulatory fragmentation across European countries complicates the establishment of a credible and comparable labelling ecosystem, which could undermine the ability of sustainable finance labels to effectively channel capital towards genuine sustainability objectives.

However, these findings take on greater significance when considered in the context of the 2030 Agenda for Sustainable Development. Integrating robust double materiality principles into sustainable finance labels is not just a technical regulatory challenge; it is a vital mechanism for achieving the United Nations Sustainable Development Goals.

Enhanced labelling frameworks that ensure financial products labelled as "sustainable" meaningfully contribute to SDG 8 (Decent Work and Economic Growth), SDG 12 (Responsible Consumption and Production) and SDG 13 (Climate Action) could help to redirect global capital flows towards activities that generate a measurable positive impact.

This analysis identifies the path towards effective, harmonized, and credible labelling systems, which directly supports SDG 17 (Partnerships for the Goals) by emphasizing the need for increased international cooperation and knowledge sharing. The challenges documented in this systematic review demonstrate that achieving the transformative vision of the 2030 Agenda necessitates coordinated global efforts to develop consistent and credible sustainable finance standards.

This review provides analytical tools and empirical evidence to support the ongoing development of sustainable finance as a catalyst for global sustainability. By providing a comprehensive framework for assessing double materiality integration and documenting current limitations, this analysis establishes a basis for future research and policy development to ensure sustainable finance labels fulfil their potential in mobilizing the essential resources required to achieve the ambitious targets of the 2030 Agenda.

AUTHOR CREDITS

Derick Moukamia: conceptualisation, methodology, formal analysis, investigation, writing the original draft, writing the review and editing;

Nathalie Lévy: conceptualisation, formal analysis, writing the original draft, writing the review and editing, supervision.

REFERENCES

Coullabé, J. (2025). Social indicators, revealing the tensions between aspirations for sustainability and the preservation of existing business models. *ACCRA,* 78-112. https://EconPapers.repec.org/RePEc:hal:journl:hal04916483

Crifo, P. (2022). The promise of green finance labels. 2-9, *Presses universitaires de Grenoble*. https://shs.cairn.info/le-virus-de-la-recherche--9782706153167-page-2?lang=fr

Crifo, P., Rodolphe, D., & Gond, J. P. (2020). The role of labels in green finance: construction and regulation of a label market in France. In R. d. financière (Ed.), *Climate Finance* (138), 209-223. *Journal of Financial Economics*. https://doi.org/DOI: 10.3917/ecofi.138.0209

De Cristofaro, T., & Gullu, C. (2023). In Search of Double Materiality in Non Financial Reports: First Empirical Evidence. *Sustainability*, *15*(2), 924. DOI: 10.3390/su15020924

De Merxem, L. G., & Tchotourian, I. (2024). Double materiality, the keystone of sustainable corporate governance. (R. i. économique, Ed.) *VARIA*, 59-91. https://doi.org/DOI: 10.3917/ride.384.0059

Desmarais, C. (2014). Systematic review. In *Practical Guide to Rehabilitation Research* (ed. Méthodes techn et outils d'intervention), De Boeck Supérieur. 161-176 https://doi.org/DOI: 10.3917/dbu.guill.2014.01.0161

European Securities and Markets Authority. (2024). ESMA Report on trends, risks and vulnerabilities: Risk Monitor. ESMA, ESMA505248213444. *European Union*. https://www.esma.europa.eu/document/trendsrisksandvulnerabilitiestrvreportno22024

International Energy Agency. (2025). *World Energy Investment 2025* (éd. 10th). *IEA Publications*. https://www.iea.org/reports/world-energy-investment-2025

Kamara, L. (2023). Socially responsible investment: the imbroglio of European regulatory developments. In Institute, C. B. (Ed.), *Sustainability Research* (pp. 405–418)., DOI: 10.3917/ems.cheva.2023.01.0405

Khan, H. H., Nabila, A., Noorlailahusna, M., & Mohammad, M. (2024). Green finance and environmental sustainability: A systematic review and future research avenues. *Environmental Science and Pollution Research International, 33*(6), 9784–9794. DOI: 10.1007/s11356-023-31809-6 PMID: 38194178

La chaire de la double matérialité. (2025). The Double Materiality in the World: Geopolitical and Critical Analysis (Report). *Fondation du Risque de l'Institut Louis Bachelier.* Chaire Double Materialité. https://www.chairedoublematerialite.org/publications.html

Nicken, D., Zulfikar, R., Mulyasari, W., & Ismawati, I. (2024). Financial Sustainability for a Sustainable Future: A Bibliometric Analysis. *International Journal of Sustainable Development and Planning*, 4653-4662. https://iieta.org/journals/ijsdp/paper/10.18280/ijsdp.191213

Novethic. (2025). Overview of European sustainable finance labels: Recalibration or identity crisis? *Novethic.* https://www.novethic.fr/decryptages-dexpert/etudes/panorama-des-labels-europeens-de-finance-durable-edition-2025

Pappalardo, M. (2024). The SRI label, an evolving tool to help investors and savers participate in sustainable finance. (I. MinesTélécom, Ed.) *Sustainable finance*, 38-42. https://doi.org/DOI: 10.3917/rindu1.243.0038

Touati, C., & Miljkovitch, R., DuboisComtois, K., Sirparanta, A., & Deborde, A.S. (2021). Risk and protective factors in placement associated with mental health: A systematic review of the literature. *Devenir, 33*(2), 135–172. DOI: 10.3917/dev.212.0135

Weefin. (2025). 2025 guide: complete comparison of sustainable finance labels in Europe. (WEEFIN) https://www.weefin.co/ressource/guide-2025-comparatif-complet-des-labels-de-finance-durable-en-europe

Compilation of References

Abeysekera, I., & Guthrie, J. (2005). An empirical investigation of annual reporting trends of intellectual capital in Sri Lanka. *Critical Perspectives on Accounting*, *16*(3), 151–163. DOI: 10.1016/s1045-2354(03)00059-5

Adams, C. A., Coutts, A., & Harte, G. (1995). Corporate equal opportunities (non-) disclosure. *The British Accounting Review*, *27*(2), 87–108. DOI: 10.1006/bare.1994.0005

Adams, R., Parry, G., Godsiff, P., & Ward, P. (2017). The future of money and further applications of the blockchain. *Strategic Change*, *26*(5), 417–422. DOI: 10.1002/jsc.2141

Agrawala, S., Carraro, M., Kingsmill, N., Lanzi, E., Mullan, M., & Prudent-Richard, G. (2011). *Private Sector Engagement in Adaptation to Climate Change: Approaches to Managing Climate Risks*. OECD., DOI: 10.1787/5kg221jkf1g7-

Agrawal, R., Wankhede, V. A., Kumar, A., Luthra, S., & Huisingh, D. (2022). Progress and trends in integrating Industry 4.0 within Circular Economy: A comprehensive literature review and future research propositions. *Business Strategy and the Environment*, *31*(1), 559–579.

Agusti Strid, A., & Ronicle, J. (2021). *Social Impact Bonds in Latin America-IDB Lab's pioneering work in the region: lessons learnt*. Technical Note No. IDB-TN-2087. Inter-American Development Bank.

Ahlers, G. K. C., Cumming, D., Günther, C., & Schweizer, D. (2015). Signaling in Equity Crowdfunding. *Entrepreneurship Theory and Practice*, *39*(4), 955–980. DOI: 10.1111/etap.12157

Ahmed, S., & Liu, H. (2023). Decentralized finance and governance in low-trust economies: Evidence from Sub-Saharan Africa. *Journal of Emerging Financial Markets*, *12*(1), 45–61.

Ahuja, R., & Khandelwal, J. (2023). Challenges, Opportunities And Risk Analysis Of Adoption Of Decentralised Finance Applications. ICTACT Journal on Soft Computing, 14(1).

Akcay, E., & Hirshleifer, D. (2020). Social finance: Cultural evolution, transmission bias and market dynamics. https://doi.org/DOI: 10.3386/w27745

Akhter, A., Javed, M. Y., & Akhter, J. (2023). Research trends in the field of Islamic social finance: A bibliometric analysis from 1914 to 2022. *International Journal of Ethics and Systems*. https://doi.org/DOI: 10.1108/ijoes-03-2023-0044

Alamsyah, A., Kusuma, G. N. W., & Ramadhani, D. P. (2024). A *Review on Decentralised Finance Ecosystems. Future Internet*, *16*(3), 76.

Alamsyah, A., Kusuma, G. N. W., & Ramadhani, D. P. (2024). A review on decentralized finance ecosystems. *Future Internet*, *16*(3), 76.

Albertson, K., & Fox, C. (2018). *Payment by results and social impact bonds: Outcome-based payment systems in the UK and US*. Policy Press.

Albertson, K., & Fox, C. (2019). The marketisation of rehabilitation: Some economic considerations. *Probation Journal*, *66*(1), 25–42.

Albertson, K., Fox, C., O'Leary, C., & Painter, G. (2020). 'Towards a Theoretical Framework for Social Impact Bonds'. *Nonprofit Policy Forum*, *11*(2).

Alenda-Demoutiez, J. (2020). 'A fictitious commodification of local development through development impact bonds?'. *Journal of Urban Affairs*, *42*(6), 892–906.

Alenda-Demoutiez, J. (2023). Financialization in development projects and new modes of governance: the case of development impact bonds. In Chiapello, E., Engles, A., & Gresse, E. G. (Eds.), *Financializations of Development: Global Games and Local Experiments* (1st ed., pp. 123–138). Routledge.

Alhammad, M. M., AlOthman, R., & Tan, C. (2021). Review of Crowdfunding Regulations Across Countries: A Systematic Review Study. *Journal of Information Systems Engineering & Management*, *6*(4), em0145. Advance online publication. DOI: 10.21601/jisem/11395

Allen, M., Babiker, M., Chen, Y., Coninck, H. de, Connors, S., Diemen, R. van, Dube, O. P., Ebi, K. L., Engelbrecht, F., Ferrat, M., Ford, J., Forster, P., Fuss, S., Guillén Bolanos, T., Harold, J., Hoegh-Guldberg, O., Hourcade, J.-C., Huppmann, D., Jacob, D., … Zickfeld, K. (2018). *Global Warming of 1.5 °C. Summary for Policymakers*. 26.

Alliance for Hydromet developement. (2021). *Hydromet Gap Report*.

Alonso, J. M., Clifton, J., & Diaz-Fuentes, D. (2015). Did new public management matter? An empirical analysis of the outsourcing and decentralization effects on public sector size. *Public Management Review, 17*, 643–660.

Alshater, M. M., Hassan, M. K., Khan, A., & Saba, I. (2020). Influential and intellectual structure of Islamic finance: A bibliometric review. *International Journal of Islamic and Middle Eastern Finance and Management.*

Alshater, M. M., Atayah, O. F., & Hamdan, A. (2021). Journal of sustainable finance and investment: A bibliometric analysis. *Journal of Sustainable Finance & Investment, 13*(3), 1131–1152. DOI: 10.1080/20430795.2021.1947116

American Meteorological Society, A. (2021). *Weather-Water-Climate Value Chain(s): Giving VOICE to the Characterization of the Economic Benefits of Hydro-Met Services and Products.*

Amuzu-Sefordzi, B., Martinus, K., Tschakert, P., & Wills, R. (2018). Disruptive innovations and decentralised renewable energy systems in Africa: *A socio-technical review. Energy Research & Social Science, 46*, 140–154.

André, K., Gerger Swartling, Å., Englund, M., Petutschnig, L., Attoh, E. M. N. A. N., Milde, K., Lückerath, D., Cauchy, A., Botnen Holm, T., Hanssen Korsbrekke, M., Bour, M., & Rome, E. (2023). Improving stakeholder engagement in climate change risk assessments: Insights from six co-production initiatives in Europe. *Frontiers in Climate, 5*. Advance online publication. DOI: 10.3389/fclim.2023.1120421

Andreu, M. (2018). 'A Responsibility to Profit? Social Impact Bonds as a Form of "Humanitarian Finance"'. *New Political Science, 40*(4), 708–726.

Andrikopoulos, A. (2019). Delineating social finance. SSRN *Electronic Journal.* https://doi.org/DOI: 10.2139/ssrn.3510056

Andrikopoulos, A. (2020). Delineating social finance. *International Review of Financial Analysis, 70*, 101519. DOI: 10.1016/j.irfa.2020.101519

Aria, M., & Cuccurullo, C. (2017). bibliometrix: An R-tool for comprehensive science mapping analysis. *Journal of Informetrics, 11*(4), 959–975. DOI: 10.1016/j.joi.2017.08.007

Arifin, M. R., Raharja, B. S., Aligarh, F., & Nugroho, A. (2023). A systematic literature review on community financing: Avenues for further research. *Cogent Business & Management, 10*(2). Advance online publication. DOI: 10.1080/23311975.2023.2211208

Arner, D. W., Buckley, R. P., Zetzsche, D. A., & Veidt, R. (2020). Sustainability, FinTech and financial inclusion. *European Business Organization Law Review, 21*(1), 7–35. DOI: 10.1007/s40804-020-00183-y

Arora, R. U., & Sarker, T. (2023). Financing for Sustainable Development Goals (SDGs) in the Era of COVID-19 and Beyond. *European Journal of Development Research, 35*(1), 1–19. DOI: 10.1057/s41287-022-00571-9 PMID: 36620200

Ascarya, A. (2021). The role of Islamic social finance during Covid-19 pandemic in Indonesia's economic recovery. *International Journal of Islamic and Middle Eastern Finance and Management, 15*(2), 386–405. DOI: 10.1108/IMEFM-07-2020-0351

Ascarya, A., Suharto, U., & Husman, J. A. (2022). Proposed model of integrated Islamic commercial and social finance for Islamic bank in Indonesia. *Eurasian Economic Review, 12*(1), 115–138. DOI: 10.1007/s40822-022-00201-z

Ascarya, A., Sukmana, R., Rahmawati, S., & Masrifah, A. R. (2022). Developing cash waqf models for Baitul Maal wat Tamwil as integrated Islamic social and commercial microfinance. *Journal of Islamic Accounting and Business Research, 14*(5), 699–717. DOI: 10.1108/JIABR-09-2020-0267

Atif, M., Hassan, M. K., Rabbani, M. R., & Khan, S. (2021). Islamic FinTech: The digital transformation bringing sustainability to Islamic finance. In *COVID-19 and Islamic Social Finance*. Routledge.

Atlantic Council. (2025). *The 2025 Crypto Policy Landscape: Looming EU and US Divergences?* Retrieved from https://www.atlanticcouncil.org/blogs/econographics/the-2025-crypto-policy-landscape-looming-eu-and-us-divergences/

Auer, R., Haslhofer, B., Kitzler, S., Saggese, P., & Victor, F. (2024). The technology of decentralized finance (DeFi). *Digital Finance, 6*(1), 55–95. DOI: 10.1007/s42521-023-00088-8

Austin, J., Stevenson, H., & Wei–Skillern, J. (2006). Social and commercial entrepreneurship: Same, different, or both? *Entrepreneurship Theory and Practice, 30*(1), 1–22.

Ayala, T. 2021. Financial technology and social impact: socialfintech sector. Soc. FinTech. https://socialfintech.org/social-fintech-sector

Ayob, N., Teasdale, S., & Fagan, K. (2016). 'How social innovation 'came to be': Tracing the evolution of a contested concept'. *Journal of Social Policy, 45*(4), 635–653.

Azemati, H., Belinsky, M., Gillette, R., Liebman, J., Sellman, A., & Wyse, A. (2013). Social impact bonds: Lessons learned so far. *Community Development Investment Review*, *9*(1), 23–34.

Baeck, P., Collins, L., & Zhang, B. (2014). Understanding alternative finance. *The UK alternative finance industry report*. Retrieved from https://media.nesta.org.uk/documents/understanding-alternative-finance-2014.pdf

Bahoo, S., Alon, I., & Paltrinieri, A. (2020). Corruption in international business: A review and research agenda. *International Business Review*, *29*(4), 101660. DOI: 10.1016/j.ibusrev.2019.101660

Bahoo, S., Alon, I., & Paltrinieri, A. (2020). Sovereign wealth funds: Past, present and future. *International Review of Financial Analysis*, *67*, 101418. DOI: 10.1016/j.irfa.2019.101418

Bain, P. G., Hornsey, M. J., Bongiorno, R., Kashima, Y., & Crimston, C. R. (2013). Collective Futures: How Projections About the Future of Society Are Related to Actions and Attitudes Supporting Social Change. *Personality and Social Psychology Bulletin*, *39*(4), 523–539. DOI: 10.1177/0146167213478200 PMID: 23456559

Baker, H. K., Kumar, S., & Pandey, N. (2020). A bibliometric analysis of European Financial Management's first 25 years. *European Financial Management*, *26*(5), 1224–1260.

Baker, H. K., Kumar, S., & Pattnaik, D. (2020). Twenty-five years of Review of Financial Economics: A bibliometric overview. *Review of Financial Economics*, *38*(1), 3–23. DOI: 10.1002/rfe.1095

Balboa, C. M. (2016). Accountability of environmental impact bonds: The future of global environmental governance? *Global Environmental Politics*, *16*(1), 33–41.

Ballandies, M. C., Dapp, M. M., Degenhart, B. A., Helbing, D., Klauser, S., & Pardi, A. (2021). Finance 4.0—A socio-ecological finance system. *SpringerBriefs in Applied Sciences and Technology*, 53-89. https://doi.org/DOI: 10.1007/978-3-030-71400-0_4

Banerjee, A., Duflo, E., & Glennerster, R. (2015). The Miracle of Microfinance? Evidence from a Randomized Evaluation. *American Economic Journal. Applied Economics*.

Banerjee, A., Karlan, D., & Zinman, J. (2015). Six Randomized Evaluations of Microcredit: Introduction and Further Steps. *American Economic Journal. Applied Economics*, *7*(1), 1–21. DOI: 10.1257/app.20140287

Bardhi, F., & Eckhardt, G. M. (2012). Access-Based Consumption: The Case of Car Sharing. *The Journal of Consumer Research, 39*(4), 881–898. DOI: 10.1086/666376

Bärnreuther, S. (2025). Financializing Maternal and Newborn Care: Temporal Tensions within a Development Impact Bond in India. *Development and Change, 56*(1), 31–55.

Barr, M. (2004). Microfinance and Financial Development. *Articles*, 271.

Basak, D., & Roy Chowdhury, I. (2024). Role of self-help groups on socioeconomic development and the achievement of Sustainable Development Goals (SDGs) among rural women in Cooch Behar District, India. *Regional Sustainability, 5*(2), 100140. DOI: 10.1016/j.regsus.2024.100140

Bautista-Bernal, I., Quintana-García, C., & Marchante-Lara, M. (2021). Research trends in occupational health and social responsibility: A bibliometric analysis. *Safety Science, 137*, 105167. DOI: 10.1016/j.ssci.2021.105167

Bayar, Y., Gavriletea, M. D., & Păun, D. (2021). Impact of mobile phones and internet use on financial inclusion: Empirical evidence from the EU post-communist countries. *Technological and Economic Development of Economy, 27*(3), 722–741. DOI: 10.3846/tede.2021.14508

Bayram, O., Talay, I., & Feridun, M. (2022). Can Fintech Promote Sustainable Finance? Policy Lessons from the Case of Turkey. *Sustainability, 14*(19), 19. Advance online publication. DOI: 10.3390/su141912414

Beckman, C., Rosen, J., Estrada-Miller, J., & Painter, G. (2023). 'The Social Innovation Trap: Critical Insights into an Emerging Field'. *The Academy of Management Annals, 17*(2), 684–709.

Begum, H., Alam, A. S. A. F., Mia, M. A., Bhuiyan, F., & Ghani, A. B. A. (2018). Development of Islamic microfinance: A sustainable poverty reduction approach. *Journal of Economic and Administrative Sciences, 35*(3), 143–157. DOI: 10.1108/JEAS-01-2018-0007

Belk, R. (2014). You are what you can access: Sharing and collaborative consumption online. *Journal of Business Research, 67*(8), 1595–1600. DOI: 10.1016/j.jbusres.2013.10.001

Belleflamme, P., Lambert, T., & Schwienbacher, A. (2014a). Crowdfunding: Tapping the right crowd. *Journal of Business Venturing, 29*(5), 585–609. DOI: 10.1016/j.jbusvent.2013.07.003

Belt, J., Kuleshov, A., & Minneboo, E. (2017). 'Development impact bonds: Learning from the Asháninka cocoa and coffee case in Peru'. *Enterprise Development & Microfinance*, *28*(1-2), 130–144.

Benedikter, R. (2011). *Social banking and social finance.* SpringerBriefs in Business., DOI: 10.1007/978-1-4419-7774-8

Benquet, M., & Bourgeron, T. (2022). *Alt-Finance: How the City of London Bought Democracy*. https://hal.science/hal-03879329

Bento, N., Gianfrate, G., & Thoni, M. H. (2019). Crowdfunding for sustainability ventures. *Journal of Cleaner Production*, *237*, 117751. DOI: 10.1016/j.jclepro.2019.117751

Bergfeld, N., Klausner, D., & Samel, M. (2019). Improving Social Impact Bonds: Assessing Alternative Financial Models to Scale Pay-for-Success. *Annual Review of Policy Design*, *7*, 1–20.

Bergman, R., Abbas, A. E., Jung, S., Werker, C., & de Reuver, M. (2022). Business model archetypes for data marketplaces in the automotive industry. *Electronic Markets*, *32*(2), 747–765. DOI: 10.1007/s12525-022-00547-x

Berka, A., & Dreyfus, M. (2021). Decentralisation and inclusivity in the energy sector: Preconditions, impacts and avenues for further research. *Renewable & Sustainable Energy Reviews*, *138*, 110663.

Berke, P., & Lyles, W. (2013). Public Risks and the Challenges to Climate-Change Adaptation: A Proposed Framework for Planning in the Age of Uncertainty. *Cityscape (Washington, D.C.)*, *15*(1), 181–208.

Bielenberg, A., Kerlin, M., Oppenheim, J., & Roberts, M. (2016). Financing change: How to mobilize private-sector financing for sustainable infrastructure. *McKinsey Center for Business and Environment*, 24-25.

Bin-Nashwan, S. A., Ismaiel, A. E. A., Muneeza, A., & Isa, M. Y. (2023). Adoption of ZakaTech in the time of COVID-19: Cross-country and gender differences. *Journal of Islamic Marketing*, *14*(11), 2949–2979. DOI: 10.1108/JIMA-08-2021-0278

BIS Committee on Banking Supervision [BIS]. (2022). *Prudential Treatment of Cryptoasset Exposures.* Retrieved from https://www.bis.org/bcbs/publ/d545.pdf

BIS Innovation Hub & Hong Kong Monetary Authority (HKMA). (2023). *A prototype for green bond tokenisation by Digital Asset and GFT.* Retrieved March 15, 2025 from https://www.bis.org/publ/othp43_report3.pdf

Block, J. H., Groh, A., Hornuf, L., Vanacker, T., & Vismara, S. (2021). The entrepreneurial finance markets of the future: A comparison of crowdfunding and initial coin offerings. *Small Business Economics*, *57*(2), 865–882. DOI: 10.1007/s11187-020-00330-2

Bocken, N. M., Short, S. W., Rana, P., & Evans, S. (2014). A literature and practice review to develop sustainable business model archetypes. *Journal of Cleaner Production*, *65*, 42–56.

Bojovic, D., Clair, A., Christel Jiménez, I., Terrado, M., Stanzel, P., Gonzalez, P., & Palin, E. (2021). Engagement, involvement and empowerment: Three realms of a coproduction framework for climate services. *Global Environmental Change*, *68*, 102271. DOI: 10.1016/j.gloenvcha.2021.102271

Bollag, B. (2017, September 8). ICRC launches World's first Humanitarian Impact Bond. Retrieved April 27, 2023, from https://www.devex.com/news/icrc-launches-world-s-first-humanitarian-impact-bond-90981

Bongini, P. A., Mattassoglio, F., Pedrazzoli, A., & Vismara, S. (2025). Crypto ecosystem: Navigating the past, present, and future of decentralized finance. *The Journal of Technology Transfer*, •••, 1–22.

Botsman, R., & Rogers, R. (2010, October 1). Beyond Zipcar: Collaborative Consumption. *Harvard Business Review*. https://hbr.org/2010/10/beyond-zipcar-collaborative-consumption

Brandstetter, L., & Lehner, O. M. (2015). Opening the market for impact investments: The need for adapted portfolio tools. *Entrepreneurship Research Journal*, *5*(2), 87–107.

Brem, A., Bilgram, V., & Marchuk, A. (2019). How crowdfunding platforms change the nature of user innovation – from problem solving to entrepreneurship. *Technological Forecasting and Social Change*, *144*, 348–360. DOI: 10.1016/j.techfore.2017.11.020

Bremer, S., Wardekker, A., Dessai, S., Sobolowski, S., Slaattelid, R., & van der Sluijs, J. (2019). Toward a multi-faceted conception of co-production of climate services. *Climate Services*, *13*, 42–50. DOI: 10.1016/j.cliser.2019.01.003

Breuer, H., & Lüdeke-Freund, F. (2017). VALUES-BASED NETWORK AND BUSINESS MODEL INNOVATION. *International Journal of Innovation Management*, *21*(03), 1750028. DOI: 10.1142/S1363919617500281

Brisbois, M. C. (2019). Powershifts: A framework for assessing the growing impact of decentralised ownership of energy transitions on political decision-making. *Energy Research & Social Science*, *50*, 151–161.

Broccardo, E., & Mazzuca, M. (2019). Social impact bonds: The evolution of research and a review of the academic literature. *Corporate Social Responsibility and Environmental Management*, *27*(3), 1316–1332. DOI: 10.1002/csr.1886

Broccardo, E., Mazzuca, M., & Frigotto, M. L. (2020). 'Social impact bonds: The evolution of research and a review of the academic literature'. *Corporate Social Responsibility and Environmental Management*, *27*(3), 1316–1332.

Brown, D., Hall, S., & Davis, M. E. (2020). What is prosumerism for? Exploring the normative dimensions of decentralised energy transitions. *Energy Research & Social Science*, *66*, 101475.

Bruton, G., Khavul, S., Siegel, D., & Wright, M. (2015). New Financial Alternatives in Seeding Entrepreneurship: Microfinance, Crowdfunding, and Peer–to–Peer Innovations. *Entrepreneurship Theory and Practice*, *39*(1), 9–26. DOI: 10.1111/etap.12143

Burand, D. (2012). Globalizing social finance: How social impact bonds and social impact performance guarantees can scale development. *NYU Journal of Law & Business*, *9*, 447.

Burtch, G., Ghose, A., & Wattal, S. (2014). Cultural Differences and Geography as Determinants of Online Prosocial Lending. *Management Information Systems Quarterly*, *38*(3), 773–794.

Calabrese, A., Costa, R., Gastaldi, M., Ghiron, N. L., & Montalvan, R. A. V. (2021). Implications for sustainable development goals: A framework to assess company disclosure in sustainability reporting. *Journal of Cleaner Production*, *319*, 128624. DOI: 10.1016/j.jclepro.2021.128624

Calvin, K., Dasgupta, D., Krinner, G., Mukherji, A., Thorne, P. W., Trisos, C., Romero, J., Aldunce, P., Barrett, K., Blanco, G., Cheung, W. W. L., Connors, S., Denton, F., Diongue-Niang, A., Dodman, D., Garschagen, M., Geden, O., Hayward, B., Jones, C., . . . Péan, C. (2023). *IPCC, 2023: Climate Change 2023: Synthesis Report. Contribution of Working Groups I, II and III to the Sixth Assessment Report of the Intergovernmental Panel on Climate Change [Core Writing Team, H. Lee and J. Romero (eds.)]. IPCC, Geneva, Switzerland.* (First). Intergovernmental Panel on Climate Change (IPCC). https://doi.org/DOI: 10.59327/IPCC/AR6-9789291691647

Cambridge Centre for Alternative Finance [CCAF]. (2024). *2nd Global Cryptoasset Regulatory Landscape Study*. University of Cambridge. Retrieved from https://www.jbs.cam.ac.uk/wp-content/uploads/2024/10/2024-2nd-global-cryptoasset-regulatory-landscape-study.pdf

Carè, R. (2018). Social Impact Bond: Beyond financial innovation. In Wendt, K. (Ed.), *Sustainable Financial Innovation* (pp. xx–xx). Taylor & Francis.

Carè, R. (2022). From New Public Management to Social Impact Bonds: The European Experience. In *The Anglo-American Model of Neoliberalism of the 1980s: Construction, Development and Dissemination* (pp. 293–317). Springer International Publishing.

Carè, R., Carè, S., Lévy, N., & Fatima, R. (2023). Missing finance in social impact bond research? A bibliometric overview between past and future research. *Corporate Social Responsibility and Environmental Management*, *30*(5), 2101–2120. DOI: 10.1002/csr.2496

Carè, R., & Cumming, D. (2024). Technology and automation in financial trading: A bibliometric review. *Research in International Business and Finance*, *71*, 102471. DOI: 10.1016/j.ribaf.2024.102471

Carè, R., & De Lisa, R. (2019). Social Impact Bonds for a Sustainable Welfare State: The Role of Enabling Factors. *Sustainability*, *11*(10), 2884.

Carè, R., & De Lisa, R. (2019). Social impact bonds: A new tool to finance social services. *Journal of Cleaner Production*, *210*, 1434–1447.

Carè, R., Fatima, R., & Agnese, P. (2025). Crowdfunding and sustainable development: A systematic review. *Finance Research Letters*, *78*, 107220. DOI: 10.1016/j.frl.2025.107220

Carè, R., Fatima, R., & Boitan, I. (2024). Central banks and climate risks: Where we are and where we are going? *International Review of Economics & Finance*, *92*, 1200–1229. DOI: 10.1016/j.iref.2024.01.057

Carè, R., & Ferraro, G. (2019). Funding innovative healthcare programs through social impact bonds: Issues and challenges. *China-USA Business Review*, *18*(1), 1–15.

Carè, R., Trotta, A., & Rizzello, A. (2018). An alternative finance approach for a more sustainable financial system. In Walker, T., Kibsey, S. D., & Crichton, R. (Eds.), *Designing a Sustainable Financial System: Development Goals and Socio-Ecological Responsibility* (pp. 17–63). Springer., DOI: 10.1007/978-3-319-66387-6_2

Carè, R., & Weber, O. (2023). How much finance is in climate finance? A bibliometric review, critiques, and future research directions. *Research in International Business and Finance*, *64*, 101886. DOI: 10.1016/j.ribaf.2023.101886

Carè, R., & Weber, O. (2023). What's in a name? Exploring the intellectual structure of social finance. *International Journal of Emerging Markets*. Advance online publication. DOI: 10.1108/ijoem-07-2022-1142

Carè, S., Trotta, A., Carè, R., & Rizzello, A. (2018). Crowdfunding for the development of smart cities. *Business Horizons*, *61*(4), 501–509.

Carter, E., FitzGerald, C., Dixon, R., Economy, C., Hameed, T., & Airoldi, M. (2018). *Building the tools for public services to secure better outcomes: Collaboration, Prevention, Innovation.* Government Outcomes Lab, University of Oxford, Blavatnik School of Government.

Carter, E. (2021). More than marketised? Exploring the governance and accountability mechanisms at play in social impact bonds. *Journal of Economic Policy Reform*, *24*(1), 78–94.

Casselman, R. M., Sama, L. M., & Stefanidis, A. (2015). Differential Social Performance of Religiously-Affiliated Microfinance Institutions (MFIs) in Base of Pyramid (BoP) Markets. *Journal of Business Ethics*, *132*(3), 539–552. DOI: 10.1007/s10551-014-2360-z

Castriotta, M., Loi, M., Marku, E., & Moi, L. (2021). Disentangling the corporate entrepreneurship construct: Conceptualizing through co-words. *Scientometrics*, *126*(4), 2821–2863.

Center for Disease Control and Prevention (CDC). (2017). *Pay for success: How-to guide for local government focused on lead-safe homes*. Retrieved from https://www.cdc.gov/nceh/lead/docs/pay_for_success_guide.pdf

Chandra, Y., Shang, L., & Roy, M. J. (2021). 'Understanding Healthcare Social Enterprises: A New Public Governance Perspective'. *Journal of Social Policy*, •••, 1–22.

Chavez, F. J., & Gupta, R. (2021). Decentralized finance: A comprehensive review of technologies, applications, and challenges. *Journal of Blockchain Research*, *10*(3), 56–72.

Chen, F., She, W., Zeng, F., Gao, M., Wen, C., Liu, G., Wu, L., Wu, Y., & Zhang, C. (2024). Resource depletion and conservation: Balancing demands on resources for green recovery and sustainability. *Resources Policy*, *89*, 104544. DOI: 10.1016/j.resourpol.2023.104544

Chen, Y., & Volz, U. (2022). Scaling up sustainable investment through blockchain-based project bonds. *Development Policy Review, 40*(3). https://www.econstor.eu/bitstream/10419/287886/1/DPR_DPR12582.pdf

Chiapello, E., & Knoll, L. (2020). Social Finance and Impact Investing. Governing Welfare in the Era of Financialization. *Historical Social Research / Historische Sozialforschung, Special Issue: Social Finance, Impact Investing, and the Financialization of the Public Interest, 45*(3), 7-30. https://www.jstor.org/stable/26918402

Chiapello, E., & Knoll, L. (2020). The welfare conventions approach: A comparative perspective on social impact bonds. *Journal of Comparative Policy Analysis, 22*(2), 100–115.

Child, C., Gibbs, B. G., & Rowley, K. J. (2016). Paying for success: An appraisal of social impact bonds. *Global Economics and Management Review, 21*(1), 36–45.

Chiu, I. H. Y., & Greene, E. F. (2019). The Marriage of Technology, Markets and Sustainable (and) Social Finance: Insights from ICO Markets for a New Regulatory Framework. *European Business Organization Law Review, 20*(1), 139–169. DOI: 10.1007/s40804-019-00138-y

Chohan, U. W. (2021). *Decentralized Finance (DeFi): An Emergent Alternative Financial Architecture* (SSRN Scholarly Paper 3791921). Social Science Research Network. https://doi.org/DOI: 10.2139/ssrn.3791921

Choi, J., Yi, S., & Lee, K. C. (2011). Analysis of keyword networks in MIS research and implications for predicting knowledge evolution. *Information & Management, 48*(8), 371–381. DOI: 10.1016/j.im.2011.09.004

Clarke, L., Chalkidou, K., & Nemzoff, C. (2018). 'Development impact bonds targeting health outcomes'. *CGD Policy Paper, 133.*

Clarke, T., & Boersma, M. (2016). *Sustainable Finance? A Critical Analysis of the Regulation, Policies, Strategies, Implementation and Reporting on Sustainability in International Finance.* https://opus.lib.uts.edu.au/handle/10453/42043

Clarke, C., & Tooker, L. (2018). Social Finance Meets Financial Innovation: Contemporary Experiments in Payments, Money and Debt. *Theory, Culture & Society, 35*(3), 3–11. DOI: 10.1177/0263276417746467

Clark, R., Reed, J., & Sunderland, T. (2018). Bridging funding gaps for climate and sustainable development: Pitfalls, progress and potential of private finance. *Land Use Policy, 71*, 335–346. DOI: 10.1016/j.landusepol.2017.12.013

Clifton, J., Comin, F., & Diaz-Fuentes, D. (2006). Privatization in the European Union: Pragmatic, ideological, inevitable? *Journal of European Public Policy, 13*(5), 736–756.

Climate Policy Initiative. (2023). *Global Landscape of Climate Finance 2023—Methodology*.

Clohessy, T., Treiblmaier, H., Acton, T., & Rogers, N. (2020). Antecedents of blockchain adoption: An integrative framework. *Strategic Change, 29*(5), 501–515. DOI: 10.1002/jsc.2360

Cobo, M. j., López-Herrera, A. g., Herrera-Viedma, E., & Herrera, F. (2011). Science mapping software tools: Review, analysis, and cooperative study among tools. *Journal of the American Society for Information Science and Technology, 62*(7), 1382–1402. DOI: 10.1002/asi.21525

Cobo, M., López-Herrera, A., Herrera-Viedma, E., & Herrera, F. (2011). An approach for detecting, quantifying, and visualizing the evolution of a research field: A practical application to the fuzzy sets theory field. *Journal of Informetrics, 5*(1), 146–166. DOI: 10.1016/j.joi.2010.10.002

Condon, M. (2023). *Climate Services: The Business of Physical Risk* (SSRN Scholarly Paper 4396826). https://doi.org/DOI: 10.2139/ssrn.4396826

Connaker, A., & Madsbjerg, S. (2019). The state of socially responsible investing. *Harvard Business Review, 17*, •••. https://hbr.org/2019/01/the-state-of-socially-responsible-investing

Conning, J., & Morduch, J. (2011). Microfinance and Social Investment. *Annual Review of Financial Economics, 3*(Volume 3, 2011), 407–434. https://doi.org/DOI: 10.1146/annurev-financial-102710-144909

Contreras, E., Herrero, J., Crochemore, L., Pechlivanidis, I., Photiadou, C., Aguilar, C., & Polo, M. J. (2020). Advances in the Definition of Needs and Specifications for a Climate Service Tool Aimed at Small Hydropower Plants' Operation and Management. *Energies, 13*(7), 1827. DOI: 10.3390/en13071827

Cooper, C., Graham, C., & Hinick, D. (2016). Social impact bonds: The securitization of the homeless. *Accounting, Organizations and Society, 55*, 63–82. DOI: 10.1016/j.aos.2016.10.003

Cosma, S., Grasso, A. G., Pagliacci, F., & Pedrazzoli, A. (2019). Is Equity Crowdfunding a Good Tool for Social Enterprises?. *Socially Responsible Investments: The Crossroads Between Institutional and Retail Investors*, 149-170.

Coullabé, J. (2025). Social indicators, revealing the tensions between aspirations for sustainability and the preservation of existing business models. *ACCRA,* 78-112. https://EconPapers.repec.org/RePEc:hal:journl:hal04916483

Crifo, P. (2022). The promise of green finance labels. 2-9, *Presses universitaires de Grenoble*. https://shs.cairn.info/le-virus-de-la-recherche--9782706153167-page-2?lang=fr

Crifo, P., Rodolphe, D., & Gond, J. P. (2020). The role of labels in green finance: construction and regulation of a label market in France. In R. d. financière (Ed.), *Climate Finance* (138), 209-223. *Journal of Financial Economics*. https://doi.org/ DOI: 10.3917/ecofi.138.0209

Crossan, M. M., & Apaydin, M. (2010). A Multi-Dimensional Framework of Organizational Innovation: A Systematic Review of the Literature. *Journal of Management Studies*, *47*(6), 1154–1191. DOI: 10.1111/j.1467-6486.2009.00880.x

Cull, R., Demirguc-Kunt, A. A., & Morduch, J. (2009). Microfinance Meets the Market. *The Journal of Economic Perspectives*, *23*(1), 167–192. DOI: 10.1257/jep.23.1.167

Cunha, F. A., Meira, E., & Orsato, R. J. (2021). Sustainable finance and investment: Review and research agenda. *Business Strategy and the Environment, 30*(8), 3821–3838. DOI: 10.1002/bse.2842

Dadabada, P. K. (2024). Analyzing the Impact of ESG Integration and FinTech Innovations on Green Finance: A Comparative Case Studies Approach. *Journal of the Knowledge Economy*. Advance online publication. DOI: 10.1007/s13132-024-02197-0

Dahbi, F., Carrasco, I., & Petracci, B. (2024). A systematic literature review on social impact bonds. *Finance Research Letters*, *62*, 105063.

Dahdal, A., Truby, J., & Ismailov, O. (2022). The Role and Potential of Blockchain Technology in Islamic Finance. *European Business Law Review, 33*(2). https://kluwerlawonline.com/api/Product/CitationPDFURL?file=Journals\EULR\EULR2022005.pdf

Danilov, Y. (2021). Sustainable finance: A new theoretical paradigm. *World Economy and International Relations*, *65*(9), 5–13. DOI: 10.20542/0131-2227-2021-65-9-5-13

Daou, A., Mallat, C., Chammas, G., Cerantola, N., Kayed, S., & Saliba, N. A. (2020). The Ecocanvas as a business model canvas for a circular economy. *Journal of Cleaner Production*, *258*, 120938. DOI: 10.1016/j.jclepro.2020.120938

Das, T. (2019). Does credit access lead to expansion of income and multidimensional poverty? A study of rural Assam. *International Journal of Social Economics*, *46*(2), 252–270. DOI: 10.1108/IJSE-12-2017-0592

De Cristofaro, T., & Gullu, C. (2023). In Search of Double Materiality in Non Financial Reports: First Empirical Evidence. *Sustainability*, *15*(2), 924. DOI: 10.3390/su15020924

de Gruyter, E., Petrie, D., Black, N., & Gharghori, P. (2020). 'Attracting investors for public health programmes with Social Impact Bonds'. *Public Money & Management*, *40*(3), 225–236.

De Merxem, L. G., & Tchotourian, I. (2024). Double materiality, the keystone of sustainable corporate governance. (R. i. économique, Ed.) *VARIA*, 59-91. https://doi.org/DOI: 10.3917/ride.384.0059

Deflorian, M. (2023). Crowdsourcing infrastructures of green everyday life: How sustainable sharing, swapping and gardening initiatives in Vienna tackle the lack of transformative agency in eco-politics. *Environmental Politics*, *32*(7), 1231–1254. DOI: 10.1080/09644016.2022.2164212

Defourny, J., & Nyssens, M. (2010). Conceptions of social enterprise and social entrepreneurship in Europe and the United States: Convergences and divergences. *Journal of Social Entrepreneurship*, *1*(1), 32–53. DOI: 10.1080/19420670903442053

Dehdarirad, T., Villarroya, A., & Barrios, M. (2014). Research trends in gender differences in higher education and science: A co-word analysis. *Scientometrics*, *101*(1), 273–290. DOI: 10.1007/s11192-014-1327-2

Del Giudice, A., & Migliavacca, M. (2019). Social impact bonds and institutional investors: An empirical analysis of a complicated relationship. *Nonprofit and Voluntary Sector Quarterly*, *48*(1), 50–70.

Delia, E. P. (with APS Bank). (2011). *Microcredit as a tool of ethical financing for sustainable development*. APS Bank.

Dell'Aquila, A., Graça, A., Teixeira, M., Fontes, N., Gonzalez-Reviriego, N., Marcos-Matamoros, R., Chou, C., Terrado, M., Giannakopoulos, C., Varotsos, K. V., Caboni, F., Locci, R., Nanu, M., Porru, S., Argiolas, G., Bruno Soares, M., & Sanderson, M. (2023). Monitoring climate related risk and opportunities for the wine sector: The MED-GOLD pilot service. *Climate Services*, *30*, 100346. DOI: 10.1016/j.cliser.2023.100346

Dell'Atti, S., Trotta, A., Iannuzzi, A. P., & Demaria, F. (2017). Corporate Social Responsibility Engagement as a Determinant of Bank Reputation: An Empirical Analysis. *Corporate Social Responsibility and Environmental Management, 24*(6), 589–605. DOI: 10.1002/csr.1430

Dellermann, D., Lipusch, N., Ebel, P., & Leimeister, J. M. (2020). The potential of collective intelligence and crowdsourcing for opportunity creation. *International Journal of Entrepreneurial Venturing, 12*(2), 183–207. DOI: 10.1504/IJEV.2020.105569

Desmarais, C. (2014). Systematic review. In *Practical Guide to Rehabilitation Research* (ed. Méthodes techn et outils d'intervention), De Boeck Supérieur. 161-176 https://doi.org/DOI: 10.3917/dbu.guill.2014.01.0161

Dileo, P. (2011). Repositioning microfinance with impact investors: Codes of conduct and 'social first' MFIs. *Enterprise Development & Microfinance, 22*(4), 276–290. DOI: 10.3362/1755-1986.2011.031

Ding, X., Li, W., Huang, D., & Qin, X. (2022). Does Innovation Climate Help to Effectiveness of Green Finance Product R&D Team? The Mediating Role of Knowledge Sharing and Moderating Effect of Knowledge Heterogeneity. *Sustainability, 14*(7), 7. Advance online publication. DOI: 10.3390/su14073926

Directorate-General for Research and Innovation. (2015). *A European Research innovation _ Roadmap for Climate Services.*

Dirie, K. A., Alam, M. M., & Maamor, S. (2023). Islamic social finance for achieving sustainable development goals: A systematic literature review and future research agenda. *International Journal of Ethics and Systems, 40*(4), 676–698. DOI: 10.1108/ijoes-12-2022-0317

Dogan, E., Majeed, M. T., & Luni, T. (2022). Are clean energy and carbon emission allowances caused by bitcoin? A novel time-varying method. *Journal of Cleaner Production, 347*, 131089. DOI: 10.1016/j.jclepro.2022.131089

Doherty, B., Haugh, H., & Lyon, F. (2014). Social enterprises as hybrid organizations: A review and research agenda. *International Journal of Management Reviews, 16*(4), 417–436.

Doh, J. P., & Guay, T. R. (2006). Corporate Social Responsibility, Public Policy, and NGO Activism in Europe and the United States: An Institutional-Stakeholder Perspective. *Journal of Management Studies, 43*(1), 47–73. DOI: 10.1111/j.1467-6486.2006.00582.x

Donthu, N., Kumar, S., Mukherjee, D., Pandey, N., & Lim, W. M. (2021). How to conduct a bibliometric analysis: An overview and guidelines. *Journal of Business Research, 133*, 285–296. DOI: 10.1016/j.jbusres.2021.04.070

Dowling, E. (2017). In the wake of austerity: Social impact bonds and the financialisation of the welfare state in Britain. *New Political Economy*, *22*(3), 294–310.

EC. (2022). *COMMISSION STAFF WORKING DOCUMENT on Common European Data Spaces.*

EC. JRC. (2020). *Destination Earth: Survey on "Digital Twins" technologies and activities, in the Green Deal area.* Publications Office. https://data.europa.eu/doi/10.2760/430025

Edmans, A., & Kacperczyk, M. (2022). Sustainable finance. *Review of Finance*, *26*(6), 1309–1313. DOI: 10.1093/rof/rfac069

Edmiston, D., & Nicholls, A. (2018). Social impact bonds: The role of private capital in outcome-based commissioning. *Journal of Social Policy*, *47*(1), 57–76.

Edmiston, D., & Nicholls, A. (2018). Social Impact Bonds: The role of private capital in outcome-based commissioning. *Journal of Social Policy*, *47*(1), 57–76.

Emerson, J. (2003). The blended value proposition: Integrating social and financial returns. *California Management Review*, *45*(4), 35–51. DOI: 10.2307/41166187

Emerson, J. (2012). Risk, return and impact: Understanding diversification and performance within an impact investing portfolio. *ImpactAssets*, *2*, 1–15.

Emerton, L., Bishop, J., & Thomas, L. (2006). *Sustainable Financing of Protected Areas: A Global Review of Challenges and Options.* IUCN.

Erskine, C. (2021). *Quality Education India Development Impact Bond: A case study produced as part of the FCDO DIBs Evaluation.* Ecorys. Retrieved April 27, 2023, from https://golab.bsg.ox.ac.uk/knowledge-bank/resource-library/quality-education-india-report/

Esmaeilian, B., Sarkis, J., Lewis, K., & Behdad, S. (2020). Blockchain for the future of sustainable supply chain management in Industry 4.0. *Resources, Conservation and Recycling*, *163*, 105064. DOI: 10.1016/j.resconrec.2020.105064

Ethereum.org. (2023). *Ethereum energy consumption: Sustainability benefits of proof-of-stake.* Retrieved from https://ethereum.org/en/energy-consumption/

Etzion, D., Gehman, J., Ferraro, F., & Avidan, M. (2017). Unleashing sustainability transformations through robust action. *Journal of Cleaner Production, 140*, 167–178. DOI: 10.1016/j.jclepro.2015.06.064

European Commission. (2016). *A recipe book for social finance.*

European Commission. (2019). *Digital Urban European Twins for smarter decision making | DUET Project | Fact Sheet | H2020.* CORDIS | European Commission. https://cordis.europa.eu/project/id/870697

European Commission. (2020). https://commission.europa.eu/index_it

European Commission. (2022). *A European strategy for data | Shaping Europe's digital future.* https://digital-strategy.ec.europa.eu/en/policies/strategy-data

European Commission. (2024). *Overview of sustainable finance.* Available at https://finance.ec.europa.eu/sustainable-finance/overview-sustainable-finance_en

European Commission. (2024). *Overview of sustainable finance.* https://finance.ec.europa.eu/sustainable-finance/overview-sustainable-finance_en

European Commission. (2025). *Overview of sustainable finance.* https://finance.ec.europa.eu/sustainable-finance/overview-sustainable-finance_en

European Investment Advisory Hub. (2021). *Social outcomes contracting in Europe: An introductory guide to social outcomes contracting in European Union Member States.* https://eiah.eib.org/publications/attachments/socialoutcomes-contracting-in-Europe-10052021.pdf

European Parliament. (2024). *Proposal for a Regulation on Markets in Crypto-assets.* Retrieved from https://www.europarl.europa.eu/legislative-train/theme-a-europe-fit-for-the-digital-age/file-crypto-assets-1

European Securities and Markets Authority. (2024). ESMA Report on trends, risks and vulnerabilities: Risk Monitor. ESMA, ESMA505248213444. *European Union.* https://www.esma.europa.eu/document/trendsrisksandvulnerabilitiestrvreportno22024

Evans, S., Vladimirova, D., Holgado, M., Van Fossen, K., Yang, M., Silva, E., & Barlow, C. (2017). Business Model Innovation for Sustainability. *Business Strategy and the Environment, 26.* Advance online publication. DOI: 10.1002/bse.1939

Farrukh, M., Meng, F., Raza, A., & Tahir, M. S. (2020). Twenty-seven years of Sustainable Development Journal: A bibliometric analysis. *Sustainable Development, 28*(6), 1725–1737. DOI: 10.1002/sd.2120

Fatima, R., Boitan, I. A., & Carè, R. (2022). How Many Shades Are There in Sustainable Finance?: A Bibliometric Review. In Gok, I. Y. (Ed.), *Handbook of Research on Global Aspects of Sustainable Finance in Times of Crises* (pp. 1–26). IGI Global., DOI: 10.4018/978-1-7998-8501-6.ch001

Fatima, R., & Carè, R. (2024a). Navigating the landscape of nature-inspired finance approaches: A bibliometric analysis. In *Reference Module in Social Sciences*. Elsevier., DOI: 10.1016/B978-0-44-313776-1.00278-6

Fatima, R., & Carè, R. (2024b). The Role of FinTech and DeFi for Sustainable Development Goals and Sustainable Development: A Comprehensive Bibliometric Review. In *Decentralized Finance and Tokenization in FinTech* (pp. 238–270). IGI Global., DOI: 10.4018/979-8-3693-3346-4.ch014

Fedele, A., & Miniaci, R. (2010). Do Social Enterprises Finance Their Investments Differently from For-profit Firms? The Case of Social Residential Services in Italy. *Journal of Social Entrepreneurship*, *1*(2), 174–189. DOI: 10.1080/19420676.2010.511812

Feng, Y., Zhu, Q., & Lai, K. (2017). Corporate social responsibility for supply chain management: A literature review and bibliometric analysis. *Journal of Cleaner Production*, *158*, 296–307. DOI: 10.1016/j.jclepro.2017.05.018

Fernandez-Alles, M., & Ramos-Rodríguez, A. (2009). Intellectual structure of human resources management research: A bibliometric analysis of the journal Human Resource Management, 1985–2005. *Journal of the American Society for Information Science and Technology*, *60*(1), 161–175. DOI: 10.1002/asi.20947

Ferreira, F. A. F., Jalali, M. S., Meidutė-Kavaliauskienė, I., & Viana, B. A. C. P. (2015). A metacognitive decision making based-framework for bank customer loyalty measurement and management. *Technological and Economic Development of Economy*, *21*(2), 280–300. DOI: 10.3846/20294913.2014.981764

Financial Stability Board [FSB]. (2012). *Global shadow banking monitoring report 2012*. Financial Stability Board. Retrieved from https://www.fsb.org/2012/11/r_121118c/

Financial Stability Board [FSB]. (2025). *Thematic Peer Review on FSB Global Regulatory Framework for Crypto Asset Activities*. Retrieved from https://www.fsb.org/2025/02/thematic-peer-review-on-fsb-global-regulatory-framework-for-crypto-asset-activities/

Firmansyah, E. A., Masri, M., Anshari, M., & Besar, M. H. A. (2023). Factors Affecting Fintech Adoption: A Systematic Literature Review. *FinTech*, *2*(1), 1. Advance online publication. DOI: 10.3390/fintech2010002

Fitzgerald, C., Carter, E., Dixon, R., & Airoldi, M. (2019). Walking the contractual tightrope: A transaction cost economics perspective on social impact bonds. *Public Money & Management, 39*(5), 327–336.

FitzGerald, C., Fraser, A., & Kimmitt, J. (2020). 'Tackling the Big Questions in Social Impact Bond Research through Comparative Approaches'. *Journal of Comparative Policy Analysis, 22*(2), 85–99.

FitzGerald, C., Fraser, A., & Kimmitt, J. (2020). Tackling the Big Questions in Social Impact Bond Research through Comparative Approaches. *Journal of Comparative Policy Analysis*, •••, 1–15.

Flammer, C. (2020). Green bonds: Effectiveness and implications for public policy. *Environmental and Energy Policy and the Economy, 1*(1), 95–128. DOI: 10.1086/706794

Flynn, J., Young, J., & Barnett, C. (2015). *Impact Investments: A literature Review*. Centre for Development Impact.

FMO. (2019, November 15). FMO supports the first Palestinian Employment Development Impact Bond (DIB). Retrieved April 27, 2023, from https://www.fmo.nl/news-detail/4f39ef8e-d43f-44c6-9d8f-47c0a8fb4ca4/fmo-supports-the-first-palestinian-employment-development-impact-bond-(dib)

Fox, C., & Morris, S. (2019). Evaluating outcome-based payment programmes: Challenges for evidence-based policy. *Journal of Economic Policy Reform*. Advance online publication. DOI: 10.1080/17487870.2019.1575217

Fox, C., & Morris, S. (2021). 'Evaluating outcome-based payment programmes: Challenges for evidence-based policy'. *Journal of Economic Policy Reform, 24*(1), 61–77.

Fox, C., Olson, H., Armitage, H., Baines, S., & Painter, G. (2022). Can a Focus on Co-Created, Strengths-Based Services Facilitate Early-Stage Innovation within SIBs? *International Public Management Journal*, •••, 1–17.

Franceschini, F., Maisano, D., & Mastrogiacomo, L. (2016). Empirical analysis and classification of database errors in Scopus and Web of Science. *Journal of Informetrics, 10*(4), 933–953.

Fraser, A., Tan, S., Lagarde, M., & Mays, N. (2018). 'Narratives of Promise, Narratives of Caution: A review of the literature on Social Impact Bonds'. *Social Policy and Administration, 52*(1), 4–28.

Fraser, A., Tan, S., Lagarde, M., & Mays, N. (2018). Narratives of promise, narratives of caution: A review of the literature on Social Impact Bonds. *Social Policy and Administration*, *52*(1), 4–28. DOI: 10.1111/spol.12260

Frei, T. (2021). Public–private engagement (PPE) in hydromet services and the role of the academic sector. *Meteorological Applications*, *28*(5), e2025. DOI: 10.1002/met.2025

FrontFundr. (n.d.). About Us. Retrieved from http://www.frontfundr.com/

Gallucci, C., Del Giudice, A., & Santulli, R. (2022). 'How to attract professional investors in developing countries? An evidence-based structure for development impact bonds'. *Finance Research Letters*, *46*, 102816.

Gallucci, C., Rosalia, S., & Riccardo, T. (2019). 'Development impact bonds to overcome investors-services providers agency problems: Insights from a case study analysis'. *African Journal of Business Management*, *13*(13), 415–427.

GAO [Government Accountability Office]. (2012). *Designing Evaluations, 2012 Revision*.

Garcia, J., & Lopez, M. (2022). Tokenized incentives for sustainable energy behavior: Evidence from Argentina. *Renewable Energy Review*, *45*(3), 223–234.

Geobey, S., Westley, F. R., & Weber, O. (2012). Enabling social innovation through developmental social finance. *Journal of Social Entrepreneurship*, *3*(2), 151–165. DOI: 10.1080/19420676.2012.726006

Germany's Energiewende. (2021, May 27). World Nuclear Association. https://world-nuclear.org/information-library/energy-and-the-environment/energiewende

Ghaouri, M. H., Kassim, S., & Rashid, H. (2023). Waqf-Linked Islamic Fintech Microfinance as a Business Enabler in Post-pandemic Economy: The Experience of Hal Microfinance, Kenya. In Hamdan, A., Harraf, A., Buallay, A., Arora, P., & Alsabatin, H. (Eds.), *From Industry 4.0 to Industry 5.0: Mapping the Transitions* (pp. 357–370). Springer Nature Switzerland., DOI: 10.1007/978-3-031-28314-7_30

Ghosh, S., Mahapatra, M. S., Tandon, N., & Tandon, D. (2024). Achieving Sustainable Development Goal of Women Empowerment: A Study among Self-help Groups in India. *FIIB Business Review*, *13*(4), 477–491. DOI: 10.1177/23197145231169074

Giacomantonio, C. (2017). Grant-Maximizing but not Money-Making: A Simple Decision-Tree Analysis for Social Impact Bonds. *Journal of Social Entrepreneurship*, *8*(1), 47–66.

Giacomantonio, C. (2018). Setting realistic expectations: The narrow use-case for Social Impact Bonds. *Journal of Community Safety & Well-being*, *3*(3), 93–95.

Gillpatrick, T., Boğa, S., & Aldanmaz, O. (2022). How Can Blockchain Contribute to Developing Country Economies? A Literature Review on Application Areas. *ECONOMICS*, *10*(1), 105–128. DOI: 10.2478/eoik-2022-0009

Global Legal Insights. (2025). *Blockchain & Cryptocurrency Laws & Regulations*. Retrieved from https://www.globallegalinsights.com/practice-areas/blockchain-cryptocurrency-laws-and-regulations/usa/

Glynn, J. J., & Murphy, M. P. (1996). Public management: Failing accountabilities and failing performance review. *International Journal of Public Sector Management*, *9*(5/6/7), 125–137.

Goda, D. R. (2021). The Evolution of Business Models in the Digital Age: Implications for Energy, Environment, and Finance. *Digitalization & Sustainability Review*, *1*(1), 41–56.

Golka, P. (2024). Epistemic gerrymandering: ESG, impact investing, and the financial governance of sustainability. *Review of International Political Economy*, *31*(6), 1894–1918. DOI: 10.1080/09692290.2024.2382241

González, D. M. L., & Rendon, J. G. (2022). Opportunities and challenges of mainstreaming distributed energy resources towards the transition to more efficient and resilient energy markets. *Renewable & Sustainable Energy Reviews*, *157*, 112018.

Gonzalez-Ruiz, J. D., Marín-Rodríguez, N. J., & Weber, O. (2024). New insights on social finance research in the sustainable development context. *Business Strategy & Development*, *7*(1). Advance online publication. DOI: 10.1002/bsd2.342

Goodall, E. (2014). *Choosing Social Impact Bonds: A Practitioner's Guide*. Bridges Ventures.

Government Outcomes Lab. (2025.). *INDIGO impact bond dataset*. https://golab.bsg.ox.ac.uk/knowledge-bank/indigo/

Grimsey, D., & Lewis, M. K. (2005). Are public private partnerships value for money? Evaluating alternative approaches and comparing academic and practitioner views. *Accounting Forum*, *29*(4), 345–378.

Grittner, A. M. (2013). *Results-based Financing: Evidence from performance-based financing in the health sector*. Discussion Paper No. 6/2013. Deutsches Institut für Entwicklungspolitik.

Guan, L., Merigó, J. M., Löfstedt, R. E., & Wardman, J. K. (2024). Twenty-five years of the Journal of Risk Research: A bibliometric overview. *Journal of Risk Research*, •••, 1–44. DOI: 10.1080/13669877.2024.2377093

Guentchev, G., Palin, E. J., Lowe, J. A., & Harrison, M. (2023). Upscaling of climate services – What is it? A literature review. *Climate Services*, *30*, 100352. DOI: 10.1016/j.cliser.2023.100352

Gugiu, P. C., & Rodríguez-Campos, L. (2007). 'Semi-structured interview protocol for constructing logic models'. *Evaluation and Program Planning*, *30*(4), 339–350. PMID: 17905433

Gunay, S., Sraieb, M. M., Kaskaloglu, K., & Yıldız, M. E. (2023). Cryptocurrencies and global sustainability: Do blockchained sectors have distinctive effects? *Journal of Cleaner Production*, *425*, 138943. DOI: 10.1016/j.jclepro.2023.138943

Gustafsson-Wright, E., Osborne, S., & Crane, E. (2021). *How have impact bond-funded projects in low-and middle-income countries fared in COVID-19?* Working Paper No. 164. Global Economy and Development at Brookings, Brookings Institution: Washington, DC.

Gustafsson-Wright, E., Osborne, S., & Shankar, A. (2022). *From Evidence to Scale: Lessons Learned from the Quality Education India Development Impact Bond*. Center for Universal Education, Brookings Institution: Washington, DC.

Gustafsson-Wright, E., Boggild-Jones, I., Segell, D., & Durland, J. (2017). *Impact Bonds in Developing Countries: Early Learning from the Field*. Global Economy and Development at Brookings, Brookings Institution.

Gustafsson-Wright, E., Gardiner, S., & Putcha, V. (2015). *The potential and limitations of impact bonds: Lessons from the first five years of experience worldwide*. Global Economy and Development at Brookings, Brookings Institution.

Gustafsson-Wright, E., Gardiner, S., & Putcha, V. (2015). *The Potential and Limitations of Impact Bonds: Lessons from the First Five Years of Experience Worldwide*. Global Economy and Development at Brookings.

Gustafsson-Wright, E., & Osborne, S. (2020a). *Are Impact Bonds Reaching the Intended Populations?* Global Economy and Development at Brookings, Brookings Institution.

Gustafsson-Wright, E., & Osborne, S. (2020b). *Do the Benefits Outweigh the Costs of Impact Bonds?* Global Economy and Development at Brookings, Brookings Institution.

Habegger, B. (2010). Strategic foresight in public policy: Reviewing the experiences of the UK, Singapore, and the Netherlands. *Futures, 42*(1), 49–58. DOI: 10.1016/j.futures.2009.08.002

Habibi, M. R., Davidson, A., & Laroche, M. (2017). What managers should know about the sharing economy. *Business Horizons, 60*(1), 113–121. DOI: 10.1016/j.bushor.2016.09.007

Hafner, S., Jones, A., Anger-Kraavi, A., & Pohl, J. (2020). Closing the green finance gap – A systems perspective. *Environmental Innovation and Societal Transitions, 34*, 26–60. DOI: 10.1016/j.eist.2019.11.007

Haigh, M. (2014). Call for papers for the social finance and sustainable finance stream: The 14th finance, risk and accounting perspectives conference oriel college, University of Oxford 22nd–24th September 2014 conference pages HTTP://www.acrn.eu/finance. *Journal of Sustainable Finance & Investment, 4*(2), 210-210. https://doi.org/DOI: 10.1080/20430795.2014.891968

Hajer, J. (2020). The national governance and policy context of social impact bond emergence: A comparative analysis of leaders and skeptics. *Journal of Comparative Policy Analysis, 22*(2), 116–133.

Halkos, G., & Gkampoura, E. C. (2021). 'Where do we stand on the 17 Sustainable Development Goals? An overview on progress'. *Economic Analysis and Policy, 70*, 94–122.

Hamadeh, N., Van Rompaey, C., Metreau, E., & Eapen, S. G. (2022, July 1). *New World Bank country classifications by income level: 2022-2023*. World Bank Blogs. Retrieved April 27, 2023, from https://blogs.worldbank.org/opendata/new-world-bank-country-classifications-income-level-2022-2023

Harding, P. (2007). Quotes on sustainability, climate change, population - Quotes corner. *philharding.net - Environmental sustainability, Green Belt advocate and photographer*. https://www.philharding.net/quotes-corner/quotes-corner-1sd.htm

Hartl, B., Sabitzer, T., Hofmann, E., & Penz, E. (2018). *"Sustainability is a nice bonus"* the role of sustainability in carsharing from a consumer perspective. *Journal of Cleaner Production, 202*, 88–100. DOI: 10.1016/j.jclepro.2018.08.138

Harvey, C. R., & Rabetti, D. (2024). International business and decentralised finance. *Journal of International Business Studies*, •••, 1–24.

Harvey, D. (2006). Neo-liberalism as creative destruction. *Geografiska Annaler, 88*(2), 145–158.

Hassan, M. K., Alshater, M. M., Hasan, R., & Bhuiyan, A. B. (2021). Islamic microfinance: A bibliometric review. *Global Finance Journal*, *49*, 100651. DOI: 10.1016/j.gfj.2021.100651

Hassan, M. K., Rabbani, M. R., & Ali, M. A. M. (2020). Challenges for the Islamic Finance and banking in post COVID era and the role of Fintech. *Journal of Economic Cooperation & Development*, *41*(3), 93–116.

Hassan, M. K., Sanchez, B., & Yu, J.-S. (2011). Financial development and economic growth: New evidence from panel data. *The Quarterly Review of Economics and Finance*, *51*(1), 88–104. DOI: 10.1016/j.qref.2010.09.001

Hera. (2022). *A Development Impact Bond to Finance the In Their Hands Project: Third Party Monitoring Final Report*. UK Foreign, Commonwealth & Development Office. Retrieved April 27, 2023, from https://iati.fcdo.gov.uk/iati_documents/D0001335.pdf

Hevenstone, D., Fraser, A., Hobi, L., Przepiorka, W., & Geuke, G. G. (2023). The impact of social impact bond financing. *Public Administration Review*, *83*(4), 930–946.

Hilario-Caballero, A., Garcia-Bernabeu, A., Salcedo, J. V., & Vercher, M. (2020). Tri-criterion model for constructing low-carbon mutual fund portfolios: A preference-based multi-objective genetic algorithm approach. *International Journal of Environmental Research and Public Health*, *17*(17), 6324. DOI: 10.3390/ijerph17176324 PMID: 32878037

Hong, H., Wang, N., & Yang, J. (2023). Welfare consequences of sustainable finance. *Review of Financial Studies*, *36*(12), 4864–4918. DOI: 10.1093/rfs/hhad048

Hörisch, J. (2015). Crowdfunding for environmental ventures: An empirical analysis of the influence of environmental orientation on the success of crowdfunding initiatives. *Journal of Cleaner Production*, *107*, 636–645. DOI: 10.1016/j.jclepro.2015.05.046

Hörisch, J. (2018). "Think big" or "small is beautiful"? An empirical analysis of characteristics and determinants of success of sustainable crowdfunding projects. *International Journal of Entrepreneurial Venturing*, *10*(1), 111–129. DOI: 10.1504/IJEV.2018.090982

Hosseini, M., Shahri, A., Phalp, K., Taylor, J., & Ali, R. (2015). Crowdsourcing: A taxonomy and systematic mapping study. *Computer Science Review*, *17*, 43–69. DOI: 10.1016/j.cosrev.2015.05.001

Howe, J. (2006). The rise of crowdsourcing. *Wired Magazine*, *14*(6), 176–183.

Hudon, M. (2009). Should Access to Credit be a Right? *Journal of Business Ethics*, *84*(1), 17–28. DOI: 10.1007/s10551-008-9670-y

Huertas-Valdivia, I., Ferrari, A. M., Settembre-Blundo, D., & García-Muiña, F. E. (2020). Social life-cycle assessment: A review by bibliometric analysis. *Sustainability*, *12*(15), 6211. DOI: 10.3390/su12156211

Huggett, S., James, C., & Palmaro, E. (2018). Field-Weighting Readership: How Does It Compare to Field-Weighting Citations? In Erdt, M., Sesagiri Raamkumar, A., Rasmussen, E., & Theng, Y.-L. (Eds.), *Altmetrics for Research Outputs Measurement and Scholarly Information Management* (pp. 96–104). Springer., DOI: 10.1007/978-981-13-1053-9_8

Hummels, H., & de Leede, M. (2014). The emergence of impact investments: The case of microfinance. In *Socially Responsible Investment in the 21st Century: Does it Make a Difference for Society?* (world; Vol. 7, pp. 91–115). Emerald Group Publishing Limited. https://doi.org/DOI: 10.1108/S2043-905920140000007004

Husain, A., Yii, K.-J., & Lee, C.-C. (2023). Are green cryptocurrencies really green? New evidence from wavelet analysis. *Journal of Cleaner Production*, *417*, 137985. DOI: 10.1016/j.jclepro.2023.137985

Hussain, N., Di Pietro, F., & Rosati, P. (2023). Crowdfunding for Social Entrepreneurship: A systematic review of the literature. *Journal of Social Entrepreneurship*, ●●●, 1–24.

Huynh, T. L. D. (2022). When 'green' challenges 'prime': Empirical evidence from government bond markets. *Journal of Sustainable Finance & Investment*, *12*(2), 375–388. DOI: 10.1080/20430795.2020.1769984

Ibe-enwo, G., Igbudu, N., Garanti, Z., & Popoola, T. (2019). Assessing the Relevance of Green Banking Practice on Bank Loyalty: The Mediating Effect of Green Image and Bank Trust. *Sustainability*, *11*(17), 17. Advance online publication. DOI: 10.3390/su11174651

Igbudu, N., Garanti, Z., & Popoola, T. (2018). Enhancing Bank Loyalty through Sustainable Banking Practices: The Mediating Effect of Corporate Image. *Sustainability*, *10*(11), 11. Advance online publication. DOI: 10.3390/su10114050

Imai, K. S., Gaiha, R., Thapa, G., & Annim, S. K. (2012). Microfinance and Poverty—A Macro Perspective. *World Development*, *40*(8), 1675–1689. DOI: 10.1016/j.worlddev.2012.04.013

Independent Evaluation Group. (2021). https://ieg.worldbankgroup.org/sites/default/files/Data/reports/ap_driveforfinancialinclusion.pdf

India, N. (2025, January 28). *Corporate filings annual reports - Equity, SME - NSE India*. NSE India. https://www.nseindia.com/companies-listing/corporate-filings-annual-reports

Indigo. (2022a, February 22). Cameroon Cataract Bond. Retrieved April 27, 2023, from https://golab.bsg.ox.ac.uk/knowledge-bank/case-studies/cameroon-cataract-bond/

Indigo. (2022b, September 4). In Their Hands. Retrieved April 27, 2023, from https://golab.bsg.ox.ac.uk/knowledge-bank/case-studies/in-their-hands/

Indigo. (2023). Impact Bond Dataset. Retrieved April 27, 2023, from https://golab.bsg.ox.ac.uk/knowledge-bank/indigo/impact-bond-dataset-v2/

International Committee of the Red Cross (ICRC). (2022, June 28). First Humanitarian Impact Bond successfully brings physical rehabilitation services to conflict-affected communities. Retrieved April 27, 2023, from https://www.icrc.org/en/document/humanitarian-impact-bond-brings-physical-rehabilitation-services

International Energy Agency. (2025). *World Energy Investment 2025* (éd. 10th). *IEA Publications*. https://www.iea.org/reports/world-energy-investment-2025

International Finance Corporation [IFC]. (2023). *Green and Social Bond Impact Report*. Retrieved from https://www.ifc.org/en/insights-reports/2024/green-social-bond-impact-report-fy23

Investment Management & Financial Services. (2024). BlackRock. https://www.blackrock.com/us/individual/literature/annual-financial-statements/afs-retail-blackrock-funds.pdf

Jackson, E. T. (2013). 'Interrogating the theory of change: Evaluating impact investing where it matters most'. *Journal of Sustainable Finance & Investment*, *3*(2), 95–110.

Jayaram, R., & Singh, S. (2020). Sustainable finance: A systematic review. *International Journal of Indian Culture and Business Management*, *21*(3), 317. DOI: 10.1504/ijicbm.2020.110452

Jochnick, C. (2012). *Systems, power, and agency in market-based approaches to poverty. Oxfam America Research Backgrounder Series*. Oxfam America., https://beamexchange.org/uploads/filer_public/2f/64/2f64190f-1213-486b-bf25-ac90553195be/systems_poweragency.pdf

Jouti, A. T. (2019). An integrated approach for building sustainable Islamic social finance ecosystems. *ISRA International Journal of Islamic Finance*, *11*(2), 246–266. DOI: 10.1108/IJIF-10-2018-0118

Jouti, A. T. (2021). Islamic FinTech and Financial Inclusion. In Billah, M. M. (Ed.), *Islamic FinTech: Insights and Solutions* (pp. 209–229). Springer International Publishing., DOI: 10.1007/978-3-030-45827-0_12

Joyce, A., & Paquin, R. L. (2016). The triple layered business model canvas: A tool to design more sustainable business models. *Journal of Cleaner Production, 135*, 1474–1486.

Joy, M., & Shields, J. (2013). Social impact bonds: The next phase of third sector marketization? *Canadian Journal of Nonprofit and Social Economy Research, 4*(2), 39–55. DOI: 10.22230/cjnser.2013v4n2a148

Kamal, J. B., & Hassan, M. K. (2022). Asymmetric connectedness between cryptocurrency environment attention index and green assets. *Journal of Economic Asymmetries, 25*, e00240. DOI: 10.1016/j.jeca.2022.e00240

Kamara, L. (2023). Socially responsible investment: the imbroglio of European regulatory developments. In Institute, C. B. (Ed.), *Sustainability Research* (pp. 405–418)., DOI: 10.3917/ems.cheva.2023.01.0405

Karakas, S., Acar, A. Z., & Kucukaltan, B. (2021). Blockchain adoption in logistics and supply chain: A literature review and research agenda. *International Journal of Production Research, 62*(22), 8193–8216. DOI: 10.1080/00207543.2021.2012613

Kashi, A., & Shah, M. E. (2023). Bibliometric review on sustainable finance. *Sustainability, 15*(9), 7119. DOI: 10.3390/su15097119

Kashif, M., Pinglu, C., Ullah, S., & Zaman, M. (2024). Evaluating the influence of financial technology (FinTech) on sustainable finance: A comprehensive global analysis. *Financial Markets and Portfolio Management, 38*(1), 123–155. DOI: 10.1007/s11408-023-00439-w

Kasmon, B., Ibrahim, S. S., Daud, D., Raja Hisham, R. R., & Dian Wisika Prajanti, S. (2024). FinTech application in Islamic social finance in Asia region: A systematic literature review. *International Journal of Ethics and Systems*. https://doi.org/DOI: 10.1108/ijoes-07-2023-0155

Katona, T. (2021). Decentralized Finance—The Possibilities of a Blockchain "Money Lego" System. *Financial and Economic Review, 20*(1), 74–102.

Kayani, U., & Hasan, F. (2024). Unveiling Cryptocurrency Impact on Financial Markets and Traditional Banking Systems: Lessons for Sustainable Blockchain and Interdisciplinary Collaborations. *Journal of Risk and Financial Management, 17*(2), 58.

Kazantsev, N., Islam, N., Zwiegelaar, J., Brown, A., & Maull, R. (2023). Data sharing for business model innovation in platform ecosystems: From private data to public good. *Technological Forecasting and Social Change*, *192*, 122515. DOI: 10.1016/j.techfore.2023.122515

Khan, A., Goodell, J. W., Hassan, M. K., & Paltrinieri, A. (2022). A bibliometric review of finance bibliometric papers. *Finance Research Letters*, *47*, 102520. DOI: 10.1016/j.frl.2021.102520

Khan, H. H., Nabila, A., Noorlailahusna, M., & Mohammad, M. (2024). Green finance and environmental sustainability: A systematic review and future research avenues. *Environmental Science and Pollution Research International*, *33*(6), 9784–9794. DOI: 10.1007/s11356-023-31809-6 PMID: 38194178

Khavul, S. (2010). Microfinance: Creating Opportunities for the Poor? *The Academy of Management Perspectives*, *24*(3), 58–72.

Kirişci, M. (2025). An integrated decision-making process for risk analysis of decentralized finance. *Neural Computing & Applications*, •••, 1–31.

Kish, Z., & Leroy, J. (2015). Bonded Life: Technologies of racial finance from slave insurance to philanthrocapital. *Cultural Studies*, *29*(5–6), 630–651. DOI: 10.1080/09502386.2015.1017137

Kitzmuller, L., McManus, J., Shah, N. B., & Starla, K. (2018). *Educate Girls Development Impact Bond: Final Evaluation Report*. IDinsight. Retrieved April 27, 2023, from https://golab.bsg.ox.ac.uk/documents/ID_Insight_2018_Educate_Girls_Development_Impact_Bond_-_Final_Evaluation_Report.pdf

Kleynjans, L., & Hudon, M. (2016). A Study of Codes of Ethics for Mexican Microfinance Institutions. *Journal of Business Ethics*, *134*(3), 397–412. DOI: 10.1007/s10551-014-2434-y

Konhäusner, P. (2021). Crowdsourcing in Sustainable Retail—A Theoretical Framework of Success Criteria. *Journal of Risk and Financial Management*, *14*(2), 2. Advance online publication. DOI: 10.3390/jrfm14020087

Krause, M., & Tolaymat, T. (2018). Quantification of energy and carbon costs for mining cryptocurrencies. *Nature Sustainability*, *1*(11), 711–718. DOI: 10.1038/s41893-018-0152-7

Kshetri, N., & Voas, J. (2018). Blockchain in Developing Countries. *IT Professional, 20*(2), 11–14. *IT Professional*. Advance online publication. DOI: 10.1109/MITP.2018.021921645

Kuanova, L. A., Sagiyeva, R., & Shirazi, N. S. (2021). Islamic social finance: A literature review and future research directions. *Journal of Islamic Accounting and Business Research, 12*(5), 707–728. DOI: 10.1108/jiabr-11-2020-0356

Kuchler, T., & Stroebel, J. (2021). Social finance. *Annual Review of Financial Economics, 13*(1), 37–55. DOI: 10.1146/annurev-financial-101320-062446

Kumar, S., Sharma, D., Rao, S., Lim, W. M., & Mangla, S. K. (2022). Past, present, and future of sustainable finance: Insights from big data analytics through machine learning of scholarly research. *Annals of Operations Research.* Advance online publication. DOI: 10.1007/s10479-021-04410-8 PMID: 35002001

Kumar, S., & Sharma, M. (2022). The role of DeFi in sustainable energy financing: Opportunities and risks. *International Journal of Renewable Energy, 45*(4), 231–249.

Kwong, R., Kwok, M. L. J., & Wong, H. S. M. (2023). Green FinTech Innovation as a Future Research Direction: A Bibliometric Analysis on Green Finance and FinTech. *Sustainability, 15*(20), 20. Advance online publication. DOI: 10.3390/su152014683

La chaire de la double matérialité. (2025). The Double Materiality in the World: Geopolitical and Critical Analysis (Report). *Fondation du Risque de l'Institut Louis Bachelier.* Chaire Double Materialité. https://www.chairedoublematerialite.org/publications.html

La Torre, M., Trotta, A., Chiappini, H., & Rizzello, A. (2019). Business models for sustainable finance: The case study of Social Impact Bonds. *Sustainability, 11*(7), 1887.

Lagoarde-Segot, T. (2016). Prolegomena to an alternative study of finance. In Paranque, B., & Pérez, R. (Eds.), *Finance Reconsidered: New Perspectives for a Responsible and Sustainable Finance* (Vol. 10, pp. 89–110). Emerald Group Publishing., DOI: 10.1108/S2043-/905920160000010024

Lagoarde-Segot, T. (2019). Sustainable finance. A critical realist perspective. *Research in International Business and Finance, 47*, 1–9.

Lagoarde-Segot, T., & Paranque, B. (2017). Sustainability and the reconstruction of academic finance. *Research in International Business and Finance, 39*, 657–662. DOI: 10.1016/j.ribaf.2016.03.002

Laing, N., Long, C., Marcandalli, A., Matthews, J., Grahovac, A., & Featherby, J. (2012). *The UK Social Investment Market: The Current Landscape and a Framework for Investor Decision Making.* Cambridge Associates.

Lam, P. T. I., & Law, A. O. K. (2016). Crowdfunding for renewable and sustainable energy projects: An exploratory case study approach. *Renewable & Sustainable Energy Reviews*, *60*, 11–20. DOI: 10.1016/j.rser.2016.01.046

Langley, P. (2018). The folds of social finance: Making markets, remaking the social. *Environment and Planning A. Economy and Space*, *52*(1), 130–147. DOI: 10.1177/0308518x17752682

Langley, P. (2020). "The folds of social finance: Making markets, remaking the social." Environment and Planning A. *Economy and Space*, *52*(1), 130–147. DOI: 10.1177/0308518X17752682

Lanzara, F. (2021). Islamic finance as social finance: A bibliometric analysis from 2000 to 2021. *International Journal of Business and Management*, *16*(9), 107. DOI: 10.5539/ijbm.v16n9p107

Larios-Hernández, G. J. (2017). Blockchain entrepreneurship opportunity in the practices of the unbanked. *Business Horizons*, *60*(6), 865–874. DOI: 10.1016/j.bushor.2017.07.012

Larosa, F., & Mysiak, J. (2020). Business models for climate services: An analysis. *Climate Services*, *17*, 100111. DOI: 10.1016/j.cliser.2019.100111

Lauesen, L. M. (2016). The landscape and scale of social and sustainable finance. In Lehner, O. M. (Ed.), *Routledge Handbook of Social and Sustainable Finance* (pp. 5–16). Routledge., DOI: 10.4324/9781315772578

Léautier, F. A. (2018). Can using geographical factors leverage private equity to deliver sustainable development results? In *Africa in the Post-2015 Development Agenda*. Routledge.

Leech, B. (2002). 'Asking Questions: Techniques for Semistructured Interviews'. *PS, Political Science & Politics*, *35*(4), 665–668.

Lee, J. (2021). *Investor Protection on Crowdfunding Platforms*. In *The EU Crowdfunding Regulation*. Oxford University Press. Available at *SSRN*: https://ssrn.com/abstract=3968572

Lehner, O. M. (2013). Crowdfunding social ventures: A model and research agenda. *Venture Capital*, *15*(4), 289–311. DOI: 10.1080/13691066.2013.782624

Lehner, O. M., & Kansikas, J. (2012). Opportunity recognition in social entrepreneurship: A thematic meta-analysis. *The Journal of Entrepreneurship*, *21*(1), 25–58. DOI: 10.1177/097135571102100102

Lehner, O. M., & Nicholls, A. (2014). Social finance and crowdfunding for social enterprises: A public–private case study providing legitimacy and leverage. *Venture Capital*, *16*(3), 271–286. DOI: 10.1080/13691066.2014.925305

Lehner, O. M., & Nicholls, A. (2016). Social finance and crowdfunding for social enterprises: A public–private case study providing legitimacy and leverage. In *Crowdfunding and Entrepreneurial Finance*. Routledge.

Le, T.-L., Abakah, E. J. A., & Tiwari, A. K. (2021). Time and frequency domain connectedness and spill-over among fintech, green bonds and cryptocurrencies in the age of the fourth industrial revolution. *Technological Forecasting and Social Change*, *162*, 120382. DOI: 10.1016/j.techfore.2020.120382 PMID: 33100414

LIU, M. (1993). Progress in documentation the complexities of citation practice: A review of citation studies. *The Journal of Documentation*, *49*(4), 370–408. DOI: 10.1108/eb026920

Liu, M. (2022). The driving forces of green bond market volatility and the response of the market to the COVID-19 pandemic. *Economic Analysis and Policy*, *75*, 288–309. DOI: 10.1016/j.eap.2022.05.012

Liu, Z.-J., Panfilova, E., Mikhaylov, A., & Kurilova, A. (2021). Assessing Stability in the Relationship Between Parties in Crowdfunding and Crowdsourcing Projects During the COVID-19 Crisis. [JGIM]. *Journal of Global Information Management*, *30*(4), 1–18. DOI: 10.4018/JGIM.297905

Lobão, J. (2022). Herding Behavior in the Market for Green Cryptocurrencies: Evidence from CSSD and CSAD Approaches. *Sustainability*, *14*(19), 19. Advance online publication. DOI: 10.3390/su141912542

Lopatta, K., & Tchikov, M. (2016). Do microfinance institutions fulfil their promise? Evidence from cross-country data. *Applied Economics*, *48*(18), 1655–1677. DOI: 10.1080/00036846.2015.1105924

Lopatta, K., & Tchikov, M. (2017). The Causal Relationship of Microfinance and Economic Development: Evidence from Transnational Data. *International Journal of Financial Research*, *8*(3), 3. Advance online publication. DOI: 10.5430/ijfr.v8n3p162

Lopatta, K., Tchikov, M., Jaeschke, R., & Lodhia, S. (2017). Sustainable Development and Microfinance: The Effect of Outreach and Profitability on Microfinance Institutions' Development Mission. *Sustainable Development*, *25*(5), 386–399. DOI: 10.1002/sd.1663

Loraque, J. (2018). 'Development Impact Bonds: Bringing innovation to education development financing and delivery'. *Childhood Education*, *94*(4), 64–68.

Lüdeke-Freund, F., Carroux, S., Joyce, A., Massa, L., & Breuer, H. (2018). The sustainable business model pattern taxonomy—45 patterns to support sustainability-oriented business model innovation. *Sustainable Production and Consumption*, *15*, 145–162. DOI: 10.1016/j.spc.2018.06.004

Luo, W., Tian, Z., Zhong, S., Lyu, Q., & Deng, M. (2022). Global evolution of research on sustainable finance from 2000 to 2021: A bibliometric analysis on wos database. *Sustainability*, *14*(15), 9435. DOI: 10.3390/su14159435

Lyons, T. S., & Kickul, J. R. (2013). The social enterprise financing landscape: The lay of the land and new research on the horizon. *Entrepreneurship Research Journal*, *3*(2), 147–159.

Macchiavello, E., & Siri, M. (2022). Sustainable Finance and Fintech: Can Technology Contribute to Achieving Environmental Goals? A Preliminary Assessment of 'Green Fintech' and 'Sustainable Digital Finance.'. *European Company and Financial Law Review*, *19*(1), 128–174. DOI: 10.1515/ecfr-2022-0005

Maier, F., Barbetta, G. P., & Godina, F. (2018). 'Paradoxes of social impact bonds'. *Social Policy and Administration*, *52*(7), 1332–1353.

Maier, F., Barbetta, G. P., & Godina, F. (2018). Paradoxes of social impact bonds. *Social Policy and Administration*, *52*(7), 1332–1353.

Maier, F., & Meyer, M. (2017). Social Impact Bonds and the Perils of Aligned Interests. *Administrative Sciences*, *7*(3), 24.

Mäkinen, S. J. (2021). Sustainable Disruptive Innovation (SDI): Initiating Systemic Changes by Reconfiguring User Preferences. In *Affordable and Clean Energy* (pp. 1205–1213). Springer International Publishing.

Malamas, V., Dasaklis, T. K., Arakelian, V., & Chondrokoukis, G. (2023). A blockchain framework for digitizing securities issuance: The case of green bonds. *Journal of Sustainable Finance & Investment*, *14*(3), 569–595. DOI: 10.1080/20430795.2023.2275212

Martino, P., Bell, G., Rasheed, A. A., & Bellavitis, C. (2022). Entrepreneurial Finance and Governance. In *Oxford Research Encyclopedia of Business and Management*. https://doi.org/DOI: 10.1093/acrefore/9780190224851.013.384

Mattera, M., & Soto, F. (2023). Dodging the bullet: Overcoming the financial impact of Ukraine armed conflict with sustainable business strategies and environmental approaches. *The Journal of Risk Finance*, *24*(1), 122–142. DOI: 10.1108/JRF-04-2022-0092

Mayor, B., Zorrilla-Miras, P., Coent, P. L., Biffin, T., Dartée, K., Peña, K., Graveline, N., Marchal, R., Nanu, F., Scrieciu, A., Calatrava, J., Manzano, M., & López Gunn, E. (2021). Natural Assurance Schemes Canvas: A Framework to Develop Business Models for Nature-Based Solutions Aimed at Disaster Risk Reduction. *Sustainability, 13*(3). *Articolo, 3*. Advance online publication. DOI: 10.3390/su13031291

Mazumder, M. S. U. (2015). Role of Microfinance in Sustainable Development in Rural Bangladesh. *Sustainable Development, 23*(6), 396–413. DOI: 10.1002/sd.1599

Mc Laren, E. M., & Baldegger, R. (2021). Crowd funders' motivations to support impact-oriented projects. *Journal of the International Council for Small Business, 2*(4), 334–339. DOI: 10.1080/26437015.2021.1938749

McGrath, A. (2023, December 22). *What is corporate social responsibility (CSR)?* IBM - United States. https://www.ibm.com/think/topics/corporate-social-responsibility

McHugh, N., Sinclair, S., Roy, M., Huckfield, L., & Donaldson, C. (2013). Social impact bonds: A wolf in sheep's clothing? *The Journal of Poverty and Social Justice : Research, Policy, Practice, 21*(3), 247–257.

Mejia-Escobar, J. C., González-Ruiz, J. D., & Duque-Grisales, E. (2020). Sustainable Financial Products in the Latin America Banking Industry: Current Status and Insights. *Sustainability, 12*(14), 14. Advance online publication. DOI: 10.3390/su12145648

Meoli, M., & Vismara, S. (2021). Information manipulation in equity crowdfunding markets. *Journal of Corporate Finance, 67*, 101866. DOI: 10.1016/j.jcorpfin.2020.101866

Messeni Petruzzelli, A., Natalicchio, A., Panniello, U., & Roma, P. (2019). Understanding the crowdfunding phenomenon and its implications for sustainability. *Technological Forecasting and Social Change, 141*, 138–148. DOI: 10.1016/j.techfore.2018.10.002

Metawa, N., Dogan, E., & Taskin, D. (2022). Analyzing the nexus of green economy, clean and financial technology. *Economic Analysis and Policy, 76*, 385–396. DOI: 10.1016/j.eap.2022.08.023

Meyer, J., & Krauss, A. (2021). The social performance of microfinance investment vehicles. *Journal of Sustainable Finance & Investment, 11*(2), 163–186. DOI: 10.1080/20430795.2020.1715094

Mia, M. A., Zhang, M., Zhang, C., & Kim, Y. (2019). Are microfinance institutions in South-East Asia pursuing objectives of greening the environment? In *Climate Change Mitigation and Sustainable Development*. Routledge.

Migliavacca, M., Patel, R., Paltrinieri, A., & Goodell, J. W. (2022). Mapping impact investing: A bibliometric analysis. *Journal of International Financial Markets, Institutions and Money*, *81*, 101679. DOI: 10.1016/j.intfin.2022.101679

Miles, I., Kastrinos, N., Bilderbeek, R., den Hertog, P., Flanagan, K., Huntink, W., & Bouman, M. (1995). *Knowledge-intensive business services: Users, carriers and sources of innovation*. https://research.manchester.ac.uk/en/publications/knowledge-intensive-business-services-users-carriers-and-sources-

Mintz-Woo, K., Dennig, F., Liu, H., & Schinko, T. (2021). Carbon pricing and COVID-19. *Climate Policy*, *21*(10), 1272–1280. DOI: 10.1080/14693062.2020.1831432

Mishra, A. K., & Dash, A. K. (2022). 'Development impact bonds in developing countries: An emerging innovation for achieving social outcomes'. *Journal of Social and Economic Development*, •••, 1–27. PMID: 36532830

Misra, N., Gupta, S., & Rao, T. J. (2024). Fintech's role in green finance: Procuring funds for sustainable energy. *International Research Journal of Multidisciplinary Scope*, *5*(02), 290–312.

Mollick, E. (2012). The dynamics of crowdfunding: Determinants of success and failure. *Journal of Business Venturing*, *29*(1), 1–16.

Mollick, E. (2014). The dynamics of crowdfunding: An exploratory study. *Journal of Business Venturing*, *29*(1), 1–16. DOI: 10.1016/j.jbusvent.2013.06.005

Montalván-Burbano, N., Velastegui-Montoya, A., Gurumendi-Noriega, M., Morante-Carballo, F., & Adami, M. (2021). Worldwide Research on Land Use and Land Cover in the Amazon Region. *Sustainability*, *13*(11), 11. Advance online publication. DOI: 10.3390/su13116039

Montgomery, H., & Weiss, J. (2011). Can Commercially-oriented Microfinance Help Meet the Millennium Development Goals? Evidence from Pakistan. *World Development*, *39*(1), 87–109. DOI: 10.1016/j.worlddev.2010.09.001

Moore, M. L., Westley, F. R., & Nicholls, A. (2012). The social finance and social innovation nexus. *Journal of Social Entrepreneurship*, *3*(2), 115–132. DOI: 10.1080/19420676.2012.725824

Morduch, J. (1999). The Microfinance Promise. *Journal of Economic Literature*, *37*(4), 1569–1614. DOI: 10.1257/jel.37.4.1569

Morgan, P. J. (2022). Assessing the Risks Associated with Green Digital Finance and Policies for Coping with Them. In Taghizadeh-Hesary, F., & Hyun, S. (Eds.), *Green Digital Finance and Sustainable Development Goals* (pp. 51–68). Springer Nature., DOI: 10.1007/978-981-19-2662-4_3

Morley, J. (2019). The ethical status of social impact bonds. *Journal of Economic Policy Reform*, *22*(3), 231–246.

Moro-Visconti, R., Cruz Rambaud, S., & López Pascual, J. (2020). Sustainability in FinTechs: An Explanation through Business Model Scalability and Market Valuation. *Sustainability*, *12*(24), 24. Advance online publication. DOI: 10.3390/su122410316

Morschheuser, B., Hamari, J., & Maedche, A. (2019). Cooperation or competition – When do people contribute more? A field experiment on gamification of crowdsourcing. *International Journal of Human-Computer Studies*, *127*, 7–24. DOI: 10.1016/j.ijhcs.2018.10.001

Motylska-Kuzma, A. (2018). Crowdfunding and Sustainable Development. *Sustainability*, *10*(12), 12. Advance online publication. DOI: 10.3390/su10124650

Municipality of Milan—Permanent citizens' assembly on the climate—Milan Cambia Aria -. (s.d.). Milan Municipality. Recuperato 9 luglio 2024, da https://www.comune.milano.it/en/web/milano-cambia-aria/cosa-puoi-fare-tu/sei-una-cittadina-o-un-cittadino/assemblea-permanente-dei-cittadini-sul-clima

Muñoz, P., & Kimmitt, J. (2019). 'A diagnostic framework for social impact bonds in emerging economies'. *Journal of Business Venturing Insights*, *12*, e00141.

Naeem, M. A., & Karim, S. (2021). Tail dependence between bitcoin and green financial assets. *Economics Letters*, *208*, 110068. DOI: 10.1016/j.econlet.2021.110068

Naeem, M. A., Karim, S., Rabbani, M. R., Bashar, A., & Kumar, S. (2022). Current state and future directions of green and sustainable finance: A bibliometric analysis. *Qualitative Research in Financial Markets*, *15*(4), 608–629. DOI: 10.1108/qrfm-10-2021-0174

Nakamoto, S. (2008). Bitcoin: A peer-to-peer electronic cash system. *Satoshi Nakamoto*. https://static.upbitcare.com/931b8bfc-f0e0-4588-be6e-b98a27991df1.pdf

Nativi, S., & Craglia, M. (2020, novembre 10). *Destination Earth: Use Cases Analysis*. JRC Publications Repository. https://doi.org/DOI: 10.2760/17457

Nazari Chamaki, F., Jenkins, G. P., & Hashemi, M. (2019). Social Impact Bonds: Implementation, Evaluation, and Monitoring. *International Journal of Public Administration*, *42*(4), 289–297.

NFGS. (2019). *A call for action: Climate change as a source of financial risk.* https://www.tcfdhub.org/resource/a-call-for-action-climate-change-as-a-source-of-financial-risk/

Ng, A., Mirakhor, A., & Ibrahim, M. H. (2015). Risk sharing and social impact partnerships. In *Social Capital and Risk Sharing* (pp. 133–156). Palgrave Macmillan.

Nguyen, T., Choudhury, M., & Okafor, N. (2023). Blockchain-enabled crowdfunding for sustainable energy: An empirical analysis. *Energy Finance Journal, 18*(2), 112–130.

Niaz, M. U. (2022). Socio-Economic development and sustainable development goals: A roadmap from vulnerability to sustainability through financial inclusion. *Economic Research-Ekonomska Istraživanja, 35*(1), 3243–3275. DOI: 10.1080/1331677X.2021.1989319

Nicholls, A., & Emerson, J. (2015). Social finance. *Social Finance*, 1-42. https://doi.org/DOI: 10.1093/acprof:oso/9780198703761.003.0001

Nicholls, A., & Tomkinson, E. (2015). Risk and return in social. *Social Finance*, 282.

Nicholls, A. (2010). The legitimacy of social entrepreneurship: Reflexive isomorphism in a pre-paradigmatic field. *Entrepreneurship Theory and Practice, 34*(4), 611–633. DOI: 10.1111/j.1540-6520.2010.00397.x

Nicholls, A., Paton, R., & Emerson, J. (2015). *Social finance.* Oxford University Press.

Nicken, D., Zulfikar, R., Mulyasari, W., & Ismawati, I. (2024). Financial Sustainability for a Sustainable Future: A Bibliometric Analysis. *International Journal of Sustainable Development and Planning*, 4653-4662. https://iieta.org/journals/ijsdp/paper/10.18280/ijsdp.191213

Nilsson, F. (2021). *Anticipating Environmental Change in Local Climate Governance: A Case Study of Gothenburg, Sweden* [B]. https://campus-fryslan.studenttheses.ub.rug.nl/70/

Noreen, U., Imran, R., Zaheer, A., & Saif, M. I. (2011). Impact of microfinance on poverty: A case of Pakistan. *World Applied Sciences Journal, 12*(6), 877–883.

Norris, M., & Oppenheim, C. (2007). Comparing alternatives to the Web of Science for coverage of the social sciences' literature. *Journal of Informetrics, 1*(2), 161–169. DOI: 10.1016/j.joi.2006.12.001

Novethic. (2025). Overview of European sustainable finance labels: Recalibration or identity crisis? *Novethic.* https://www.novethic.fr/decryptages-dexpert/etudes/panorama-des-labels-europeens-de-finance-durable-edition-2025

NSF [National Science Foundation]. (2010). *The 2010 User-Friendly Handbook for Project Evaluation.*

O'Donohoe, N., Leijonhufvud, C., Saltuk, Y., Bugg-Levine, A., & Brandenburg, M. (2010). Impact investments. *An Emerging Asset Class*, *96*, 1–96.

O'Flynn, L., Schweinsberg, S., & Wearing, S. (2022). Financing Protected Areas: The Social and Environmental Impact Bond's Role in Terrestrial Protected Area Sustainability. *Journal of Park and Recreation Administration*, *40*(3), 123–139. DOI: 10.18666/JPRA-2021-10870

OECD. (2017). *Mobilising financing for the transition.* OECD., DOI: 10.1787/9789264273528-9-

OECD. (2024). *Better policies for better lives.* OECD. https://www.oecd.org/en.html

Olson, H., Painter, G., Albertson, K., Fox, C., & O'Leary, C. (2022). 'Are Social Impact Bonds an innovation in finance or do they help finance social innovation?'. *Journal of Social Policy*, •••, 1–25.

Olumekor, M., & Oke, A. (2024). Support for sustainable finance and investment in Europe. *Journal of Cleaner Production*, *449*, 141769. DOI: 10.1016/j.jclepro.2024.141769

Olutimehin, A. T. (2025). Assessing the effectiveness of cybersecurity frameworks in mitigating cyberattacks in the banking sector and its applicability to decentralized finance (DeFi). Available at *SSRN* 5133050.

Ometto, M. P., Gegenhuber, T., Winter, J., & Greenwood, R. (2019). From balancing missions to mission drift: The role of the institutional context, spaces, and compartmentalization in the scaling of social enterprises. *Business & Society*, *58*(5), 1003–1046.

O'Neil, S., Vohra, D., Spitzer, M., Kalyanwala, S., & Rotz, D. (2021). *Maternal Health Care Quality Improvement in Rajasthan, India: A Series of Insights from a Development Impact Bond Verification Agent.* Mathematica.

Ormiston, J., Moran, M., Castellas, E. I., & Tomkinson, E. (2020). 'Everybody wins? A discourse analysis of competing stakeholder expectations in Social Impact Bonds'. *Public Money & Management*, *40*(3), 237–246.

Ormiston, J., Moran, M., Castellas, E. I., & Tomkinson, E. (2020). Everybody wins? A discourse analysis of competing stakeholder expectations in social impact bonds. *Public Money & Management*, *40*(3), 237–246.

Oroxom, R., Glassman, A., & McDonald, L. (2018). *Structuring and funding development impact bonds for health: nine lessons from Cameroon and beyond*. Center for Global Development.

Ortas, E., Burritt, R. L., & Moneva, J. M. (2013). Socially Responsible Investment and cleaner production in the Asia Pacific: Does it pay to be good? *Journal of Cleaner Production*, *52*, 272–280. DOI: 10.1016/j.jclepro.2013.02.024

Osborne, S. P. (2006). 'The New Public Governance?'. *Public Management Review*, *8*(3), 377–387.

Osterwalder, A., & Pigneur, Y. (2010). *Business Model Generation: A Handbook for Visionaries, Game Changers, and Challengers*. John Wiley & Sons.

Osterwalder, A., Pigneur, Y., & Tucci, C. L. (2005a). Clarifying Business Models: Origins, Present, and Future of the Concept. *Communications of the Association for Information Systems*, *16*. Advance online publication. DOI: 10.17705/1CAIS.01601

Over 540 million bank accounts opened under Pradhan Mantri Jan Dhan Yojana. (2024, December 12). *Mint*. https://www.livemint.com/industry/banking/pradhan-mantri-jan-dhan-yojana-jan-dhan-accounts-financial-inclusion-financial-literacy-msmes-credit-gap-rupay-11733996410678.html

Ozcan, R. (2021). Decentralized Finance. In Hacioglu, U., & Aksoy, T. (Eds.), *Financial Ecosystem and Strategy in the Digital Era: Global Approaches and New Opportunities* (pp. 57–75). Springer International Publishing., DOI: 10.1007/978-3-030-72624-9_4

Ozili, P. K. (2021). Digital finance, green finance and social finance: Is there a link? SSRN *Electronic Journal*. https://doi.org/DOI: 10.2139/ssrn.3786881

Ozili, P. K. (2021). Digital Finance, Green Finance and Social Finance: Is there a Link? *Financial Internet Quarterly*, *17*(1), 1–7. DOI: 10.2478/fiqf-2021-0001

Ozili, P. K. (2022). Assessing global interest in decentralized finance, embedded finance, open finance, ocean finance and sustainable finance. *Asian Journal of Economics and Banking*, *7*(2), 197–216. DOI: 10.1108/AJEB-03-2022-0029

Ozili, P. K. (2024). *Social finance: What is social about it*. Reference Module in Social Sciences., DOI: 10.1016/b978-0-44-313776-1.00286-5

Palshikar, G. K. (2007). Keyword Extraction from a Single Document Using Centrality Measures. In Ghosh, A., De, R. K., & Pal, S. K. (Eds.), *Pattern Recognition and Machine Intelligence* (pp. 503–510). Springer., DOI: 10.1007/978-3-540-77046-6_62

Paltrinieri, A., Hassan, M. K., Bahoo, S., & Khan, A. (2019). A bibliometric review of sukuk literature. *International Review of Economics & Finance, 86*, 897–918. DOI: 10.1016/j.iref.2019.04.004

Pandey, N. (2012). Human resources. *Management and Labour Studies, 37*(4), 323–335. DOI: 10.1177/0258042x13484869

Pandey, S., Cordes, J. J., Pandey, S. K., & Winfrey, W. F. (2018). Use of social impact bonds to address social problems: Understanding contractual risks and transaction costs. *Nonprofit Management & Leadership, 28*(4), 511–528.

Pappalardo, M. (2024). The SRI label, an evolving tool to help investors and savers participate in sustainable finance. (I. MinesTélécom, Ed.) *Sustainable finance*, 38-42. https://doi.org/DOI: 10.3917/rindu1.243.0038

Park, K., & Jun, H. (2024). Win-win or tradeoff? Investigating the hybridity of impact investing in Cambodia's microfinance industry. *Journal of International Development, n/a*(n/a). https://doi.org/DOI: 10.1002/jid.3954

Passador, M. L. (2023). *Crowdfunding Regulation*. In *The Palgrave Encyclopedia of Private Equity* (edited by D. Cumming & B. Hammer, forthcoming 2024). Palgrave Macmillan. Available at *SSRN*: https://ssrn.com/abstract=4603816

Patel, N., & Wang, L. (2020). Blockchain and decentralized finance: Transforming energy markets and investment structures. *Energy Economics, 42*(6), 102–118.

Patel, R., Migliavacca, M., & Oriani, M. E. (2022). Blockchain in banking and finance: A bibliometric review. *Research in International Business and Finance, 62*, 101718. DOI: 10.1016/j.ribaf.2022.101718

Pearson, M. (2011). *Results based aid and results based financing: What are they? Have they delivered results*. HLSP Institute.

Pereira, Á., & Vence, X. (2021). The role of KIBS and consultancy in the emergence of Circular Oriented Innovation. *Journal of Cleaner Production, 302*, 127000. DOI: 10.1016/j.jclepro.2021.127000

Pereira, G. I., Niesten, E., & Pinkse, J. (2022). Sustainable energy systems in the making: A study on business model adaptation in incumbent utilities. *Technological Forecasting and Social Change, 174*, 121207.

Pham, L., Huynh, T. L. D., & Hanif, W. (2023). Time-varying asymmetric spillovers among cryptocurrency, green and fossil-fuel investments. *Global Finance Journal, 58*, 100891. DOI: 10.1016/j.gfj.2023.100891

Phillips, W., Lee, H., Ghobadian, A., O'Regan, N., & James, P. (2015). Social innovation and social entrepreneurship: A systematic review. *Group & Organization Management, 40*(3), 428–461. DOI: 10.1177/1059601114560063

Piñeiro-Chousa, J., López-Cabarcos, M. Á., Sevic, A., & González-López, I. (2022). A preliminary assessment of the performance of DeFi cryptocurrencies in relation to other financial assets, volatility, and user-generated content. *Technological Forecasting and Social Change, 181*, 121740.

Pizzi, S., Rosati, F., & Venturelli, A. (2021). The determinants of business contribution to the 2030 Agenda: Introducing the SDG reporting score. *Business Strategy and the Environment, 30*(1), 404–421. DOI: 10.1002/bse.2628

Podsakoff, P. M., MacKenzie, S. B., Bachrach, D. G., & Podsakoff, N. P. (2005). The influence of management journals in the 1980s and 1990s. *Strategic Management Journal, 26*(5), 473–488. DOI: 10.1002/smj.454

Popescu, A. D. (2020). Decentralised finance (defi)–the lego of finance. *Social Sciences and Education Research Review, 7*(1), 321–349.

Popescu, A.-D. (2020). Decentralized finance (defi) – The lego of finance. *Social Sciences and Education Research Review, 7*(1), 321–349.

Pretty, J. N., Williams, S., & Toulmin, C. (2011). Sustainable intensification: Increasing productivity in African food and agricultural systems. *International Journal of Agricultural Sustainability, 9*(1), 3–289. DOI: 10.3763/ijas.2011.91ED

Price, D. J. (1965). Networks of scientific papers. *Science, 149*(3683), 510–515. DOI: 10.1126/science.149.3683.510 PMID: 14325149

Prior, F., & Argandoña, A. (2009). Credit accessibility and corporate social responsibility in financial institutions: The case of microfinance. *Business Ethics (Oxford, England), 18*(4), 349–363. DOI: 10.1111/j.1467-8608.2009.01568.x

Purnomo, A., Sari, A. K., Susanti, T., Mannan, S. S., & Lumentut, T. M. (2021). Sustainable finance study of bibliometric overview. *IOP Conference Series. Earth and Environmental Science, 729*(1), 012124. DOI: 10.1088/1755-1315/729/1/012124

Puschmann, T., Hoffmann, C. H., & Khmarskyi, V. (2020). How green FinTech can alleviate the impact of climate change—The case of Switzerland. *Sustainability, 12*(24), 10691.

PwC. (2023). *Global Crypto Regulation Report*. Retrieved from https://www.pwc.com/gx/en/new-ventures/cryptocurrency-assets/pwc-global-crypto-regulation-report-2023.pdf

Rabbani, M. R., Bashar, A., Nawaz, N., Karim, S., & Ali, M. A. Mohd., Rahiman, H. U., & Alam, Md. S. (2021). Exploring the Role of Islamic Fintech in Combating the Aftershocks of COVID-19: The Open Social Innovation of the Islamic Financial System. *Journal of Open Innovation*, *7*(2), 136. DOI: 10.3390/joitmc7020136

Raineri, E. M., & Reno, L. S. E. (2022). A Study of Crowdsourcing in Undergraduate Entrepreneurship Education. *Journal of Higher Education Theory and Practice*, *22*(5), 5. https://articlearchives.co/index.php/JHETP/article/view/3398

Ramos-Rodríguez, A.-R., & Ruíz-Navarro, J. (2004). Changes in the intellectual structure of strategic management research: A bibliometric study of the Strategic Management Journal, 1980–2000. *Strategic Management Journal*, *25*(10), 981–1004. DOI: 10.1002/smj.397

Ravi, S., Gustafsson-Wright, E., Sharma, P., & Boggild-Jones, I. (2019). *The Promise of Impact Investing in India*. Brookings India Research Paper No. 062019. Brookings Institution India Center: New Delhi, India.

Ren, Y.-S., Ma, C.-Q., Chen, X.-Q., Lei, Y.-T., & Wang, Y.-R. (2023). Sustainable finance and blockchain: A systematic review and research agenda. *Research in International Business and Finance*, *64*, 101871. DOI: 10.1016/j.ribaf.2022.101871

Rey-Martí, A., Mohedano-Suanes, A., & Simón-Moya, V. (2019). Crowdfunding and social entrepreneurship: Spotlight on intermediaries. *Sustainability*, *11*(4), 1175.

Rhee, W. W., & Ha, H. (2022). Does public-loan management matter for sustainable finance and operation risk? *Sustainability*, *14*(3), 1453. DOI: 10.3390/su14031453

Richter, C. (2015). Crowdcreation as a dimension of crowdsourcing: Conditions for entrepreneurs. *International Journal of Entrepreneurial Venturing*, *7*(4), 324–340. DOI: 10.1504/IJEV.2015.073645

Richter, M. (2013). Business model innovation for sustainable energy: German utilities and renewable energy. *Energy Policy*, *62*, 1226–1237.

Rijpens, J., Bouchard, M. J., Gruet, E., & Salathe-Beaulieu, G. (2020). *Social impact bonds: Promises versus facts. What does the recent scientific literature tell us?* (Working Paper, CIREC 2020/15) Liege University.

Rios, J., & Zhang, X. (2021). Blockchain technology and decentralized finance: A critical review of its implications for investment and energy markets. *Journal of Financial Innovation*, *8*(2), 1–19.

Rizzello, A., & Kabli, A. (2020). Social finance and sustainable development goals: A literature synthesis, current approaches and research agenda. *ACRN Journal of Finance and Risk Perspectives, 9.*

Rizzello, A., & Kabli, A. (2020). Social Finance and Sustainable Development Goals: A Literature Synthesis, Current Approaches and Research Agenda. *ACRN Journal of Finance and Risk Perspectives, 9.*

Rizzello, A., & Carè, R. (2016). Insight into the social impact bond market: An analysis of investors. *ACRN Oxford Journal of Finance and Risk Perspectives*, *5*(3), 145–171.

Rizzello, A., & Kabli, A. (2020). 'Sustainable Financial Partnerships for the SDGs: The Case of Social Impact Bonds'. *Sustainability (Basel, Switzerland)*, *12*(13), 5362.

Rizzi, F., Pellegrini, C., & Battaglia, M. (2018). The structuring of social finance: Emerging approaches for supporting environmentally and socially impactful projects. *Journal of Cleaner Production*, *170*, 805–817. DOI: 10.1016/j.jclepro.2017.09.167

Robert, F. C., Frey, L. M., & Sisodia, G. S. (2021). Village development framework through self-help-group entrepreneurship, microcredit, and anchor customers in solar microgrids for cooperative sustainable rural societies. *Journal of Rural Studies*, *88*, 432–440. DOI: 10.1016/j.jrurstud.2021.07.013

Robison, R. (2006). *Neo-liberalism and the market state: What is the ideal shell?* Palgrave Macmillan.

Rogers, D. P., Staudinger, M., Tsirkunov, V., Suwa, M., & Kootval, H. (2022). *Affordability of National Meteorological and Hydrological Services*. GFDRR.

Rogers, D., Bogdanova, A.-M., Tsirkunov, V., & Suwa, M. (2021). *Public and Private Engagement in Hydromet Services: From Rivalry to Coproduction in Meteorological and Hydrological Service Delivery*. GFDRR.

Rogers, P. J. (2000). 'Causal models in program theory evaluation'. *New Directions for Evaluation*, *2000*(87), 47–55.

Rohrbeck, R., Konnertz, L., & Knab, S. (2013). Collaborative business modelling for systemic and sustainability innovations. *International Journal of Technology Management*. https://www.inderscienceonline.com/doi/10.1504/IJTM.2013.055577

Rosati, F., & Faria, L. G. D. (2019). Addressing the SDGs in sustainability reports: The relationship with institutional factors. *Journal of Cleaner Production*, *215*, 1312–1326. DOI: 10.1016/j.jclepro.2018.12.107

Rotolo, D., Rafols, I., Hopkins, M. M., & Leydesdorff, L. (2017). Strategic intelligence on emerging technologies: Scientometric overlay mapping. *Journal of the Association for Information Science and Technology, 68*(1), 214–233. DOI: 10.1002/asi.23631

Roundy, P., Holzhauer, H., & Dai, Y. (2017). Finance or philanthropy? Exploring the motivations and criteria of impact investors. *Social Responsibility Journal, 13*(3), 491–512.

Rubio-Martin, A., Mañez Costa, M., Pulido-Velazquez, M., Garcia-Prats, A., Celliers, L., Llario, F., & Macian, J. (2021). Structuring Climate Service Co-Creation Using a Business Model Approach. *Earth's Future, 9*(10), e2021EF002181. https://doi.org/DOI: 10.1029/2021EF002181

Ruiz-Parrado, V., Heradio, R., Aranda-Escolastico, E., Sánchez, Á., & Vélez, J. F. (2022). A bibliometric analysis of off-line handwritten document analysis literature (1990–2020). *Pattern Recognition, 125*, 108513.

Rupeika-Apoga, R., & Thalassinos, E. I. (2020). *Ideas for a regulatory definition of FinTech.* https://www.um.edu.mt/library/oar/handle/123456789/55195

Rush, B., & Ogborne, A. (1991). 'Program logic models: Expanding their role and structure for program planning and evaluation'. *The Canadian Journal of Program Evaluation, 6*(2), 95.

Saha, S., Kermode, M., & Annear, P. L. (2015). Effect of combining a health program with a microfinance-based self-help group on health behaviors and outcomes. *Public Health, 129*(11), 1510–1518. DOI: 10.1016/j.puhe.2015.07.010 PMID: 26304181

Santiago, V., Charifzadeh, M., & Herberger, T. A. (2025). Risks of decentralized finance and their potential negative effects on capital markets: The Terra-Luna case. *Studies in Economics and Finance, 42*(3), 427–448.

Sas, A., Lw, M., & Sm, M. (2019). Comparing Bibliometric Analysis Using PubMed, Scopus, and Web of Science Databases. *Journal of Visualized Experiments, 152*. Advance online publication. DOI: 10.3791/58494

Savell, L., & Eddleston, C. (2021). Cameroon Kangaroo Mother Care Development Impact Bond 2018- 2021: End of programme report. Social Finance. Retrieved April 27, 2023, from https://www.socialfinance.org.uk/sites/default/files/publications/cameroon_kmc_development_impact_bond_report_-_en.pdf

Schaltegger, S. (2002). A Framework for Ecopreneurship: Leading Bioneers and Environmental Managers to Ecopreneurship. *Greener Management International, 38*, 45–58.

Schaltegger, S., & Wagner, M. (2011). Sustainable entrepreneurship and sustainability innovation: Categories and interactions. *Business Strategy and the Environment*, *20*(4), 222–237. DOI: 10.1002/bse.682

Schaper, M. (2010). Understanding the Green Entrepreneur. In *Making Ecopreneurs* (2nd ed.). Routledge.

Schär, F. (2021). *Decentralized Finance: On Blockchain- and Smart Contract-Based Financial Markets* (SSRN Scholarly Paper 3843844). Social Science Research Network. https://doi.org/DOI: 10.20955/r.103.153-74

Schinckus, C. (2017). Financial innovation as a potential force for a positive social change: The challenging future of social impact bonds. *Research in International Business and Finance*, *39*, 727–736.

Schinckus, C. (2018). The valuation of social impact bonds: An introductory perspective with the Peterborough SIB. *International Review of Financial Analysis*, *59*, 1–6.

Schoenmaker, D., & Schramade, W. (2019). Investing for long-term value creation. *Journal of Sustainable Finance & Investment*, *9*(4), 356–377. DOI: 10.1080/20430795.2019.1625012

Schreiner, M. (2002). Aspects of outreach: A framework for discussion of the social benefits of microfinance. *Journal of International Development*, *14*(5), 591–603. DOI: 10.1002/jid.908

Scognamiglio, E., Di Lorenzo, E., Sibillo, M., & Trotta, A. (2019). Social uncertainty evaluation in Social Impact Bonds: Review and framework. *Research in International Business and Finance*, *47*, 40–56.

Scott, B. (2016). *How can cryptocurrency and blockchain technology play a role in building social and solidarity finance?* (Working Paper 2016–1). UNRISD Working Paper. https://www.econstor.eu/handle/10419/148750

SEC. (2024). *Securities and Exchange Commission*. https://www.sec.gov/newsroom/press-releases/2022-46

Setyowati, A. B. (2020). Governing sustainable finance: Insights from Indonesia. *Climate Policy*, *23*(1), 108–121. DOI: 10.1080/14693062.2020.1858741

Seychelles launches world's first sovereign blue bond. (2018, October 29). World Bank. https://www.worldbank.org/en/news/press-release/2018/10/29/seychelles-launches-worlds-first-sovereign-blue-bond

Shafer, S. M., Smith, H. J., & Linder, J. C. (2005). The power of business models. *Business Horizons*, *48*(3), 199–207. DOI: 10.1016/j.bushor.2004.10.014

Shahid, M., Sulub, Y. A., Mohtesham, M. M., & Abdullah, M. (2023). Analyzing the commonalities between Islamic social finance and sustainable development goals. *International Journal of Ethics and Systems*, *40*(2), 381–394. DOI: 10.1108/ijoes-04-2022-0082

Shaikh, S. A. (2020). Using Fintech in scaling up Islamic microfinance. *Journal of Islamic Accounting and Business Research*, *12*(2), 186–203. DOI: 10.1108/JIABR-10-2019-0198

Sharma, G. D., Tiwari, A. K., Chopra, R., & Dev, D. (2024). 'Past, present, and future of block-chain in finance'. *Journal of Business Research*, *177*, 114640.

Sharma, G. D., Tiwari, A. K., Chopra, R., & Dev, D. (2024). Past, present, and future of block-chain in finance. *Journal of Business Research*, *177*, 114640. DOI: 10.1016/j.jbusres.2024.114640

Shashi, Centobelli, P., Cerchione, R., & Mittal, A. (2020). Managing sustainability in luxury industry to pursue circular economy strategies. *Business Strategy and the Environment*, *30*(1), 432–462. DOI: 10.1002/bse.2630

Siano, A., Raimi, L., Palazzo, M., & Panait, M. C. (2020). Mobile Banking: An Innovative Solution for Increasing Financial Inclusion in Sub-Saharan African Countries: Evidence from Nigeria. *Sustainability*, *12*(23), 10130. DOI: 10.3390/su122310130

Siemiatycki, M., & Farooqi, N. (2012). Value for money and risk in public–private partnerships: Evaluating the evidence. *Journal of the American Planning Association*, *78*(3), 286–299.

Silva, H. P., Lehoux, P., & Sabio, R. P. (2024). The multifaceted role of social finance in supporting social entrepreneurship: A qualitative inquiry into business tools and value-adding and subtracting activities. *Journal of Social Entrepreneurship*, •••, 1–26. DOI: 10.1080/19420676.2024.2418867

Sinclair, S., McHugh, N., & Roy, M. J. (2021). 'Social innovation, financialisation and commodification: A critique of social impact bonds'. *Journal of Economic Policy Reform*, *24*(1), 11–27.

Sinclair, S., McHugh, N., & Roy, M. J. (2021). Social innovation, financialisation and commodification: A critique of social impact bonds. *Journal of Economic Policy Reform*, *24*(1), 11–27.

Sinclair, S., McHugh, N., & Roy, M. J. (2021). Social innovation, financialization and commodification: A critique of social impact bonds. *Journal of Economic Policy Reform*, *24*(1), 11–27.

Singh, A., & Singh, S. (2023). Regulatory frameworks for decentralized finance in energy investments: Challenges and opportunities. *Journal of Energy Regulation and Policy*, *12*(1), 89–101.

Singhania, M., Chadha, G., & Prasad, R. (2023). Sustainable finance research: Review and agenda. *International Journal of Finance & Economics*, *29*(4), 4010–4045. DOI: 10.1002/ijfe.2854

Singh, D., & Stakic, N. (2021). Financial inclusion and economic growth nexus: Evidence from SAARC countries. *South Asia Research*, *41*(2), 238–258. DOI: 10.1177/0262728020964605

Singh, V. K., Singh, P., Karmakar, M., Leta, J., & Mayr, P. (2021). The journal coverage of Web of Science, Scopus and Dimensions: A comparative analysis. *Scientometrics*, *126*(6), 5113–5142. DOI: 10.1007/s11192-021-03948-5

Sisodia, A., & Maheshwari, G. C. (2023). Exploring sustainable finance: A review and future research agenda. *Vision: The Journal of Business Perspective*. https://doi.org/DOI: 10.1177/09722629231209177

Small, H. (1973). Co-citation in the scientific literature: A new measure of the relationship between two documents. *Journal of the American Society for Information Science*, *24*(4), 265–269. DOI: 10.1002/asi.4630240406

Smith, L., Kim, D., & Mwangi, J. (2023). Decentralized finance and peer-to-peer energy systems: A case study from Kenya. *International Journal of Green Finance*, *9*(4), 178–196.

Snick, A. (2021). Social finance in the Anthropocene. In Walker, T., McGaughey, J., Goubran, S., & Wagdy, N. (Eds.), *Innovations in Social Finance* (pp. 13–34). Palgrave Macmillan., DOI: 10.1007/978-3-030-72535-8_2

So, I., & Jagelewski, A. (2013). *Social Impact Bond: Technical Guide for Service Providers*. MaRS Centre for Impact Investing.

Social Finance, U. K. (2016). *Social Impact Bond. The Early Years*. Retrieved from https://www.socialfinance.org.uk/sites/default/files/publications/sibs-early-years_social_finance_2016_final.pdf

Solesbury, W. (2003). *Sustainable livelihoods: A case study of the evolution of DFID policy*. Overseas Development Institute London. https://cdn.odi.org/media/documents/172.pdf

Spiess-Knafl, W., & Jansen, S. A. (2014). Social enterprises and the financing of different scaling strategies. *Emerging research directions in social entrepreneurship*, 67-83.

Spiller, P. T. (2008). *An Institutional Theory of Public Contracts: Regulatory Implications (No. w14152)*. National Bureau of Economic Research.

Staccione, A., Brown, C., Arneth, A., Rounsevell, M., Hrast Essenfelder, A., Seo, B., & Mysiak, J. (2023). Exploring the effects of protected area networks on the European land system. *Journal of Environmental Management, 337*, 117741. DOI: 10.1016/j.jenvman.2023.117741 PMID: 36966632

Stid, D. (2013). Pay for success is not a panacea. *Community Development Investment Review, 9*(1), 13–18.

Stolz, D., & Lai, K. P. Y. (2020). Impact Investing, Social Enterprise and Global Development. In *The Routledge International Handbook of Financialization*. Routledge.

Stone Family Foundation, & iDE. (n.d.). The Cambodia Rural Sanitation Development Impact Bond: Two Years of Delivering Results through Innovative Finance. Retrieved April 27, 2023, from https://www.thesff.com/wp-content/uploads/2022/05/Cambodia-Rural-Sanitation-Development-Impact-Bond-Year-2-Report.pdf

Streimikiene, D., Mikalauskiene, A., & Burbaite, G. (2023). The role of sustainable finance in achieving sustainable development goals. *Economia e Sociologia, 16*(1), 271–298. DOI: 10.14254/2071-789x.2023/16-1/17

Strid, A. A. (2021). *Cameroon Cataract Bond: A case study produced as part of the Cameroon Cataract Bond Evaluation*. The Government Outcomes Lab. Retrieved April 27, 2023, from https://golab.bsg.ox.ac.uk/knowledge-bank/resource-library/cameroon-cataract-bond-eval/

Suprayitno, D., Iskandar, S., Dahurandi, K., Hendarto, T., & Rumambi, J. (s.d.). *Public Policy In The Era Of Climate Change: Adapting Strategies For Sustainable Futures*.

Suryono, R. R., Budi, I., & Purwandari, B. (2020). Challenges and Trends of Financial Technology (Fintech): A Systematic Literature Review. *Information (Basel), 11*(12), 12. Advance online publication. DOI: 10.3390/info11120590

Sustainability-related disclosure in the financial services sector. (2024, May 3). Finance. https://finance.ec.europa.eu/sustainable-finance/disclosures/sustainability-related-disclosure-financial-services-sector_en

Svartzman, R., Bolton, P., Despres, M., Pereira Da Silva, L. A., & Samama, F. (2020). Central banks, financial stability and policy coordination in the age of climate uncertainty: A three-layered analytical and operational framework. *Climate Policy*, *21*(4), 563–580. DOI: 10.1080/14693062.2020.1862743

Swamy, V., & Tulasimala, B. K. (2011). Financial Intermediaries and Economic Development: Evidence on Transaction Costs of Borrowing by the Poor. *International Journal of Banking and Finance*, *8*(3), 3.

Swart, R., Celliers, L., Collard, M., Prats, A. G., Huang-Lachmann, J.-T., Sempere, F. L., de Jong, F., Máñez Costa, M., Martinez, G., Velazquez, M. P., Martín, A. R., Segretier, W., Stattner, E., & Timmermans, W. (2021a). Reframing climate services to support municipal and regional planning. *Climate Services*, *22*, 100227. DOI: 10.1016/j.cliser.2021.100227

Szennay, Á., Szigeti, C., Kovács, N., & Szabó, D. R. (2019). Through the blurry looking glass—SDGs in the GRI reports. *Resources*, *8*(2), 101.

Talan, G., & Sharma, G. D. (2019). Doing well by doing good: A systematic review and research agenda for sustainable investment. *Sustainability*, *11*(2), 353. DOI: 10.3390/su11020353

Tang, S., & Dessai, S. (2012). *Usable Science? The U.K. Climate Projections 2009 and Decision Support for Adaptation Planning*. https://doi.org/DOI: 10.1175/WCAS-D-12-00028.1

Tangcharoensathien, V., Calleja, N., Nguyen, T., Purnat, T., D'Agostino, M., Garcia-Saiso, S., Landry, M., Rashidian, A., & Hamilton, C., AbdAllah, A., Ghiga, I., Hill, A., Hougendobler, D., Andel, J. van, Nunn, M., Brooks, I., Sacco, P. L., Domenico, M. D., Mai, P., … Briand, S. (2020). Framework for Managing the COVID-19 Infodemic: Methods and Results of an Online, Crowdsourced WHO Technical Consultation. *Journal of Medical Internet Research*, *22*(6), e19659. DOI: 10.2196/19659 PMID: 32558655

TCFD. (2023). *2023 TCFD Status Report: Task Force on Climate-related Financial Disclosures*. https://www.fsb.org/uploads/P121023-2.pdf

Tekolste, R., Eldridge, M., & Hawkins, R. (2016). *Managing Investors' Risk in Pay for Success Projects*. Urban Institute.

Tennekes, M. (2018). tmap: Thematic Maps in R. *Journal of Statistical Software*, *84*, 1–39. DOI: 10.18637/jss.v084.i06

Tenner, I., & Hörisch, J. (2021). Crowdfunding sustainable entrepreneurship: What are the characteristics of crowdfunding investors? *Journal of Cleaner Production, 290*, 125667.

Testa, S., Roma, P., Vasi, M., & Cincotti, S. (2020). Crowdfunding as a tool to support sustainability-oriented initiatives: Preliminary insights into the role of product/service attributes. *Business Strategy and the Environment, 29*(2), 530–546. DOI: 10.1002/bse.2385

TFCD. (2024). *Task Force on Climate-Related Financial Disclosures*. Task Force on Climate-Related Financial Disclosures. https://www.fsb-tcfd.org/

Thakor, A. V. (2020). Fintech and banking: What do we know? *Journal of Financial Intermediation, 41*, 100833. DOI: 10.1016/j.jfi.2019.100833

Thorpe, A. (2022). The global weather enterprise, part 1: The jigsaw pieces. *Weather, 77*(10), 349–351. DOI: 10.1002/wea.4261

Thorpe, A. (2023). The global weather enterprise, part 3: An evolving picture. *Weather, 78*(3), 74–78. DOI: 10.1002/wea.4347

Tian, X., Geng, Y., Sarkis, J., & Zhong, S. (2018). Trends and features of embodied flows associated with international trade based on bibliometric analysis. *Resources, Conservation and Recycling, 131*, 148–157. DOI: 10.1016/j.resconrec.2018.01.002

Tiko. (2023, November 20). How Real-Time Data Spurred Success in World-First Adolescent Sexual Reproductive Health Development Impact Bond. Retrieved January 16, 2025, from tiko.org/2023/11/20/how-real-time-data-spurred-success-in-world-first-adolescent-sexual-reproductive-health-development-impact-bond/

Todorof, M. (2018). Shariah-compliant FinTech in the banking industry. *ERA Forum, 19*(1), 1–17. https://doi.org/DOI: 10.1007/s12027-018-0505-8

Tomlinson, B., Boberg, J., Cranefield, J., Johnstone, D., Luczak-Roesch, M., Patterson, D. J., & Kapoor, S. (2021). Analyzing the sustainability of 28 'Blockchain for Good' projects via affordances and constraints. *Information Technology for Development, 27*(3), 439–469. DOI: 10.1080/02681102.2020.1828792

Touati, C., & Miljkovitch, R., DuboisComtois, K., Sirparanta, A., & Deborde, A.S. (2021). Risk and protective factors in placement associated with mental health: A systematic review of the literature. *Devenir, 33*(2), 135–172. DOI: 10.3917/dev.212.0135

Trotta, A., Care, R., Carida, R., & Migliazza, M. C. (2021). Fighting poverty and inequalities through social impact bonds: Learning from case studies to support the Covid-19 response. In *Contemporary Issues in Sustainable Finance: Financial Products and Financial Institutions* (p. 37). Springer.

Trotta, A., Rania, F., & Strano, E. (2024). Exploring the linkages between FinTech and ESG: A bibliometric perspective. *Research in International Business and Finance*, *69*, 102200. DOI: 10.1016/j.ribaf.2023.102200

Tse, A. E., & Warner, M. E. (2020). The razor's edge: Social impact bonds and the financialization of early childhood services. *Journal of Urban Affairs*, *42*(6), 816–832.

Umar, U. H., Baita, A. J., Haron, M. H., & Kabiru, S. H. (2021). The potential of Islamic social finance to alleviate poverty in the era of COVID-19: The moderating effect of ethical orientation. *International Journal of Islamic and Middle Eastern Finance and Management*, *15*(2), 255–270. DOI: 10.1108/imefm-07-2020-0371

UN environmental programme. (2024). *The climate data challenge: The critical role of open-source and neutral data platforms. Technical Supplement to the 2024 Climate Risk Landscape Report.* https://www.unepfi.org/themes/climate-change/the-climate-data-challenge-the-critical-role-of-open-source-and-neutral-data-platforms/

United Nations Environment Programme. (2021, settembre 1). *Adaptation Gap Report 2020*. UNEP - UN Environment Programme. https://www.unep.org/resources/adaptation-gap-report-2020

United Nations. (2024). *The Sustainable Development Goals Report 2024*. United Nations. Retrieved from https://unstats.un.org/sdgs/report/2024/The-Sustainable-Development-Goals-Report-2024.pdf

Uzougbo, N. S., Ikegwu, C. G., & Adewusi, A. O. (2024). Regulatory frameworks for decentralized finance (DEFI): Challenges and opportunities. *GSC Advanced Research and Reviews*, *19*(02), 116–129.

Van der Waal, J. W., & Thijssens, T. (2020). Corporate involvement in sustainable development goals: Exploring the territory. *Journal of Cleaner Production*, *252*, 119625.

van Eck, N. J., & Waltman, L. (2014). Visualizing Bibliometric Networks. In Ding, Y., Rousseau, R., & Wolfram, D. (Eds.), *Measuring Scholarly Impact: Methods and Practice* (pp. 285–320). Springer International Publishing., DOI: 10.1007/978-3-319-10377-8_13

Van Eck, N. J., & Waltman, L. (2023). VOSviewer manual. *Leiden. Univeristeit Leiden*, *1*(1), 1–54.

van Eck, N. J., Waltman, L., van den Berg, J., & Kaymak, U. (2006). Visualizing the computational intelligence field [Application Notes]. *IEEE Computational Intelligence Magazine, 1*(4), 6–10. *IEEE Computational Intelligence Magazine*. Advance online publication. DOI: 10.1109/MCI.2006.329702

van Eck, N., & Waltman, L. (2010). Software survey: VOSviewer, a computer program for bibliometric mapping. *Scientometrics*, *84*(2), 523–538. DOI: 10.1007/s11192-009-0146-3 PMID: 20585380

Vandemeulebroucke, V., Beck, K., & Kauefer, K. (2010). *Networking Social Finance*. INAISE.

Vanroose, A., & D'Espallier, B. (2013). Do microfinance institutions accomplish their mission? Evidence from the relationship between traditional financial sector development and microfinance institutions' outreach and performance. *Applied Economics*, *45*(15), 1965–1982. DOI: 10.1080/00036846.2011.641932

Vasileiadou, E., Huijben, J. C. C. M., & Raven, R. P. J. M. (2016). Three is a crowd? Exploring the potential of crowdfunding for renewable energy in the Netherlands. *Journal of Cleaner Production*, *128*, 142–155. DOI: 10.1016/j.jclepro.2015.06.028

Vaughan, C., Dessai, S., Hewitt, C., Baethgen, W., Terra, R., & Berterretche, M. (2017). Creating an enabling environment for investment in climate services: The case of Uruguay's National Agricultural Information System. In *Climate Services* (Vol. 8, pp. 62–71). https://doi.org/DOI: 10.1016/j.cliser.2017.11.001

Vaz, J., & Brown, K. (2020). Sustainable development and cryptocurrencies as private money. *Economia e Politica Industriale*, *47*(1), 163–184. DOI: 10.1007/s40812-019-00139-5

Vecchi, V., & Casalini, F. (2019). Is a social empowerment of PPP for infrastructure delivery possible? Lessons from social impact bonds. *Annals of Public and Cooperative Economics*, *90*(2), 353–369.

Vecchi, V., Casalini, F., & Caselli, S. (2017). Impact investing as a societal refocus of venture capital: The perspective of mature economies. In *Principles and Practice of Impact Investing* (pp. 62–80). Routledge.

Velez-Valencia, C., Herrera-Cano, C., Gonzalez-Perez, M., Alvarez, P., & Vergara Garavito, J. (2025). *'Aligning Investment with Impact: Exploring Social Impact Bonds in Emerging Markets for Sustainable Development.' Corporate Social Responsibility and Environmental Management*. EarlyView.

Vermicelli, S., Cricelli, L., & Grimaldi, M. (2021). How can crowdsourcing help tackle the COVID-19 pandemic? An explorative overview of innovative collaborative practices. *R & D Management, 51*(2), 183–194. DOI: 10.1111/radm.12443

Vermicelli, S., Cricelli, L., Grimaldi, M., Mignacca, B., & Strazzullo, S. (2022). Crowdsourcing initiatives during the COVID-19 pandemic: Empirical evidence from the Italian context. *European Journal of Innovation Management, 27*(3), 1042–1055. DOI: 10.1108/EJIM-06-2022-0341

Vickers, J., & Yarrow, G. (1988). *Privatization: An economic analysis*. MIT Press.

Vigna, P., & Casey, M. J. (2015). *The Age of Cryptocurrency: How Bitcoin and Digital Money Are Challenging the Global Economic Order*. St. Martin's Press, Inc.

Vinoth, S., & Srivastava, N. (2024). Disruptive Business Models and the Shift Towards Decentralised Marketplaces. In *Digital Technologies, Ethics, and Decentralisation in the Digital Era* (pp. 34–58). IGI Global.

Vismara, S. (2019). Sustainability in equity crowdfunding. *Technological Forecasting and Social Change, 141*, 98–106. DOI: 10.1016/j.techfore.2018.07.014

Vizcaíno, C. F. O., Valle, C. T., & Puig, P. G. (2024). Spillover effects of microcredit on the GDP of surrounding cantons in Ecuador. *Journal of Strategy and Management, ahead-of-print*(ahead-of-print). https://doi.org/DOI: 10.1108/JSMA-07-2023-0199

Vuontisjärvi, T. (2006). Corporate social reporting in the European context and human resource disclosures: An analysis of Finnish companies. *Journal of Business Ethics, 69*(4), 331–354. DOI: 10.1007/s10551-006-9094-5

Wang, Y., & Zeng, Q. (2024). Smart contracts and tokenization in green energy: A quantitative review of DeFi platforms. *Journal of Sustainable Finance & Investment, 14*(1), 55–78.

Warner, M. (2012, September). Profiting from public value? The case of social impact bonds. Draft paper prepared for *Creating Public Value Conference*. University of Minnesota.

Warner, M. E. (2013). Private finance for public goods: Social impact bonds. *Journal of Economic Policy Reform, 16*(4), 303–319.

Watson, R., Nielsen, K. R., Wilson, H. N., Macdonald, E. K., Mera, C., & Reisch, L. (2023). Policy for sustainable entrepreneurship: A crowdsourced framework. *Journal of Cleaner Production, 383*, 135234. DOI: 10.1016/j.jclepro.2022.135234

WB. (2019). *The Power of Partnership: Public and Private Engagement in Hydromet Services*. The World Bank.

Webber, S., & Donner, S. D. (2017). Climate service warnings: Cautions about commercializing climate science for adaptation in the developing world. *Wiley Interdisciplinary Reviews: Climate Change, 8*(1). *Scopus.* Advance online publication. DOI: 10.1002/wcc.424

Weber, O. (2012). Sustainable banking – History and current developments. SSRN *Electronic Journal.* https://doi.org/DOI: 10.2139/ssrn.2159947

Weber, O. (2019). Sustainable finance and the SDGs: The role of the banking sector. In *Achieving the Sustainable Development Goals: Global Governance Challenges* (pp. 226–239). Scopus. https://doi.org/DOI: 10.4324/9780429029622

Weber, O., & Duan, Y. (2012). Social finance and banking. *Socially Responsible Finance and Investing*, 161-180. https://doi.org/DOI: 10.1002/9781118524015.ch9

Weber, O., & Duan, Y. (2012). Social finance and banking. *Socially responsible finance and investing: Financial institutions, corporations, investors, and activists*, 161-180.

Weber, R. P. (1988). Basic content analysis. *Sage University Paper Series on Quantitative Applications in the Social Sciences, 07*(49). Advance online publication. DOI: 10.4135/9781412983488

Weefin. (2025). 2025 guide: complete comparison of sustainable finance labels in Europe. (WEEFIN) https://www.weefin.co/ressource/guide-2025-comparatif-complet-des-labels-de-finance-durable-en-europe

Wefunder. (2021). Impact Report. Retrieved from https://wefunder.com/pbc

What is impact investing? Meaning, types and examples. (2024, April 5). Fintrakk: Personal Finance Blog. https://fintrakk.com/what-is-impact-investing-meaning-types-examples/

White, H. D., & McCain, K. W. (1998). Visualizing a discipline: An author Co-citation analysis of information science, 1972–1995. *Journal of the American Society for Information Science, 49*(4), 327–355. DOI: 10.1002/(sici)1097-4571(19980401)49:43.0.co;2-4

White, H., & Phillips, D. (2012). *Addressing attribution of cause and effect in small n impact evaluations: towards an integrated framework.* International Initiative for Impact Evaluation.

Widiarto, I., & Emrouznejad, A. (2015). Social and financial efficiency of Islamic microfinance institutions: A Data Envelopment Analysis application. *Socio-Economic Planning Sciences, 50*, 1–17. DOI: 10.1016/j.seps.2014.12.001

Wieczorek, A. J., Rohracher, H., Bauknecht, D., Kubeczko, K., Bolwig, S., Valkering, P., & Maggiore, S. (2024). Citizen-led decentralised energy futures: Emerging rationales of energy system organisation. *Energy Research & Social Science*, *113*, 103557.

Williams, J. W. (2020). 'Surveying the SIB economy: Social impact bonds, "local" challenges, and shifting markets in urban social problems'. *Journal of Urban Affairs*, *42*(6), 907–919.

Williams, J. W. (2024). 'Finance interrupted: Social impact bonds, spatial politics, and the limits of financial innovation in the social sector.' *Environment and Planning A. Economy and Space*, *56*(1), 42–58.

Wilson, K. E., Silva, F., & Richardson, D. (2015). *Social Impact Investment: Building the Evidence Base*. OECD Reports World Bank. (2019). *The Global Partnership for Results-Based Approaches. Impact Bonds: Considerations for Investment Returns and Pricing of Outcomes.*

WMO. (2018). *Step-by-step Guidelines for Establishing a National Framework for Climate Services. 1206.*

WMO. (2020). *2020 State of Climate Services: Risk Information and Early Warning Systems* (WMO-No. 1252; p. 25). World Meteorological Organization. https://library.wmo.int/idurl/4/57191

Wójcik, D., & Bratton, W. (2024). Theory, explanation, and economics in financial geographies. *Dialogues in Human Geography*, *20438206241280659*. Advance online publication. DOI: 10.1177/20438206241280659

World Bank. (2022). *Financial Inclusion* [Text/HTML]. World Bank. https://www.worldbank.org/en/topic/financialinclusion/overview

World Bank. (Director). (2020). Reversing the Inequality Pandemic: Speech by World Bank Group President David Malpass [Broadcast]. In *World Bank Live*. https://www.worldbank.org/en/news/speech/2020/10/05/reversing-the-inequality-pandemic-speech-by-world-bank-group-president-david-malpass

Xu, H., Liu, L., & Ding, P. (2021). Building Climate Resilient City through Multiple Scale Cooperative Planning: Experiences from Copenhagen. *IOP Conference Series. Materials Science and Engineering*, *1203*(3), 032063.

Xu, J. (2024). AI in ESG for financial institutions: An industrial survey. https://doi.org/DOI: 10.2139/ssrn.4949354

Yang, J., & Jung, S. U. (2024). ‘Harnessing FinTech for Sustainable Finance in Developing Countries: An Integrated SWOT–Multi-Level Perspective Analysis of Mongolia’. *Sustainability*, *16*(10), 4102.

Yang, J., & Jung, S. U. (2024). Harnessing FinTech for Sustainable Finance in Developing Countries: An Integrated SWOT–Multi-Level Perspective Analysis of Mongolia. *Sustainability*, *16*(10), 4102. DOI: 10.3390/su16104102

Yi, X., Bai, C., Lyu, S., & Dai, L. (2021). The impacts of the COVID-19 pandemic on China’s green bond market. *Finance Research Letters*, *42*, 101948. DOI: 10.1016/j.frl.2021.101948 PMID: 34566534

Zanotto, E. D., & Carvalho, V. (2021). Article age- and field-normalized tools to evaluate scientific impact and momentum. *Scientometrics*, *126*(4), 2865–2883. DOI: 10.1007/s11192-021-03877-3

Zauro, N. A., Saad, R. A. J., Ahmi, A., & Hussin, M. Y. M. (2020). Integration of Waqf towards enhancing financial inclusion and socio-economic justice in Nigeria. *International Journal of Ethics and Systems*, *36*(4), 491–505. DOI: 10.1108/IJOES-04-2020-0054

Zhang, D. (2023). Fiscal policy benefits and green recovery of firms: An experimental exploration of Chinese listed firms in post-Covid-19. *Economic Change and Restructuring*, *56*(5), 2921–2942. DOI: 10.1007/s10644-021-09344-6

Zhao, X. (2022). How Blockchain Can Empower the Growth in Green Finance. In Y. Jiang et al. (Eds.), Proceedings of the 2022 International Conference on E-Business and Digital Commerce (ICEDBC 2022), AEBMR 225 (pp. 412-416). Atlantis Press. https://doi.org/DOI: 10.2991/978-94-6463-036-7_60

Zhou, S. (2024). Financial Innovation and Market Transformation in the Age of Digital Finance. Transactions on Economics. *Business and Management Research*, *6*, 118–127.

Zhuk, A. (2025). From Cypherpunks to Decentralized Finance: How Crypto-Anarchy is Redefining Legal and Economic Systems. Markets, *Globalization &. Developmental Review*, *9*(3).

Ziolo, M., Bak, I., & Cheba, K. (2020). The role of sustainable finance in achieving sustainable development goals: Does it work? *Technological and Economic Development of Economy*, *27*(1), 45–70. DOI: 10.3846/tede.2020.13863

Zumbansen, P. (2023). Runaway train? Decentralised finance and the myth of the private platform economy. *Transnational Legal Theory*, *14*(4), 413–452.

Zupic, I., & Cater, T. (2013). Bibliometric methods in management and organization: A review. SSRN *Electronic Journal*. https://doi.org/DOI: 10.2139/ssrn.2267251

Zupic, I., & Čater, T. (2015). Bibliometric Methods in Management and Organization. *Organizational Research Methods*, *18*(3), 429–472.

About the Contributors

Rosella Carè, University Magna Graecia of Catanzaro (Italy) & University of Waterloo (Canada) Rosella Carè is Assistant Professor of Sustainability & Financial Management at the University of Waterloo (Canada) and Assistant Professor of Banking and Finance at the University of Catanzaro (Italy). Her works have been published by outstanding international academic editors and publishers such as Routledge, Springer, Taylor and Francis, Palgrave MacMillan, and Elsevier. Rosella's primary research areas – where she is the author and editor of several works – include social and sustainable finance, alternative finance, impact investing, sustainable banking, ESG, climate risks, and financial stability.

***

Chiara Bidoli is a PhD student in Science and Management of Climate Change and a junior researcher at the RAAS Department. Her research focuses on financial instruments to support the implementation of nature-based solutions in coastal and marine areas, contributing to climate adaptation and mitigation. She adopts a transdisciplinary approach, combining economic expertise with environmental and social perspectives. Chiara holds a Master's degree in Business Economics from Ca' Foscari University of Venice (2020). Before starting her PhD, she worked for two years as a researcher at the Governance and Social Innovation Center in Venice, where she focused on digital healthcare and organizational models for health and social enterprises.

Rabia Fatima is Lecturer/Researcher of Sustainable Transition in Finance at the International School of Business, HAN_University of Applied Sciences (Netherlands). She holds a Ph.D. in Economics and Business at the University of Cagliari (Italy). Prior to her Ph.D., she served as a Lecturer in the Department of Business Administration at Iqra National University (Pakistan). Her research interests are primarily focused on social and sustainable finance.

Nathalie Lévy is Professor of Economics at the University of Tours, in the University Institute of Technology of the University of Tours, and researcher at IRJI (François Rabelais Institute of Legal and Interdisciplinary Research). She has been the Deputy Director in charge of training programs and pedagogy at the UIT of Tours since October 2024. Her research in monetary macroeconomics focuses mainly on three areas: (i) the transformation of banking structures and financing, by questioning banking organization models and the destination of household savings in Europe; (ii) the spread of Anglo-American neoliberalism in Europe and its impact on financial structures; (iii) the transparency of institutional forms of monetary policy and financing of the economy, particularly examining the independence of central banks and financial transparency in the context of sustainable finance.

Marina Mattera is a multilingual Business Consultant with 15+ years of collective experience in Sustainability and Innovation consultancy, Project Management (including EU and WB projects) and Academia. Accredited by the Spanish Ministry of Education as a University Professor for Public and Private Universities, currently working as an Associate Professor at EAE Barcelona Business School and Project Manager for the EU Adaptation AGORA Project. Possess a comprehensive background in corporate engagement, sustainability and strategic business consulting in EU, US and LATAM frameworks. Career supported by a Doctorate Degree (PhD) in Business / Economics, an LLM in Global Corporate Compliance and Project Management Professional (PMP) Certification.

Derick Moukiama is an expert in sustainable finance and responsible wealth management. Founder of Derick Patrimoine, he advises on investments with social and environmental impact. PhD student in économies at the François-Rabelais Interdisciplinary Legal Research Institute and the University of Tours, he studies the influence of European labels on savings behaviors to promote transparent and ethical finance.

Jaroslav Mysiak is a principal scientist (since 2023) and Founding director of the research division Risk assessment andadaptation strategies (RAAS) (2014-2024). He is also an external teacher at the Ca' Foscari University of Venice. Jaroslav holds a PhD from the University of Göttingen (Germany) and MSc. from the Technical University Zvolen (Slovakia). Jaroslav is a member and rapporteur of the EC Horizon Europe's Mission Board on Climate adaptation and Societal Transformation (2019-2021), a member of the Scientific Committee of the European Environmental Agency (EEA) (2020-2023), a member of the European Science and Technology Advisory

Group (E-STAG) (since 2018) of the United Nations Office for Disaster Risk Reduction (UNDRR), and a member of the Expert Group on slow-onset event (SOE) (2021-2023) established by the Executive Committee of the UNFCCC Warsaw International Mechanism on Loss and Damage (L&D). Jaroslav is involved and actively contribute to the Technical Expert Network on Catastrophe Risks of the European Insurance and Occupational Pensions Authority (EIOPA), the Future Earth's Knowledge Action Network on Emergent Risks and Extreme Events (www .risk-kan.org), the Ecosystems for Adaptation and Disaster Risk Reduction network (pedrr.org), INFORM Global Risk Index consortium (https://drmkc.jrc.ec.europa.eu/ inform-index), and the EEA's Topic Centre on Climate Change impacts, vulnerability and adaptation (ETC-CCA). Jaroslav's research focusses on risk assessment and governance, including behavioural responses to risks and risk-reduction measures, risk perception and transformational social change, environmental economics, sustainable finance, climate adaptation and services. Previously he contributed to the sustainable taxonomy as a member of the expert network established by the Technical Expert Group (TEG) on sustainable finance, and member of the EU Disaster Loss Data System working group. He acted as team leader of the UNDP coordinated project's developing the disaster risk reduction strategy and action plan for the Republic of Mauritius, and contributed to similar assessments elsewhere (e.g., Nigeria, St. Lucia). He coordinated several and contributed to many European research and innovation projects, such as CLARA (Climate forecasts enabled knowledge services, H2020 2017-2020), ENHANCE (Enhancing risk management partnerships for catastrophic natural disasters in Europe, FP7 2012-2016), EPI-WATER (Economic policy instruments for sustainable water resource management, FP7 2011-2013), XEROCHORE (An exercise to assess research needs and policy choices in areas of drought, FP7 2009-2011) and many more.

Hilary Olson earned her PhD in Public Policy and Management from the Price School of Public Policy at the University of Southern California. With extensive experience using both quantitative and qualitative methodologies, her work focuses on bridging theory and practice to tackle complex global challenges. As a research assistant at the Price Center for Social Innovation, Hilary contributed to a number of projects analyzing Social Impact Bonds and Emergency Aid funds. Her dissertation, entitled "Outcomes-Based Contracting through Impact Bonds: Ties to Social Innovation, Systems Change, and International Development," examined the use of social outcome contracts in a variety of contexts, including in low- and middle-income countries. Specializing in social innovation and program evaluation, her research is driven by a passion for international development, social finance, collaborative governance, co-production, and systems change.

Gagandeep Singh is an Associate Professor, with the Mittal School of Business

Simone Taddeo, Holding a Ph.D. in Economics, Statistics, and Sustainability from the University of Naples "Parthenope," Simone joined LUISS Guido Carli University in Rome as post-doc researcher, focusing on the impact of strategic alliances on organizational resilience in response to climate changes. Previously, he has conducted extensive international academic research, serving as a Visiting Ph.D. Researcher at the University of Waterloo in Canada and Leuphana University in Germany, where he delved into sustainability, ESG (Environmental, Social, and Governance), and climate-related studies. Beyond academia, Simone's international academic experiences include being a Visiting Bachelor Student at the University of Groningen in the Netherlands and a Visiting Master student at the New Jersey Institute of Technology (NJIT) in the United States. With prior experience as a Corporate Governance Research Analyst in Brussels, Simone is focusing his research interests on advancing studies related to governance climate risks, sustainability, ESG factors, and climate impact.

Jasdeep Walia is an Assistant Professor, at Lovely Professional University

Index

A

B

C

D

E

F

G

I

M

N

O

P

R

S

T

www.ingramcontent.com/pod-product-compliance
Lightning Source LLC
LaVergne TN
LVHW081345300926
849161LV00008B/2067
9798369395516